A Fear Not for

Every Day

365 Devotionals

By

Chris Boelter

With
Virginia Ann Work

ISBN: 13:9781497378421
10: 1497378427

Introduction

Fear is a crippling emotion. When it is accompanied or fueled by worry or selfishness, fear is sin. Think about what fear does. It hinders us from making wise decisions. It causes us to lose hope. It dampens or destroys our faith. In most cases, we must choose between fear and faith. Fear is a tool of Satan to defeat us, discredit God and keep us enslaved to our own interests.

And yet fear has a positive side. Solomon, the wisest of all men, wrote, "The fear of the Lord is the beginning of wisdom and the knowledge of the Holy One is understanding." (Prov. 9:10) What did Solomon mean when he used the word *fear*?

Even something as joyful and hopeful as a wedding can be hedged in with fear: fear of the future, fear of the unknown, fear of divorce. As far back as I can remember, my family observed the ceremony of exchanging marriage vows in church. My grandparents, who came from Armenia and were married in Armenia, said those vows. My aunts, uncles, and parents all did the same.

I took those vows with Bob Boelter in front of my family and the pastor on July 20, 1968. Little did I know that on a sunny day in Pennsylvania many years later, I would be called upon to keep the vows I uttered so glibly. *For better or worse. In sickness and in health. For richer or poorer.* Reciting something at the altar of a church when you are twenty years old is easy. Honoring those vows at the age of fifty under the most extreme circumstances imaginable is another story.

Fear, with all its ramifications, rears its ugly head when you stand beside the hospital bed where your husband is lying in a coma from a massive cardiac arrest. The nightmare of what happened to Bob did not end in a few days, or weeks, or years. I have had to keep fear, which creeps in at every chance, at bay. I have had to keep my focus on God and on the vows I made at that church altar. I have had to reject, time and again, the option of going the easy route.

How can we live without fear? What is the meaning of godly fear? How can we deepen our trust and faith in God? What does it mean to fear God?

When life throws a hard ball, crashing into our neat, ordered world, when fear raises its ugly head while you sit at the bedside of your beloved and know deep in your soul they will never recover, when life seems unbearable, *what then?*

Will you turn from the life-giving God or retreat into a frozen corner of the world and exist with the cancer of bitterness and anger eating away your heart?

Many people go this route. Have you done it already? My prayer is that this devotional will make you aware of the debilitating effects of fear in your life and help you chose faith and fear of God, no matter what happens.

When worry takes over your mind, you are giving in to fear, and you are trying to control a situation that is beyond you. How can you conquer fear and worry? Why should you live this way when God offers life, joy, freedom and hope?

Take the high road, even if it is the most difficult. I know about that road because I've been on it for fourteen years. When Bob had a near-fatal cardiac arrest in the fall of 2000 and was severely brain damaged, I had a choice to make: would I abandon him and go my own way, or would I remain with him and care for him? I chose to take the high road.

Come explore the whole realm of fear as it is found in Scripture. Apply it to every aspect of your life.

January 1
Reason Not to Fear #1: Live In Obedience to God

"So he said, "I heard Your voice in the garden, and I was afraid because I was naked; and I hid myself." Genesis 3:10

Bob Boelter was everything I had ever dreamed of in a man and in a husband. I saw reflected in his eyes the love and admiration I had for him. Fear was not on my horizon when we exchanged vows that bright summer day. Like most newlyweds, we were lost in a world that beckoned with hope, life, love and joy.

But fear did knock at my door many times as we raised our four children and began a ministry in the inner city of Chicago. In fact, sometimes fear barged in and tried to dominant in my life. What if I had feared to take those vows with Bob? What if I feared to have children? What if we feared to participate with God in ministry?

Adam and Eve learned about the wrong kind of fear. In the beginning, they feared God in the sense of awesome wonder, respectful worship and deep trust. Yet one day Satan came tiptoeing into their lives and they succumbed to temptation. They ate the forbidden fruit and suddenly they were afraid.

They stepped into the world of disobedience and immediately a new type of fear overtook them. Notice the immediate consequences of sin: shame and fear. Our first parents, citizens of that lovely garden, no longer enjoyed their time with the Lord. Instead, they longed intensely to avoid His presence. God's voice was no longer a comfort; it was a conviction.

Fear cripples. Fear hinders God's work. Fear separates you from God's grace and love. Fear is the heart and soul of sin. It answers to the name of terror and dread. Meeting with God had never been a chore or a duty or a fearsome thing before Adam and Eve sinned, but now it was. They became aware of their disobedience, and God became a stranger.

My dear friend, sin calls to your basic desires to disobey God. Sin will do to you what it did to Adam and Eve – make you terrified of God. It will make you loathe His presence. Do you look forward to your time with the Lord on a daily basis -- or do you dread it?

The remedy is to confess your sin and live in the realm of the fear of God. List your fears now. Commit each one to God. Allow His Spirit to so fill your heart that you will sing for joy and live each day in peace.

January 2

Reason Not to Fear #2: God, the Great I AM, Is My Reward

"After these things the word of the Lord came to Abram in a vision, saying,
"Do not be afraid, Abram. I am your shield, your exceeding great reward."
Genesis 15:1

I will never forget one New Year's Eve day when we lived in the inner city of Chicago. Bob decided to walk to the local drug store to buy a newspaper, but when he arrived at the drug store, he realized a robbery was in progress. The druggist was lying in a pool of blood. Two masked men ordered Bob to lie on his stomach and proceeded to tie his hands behind his back. In short order, the thieves thrust all three into a small closet.

The mailman was so terrified he didn't want to stand next to the door as he thought the young men would shoot through the door and he would be killed. When the robbers left, Bob called the police. The officers were amazed when Bob was able to recognize the robber's voices, and Bob was able to help the police apprehend the robbers.

I wondered what was taking Bob so long to return from his errand, and I was urged by the Spirit to pray for him. I fended off my fear and God gave me peace. Then I heard the front door open and relief flooded my heart. God not only protected Bob from serious harm, He also gave peace and strength so Bob could comfort the other victims and help the police.

Abraham might have also opened his heart's door to fear. He and his men had just successfully defeated four invading kings. Yet he knew that they might gather with more armies and come for revenge. How could he survive? He felt vulnerable and weak.

Abraham had a choice. He could have yielded to fear, but he went to prayer instead. I can imagine him up on the mountain, on his knees, hands spread out as he pled for wisdom and guidance. That is when God told Abraham, "Do not be afraid. I am your shield and exceeding great reward." This is the first time in the Scripture that the words *reward* and *shield* are used. Abraham was encouraged to give his fears to the Lord.

Dear friend, do you see how those who are protected by God really have no reason to fear? He takes care of His children. Today you may be facing something that tempts you to fear. To you God is saying, "Do not fear!" He is your shield. He is ever ready to defend you. You have a choice: fear or faith. Commit your situation to God right now and chose faith.

January 3

Reason Not to Fear #3: God Is Bigger Than My Wrong Choices

"And Abraham said, "Because I thought surely the fear of God is not in this place and they will kill me on account of my wife." Genesis 20:11

Wrong choices. We all make them. But it seems some people are more prone to chose badly. We witnessed this many times during the days Bob and I ministered to the young people who lived in Cabrini Green in Chicago. Bob interacted with boys who made the decision to join a gang and then wanted out.

It was a difficult process to leave a gang, and many kids didn't survive. As Bob attempted to help them escape, his life was also on the line. Numerous times our car was vandalized with broken windows, slashed tires and dents where rocks were thrown. Bob resorted to taking the "L" to work at the mission.

Fear can dominate a situation that goes swiftly downhill with death threats, physical damage, and hatred. The boys who attempted to flee the gangs paid highly for their wrong choices.

Abraham was a great man of faith. During a time of famine, he decided to travel south for food in the land of the Negev. As Abraham entered this land with his beautiful wife, he realized that he was among ungodly people and his fear awakened. He and Sarah agreed to say that she was his sister, not his wife. They thought this would protect Abraham from evil men killing him. But it did not protect Sarah from the greatest danger of all – from Abimelech, the king of Gerar.

Can you imagine how Abraham felt when he returned to the tent one day to find Sarah gone? His fear made him chose wrongly and now he had paid for it dearly. I love verse three, *"But God…"* God intervened and the truth was revealed. While Abraham feared in the wrong way, this ungodly king feared God in the right way -- he was afraid to harm Sarah.

God does not want you to become immobilized because of your fears. He certainly doesn't want you to make wrong choices. There really was no need for Abraham to lie. God was his protector.

God is bigger than our wrong choices. If you are on a destructive path of bad decisions, repent now. Turn from your own way of thinking, leave fear aside, and come to God by faith. In Jesus Christ, we can find forgiveness of our past sins, freedom to live in peace, and the way out of our bad choices.

January 4

Reason Not to Fear #4: God Is Bigger Than Your Impossible Situation

"And God heard the voice of the lad. Then the angel of God called to Hagar out of heaven, and said to her, 'What ails you, Hagar? Fear not, for God had heard the voice of the lad where he is.'" Genesis 21:17

I can't do this, Lord. Not this. Not again.

I had married Bob, joined him in his ministry with street kids in Chicago, and proceeded to fill our home with four children, two boys and two girls. I wanted the best for my children, and I knew Bob wanted that, too. But he often came home with a bedraggled specimen of humanity in the form of a young man or woman who had reached the end of their rope on the street.

I was tense. The tension I felt was between doing what we felt called to do and the safety for our family. Even my personal privacy was often invaded and I found I had to find God's peace over the fear of danger. We opened our home to anyone and often hid young men who wanted to escape the gangs. I didn't mind sharing my home, but I *did* mind it when I discovered that the gang was aiming to shoot and kill Bob.

He told me later that they shot at him as he walked the streets, but never once did the bullets touch him. He would often say, "I'm a big target, but God is bigger and He protects me."

Maybe Hagar felt the same way – fear for her child, Ishmael, who was about sixteen years old. He and his mother were suddenly thrust from Abraham and Sarah's home and forced on a long march through the scorching desert. After wandering alone for most of the day, Ishmael fell to the ground, more dead than alive. Hagar wept before God for the life of her son. God allowed this mother and son to come to an end of their own strength and now they were totally dependent on Him. God heard and sympathized with their distress.

Oh, dear friend, I want to assure you that not a groan, not a sigh, not a tear escapes your Father's vision. Wherever you are, that is also true for you. God is ready and able to help you when you are in trouble. Are you at the end of your rope? That is a good place to be, because underneath are the everlasting arms of God. Hagar and Ishmael found this to be true. God is listening to you today. You do not need to fear. You only need to cry out to Him and He will help you.

January 5

Reason Not to Fear #5: God Provides

"And He said, 'Do not lay your hand on the lad, or do anything to him; for now I know that you fear God, since you have not withheld your son, your only son, from Me.'" Genesis 22:12

It seems a strange request that God made of Abraham. "Take Isaac, the son whom you love, and sacrifice him on the mountains of Moriah." Wait a minute! Abraham lived in a society that practiced the worship of idols where they regularly sacrificed humans to appease their god and to gain his blessing on their lives. Why would God ask this of him?

Abraham had obeyed God's voice when He called him from the land of Ur and from his family's lands in Haran. He walked with God for a long time and over that time had grown in his faith, patience and understanding. He knew that the God he served would not ask anything of him that was wrong. He knew that this God would keep His promises to make him the father of the promised race, who would one day be known as the Israelites.

It doesn't seem from the text that Abraham questioned God. I am sure Moses would have included it if he had. No, it seems he quietly rose with the dawn, gathered his things, told Isaac they were going to travel to a place and offer a sacrifice to God. I don't know what he told Sarah, but perhaps he told her the same thing.

Isaac is another interesting study in this story. He was probably sixteen or seventeen, a strapping young boy who could have overpowered his father easily. Yet the Word does not record that he struggled against his father's directions. He laid down obediently without needing to be bound, nor did he seek to flee even when the knife in his father's hand was descending.

What kept these two people steady on the line of obedience? God gives the explanation in this verse. They feared God. Abraham did not flinch at giving back to God the thing he loved the best: his son. In fact, it appears that Abraham believed that God would raise him from the dead. (Heb. 11:19)

How about you? What are you willing to give up for God? Some of your time? Your money? Your talents and gifts? Search your heart today and see if there are any areas in which you love the things of this world more than God. Confess this and walk out freed from the chains of sin. Rejoice in Him and give Him thanks, for He is good, and He loves you.

January 6

Reason Not to Fear #6: God Is Able to Deliver Me

"Then Jacob woke from his sleep and said, 'Surely the Lord is in this place, and I did not know it.' And he was afraid and said, 'How awesome is this place! This is none other than the house of God, and this is the gate of heaven!'" Genesis 28:16, 17

When we lived and worked with street people in Chicago, the gangs hated us and wanted to kill us. We walked in the constant awareness that angels protected us from harm. I taught a ladies Bible study in an apartment building, and had to ride the elevator to the 19th floor. Every week I prayed a lot before I got on the elevator, because you never knew who would get on with you at different floors, or if you would be alive when you reached your destination.

One day, as I waited for the elevator door to open, a group of young men formed a half-circle around me. I was being hemmed in and I knew their intent was evil.

I began to panic and ran right through their circle and into the apartment of a woman who came to my Bible study. As I burst into the room and slammed the door, she asked me why I was so afraid. I could hardly speak, but managed to blurt out, "They … they were circling me. They were going to kill me!"

She regarded me solemnly. "But you tell us not to be afraid because God will help us and protect us. Why are you acting like this?" Yes, I had to admit, she was right, and I confessed my fear and went on in peace.

Jacob was alone, scared and conflicted in his heart. When he camped at Bethel, he settled down for the night, a stone for his pillow. In his dream, a ladder reached to heaven and angels were going up and down on it, and God Himself was at the top! Jacob encountered God in a new dimension that night and said, "What an awesome place this is!" He had seen God, and that is what made him experience fear and reverence. It was not Jacob's *location* that caused him fear; rather it was the *Person* he saw.

God is much nearer to us than we realize. You are surrounded by His continual presence. Your encounter with God can begin right where you are today. You do not need a dream of ladders and angels. You only need a quiet, humble heart and a repentant spirit. You will find the strength for your journey, wisdom for each decision, and love for each person God brings in your life.

You will be able to walk the path He has for you in peace and safety.

January 7

Reason Not to Fear #7: God Is Able to Protect Us

"Deliver me, I pray, from the hand of my brother, from the hand of Esau;
for I fear him, lest he come and attack me and the mothers with the children."
Genesis 32:11

Jacob had a reason to be afraid of Esau. The last time he'd seen his brother was after he'd cheated him out of the blessing and Esau was vowing to kill him. Esau was a big, blustery fighting type of man who settled things with his fists and his weapons. He was not a pleasant memory to Jacob and even after all those years, Jacob trembled when he heard that his brother was coming with four hundred armed men.

Notice several things about this prayer request from Jacob regarding his brother Esau.

First, Jacob believed in the power of God to rescue him. Second, he knew he should address his prayer to God along with his specific requests and specific difficulties. Third, Jacob knew Esau might want to destroy him, therefore he knew God was the only one who could deliver him.

There are people from my past who are truly scary, too. I think of some of the young people we ministered to in Chicago and Pennsylvania, people I allowed to stay in my home with my young children, people who regularly took advantage of us and could have easily harmed us. I think of others who have opposed my ministry, knocked me down a time or two, and been a thorn in my side. I'm sure you can think of ones who make you tremble, as well.

People can scare me and they can interrupt my relationship with the Lord. When that happens, the presence of God, the voice of God, and the peace of God vanishes.

Times of fear should cause you to have deep, straight times of prayer. Your fears should drive you to your knees. Jacob found the Lord to be his strong tower. He did not sink into despair because of his fear of his brother, and eventually Jacob and Esau were reconciled to each other.

John Calvin hit the nail on the head when he wrote, "The world's threatenings should drive us to God's promises." Who are the people who cause you to be afraid? Take them to the Lord in prayer. Confess any sin you might have. Give your fear over to the Lord and allow Him to transform that relationship. Claim the promises of God. Do it today.

January 8

Reason Not to Fear #8: God Will Never Leave You

"On the third day Joseph said to them, 'Do this and live, for I fear God.'"
Genesis 42:18

After serving in Chicago for fifteen years, we felt called of God to move to Pennsylvania. Bob worked with a church and also had a secular job. But Bob's heart was still with the troubled youths he saw on the streets of the city. With the encouragement and backing of the church, he began a mission for teens, and at first the kids did not trust him.

My heart went out to him as night after night for a year he would leave home at midnight. He did this for one year, walking the streets all night long, talking with anyone who would talk to him. At first many thought he was an undercover policeman and gave him a wide berth. They hid from him, laughed at him, mocked him. Finally one brave teenager sidled up to him and started a conversation. The teen needed some ready cash. Bob gave him what he had. The teen snatched it and left.

After that, more kids started talking to Bob. Slowly they learned to set aside their fears and trust him. Once they trusted him, he was able to sit and talk with them. He discovered how lonely they were. After a time, other hurting people began seeking him out. He was finally able to help the kids on the streets.

After a long time, the years of unfairness and frustration that characterized Joseph's life ended. When his brothers come to Egypt seeking food because of the famine, he could have taken his revenge. But an authority higher than revenge ruled Joseph and spoke to his heart. When Joseph told his brothers *I am a God fearing man*, he was conveying to them that he was a worshipper of the true God and they had nothing to fear.

Joseph's brothers did not fear God. They followed their self-ruling impulses. They were jealous, resentful and hostile towards Joseph, so they got rid of him. They feared that their flimsy pretense would collapse. When your existence is based on a lie, fear is the foundation. Joseph had to help them get past their fears and become men who feared God.

God is with you, too, despite other people's actions towards you. God will never leave you, nor forsake you. Even though you might be misunderstood and talked about, you can trust God to help. Close your devotional time by thanking God for His presence and love.

January 9

Reason Not to Fear #9: Have A Good Conscience Before God

"So he said to his brothers, 'My money has been restored, and there it is in my sack!' Then their hearts failed them and they were afraid, saying to one another, 'What is this that God has done to us?'" Genesis 42:28

One of the many wonderful gifts God has given us is conscience. When we violate our conscience, we feel guilty and afraid.

Many of the young people we knew and ministered to in Chicago lived with guilt and fear. Most of them had no idea that the gnawing pain within them could be taken away. It was our job to tell them the good news that Christ died for their sins and through His forgiveness they could find freedom from fear and guilt.

We opened our home to anyone in need. One time a young man named Bud came to live with us. We had to leave him home alone while I went to teach a ladies Bible study and Bob went to work. After a long time of suspecting that Bud was pawing through our personal belongings and stealing, we confronted him with the proof. He had even stolen my wedding rings by taking our bedroom door (which we'd left locked) off the hinges! When he denied he had done anything wrong, we asked him to leave. I felt sorry for him and still pray for him.

The ten sons of Jacob headed for Egypt because of a famine in Canaan. They had no idea they would encounter their brother Joseph, who hid his identity. After a brief exchange of words, Joseph put them in prison, where fear visited each man. After he released all but Simeon and allowed them to make the journey home, they discovered their returned money in their sacks and became frightened. Conscience had been awakened, their hearts faltered and their alarm was directed to God. They feared vengeance from God.

Has this ever happened to you? You are reading God's Word and suddenly a verse hits you right between the eyes. He has given us a conscience and the Word. He wants to conform you to the image of His Son in righteousness and truth. What is your reaction to His prompting? Do you confess your sin, turn from it and believe God has wiped the slate clean? This is the only way to find freedom from a guilty conscience.

Close your devotional time by confessing any sin God has brought to your mind. Thank Him for His forgiveness and grace. You will find peace, joy and a clear conscience.

January 10

Reason Not to Fear #10: We Can Forgive Others

"Joseph said to them, 'Do not be afraid of me, for am I in the place of God? But as for you, you meant evil against me, but God meant it for good in order to bring it about as it is this day to save many people alive.'"
Genesis 50:19

Choices. We all have them; we all make them. The choices we make today affect us for the rest of our lives. The most miserable people I know are those who live with bitterness, anger and resentment eating at their souls because they have chosen to hold a grudge or resentment or hurt rather than forgive and grant grace to others.

When we lived in Chambersburg, Pennsylvania, Bob and I taught Bible studies in the local prison – I with the women and Bob with the men. Over the years we listened to the grievances these people carried with them – both real and imagined. We urged them to forgive each offense, but it was so hard for them to grasp this and actually do it.

Joseph knew something about forgiveness. If anyone had a grievance to bear and injustice to hug to his heart, he did. But Joseph learned the important lesson of forgiveness. He didn't carry that baggage around with him. How could he be successful, even in prison? Because he forgave his brothers and refused to carry a grudge against them. In due time God honored him with great achievements, and when he finally came face to face with his brothers, his words were not judgmental but full of mercy.

Forgiveness is powerful. It frees us from fear and bondage. It gives us peace. It helps us live in harmony with others. Perhaps you will have to forgive many times, over and over again, as often as the offense reappears in your mind. But eventually, as you bring these hurts to the Lord and leave them there with Him, He will heal your heart and bring you peace.

Oh, my dear friends, if you harbor ill feelings toward another person, give it to God and *forgive that person*. I challenge you: write everything you can think of that is bothering you down on a piece of paper. Yes, do it *right now*. Then forgive each person and each offense. Ask God to wipe the slate clean.

Now burn the paper. As the paper burns, imagine that all your hurts are burning with it. They are gone! Thank God that you can live this day without bearing anyone a grudge, and determine that you will never do that again. Forgive quickly. Forgive completely. It is how Christ forgave you.

January 11

Reason Not to Fear #11: We Reverence God

"Moreover He said, "I am the God of your father -- the God of Abraham, the God of Isaac, and the God of Jacob.' And Moses hid his face, for he was afraid to look upon God." Exodus 3:6

We have no fear because we fear. There are two different meanings for this word. In Proverbs we are told that the fear of the Lord is the beginning of wisdom (Prov. 1:7). To fear God does not mean to be in dread of Him or to have horror or fright when we approach Him. In the Hebrew language, the fear of the Lord is always associated with true religion. It describes a person who keeps God's laws, who obeys His voice, who walks in His ways. It means we reverence Him to the point of committing our entire life to Him. We acknowledge Him as our Master and Lord.

How many people, even in America, are ignorant of God's laws? They have taken the Bible and His commandments out of our schools, our government, our media, and would probably like to take them out of our homes and our churches. So how can people fear the Lord when they do not even know His Word?

We must begin at the beginning. It is not enough to say you believe there is a god. Or that you acknowledge His presence. Or even that He died for your sins. It goes way beyond that – it must pierce your heart and change your life. This fear must so rule your heart that you can do nothing but lay your life down for Him in obedience and service. We begin to know the fear of the Lord by making God's Word a living and vital part of our lives.

Moses had been raised with the laws and commands of God. He was cast out of Egypt and spent forty long years tending sheep in the desert. When God spoke to him, he hid his face in fear. Because of his godly fear, Moses obeyed God and served him throughout his whole life.

The more you worship God and learn His Word, the more you will experience a godly fear. You will understand that He demands more of you than a casual Sunday morning service. He demands your life. How committed are you to this One who calls to you from your burning bush? Do you give Him obedience and reverence, or do you hide from Him? Do you follow the ways of the world and only give Him a nod, or have you given Christ your entire life?

Commit yourself totally to Him today. Do it now.

January 12

Reason Not to Fear #12: We Obey God

"But as for you and your servants, I know that you will not yet fear the Lord God." Exodus 9:30

People do not connect the dots. The reason for this is because they lack godly wisdom. The beginning of wisdom is to *fear the Lord* (Prov. 1:7). We often think we can figure life out by ourselves and that is when we fall into difficulties. Like flies caught in a spider's web, we struggle to extricate ourselves from our troubles, and we become more and more entangled.

When I taught a Bible study for women in our local prison in Pennsylvania, I loved every woman I met. They taught me more than I taught them. Some were in for murder, others for stealing, others for robbery. They were people who did not know God's Word and who had made many wrong decisions. It was a joy for me to see their lives change as they put their trust in Christ and decide to walk in His ways.

These people became a part of our extended family, for we opened our home to them to stay with us after they got out of prison. When others in the community learned what we were doing, they frequently asked, "Aren't you afraid to have those prisoners in your house, when you have your children and two of them are girls?"

The answer was always *no*. We never had any fear that made us stop being obedient to God. This is what it means to fear God and not others. To this day, I consider those who lived with us some of my dearest friends.

God commanded Pharaoh to let His people go, and time and time again, Pharaoh did not obey. God displayed His power to Pharaoh through ten plaques, yet Pharaoh remained fearless of God, and he resisted the will of God to the end. Why did Pharaoh not obey God? He did not want to lose his slaves. They were important to the economy in Egypt. He did not fear God, and he did not connect the dots. He lost his life because of it.

How about you? Are you connecting the dots? Think about it honestly. How often do you make decisions without consulting God or His Word? How much godly wisdom do you have in your life? Are you resisting the will of God? Confess this to Him and begin to walk in the wisdom of the Lord.

January 13

Reason Not to Fear #13: Even In Our Fear, God Is Able

"And when Pharaoh drew near, the children of Israel lifted their eyes, and behold, the Egyptians marched after them. So they were very afraid, and the children of Israel cried out to the Lord." Exodus 14:10

When we lived and ministered in Chicago, Bob held a Bible study every Friday evening for young teenage men and women, which went from 9pm to past midnight and included food, soft drinks, and basketball. Bob ran a basketball league and you could only be on this league if you attended the Bible study.

One evening a team was very upset at Bob and his call as ref, and before he knew it, a young man was coming after him with a lead pipe. Several times he swung it at Bob, but missed. Within minutes the police put an end to the violent activity. Why did the young man miss Bob? It wasn't because he lacked experience with a lead pipe. We can only conclude that it was God's mighty hand that saved him from serious injury that night.

The nation of Israel had been released from bondage, but their problems were not over once they left Egypt. Behind them came the armored, disciplined, and furious Egyptian army, determined to recover their lost slaves. In front of the Israelites lay the Red Sea. They were trapped. Suddenly the people experienced fear. This was terror, horror, and panic.

They resorted to the only response they knew: they complained to Moses angrily. Fear makes us do that. We lash out at everyone in our path, but the problem is really deep within our own hearts: we are afraid and we selfishly demand that others move heaven and earth to make us happy again.

What is causing you to fear today? Loss of a job? Illness? Wars and earthquakes in the world? The economic crisis in America? Family members giving you a hard time? A bad job situation? Church fights? When we get our eyes off God and onto ourselves, when we forget His Word and begin to fear, that is when we have problems.

The other path to follow is to trust God and fear Him. The choice is yours. I challenge you to turn away from your fears and turn to God. One of the underlining ideas of *the fear of the Lord* is loyalty and faithfulness. In the midst of your trial, can you find this in your heart for the Lord? Do you love Him? Can you trust Him? Confess your anger and lack of trust and learn to live this day with the peace of God ruling and reigning in your heart.

January 14

Reason Not to Fear #14: He Can Do the Impossible

*"And Moses said to the people, 'Do be afraid! Stand still, and see the salvation of the Lord, which He will accomplish for you today. For the Egyptians you see today, you shall see again no more forever.''*Exodus 14:13

When some pastors in Chambersburg learned of Bob's work in Chicago, they asked him to start a mission like that there. Even though we would have to raise our own support, Bob was very eager to start working, so with only a handful of supporters, we began.

I must admit I was fearful. We had three children to care for, a house payment, and medical bills. Stepping out in faith is a very scary thing to do when your only resource is the unseen hand of God. Is God faithful? Would He provide when the bills come due?

In our affluent American society, we find ourselves relying on our pay checks, our CDs and other securities, our insurance policies, our hospitals and doctors, our properties, stocks and bonds, yes, even on the government to provide us with health care and living expenses when we retire. Yet with the recent economic crisis, I might be writing to many who have lost everything. Suddenly we are cast solely upon the loving hands of God to provide.

I am thrilled to report that my fears were unfounded when we were living in Pennsylvania, and that God is truly faithful. Every month we had sufficient money to cover our needs.

God was faithful to the Israelites, too. He told them that all they needed to do was to *stand by*. Stand by and see the salvation of the Lord! He provided a shield for them throughout the night and a wind to blow the water into high walls. While Moses held his staff over the sea, the nation walked over dry land to the other side.

The Israelites knew how strong Pharaoh's men were and they also knew how weak they were. They had no way to escape. The vast Red Sea was staring them in the face. Truthfully, their only hope to get to the other side was to look upwards. The Israelites crossed the Red Sea by the miraculous hand of God.

That is the key to our victory today: focus on God and the promises in His Word. Find a promise and write it down on a 3x5 card. Carry the card with you today and commit it to memory.

January 15

Reason Not to Fear #15: God Provides Help

"Moreover you shall select from all the people some able men, such as fear God, men of truth, hating covetousness, and place such men over them to be rulers of thousands, rulers of hundreds, rulers of fifties, and rulers of tens."
Exodus 18:21

The simple solution to over-loaded, burned-out, harried people is to delegate responsibility. But that solution is often ignored because people in leadership tend to cling tenaciously to control and power. Yet when our energy level dips dangerously low, when stress from our job, home, church and families press upon us, we break.

None of us like to be thought of as weak or needy. Pride and lust for control enters our lives so easily in this area. In our times of exhaustion, we often respond to others in the flesh and the damage is irreparable. In our ministry of reaching young people and others for the Lord, we found the work sometimes beyond what we could handle. In those times, we realized we had to let go and ask for help.

There are two reasons to delegate responsibility. First, we help others exercise their spiritual gifts. If we do not delegate, Christians around us can do nothing but warm the pews. This is wrong. We need to recognize that others can do the ministry, too. The second reason to delegate is the care we need for our own personal lives. If we do not delegate responsibility, we will be no good for the Lord in anything we attempt to do.

Moses was working way too much and his father-in-law, Jethro, noticed. He strongly urged Moses to select some *capable, honest men who feared God* to help him. Jethro knew that only honest, and God-fearing men could be entrusted with the souls of people.

When you delegate, chose people who are proven in their spiritual lives to be mature Christians, who have a desire to serve the Lord, and are willing to learn.

As you train them, take them alongside you, walk them through it. Let them observe you, teach them how to do it, watch as they do it, then turn them loose. You will find joy in delegating and you will find rest as you enable others to exercise their spiritual gifts. Begin to put this lesson into practice. Trust God and rest in His provision for your needs.

January 16

Reason Not to Fear #16: God Is Holding My Hand

"I will send My fear before you, I will cause confusion among all the people to whom you come; and will make all your enemies turn their backs to you." Exodus 23:27

The state fair is going on here in Arizona. I decided that would be a fun activity to take my grand-daughter, Boo, to it. (Boo is my name for her.) It would be a day just for Boo and Menzie (her name for me). She had never been to the fair and for a four-year- old, it can be rather overwhelming.

As we walked through the gates, Boo grabbed my hand tighter. I could tell she was afraid of all the people and noises. However, being the good Menzie that I am, I assured her that I would be there for her, and that she didn't have to be afraid because I had already been to a fair and I would take care of her.

The Israelite nation, under the direction of Moses, was camped at Mt. Sinai where Moses would receive the law and commandments from God. The Israelites had long way to go from Mt. Sinai to the Promised Land. How could a bunch of newly freed slaves hope to arrive at their destination safely and conquer the nations who occupied the promised land? In this verse, God is telling them He will go before them, prepare them, and protect them. It is only by His strength, His power and His wisdom that they could hope to accomplish this.

God has the ability to go ahead of you, to prepare you for the task ahead, and to protect you from danger and evil along the way. Do you believe that? Many of us understand that truth, but we have a hard time living it out. We can relate to my little Boo's feelings. We want to move ahead, but we have some fears.

Dear friends, God has your hand in His if you are walking with Him. He has a plan for your spiritual development, and He can bring it to pass. Believe Him and walk out today in that awareness, freedom and joy. Grab His hand just a little tighter, walk through the gates and enjoy the fair!

January 17

Reason Not to Fear #17: God Can Change My Heart to Reflect His Glory

"So when Aaron and all the children of Israel saw Moses, behold, the skin of his face shone, and they were afraid to come near him."
Exodus 34:30

Cecil B. DeMille's movie, *The Ten Commandments,* is one of the greatest movies of all time, and even today it stands not only as a work of art, but as a reminder of God and His servant, Moses. Do you remember the scene when Charlton Heston came down from the mountain after talking with God? His hair had gone white and his face was wiser and stronger. The movie makers attempted to show what really happened many years ago on Mt. Sinai in the desert, and even though Charlton Heston was a great actor, the movie couldn't completely portray the awesome presence of God when He appeared to Moses that day.

Moses' face glowed so much they had to put a veil over it so he could go about his duties without the people being distracted by the glory. The change, the real, and authentic change, took place in Moses' heart, and it was displayed on his shining face. At the burning bush was where he got real with God. See, there is a huge difference between someone who merely imitates or fakes an encounter and someone who has an authentic one.

The people were afraid of this supernatural occurrence, yet they had no cause to be. If they only would have looked deeply into Moses' eyes, they would have seen God's joy welling up, His love overflowing, His peace like a deep river in his soul. Yet like foolish children, they allowed this change to throw them, and they veered away from Moses as if he had become a leper.

I have heard that you either have a "yes" face or a "no" face. Think about it. What does your face say about your attitudes, your thoughts, your heart? If we truly trust God as we profess to do, then people should be able to glimpse Him in our countenance. People all around us need God's love in their lives and it is our job to communicate it with them.

What are you focused on today? What does your face say about your relationship with God? Does it glow with the joy of the Lord? Check your heart and get it right with the One who longs to bring you closer to Himself in love and peace.

January 18

Reason Not to Fear #18: God Provides Help

"You shall not curse the deaf, nor put a stumbling block before the blind; but you shall fear your God; I am the LORD." Leviticus 19:14

Bernard Madoff was a man on a roll. It seemed he had the Midas touch -- everything he became involved in turned to gold and he became a big time investor on Wall Street. Yet he cheated and lied and schemed to gain money for himself. According to the original federal charges, Madoff said that his firm had "liabilities of approximately $50 billion" -- the amount of money people who had invested with his company and subsequently lost. Prosecutors estimated the size of the fraud to be $64.8 billion, based on the amounts in the accounts of Madoff's 4,800 clients. On June 29, 2009, he was sentenced to 150 years in prison with restitution of $170 billion. Bernard Madoff was arrested because of a $50 billion scam in what may rank among the biggest fraud cases ever.

While you or I may not operate on that level, it is astounding what people will do to make money. Do you realize in the retail business there is a bait cast to get you into the store? The retailer advertises or promotes an item at an extremely low price. You go in the store and find many other things to purchase while you are there. Then when you are at the register, you discover you have picked up the wrong item and that the item advertised is not available. You are encouraged to buy the slightly higher, the slightly more expensive item instead. While some people call this wise business practices, God's Word calls it cheating. It is sin.

If you fear the Lord, you will extend your faith and respect for God even into the small details of your business life and your dealings with others. The word *blind* in this verse holds the meaning of not taking advantage of the weak or helpless. In fact, this verse calls us to help those who are vulnerable and helpless. When you obey what this verse says, and put feet to it, you are showing the fear and reverence you have for God.

Rather than taking advantage of those who are weaker than you, how can you show God's love to them today? Take special notice of the details of your life and bring them into conformity to God's Word. His blessing and peace will abide with you forever if you are obedient. Just think about Bernard Madoff as he sits in his prison cell for the rest of his life.

It just isn't worth it.

January 19

Reason Not to Fear #19: We Honor Our Senior Citizens

"You shall rise before the grey headed and honor the presence of an old man, and fear your God, I am the LORD." Leviticus 19:32

We live in a culture that is given over to youth and beauty. Sadly, it is one in which the older generation finds themselves more and more looked down upon, marginalized and degraded. In fact, many beauty products are sold to color whitened or graying hair or remove wrinkles and age spots.

In Leviticus, the Israelite people were instructed to show honor and deference toward the elderly. In the New Testament, we read that elders are to be held in honor in this way, as well. Why should we do that?

God wants us to honor the senior citizens in your life because of their perseverance, hard work and their faith. Honor them for their example of hope and optimism. They have endured a lot in their lifetime. In the tough times, the elderly have learned that God is greater than their problems. They have learned to fear and trust in Him because He has never let them down. I remember watching my mother's hair turn gray, wondering when my black hair would change, too. Funny, now that it has, I find that gray is one of my favorite colors!

I am writing to young and old, and there are things each of us must learn from this lesson. For those of us over fifty, my advice is to be more aware of the feelings toward the younger generation and try to understand them. Show kindness whenever you can. A smile is a bridge to a good relationship. You need to continue to encourage the younger generation behind you. Show your reverence for God to your grandchildren and teach them to fear God.

For those of you under fifty, heed these words of wisdom. Hold the door for an elderly person. Be patient when they take a long time to get their money out at the check stand. Smile. Listen to them when they talk, even if the talk is all about their physical ailments. Someday you, too, will be there and you will appreciate kindness and honor.

The injunction in Leviticus is to *stand in the presence of an elderly person.* I love that idea, yet I don't expect to see it much in our culture and society today! Do the next best thing. By your attitude make the next elderly person you see feel very special. It will warm your heart, too.

January 20

Reason Not to Fear #20: We Act Kindly

"Therefore you shall not oppress one another, but you shall fear your God; for I am the LORD your God." Leviticus 25:17

One of the basic ways to show we fear God is to walk in His ways and obey His commandments. If you respect someone and honor them as being in authority over you, you will do what that person says to do. We all understand that principle. Yet respect for authority is being undermined in our lives every day.

The result is a society that is cruel, violent, heartless and unkind. God calls us to be different. There are many ways to show kindness. I remember one time when we worked in the mission in Chicago that I needed a winter coat. We had very little to live on, for when the mission was low on funds they could not pay us much.

Winters in Chicago are harsh and cold and I desperately needed a warmer winter coat. So I squirreled away the little extra bits of change I had, denied myself treats, and managed to collect enough money to buy a coat. I had already been looking at them in the stores and I could not wait to go and buy the one I had picked out. But then I found out that the furnace in the mission was defunct and needed to be replaced. How could I buy a coat when dozens of men and women would suffer from the cold if we could not get another furnace? And so I gave my money to the mission to help buy another furnace.

The next time I saw *my* coat hanging in the store window, I did not cry for want of it. When the ladies of the church we attended found out about my need, raised the money, and bought me a warm winter coat! *Imagine my surprise! That is when I cried!*

I experienced kindness and grace that day. How about you? Would people characterize your actions as kind and graceful? Cruelty is against God's character, for He is just, merciful, and fair. Because you fear God, you must act justly, give love to all, and forgive when you are wronged. As God's child you are to respect everyone.

The next time you are tempted to lose your temper, cut someone off on the freeway or respond with anger to someone in your family, remember these words: *show your fear of God by not taking advantage of others.* "Be kind to one another, tender-hearted, forgiving each other just as God in Christ has forgiven you." Eph. 4:32

January 21

Reason Not to Fear #21: We Help Others in Need

"Take no usury or interest from him, but fear your God, that your brother may live with you." Leviticus 25:36

In 1989, we moved to Chambersburg, PA, where Bob accepted a teaching position in a Mennonite school. When we first arrived we did not have the finances to buy a home, so we rented. Within a few weeks after our arrival, Bob got a call from a realtor we knew. This man informed Bob that he had been approached by an elderly man and wife who wanted to help a younger Christian family buy a home. We had never met this couple, never heard about them and had not solicited their help.

I could not believe that we were sitting across the table, talking with them about a loan to purchase a house! They made it possible for us to buy a home which would be used by God in many practical ways as we served Him in Chambersburg. God knew what we needed and He used a faithful man and his wife to meet our needs.

In biblical times, the law of Moses prohibited the Israelites from charging interest to those who were poor. Charging them interest, or even charging a down payment, would make their situation worse. Anything like that would have prohibited us from buying our own home back in 1989. To bypass interest or down payment is a sign of mercy.

The Lord has extended grace to you, my friend. He reached down and saved you by His death on the cross. Salvation, power, glory and eternal life belong to those who put their trust in Him, and these are all gifts of grace. God was not forced to save you. The wideness of His grace will be a matter of wonder and awe throughout all eternity.

Can you do less for your fellow Christian? Christ expects you to show forgiveness, mercy, help and grace to those who need it. And who knows? You might be the next one with your hand out, asking for help. Proverbs 3:27 says, "Do not withhold good from those to whom it is due, when it is in your power to do it." Proverbs 28:27 it says, "He who gives to the poor will never want, but he who shuts his eyes will have many curses."

Be kind to those in need. Do not only just pray for them but think of practical ways to give and help them out. Find one act of kindness and mercy that you can do today.

January 22

Reason Not to Fear #22: We Are Kind to the Poor

"Now in case a countryman of yours becomes poor and his means with regard to you falter, then you are to sustain him, like a stranger or sojourner that he may live with you. Take no usury or interest from him, but fear your God, that your brother may live with you." Leviticus 25:35, 36

Money matters affect all of us. We are taught that if we are careful with our money, save ahead for the future, and do not use our credit cards to excess, we will have enough money to live on and be secure for the future. But in these days of nationwide economic troubles, these enjoinders do not cover all the situations in which a person might find themselves.

What about the person who loses his job, his pension, his home and his livelihood? What about the person who has fallen ill and is no longer capable to work? What about the person who has sacrificed to serve God and has no means to provide for themselves when they grow older?

This verse from Leviticus tells us that at times even the best money manager in the world might fall into difficult times, and that others around them who are better off have the responsibility to help, to loan money with little or no interest, and to see that this person gets back on their feet.

There are two truths here: first, God owns everything, and second, you are only a steward of all that you have. As you put these truths into practice, you display the fear of God to those around you.

Those who have a healthy reverence for the Lord will not take advantage of other people. If you fear the Lord, it should show in the way you treat others, with love and kindness and respect. Over the years, I have been a recipient of some loans and at other times I have been the one loaning the money. When I loan money, I have never charged anyone interest.

The Israelites never learned this lesson. Many times they took advantage of each other. The truth is, they never learned to honor the Lord properly. Slowly they got to a place where they did not want God telling them how to run their businesses and lives, and they descended the slippery slope of greed to outright rebellion against God.

Treat people fairly and with kindness, and watch the Lord take care of you.

January 23

Reason Not to Fear #23: We Follow the Rules

"I will give peace in the land, and you shall lie down, and none will make you afraid; I will rid the land of evil beasts, and the sword will not go through your land." Leviticus 26:6

A lawyer questioned Jesus one day about the law. "Teacher," he said pompously, "which is the greatest commandment in the Law?"

Jesus answered, "You shall love the Lord your God with all your heart, and with all your soul, and with all your mind. This is the great and foremost commandment. The second is like it, you shall love your neighbor as yourself." (Matt. 22:36-39) Jesus condensed the Ten Commandments and the law into two simple sentences. Love is the key to obeying God's requirements for mankind.

The essence of life is to love and be loved. God's love is greater than anything we can achieve, yet by His Spirit dwelling within believers, we can experience this kind of success in our lives. If you want to know what it means to love with God's love, read I Corinthians 13.

Anything that hinders love leads us down a path of disobedience and pain. There are many things we can indulge in that would take us away from God. He instructs His people to follow His Word, His ways, and His rules to achieve success in their lives.

There are three important words I tried to have my children follow when they were growing up in our home. Now I try and have my grandchildren follow them when they come for a visit. The three words are: "Follow the rules." I think that is a pretty simple rule, but my children and grandchildren all had trouble with following that instruction.

First they had to know what the rules were in my house (and I made that clear to them), then they had to decide whether they would obey or disobey the rules. The Lord made it clear to the children of Israel, that if they would follow the rules given in His Word, they would be able to sleep without any type of fear. It is just that simple. If you want to get a good night's sleep, follow the rules.

If you want to life a peaceful life; if you want have your needs met; if you want your prayers to be heard and answered; if you want rest; if you want to success in your Christian life, **follow the rules!** The choice is yours. Make the right one.

January 24
Reason Not to Fear #24: Be Fair to All, Rich and Poor

"You shall not show partiality in judgment; you shall hear the small as well as the great; you shall not be afraid in any man's presence, for the judgment is God's. The case that is too hard for you, bring to me, and I will hear it."
Deuteronomy 1:17

Murder, rape, drugs, incest, those were all part of the normal life for the kids Bob and I worked with -- who lived in Cabrini Green downtown Chicago. Many times the children would come to the mission for our kid's program with black eyes, broken noses or broken arms. I remember one young girl who was normally happy; her cheerful face was always a boost to my spirits. But one day she entered with her head down, her hair covering her face. My heart wrenched at the misery I saw in her eyes.

After kids club was over, I walked her home and gently asked her why she was so sad. She told me that her uncle had been repeatedly sexually abusing her. I was shocked and horrified. She said she would not tell the police because of fear that they would not believe her. This young girl was a powerless victim of violence and lust. Even in a society that gives mouth service to helping the helpless, we see these types of people all the time, people who suffer because of injustice, weakness, poverty and lack of knowledge.

Moses gave instructions to the judges who ruled in Israel: *be fair to all, even to the poor, and do not give regard to the rich and powerful.* This verse cautions us to make sure our judgments are based on facts and that we hear both sides of the argument. We are not to fear those who are powerful because God will protect us from them.

We are prone to respect people because of their influence, position, or wealth. What is the divine remedy for judging fairly? The fear of God. Honoring God should govern your decisions. As God's child do not let the rich entice you to unrighteous decisions and do not let the poor entice you to favor him. Instead, seek the Lord and act accordingly. Do you allow money, prestige and power to influence your judgments?

Search your heart and see if there is any partiality there toward the wealthy and powerful. God calls us to protect the poor, show mercy to those who are without power, and be fair to all. Read James 2:1-10 and think about ways you can avoid partiality in your church, in your home, in your life. Determine to change your ways and to be kind to all.

January 25

Reason Not to Fear #25: God Is in All My Changes

*"'Where can we go up? Our brethren have discouraged our hearts, saying,
'The people are greater and taller than we; the cities were great and fortified
up to heaven; moreover, we have seen the sons of the Anakim there.' Then I
said to you, 'Do not be terrified or afraid of them.'"*
Deuteronomy 1:28, 29

Changes. We all have to make them. At times, fear can creep into our lives.

In August of 2000, Bob and I were involved one hundred percent in the ministry and we loved each moment of it. He was director of the mission downtown Chambersburg, PA, and I taught a large ladies Bible study, among other things. We'd completed a day full of purpose and God's blessings in the ministry and had time left over for a quiet dinner together. Then we went to an Amish auction which we loved to attend.

We made a bid on a table and bought it. Bob went to get the pickup, and I got in line to pay for our purchase. But Bob didn't return, and I began feeling uneasy. Finally I left the line and went out to the parking lot. To my dismay and shock, I saw a crowd of people around our pickup. Bob was slumped over the steering wheel, unconscious. After what seemed a lifetime, the ambulance arrived and he was rushed to the hospital.

We were told that he had suffered a cardiac arrest and that because his brain had gone so long without oxygen, the prognosis on his recovery was not good. We waited and prayed in his room for days. Finally he awakened.

But we discovered that he had extensive brain damage and that the man I took home from the hospital several weeks later was not the man I had married and lived with for thirty-two years. This man had the mental capacity of an eight year old. I suddenly realized I had to care for him, love him and put up with all the problems inherent in such a situation for the rest of his life. It was like my husband had died and I was a single mom.

I had spent my life serving God, raising our children, teaching Bible studies to women in prison and out, helping young people rebuild their lives, and running my feet off in the busyness of a life of ministry. Suddenly I found myself taking care of my husband who had become a stranger and, worse, a little boy.

It was beyond my ability to cope, and so I came back to my faith in God in a deeper way than I had ever known. I cried out to God for help, wisdom, strength and patience. God answered my prayers. Whenever I needed an answer, it would be there. He graciously saw me through the changes in my life. I did not need to fear if I kept my eyes on Him.

Fear can assault us when we face changes in our lives.

The Israelites faced a huge change as they stood on the banks of the Jordan River and gazed into the promised land. They knew that God made a promise to them -- that He would help them drive out the Canaanites from the land. However, after the spy expedition, they lost trust in the promises of God. They lost their faith in God. And if we would take this a step further, they even lost faith in themselves.

They saw the giants and became full of fear. From the top of their head to bottom of their toes, they were frightened. Twelve men went together to view the same land and ten came back with a negative report; two with a positive report. The ten men were fearful; two were full of courage and faith. Ten could not see past the giants and the other obstacles that stood in the way of gaining the land. Two focused on God; they believed the promise, they were obedient.

Corrie ten Boom wrote, "No matter how deep the pit into which evil may cast you, underneath are the everlasting arms of God." I can stand before you and look you in the eyes and tell you that this is true. As a child of God, you have no reason to fear the future. No matter what circumstances or Satan throws at you, you are safe and protected by the power of God.

Dear friend, are you struggling with changes this day? Have you succumbed to fear when you consider the future and what it entails? Do you feel your courage ebbing at low tide? Remember: those who put their trust in God will always have enough courage to obey Him.

Chose today to be like those two men who had the audacity to embrace their changes and the future because they believed the promises of God and focused on Him. Thank Him for His grace, love and protection. Confess your sin of fearing. Turn your eyes on Jesus and focus on Him today, even when your faith wavers and fears creep in. He will protect you and your loved ones. Instead of fear, trust God and fear Him.

January 26

Reason Not to Fear #26: God Will Make Your Enemies Fear You

"And command the people saying, 'You are about to pass through the territory of your brethren the descendants of Esau, who live in Seir, and they will be afraid of you. Therefore watch yourselves carefully.'" Deuteronomy 2:4

Deuteronomy is written by Moses just before his death. The children of Israel are about to enter the promise land *without their leader*. In Moses' farewell speech, he reminded the Israelites of the covenants they made to the Lord to keep the law. If they kept His law, God's blessing will rest on them, they will enter the land, be victorious over their enemies, and enjoy peace and security. Moses reminded them of the time they passed through the territory of Esau. The Edomites once made the Israelites fearful, but now things were reversed -- now *they* feared the Israelites! How like God to take what you once feared and have that very same person or group of people fear *you*!

As I enter my fourteenth year of taking care of my husband, I have experienced numerous fears. I wonder how Bob will die. If he has a stroke, which they tell me is possible, this will incapacitate him even more than he is now and will put more work and responsibility on me. I am tempted to fear for my health and who will help me. I struggle with the fear of placing him in a facility and having enough money. I fear another twelve years, or more, of caring for him.

You know what those fears have done to me? Nothing! They have caused me to walk in circles in the wilderness. My strength to carry on lies in turning my focus daily on Christ and His sufficiency and to trust Him for my future. When I do that, my fears evaporate into thin air. My head clears. My heart is at rest. I can enjoy the day He gives me without worry or consternation. The very issues that caused me to fear are now nothing -- they are at my feet like conquered enemies, fearing *me*.

He can strengthen me and He can strengthen you. What are you facing today that causes you to fear? Whatever it is, turn away from it and focus on Jesus Christ. Walk in obedience to Him and God will cause those fears to melt away. Wherever God leads you to walk, in familiar or unfamiliar territory, He is ahead of you dispelling all the fears. Start walking. Look at your Leader. He is in front of you, and He will give you peace.

January 27

Reason Not to Fear #27: God Will Fight for Me

"You must not fear them, for the LORD your God Himself fights for you."
Deuteronomy 3:22

I have eight wonderful grandchildren -- they are my next generation to influence. Each child is unique and special to me, and I spend time daily with them, taking them on little trips, having them in my home to work on projects or read a book, talking to them, praying with them, teaching them my values and faith. I wish I could show you their pictures! My desire is to pass on to them the foundation of my faith in God that I have learned over the years as I have walked with Him. I want each of them to understand that God does not change and just as he worked in my life, He will to work in each of their lives.

Moses wanted to encourage the people of Israel to face what lay ahead without fear. Their task was awesome: they had to enter a foreign land and overcome giants, people who outnumbered them and whose weapons were bigger and more developed. It would have been easy to freeze with fear and not go ahead to claim the land God had given them.

Moses directed many of his comments to Joshua, the young man who would succeed him. He wanted to make sure Joshua understood all that the Lord had done for the children of Israel, and that all that He would continue to do if they followed Him.

Yet it was a scary situation for the people and for Joshua to lose Moses and face the giants in the land of Canaan! What source of strength enabled them to do what God commanded them to do?

It is simply this: *their faith in God*, rather than *their fear of the people*.

What God has promised us should cause our fears to flee. Moses wanted to leave a legacy of faith and not fear, and that is the responsibility of every godly leader, parent or grandparent, aunt, uncle or friend. What are you leaving behind to the next generation? Will you leave a legacy of faith or fear? Of trust or worry? Of confidence or doubt? When a person lives by faith day by day, they can say to those coming after them, "Do not be afraid, the Lord will fight for you, just as He has done for me."

May the Lord help you by His wisdom to pass on faith to those who come after you. Fear the Lord and pass it on.

January 28

Reason Not To Fear #28: God Always Sees You

"Then the LORD heard the voice of your words when you spoke to me, and the LORD said to me: 'I have heard the voice of the words of this people which they have spoken to you. They are right in all that they have spoken. Oh, that they had such a heart in them that they would fear Me and always keep all My commandments, that it might be well with them and with their children forever!'" Deuteronomy 5:28, 29

Every summer we would take the kids from the inner city of Chicago to the youth camp in Michigan that the mission owned. Bob was the bus driver, life guard, camp director, and parent all rolled into one. Every Saturday he drove a load of kids for three hours on the bus that was held together with super-glue, duck tape, and prayer. One day when the bus broke down (again!), he was on the turnpike and was able to stop at a truck stop. After calling for help, he discovered it would be hours before help would arrive. When the boys went into the restaurant and gift shop, they stole many things from the shop and loaded them onto the bus.

The proprietor discovered the missing items and called the police, who charged Bob with grand theft. A search was made of the bus and sure enough, they discovered the items. They cuffed Bob and said they would only let him free if the ones who stole confessed. The boys did confess and finally my husband was freed. He talked to the owner of the store and explained the situation. Astonishingly, the owner did not press charges.

When the boys lost their fear of God and of the laws of the land, they succumbed to temptation. They did not think that someone had seen them. Even if they'd gotten away with the thefts, God would have seen them and held them accountable.

God desires steadfast obedience and a heart that will fear Him. That is why He says what He does in this verse. "Oh, that they had such a heart in them that they would fear Me … always.…"

Do you only fear God when you encounter Him at church on Sunday mornings? Do you walk on the narrow path only when you feel like God has His eye on you? How about during the week at work? Do you not realize God sees you? He honors those whose hearts always reverence and respect Him, no matter who is watching. Check your actions today. Bring them into conformity to God's laws and learn to fear Him each moment.

January 29

Reason Not to Fear #29: We Know God's Word and His Will

"That you may fear the LORD your God, to keep all His statutes and His commandments which I command you, you and your son and your grandson, all the days of your life, and that your days may be prolonged."
Deuteronomy 6:2

Who doesn't love hanging around with their grandchildren? I sure do. In fact, as I am writing this, one of my grandsons, Peyton, is at my home for the day. Already today we have gone to the grocery store to buy his favorite rolls, to the Quick Trip gas station to buy his favorite drink, and we have played two games of Sorry.

When we interact with our children and grandchildren, we teach them daily the Word of the Lord. We are laying the foundation in their lives to learn the reverence and fear the Lord.

"Hear, O Israel!" (Deut. 6:4) Thus begins the great *Shema* (from the Hebrew word *hear*) that is quoted in Jewish services and taught in Jewish home. What were they to hear with both ears? The law of God given on Mt. Sinai. God desired that as they moved into the promised land of Canaan, they would hear, remember, and obey the commands He gave them.

Read all of chapter six to see how deeply God wanted them to be committed to His Word and His will. They were to teach their children when they sat down, when they arose, when they walked about on their daily routines. They were to write the commands on little plaques that would be bound to their hands and their foreheads. They were to write them on the doorposts of their houses.

I know people who write themselves reminders on their hands, but I have never seen anyone write the Word of God there. How highly do you rate the Word of God and what prominence does it have in your life on a daily basis? Do you memorize it? Talk about it? Think about it? Teach it to your children and grandchildren?

This passage says that when we are obedient to God's Word and keep His commands, He blesses us in many ways. We must know God's Word before we can obey it and live by it. It is worth it! Believe God and obey Him.

January 30

Reason Not to Fear #30: We Fear God Alone

"You shall fear the Lord your God and serve Him and shall take oaths in His name. You shall not go after other gods, the gods of the peoples who are all around you." Deuteronomy 6:13, 14

When my husband suffered another major cardiac arrest in the year 2000, great fear came over me. Fear that he might not survive and would die. Fear of our future. Fear of taking care of him. Could I do it? How?

The truth is, I faced many fears and it resulted in many sleepless nights. My fear so consumed me that I found myself only believing the worst possible future for us. My hope diminished as my fear took over, and I found myself struggling to hold onto my faith because my fear wanted to push it aside.

Fear does that. It makes us lose focus, it makes problems grow larger than they are, and it causes us to lose faith and courage in God. People fear many things, but we do not often think of fear in connection with worship.

If you think about it, fear and worship are cause and effect. What I fear, I worship. I fear being looked at like a fool in front of people, so I spend too much time thinking about how I look and what I say to them. I am worshipping these people and putting them above God. If you fear being poor, you will spend an inordinate amount of time trying to become rich. You are worshipping money as a way of escaping the pain you felt as a child.

What do you fear? How does your fear affect your life? What are you worshipping instead of God?

I heard a good quote the other day. It said, "Fear is the signal to turn your focus from yourself to God."

This verse simply states, "Fear the Lord your God." In other words, hold fast to Him. Cling to Him. Every day grow closer to Him. Run to Him. Increase in reverent fear for Him alone.

The fear of the Lord will give you victory. It will move you to obedience and holiness. It will fill you with strength to face whatever is ahead. It will cause you to stand tall in Him.

Can you turn your fear to faith? Focus on the Lord and He will do it for you.

January 31

Reason Not to Fear #31: Teach Your Children the Word of God

"And the LORD commanded us to observe all these statutes, to fear the LORD our God, for our good always, that He might preserve us alive, as it is this day." Deuteronomy 6:24

The TV show, *Survivor,* portrays a young man in extreme conditions who must find a way to take care of his bodily needs and survive the cold, heat, deprivation, or wild animals of nature. Recently an expose on the show revealed that he actually got a motel room whenever he was on location shooting the show!

The children of Israel completed forty years of survival training in the desert, yet God told them through Moses that obeying His commands is the *one thing* that they must do to survive as they entered the Promised Land. They faced armies who outclassed them in size, armor, horses, chariots and ferocity. The people who lived in the valleys had walled cities and an advanced civilization. The Israelites were a nomadic tribe of people who had little experience in warfare, small amounts of weapons, and who lived and camped in the hills.

How could they survive on the mission God gave them -- to conquer and live in the land? They were cast completely on faith and the grace of God. They had to fear God and trust in Him to survive.

Have you ever been at that place, my friend? Have you been on your face before God, knowing that the situation you faced was out of your control? That you could not survive one moment, let alone a whole lifetime, in this situation? How did you cope? What are your survival techniques?

Spend time teaching the Word of God to your children and grandchildren. This is *intentional*: we must plan to do it. Plan regular times to sit down with your children and teach them the Word of God. When a problem arises, open the Bible and find a principle that will give you wisdom about it. Include them in your prayer times. Study the Bible together. Decide what Bible study or passage you are going to go through with your family and make time for it.

It's time to take God's Word seriously. You must learn the Word and obey the Word. It is for your survival; for your good, for the good of your family. Do it now.

February 1

Reason Not to Fear #32: Remember God's Power

"You shall not be afraid of them; you shall remember well what the LORD your God did to Pharaoh and to all Egypt." Deuteronomy 7:18

Are you about to step into a new job, position or responsibility that makes you fearful?

Bob and I experienced similar fears many times as God led us into the rescue mission work in Chicago. You want to experience real fear? Try walking down a littered street in the inner city around midnight. You might see a group of young people huddled around a central figure, armed to the teeth. You see they are eyeing you with aggression, with animosity, with the intent to do you harm. They converse with each other and cast you dark looks.

You know you've invaded their territory, and you know you're out of your depth. You have no weapon, defense or strategy to protect yourself if it actually comes to an attack. Your only resource is Jesus Christ and you hope He has some pretty strong angels hovering nearby. Your strategy is love. Your game plan is mercy. Your hope is eternal life.

These kids understand nothing of why you are here, but God has led you to this place and you must follow through. Fear has to be conquered with faith in an all-powerful God. This lesson is true for all of us who have begun a new ministry or stepped out in faith in obedience to God's command.

Moses talked about how they had seen God deliver them from Egypt. Remember, remember, remember, he said! God promises to impart blessings on His children every day. The catch is this: *in order to receive the blessings, you have to be obedient to Him.* God wants to release you from any remembrance of fear, and to remember instead the victories He has brought into your life.

Remember what God has brought you through, and step out in faith to be obedient to Him. Say that word to your neighbor. Teach that class. Don't be afraid of what people think of you. Remember He has saved you, delivered you, given you new life and peace. Let those memories take away any fear you may have that is still residing in you today.

Step out in faith. God will protect you.

February 2

Reason Not to Fear #33: His Eye Is On Us

"The great trials which your eyes saw, the signs and the wonders, the mighty hand and the outstretched arm, by which the LORD your God brought you out. So shall the LORD your God do to all the people of whom you are afraid." Deuteronomy 7:19

A mother went in to her little boy's room to read him a bedtime story. While she was reading, a big thunderstorm started. The little boy became very frightened and said to his mother, "Can't you stay with me tonight, Mom?" The mother pulled her son closer and said softly, "I can't. I have to stay in Daddy's room." To which the little boy replied, "That big sissy!"

All of us have fears. Some fears are beneficial and some are not. Fearing to touch a hot stove is a beneficial fear we teach our children. Fearing to walk too close to the edge of a crumbling embankment that leads to a long fall is a good kind of fear. I heard of a young man recently who climbed a mountain in Alaska while on a short term mission's project. He ventured out on a long, loose rocky area. Suddenly the whole side of the mountain gave way and he slid along with the small rocks to the very edge of a drop-off that went down for several thousand feet.

There he stopped. To this day, he does not know why he stopped, except that God worked a miracle that saved his life. As he sat on the edge of that cliff, he thanked God for his deliverance, committed his life to Him, then carefully inched away from that precipice, a healthy fear of death gripping his very soul.

In this verse, the Lord reminded the children of Israel how He protected them when they became terrified of their enemies. He reminded them that that same power which protected them will be used over and over again. Therefore they need not fear. They can rest secure in His care. His presence would protect them daily.

I love to visualize the presence of the Lord keeping an eye on me as I live my daily life. The truth is, the more I think about His presence, the less fear I have. His presence calms my fears. Does it calm your fears, too? Write down the fears you are facing right now and commit them to God. He will take care of you today. Trust Him.

February 3

Reason #34 Not to Fear: Unstinting Obedience Gives You Peace of Mind

"Therefore you shall keep the commandments of the LORD your God, to walk in His ways and to fear Him." Deuteronomy 8:6

The little boy had tried his mother's patience sorely that day. When he was asked to pick up his toys, he refused. When he was told to wash his hands for lunch, he replied that he didn't need to. When his mother reminded him to feed the dog, he kicked the dog's dish across the floor and stomped outside. At her wit's end, she finally made him go and sit in the corner on his little chair until he could obey. As he sat there, his face still puckered into a stubborn frown, he said, "I may be sittin' down on the outside, but I'm standin' up on in the inside!"

The children of Israel were like that little boy. They tried God's patience to the utmost limits during the forty years they had wandered in the wilderness. Yet God graciously provided for their needs, protected them from harm, and forgave them when they repented. Again and again God reminded them through Moses that if they wanted a full, abundant life they should walk in His ways and be obedient to His commands.

Yet they were a stubborn, stiff-necked people. While they conformed to God's will outwardly, they rebelled against Him in their hearts. Moses had come to the end of his life and gave his farewell address to the people. He wanted them to remember God's Word and God's laws, and above all, to remember to be obedient. God was not trying to make the Israelites miserable when He asked them to fear and obey Him. Every child of God should realize that God takes obedience seriously. And if He takes it seriously, so should you. There are no blessings without plain old-fashioned obedience.

If I would be honest with you, my flesh does not naturally obey the Lord. It doesn't like to be denied. However, I know that I must say *yes* to Jesus and *no* to disobedience. I have learned the hard way that when I allow my will to prevail over God's, I end up in a disastrous, uncomfortable situation. How about displaying some radical, outrageous obedience today?

What is God asking you to do -- or not to do? Determine in your heart that you will give Him your heart, your will and your obedience. Now you can rest in His blessing and not be tormented by fear.

February 4

Reason #35 Not to Fear: Do His Will

"And now, Israel, what does the Lord your God require of you, but to fear the LORD your God, to walk in all His ways and to love Him, to serve the LORD your God with all your heart and with all your soul." Deuteronomy 10:12

After graduating from Moody Bible Institute, my husband, Bob, was offered a good job with the government doing mechanical work on their jeeps. Yet at the same time, the Sunshine Gospel Mission downtown Chicago approached him with the offer of the position as director of the mission. We were in a quandary, for we had a small child and needed to provide for our family. Which way should we go? We had school debts and other obligations that had to be met. We went to the Lord in prayer and laid it all out before Him. "If You want us to minister in the mission, Lord," Bob said very earnestly, "please provide for our needs."

Bob told the board at the mission that he had to have his debts paid. Within the next week, enough money came in that we could pay every debt and even had some left over for living expenses while we got settled! Bob took the job at the mission and loved every moment of it. But what if we hadn't prayed about it? What if we'd determined we wanted more money, a better house, and nicer things for our children? We would have missed major blessings in our lives through disobedience to God's will.

What does God really want from you? What does He expect from you? What pleases Him? In Deuteronomy 10:12, God told Moses the answer to these questions. These are things you should pay attention to, as well.

#1-- Fear Him. In this case, fear means to honor and reverence Him

#2-- Do His will. We can understand His will through the Word of God.

#3-- Love Him. Love Him in return for all He has done for you.

#4-- Worship Him. Worship Him with all your heart and your affections, your mind, your will, your body. Worship involves commitment and cleansing. See to it that you worship God this way.

These are four instructions from God's Word for you to live by. Which one of the four do you need to focus on today? How can you do this one thing more excellently? More whole-heartedly? More obediently? Follow these truths, for nothing else is more vital for lasting peace of heart and mind.

February 5

Reason #36 Not to Fear: God Walks Beside Us When We Fear Him

"You shall walk after the LORD your God and fear Him, and keep His commandments and obey His voice; you shall serve Him and hold fast to Him."
Deuteronomy 13:4

Have you ever been tempted to feel sorry for yourself and forget God?

After Bob's heart attack, I was at a loss to know what to do.

Instead of having a day full of activities, I was trapped in a house with a man to care for, and a huge load of responsibility cast upon me. I was lonely, frustrated and afraid of what the future held. There were many changes that came into my life after Bob's heart attack and brain injury. We moved from Pennsylvania to Arizona to be near my daughter. We were no longer involved in ministry -- in fact, we *became* the ministry as we accepted help and prayers from God's people. Instead of being the teacher, I became the student. Instead of relying upon a strong and very capable man, I had to make all the decisions and do all the work.

It was then that I realized I could only accomplish the task He had given me if I relied on Christ alone. It was not easy. My flesh shrank from it. But I was cast upon God in a way I'd never been before, and as I cried out to Him, I came to understand that He is sufficient. God had taken my beloved Bob and changed the direction of my life. I cannot say I thanked God immediately, but I'm learning to worship Him despite the situations with which I am faced. The fear of God became my rock and my life.

The Israelites were warned countless times not to listen, cling to, or worship anyone or anything other than God Himself. They were not to listen to any false prophets. They were not to abandon God and His commands. The fear of the Lord was to protect them. Yet they did not obey this command. They wandered away from Him and their sins became worse than those they conquered when they came into the land. He had to discipline them and send them into captivity before they learned to fear God and worship Him.

If you, as a child of God, live by this verse, be assured your Shepherd will protect and cover you, too. He will go before you, walk beside you, and come behind you. He will protect you securely. Even when you cannot see Him, He will be there. You never need to fear.

February 6

Reason #37 Not to Fear: We Give God Everything

"You shall eat before the Lord your God, in the place where He chooses to make His name abide, the tithe of your grain, your new wine, and your oil, of the firstborn of your herds and your flocks, that you may learn to fear the LORD your God always."
Deuteronomy 14:23

From my youth, I watched different people in my family put their money in the offering plate when it was passed from person to person in church. When I was little, sometimes my dad would give me some change to put in the offering plate. I didn't understand all that was transpiring. However, I did enjoy dropping the coins in the plate.

Now that I am an older adult, I understand about offerings and tithing. For some, they are uncomfortable subjects, but not for me. We are to set aside a certain amount of money for the Lord, and I believe that ten percent is the starting place. In the New Testament, we are not under the law that required the tithe, for we are told to give without compulsion, to give freely, and with a generous heart. We are instructed to give it first, before the bills are paid and the groceries are bought.

The story is told about missionaries who asked the poor people in their church to bring a special Christmas offering and they would use it to meet some of the direst needs in the church. One little boy had nothing at all to bring, but when they passed him the plate, he carefully carried it to the aisle, laid it on the floor, and stepped into it. He was giving what he could -- his all!

When you give your offering, you are not giving it to the church, but to the Lord. Jesus is not interested in how much money you give. He desires a cheerful (the word means *hilarious* in Greek) giver, II Cor. 9:7. If you aren't a cheerful giver, you lose the blessing. God has blessed me many times over what I have given. I am not a rich woman, but I have enough, my needs are met and at times, I have some money left over!

In this verse, the Lord is telling the children of Israel that their consistent tithing shows their reverence for Him. They were to learn that there is great joy in giving. You see, when you decide to give, and you do it in the right spirit, your offering is a sign of your reverence for the Lord. Therefore, freely give.

February 7

Reason #38 Not to Fear: Knowing That I Am in the Will of God

"Now the man who acts presumptuously and will not heed the priest who stands to minister there before the LORD your God, or the judge, that man shall die. So you shall put away the evil from Israel. And all the people shall hear and fear, and no longer act presumptuously." Deuteronomy 17: 12, 13

We needed a building for our work with the youth in Chambersburg, PA, and finally one was located and purchased. But we faced almost immediate opposition from the gangs who operated there. They felt threatened and surmised that their territory was being invaded. They were afraid of the mission and thought it might hinder people from joining their gang or encourage them to leave.

We stood our ground and began a youth ministry in the new building. Many times Bob's life was threatened. The young men in the gangs hoped that he would become so fearful he would leave. That did not happen. We knew the will of God -- that He wanted a light in that dark place -- and we did not fear. The work grew and flourished and is still impacting and changing lives today.

Behavior that turns you away from the will of God is arrogant and self-righteous. So many Christians in today's world take the Word of God lightly. They may attend church once in a while and doze off during the sermon, but don't ask them to make a long-term commitment to serve.

Satan is the author of fear. Never forget he wants to convince you that your will is more important than God's. He is there to build up your arrogance and self-importance. He wants you to continually reject God's plans. Perhaps God is telling you what He wants to do in your life, but your pride and arrogance stands in the way. You question His plans and worry about the future as fear runs through your bones.

Remember God can accomplish the task He has given you; He just asks that you stop acting overconfident and instead lean on Him for continued guidance. Can you do that? How much time do you spend in prayer and Bible study? Can you honestly say you've prayed for the will of God to be done in your life? God calls you to repent today and begin a new way to live.

February 8

Reason #39 Not to Fear: We Make a Habit to Read God's Word

"And it shall be with him, and he shall read it all the days of his life, that he may learn to fear the LORD his God and be careful to observe all the words of this law and these statutes." Deuteronomy 17:19

Yesterday America chose President Barack Obama as their choice for the leader of our great country for the next four years. Whether that was your choice or not, we are facing another four years under this man as our "king". What lies ahead for us in the days to come? No one knows, yet we are told not to fear, but to trust in God who is in control of all things.

In the law recorded in this verse, God instructed the kings of old to make a copy of the law and the books of Moses and to read them, study them, and apply the principles to the decisions he would make as king. "All the days of his life."

Why was this? "That he would learn to fear the Lord his God." To fear God meant to trust Him, obey Him and give Him reverence. The kings of Israel and Judah were not supposed to rule according to their own wishes, mental acuity, skills or whims. They were to read the Word of God and apply it to their task as ruler.

Do you make it a regular habit to spend time in the Word of God? Do you really *hunger* to read God's Word? When I get up in the morning, I get out my Bible and my other devotional books, along with my coffee and spend time reading my Bible. Each year I read through the Bible.

This verse makes it clear that God instructs His people to read His Word all the days of their lives. If your mind wanders, read it aloud. Make it a regular habit to read God's Word. Not for just five minutes, but really get into it. We all understand that we must eat food to maintain our physical bodies. The same is true in the spiritual realm. To mature spiritually, you have to read and study God's Word.

What would it be like to have a king or a president who obeyed this command of the Lord? How would it change the decisions he made daily for millions of people?

We can't change the president's life style, but we can change our own. I encourage you to read God's Word daily to stay spiritually strong. God says it. Do it.

February 9

Reason #40 Not to Fear: I Do Not Listen to False Prophets

"When a prophet speaks in the name of the LORD, if the thing does not happen or come to pass that is the thing which the LORD has not spoken: the prophet has spoken it presumptuously: you shall not be afraid of him."
Deuteronomy 18:22

I have some friends who are involved with having the palms of their hands read, and they call these so-called "spiritual" people for advice and guidance. It is beyond me how they can believe what this person is telling them. I once ventured to ask, "Does everything she predict happen?"

"No," they said.

"Then why do you listen to and trust that person?" I inquired.

"Because sometimes she provides me with good advice," was their response.

I have no interest in seeking any kind of advice from mediums, palm readers, horoscopes; these are demonic and evil. Yet how many Christians depend upon false information to live their lives? How many times do you listen to CNN or Fox News or Oprah Winfrey or Dr. Phil for advice and counsel, and are swayed by humanistic wisdom?

There is no denying that there is a huge amount of false information being passed off as truth in the Lord's name. People long for significance and making predictions in the Lord's name is how they achieve it. Despite warning after warning from the Lord, false prophets grew in number in Israel during the days of the kings. The Lord makes a distinction between His divine appointed prophets who should be feared, and the false ones who should not be feared.

God does not resort to making false predictions, nor should His people. If you are searching for answers to issues in your life, read God's Word. It is absolutely true. Don't get involved in magic, witchcraft, astrology, or horoscopes. God is not in those types of messages. His Word holds all the information you need for your daily life.

Don't be fooled by the appearance, the form, or the outer shell of a person. Make certain those who give you guidance are true people of God. Consider what you listen to and fill your mind with: if it is not God's Word, cut back on this source of false information and put your trust in God alone.

February 10

Reason #41 Not to Fear: God Provides Justice to Wrong-doers

"And those who remain shall hear and fear, and hereafter they shall not commit such evil among you." Deuteronomy 19:20

In the middle of the night I heard someone trying to enter our back door. We lived at the time in a high crime area in Chicago in a row house and as I peered out the window from our upstairs bedroom, I saw two men fleeing across the narrow patch of grass. Bob was at a ministry function, and so I dashed down the stairs and out of the door in pursuit. They got away, but I did get a good look at each of them. I called the police and they apprehended the men. The police called the next day and had me come in to identify them. They stood the men in front of me and asked if these were the men who were trying to break into our home. I recognized them and said, "Yes!"

Several weeks later, I was in court and testified against them. The judge found them guilty and sentenced them accordingly. Justice had been done in this case, but in many cases *justice* is a foreign word. There are clever lawyers and judges who cave into pressure and bribes and allow the guilty to go free and punish the innocent. Because of that, crime is growing to become mammoth proportions across our land.

God planned that those who committed a crime should be tried before an impartial judge and jury. If the perpetrators are justly tried and punished, others would be encouraged not to commit crimes. When justice is done, law and order prevail and innocent people can live in peace.

Even if justice is not done, God calls us to forgive and let Him execute His justice upon evil. When we are unwilling to forgive a wrong or seek revenge, we are taking the role God has given Himself and human government. This attitude can only lead to great pain, illness and depression in our lives. "Never take your own revenge, beloved, but leave room for the wrath of God, for it is written, "Vengeance is Mine, I will repay, says the Lord." Rom. 10:19

Am I writing to someone who needs this message today? Is there someone in your life you need to forgive? Do it now. Turn it over to God. Leave room for the wrath and justice of God and you will walk with peace in your heart and renewed fellowship with your Lord.

February 11

Reason #42 Not to Fear: God Is With Me Even in the Dark

"When you go out to battle against your enemies and see horses and chariots and people more numerous than you, do not be afraid of them; for the LORD your God is with you, who brought you up from the land of Egypt."
Deuteronomy 20:1

From time to time, we all fight feelings of hopelessness, weariness and bleakness. This past week, I have fought all three. In fact, just last night I told my pastor's wife that for two cents I would walk away from all my responsibilities with my husband. I am so exhausted. I want this to end. Yes, I find myself drained today.

The truth is, I feel like I am in the dark, and yet I know that even in this darkness, God's presence is with me in this room and He has promised that He will never leave me or forsake me. (Heb. 13:6)

Many years ago, Virginia and her fiancé, Dan, went for a walk down along a river. They had a choice to either go through a long railroad tunnel or climb over steep rocks. They chose the tunnel. In the very midst of it, the blackness was like a deep cave. There was absolutely no light, only the eerie *drip, drip* of water, the smell of dank places and the echo of their voices.

Suddenly they looked up and saw what they most dreaded: the light of a train approaching! Getting off the tracks, they wrapped their arms around each other tightly and waited for the train. It came with a thunder of diesel motor, the blast of the horn, the screech of metal on metal, the explosion of wind that rocked them to the core. The darkness was very dark in that moment.

Yet there was an end to the thunder, noise and terror. God brought them through it and they laugh about it to this day.

If we would be honest, we are all afraid of dark situations that arise in our lives. However, in those times, we need to remind ourselves that no matter how black the darkness gets, God is with us. This promise from God's Word today encourages us to trust God, obey Him, and walk in His ways. Then He will cause us not to fear anything, not even the darkness.

Are you struggling today? Fearful of what might happen next? God is stronger than your negative feelings. I have decided I will give each fear to Him today and be a dependable worker for Him. You can do that, too.

February 12

Reason #43 Not to Fear: Greater Is He Who Is In You

"And he shall say to them, 'Hear, O Israel: Today you are on the verge of battle with your enemies. Do not let your heart faint, do not be afraid, and do not tremble or be terrified because of them.'" Deuteronomy 20:3

When I am faced with a spiritual battle, I often lose heart and panic. I begin to doubt my faith and fear begins to invade areas of my life. Why is this? Why do I take my eyes from my all-powerful Lord and put them on myself? Maybe it is because I fear loss of control. The Unknown looms over me like a monster and I yield to fear. I also am keenly aware that I am without a covering; my husband who was so strong and capable for thirty-two years is now a little boy in a man's body. My covering since Bob's heart attack is the Lord Himself, and it is a scary proposition to face the enemy of my soul without Bob's help and prayers.

When the Israelites entered Canaan, they were facing enemies who were organized, armed and experienced. Without God's help, they were as children throwing rocks at armored tanks. Yet Moses encouraged them to trust in God. He said that if they obeyed God and His law, they could face any enemy and expect victory. One of them would chase one hundred of the Canaanites!

Just as God desired to give victory to the Israelites in their battles against their enemies, so He does with you and me. God wants you to have victory over sin and self. He wants you to walk with Him and trust Him for your every need.

Perhaps you need to confront your fears so you can win the battle. Whenever I am in a spiritual battle, my greatest need is to first pray about what is causing my fear. When I face it and confess it, then God gives me strength to deal with it. I rely totally on God and in the name of Jesus Christ, I rebuke the enemy and command that he leave me. Then I ask for cleansing, protection and guidance from my Lord. He always hears me. Fears disappear like mist on the mountains.

Jesus Christ defeated Satan at the cross. Claim that victory today over your fears. Depend on the Greater One to fight your battles and take whatever action is necessary so you won't lose heart and panic. Be aggressive against your fears. Let this day be a turning point for you.

As you defeat your enemy and fear, get ready to really enjoy life!

February 13

Reason #44 Not to Fear: We Utterly Destroy Our Enemies

"How he met you on the way and attacked your rear ranks, all the stranglers at y our rear, when you were tired and weary; and he did not fear God." Deuteronomy 25:18

The Amalekites were a tribe of desert people descended from Esau. They occupied the territory of the Sinai Peninsula and were fierce warriors, known for their cruelty and inhumane fighting tactics. Their favorite method of attack was to hide behind large rocks or in ravines (*wadis*) and spring out to kill and capture those who strayed from the main group, the old and infirm, young children, and pregnant women.

Joshua led an attack on them, recorded in Ex. 17:8-16, in which the Israelites won a great victory because of God's intervention. Yet the Amalakites continued to hound the heels of Israel, following them on their journey, ever a threat and problem to the newly-born nation.

Moses was old and he was turning the reins of the leadership over to Joshua. In his final series of messages to the people, he reminded them to fight aggressively against Amalek.

They were supposed to blot out the memory of them from heaven and utterly destroy them. They did not do this; in fact, it wasn't until the days of King Hezekiah, some 700 years later, that they completed this task.

At times we all need to be reminded of what happened in the past, because there are lessons to be learned. What problems or sins from the past are hounding your heels? Some problems keep on pestering us and attacking us from our blind side, if we allow it. Maybe it is anger that erupts into a raging temper at times. Maybe it is guilt or fear. Maybe it is remorse over a wrong decision. Maybe it's an old love affair that keeps cropping up again and again. Maybe it is doubt.

Whatever it is, we should bring it under the blood, confess it and turn from it completely. We should wipe the memory of that thing from our minds. Ask God to transform our minds so we can walk in purity, freedom and joy.

In closing today, read II Cor. 10:5. I challenge you to take captive those errant thoughts, bring them to Christ. Purge the memory of sin from your mind. Kill those Amalakitish thoughts, dear friends. Kill them by bringing them to Christ.

February 14

Reason #45 Not to Fear: Obedience Has Its Rewards

"That all the peoples of the earth shall see that you are called by the name of the LORD, and they shall be afraid of you." Deuteronomy 28:10

Israel is about the size of the state of Vermont, and that's not very big. Now look at the surrounding countries that are sworn enemies of Israel, nations who have declared they would like nothing better than to sweep the Israelites into the sea and destroy each and every one of them. Do you see how large they are and how much land they occupy?

It's quite astounding that Israel exists.

As Moses addressed the people just before he went up on the mountain to die, he reminded them that they needed to keep God's commands and laws so they could continue to dwell in the land undisturbed. The history of Israel tells us that they did not heed His law, not past Joshua and his generation, and that eventually they were taken into captivity by the Assyrians, and at a later time, the Babylonians captured Judah.

Yet Israel stands today as a testimony to a God who keeps His promises. Their ancient enemies are gone, and they stand again in their promised land.

As you raised your children, or if you are in that process, most likely you have given your children rewards for obedience and good behavior. Obedience has its' rewards and benefits. When you live your life in obedience to the Lord, His blessing is with you wherever you go.

Practice obedience and no matter where you work, live, or go in life, God will bless you. He will watch over your comings and goings. He will give you joy and contentment and love. The bottom line is that if you obey the Word of the Lord, you will be blessed by Him in ways you never imagined. And others will stand in awe of what God is doing in your life.

When God starts working in your life, people will take notice. When you allow God's Word to transform you more and more into His Son's likeness, people are going to realize that something supernatural is going on. They will stand in awe of you.

Let us put God first in our lives and when we do that, we will experience the blessings of the Lord. Try it today and see if it doesn't work for you.

February 15

Reason #46 Not to Fear: We Fear His Glorious Name

"If you do not carefully observe all the words of this law that are written in this book, that you may fear this glorious and awesome name, THE LORD YOUR GOD, then the LORD will bring back on you all the diseases of Egypt, of which you were afraid, and they shall cling to you." Deuteronomy 28:58-60

In 1986, my husband and I were invited by the Billy Graham Association to go Amsterdam to their conference on evangelism. Billy Graham is a name many people recognize. He is a very respected and admired man of God.

While we were in Amsterdam, we met many popular people, George Beverly Shea and Cliff Barrows, among others. But we met Billy Graham quite by accident. After dinner one evening, we were leaving the dining hall to walk over to the conference building when almost out of nowhere stepped Mr. Graham. Our eyes made contact, and without hardly thinking about it, I began speaking with him.

Even though Billy Graham has a name that is popular and acknowledged, the Bible makes it abundantly clear that we are to fear and reverence only one name—the Lord (Jehovah) God (Elohim).

In these verses, the Israelites were urged by Moses to fear and respect one name alone -- the Lord (Jehovah) God (Elohim). No human has a name as great or glorious as His. God's name was to be exalted in Israel. His name is to be great because He is the one true, living God.

How do we fear God's name? By listening to His Voice, by heeding His Word, by obeying Him, honoring Him and putting Him first in our lives. God warned His children of dire events that would happen if they did not fear Him and went off to worship other gods.

That warning is applicable for our lives, as well. When you do not fear and honor the name of the Lord, when you exhibit disobedience and disregard for the glorious and awesome presence of the Lord, your heart is hardened and you choose other gods to serve.

Be careful. There is only one true and living God. If you know Him, you must love, obey, and serve Him as best you can. Give Him the glory and honor in your life today. His name is above all names and He is a God to be feared.

February 16

Reason #47 Not to Fear: God Is With You

"Be strong and of good courage, do not fear nor be afraid of them; for the LORD your God, He is the One who goes with you. He will not leave you nor forsake you." Deuteronomy 31:6

When Eli, one of my eight grandchildren, was four years old, I took him one day to McDonald's for a special time alone with him. As we ate our chicken nuggets, the conversation turned to the subject of heaven. Eli was intrigued with heaven. I mentioned the fact that I would probably go to heaven before he did. His eyes almost came out of their sockets.

He said, "No! I want to go first!"

So I asked him, "When would you like to go?" He put another nugget in his mouth and said, "In three minutes!"

I said, "I don't think your mother would think *that's* such a great idea." After we settled the issue of who would go first, I told Eli that he must love God and be faithful to Him every day.

He regarded me with those incredibly big brown eyes and said, "Then that's what I want to do."

Moses was one hundred and twenty years old, about to die, and wanted to leave some final words to Joshua and the people of Israel. In his last sermon, Moses encouraged them to be obedient. He knew he was about to be taken to heaven, and he desired that his people would be faithful to the Lord.

Is your desire to be faithful to the Lord and to pass your faith and devotion on to the next generation? More than anything else I might leave my family, I want them to remember my voice telling them frequently to remain faithful to the Lord.

This simple trust and confidence in the Lord can remove fear and set our feet on the right path. Remember: in God's economy, faithfulness is equal to success.

How faithful are you? Take stock of your life. Recommit your life to God, and begin anew to be faithful to Him.

Like Eli, say, "Then that's what I want to do."

February 17

Reason #48 Not to Fear: God Will Help Me Through All My Tomorrows

"And the Lord, He is the One who goes before you. He will be with you. He will not leave you nor forsake you; do not fear nor be dismayed." Deuteronomy 31:8

Do you long to be out of this life and home in glory with the Lord? Out of your pain, troubles, sorrows and problems? Out of a body that keeps breaking down? Yet God does not take us home. We have to face situations in this life whether they are painful or pleasant.

When I began caring for Bob after his heart attack and brain damage, I didn't know how hard it would be. Sometimes He allows us to laugh at our own mistakes, and sometimes laughter is about the only thing that got me through the day.

Bob comes out with some exceptional one-liners: like when he told me he played professional football. I remember the time when he said I was really his sister pretending to be his wife. Then there was the time he answered the door when I was in the shower, and allowed the Jehovah Witness men into our home. I came into the front room to hear Bob say, *yes, he wanted to join their church!*

God led the Israelites to the edge of the Promised Land. There were still giants in that land and wars to be fought and temptations to overcome. As they gazed across the Jordan River, they might have felt fear. They might have questioned God's direction. But Moses reassured them that God was with them and He was faithful to keep His promises. He reminded them that as long as they were obedient to God, they did not have to worry or fear.

God knows that you cannot do anything without Him. He will continue to help you just as He continued to help the stubborn Israelites. Understanding this verse could be a defining moment in your life. Let the presence of God go before you today. Let His favor undertake any responsibility no matter how dangerous, difficult, or risky it may be. Do not fear or be alarmed, the Lord goes before you today.

God may give you a moment of laughter to lift you above the nitty-gritty of the grind of life. Enjoy it and thank Him. He is faithful. Pray and commit your day to Him. Then walk as close to Him as you can get.

February 18

Reason #49 Not to Fear: We Assemble Together

"Assemble the people, the men and the women and children and the alien who is in your town, in order that they may hear and learn and fear the Lord your God, and be careful to observe all the words of this law."
Deuteronomy 31:12

Moses was about to die. Before he left, he commanded the people of Israel to meet together to hear the Word of God. After the Israelites entered the land, God appointed Jerusalem as the place He would meet with them. Men, women and children were all supposed to come together three times a year at this sacred place to be reminded of what the law said to them.

I can imagine the large congregation of people meeting together as Moses, now an old man, stood up before them and taught them the law and the Word of God. Maybe some of them became hot and thirsty. There might have been some babies there who cried. Perhaps they served food during this long sermon. But they put aside all their other important things to do and came and listened respectively to the Word of God.

Americans love to come together for football, baseball, basketball and political events. Think about it. We put aside our work schedules, family meetings, and other important business and set aside the time to attend a concert, to see a movie, to see a relative graduate, to see a parade or a school play. Yet when it comes to hearing God's Word, how many times do we relegate that as second or third or fourth priority?

It is important to gather together, as we do on Sunday mornings in our local churches, to hear God's Word. God knows that we have short memories! He knows we need to be reminded of what He has instructed us to do, that we should fear and respect Him always and walk in His ways. He knows we need the encouragement of others of like faith.

What priority do you make of worshipping together with other Christians, not in front of your TV in your sweats, but at *church*? In some people's lives, this takes last place. They would rather watch TV, sleep in, mow the lawn, play golf, go fishing, travel, go shopping or do anything rather than meet together at church.

Search your heart, and this Sunday get up, get dressed and get in the car. Drive to church and listen to God's Word. You will be blessed if you do.

February 19
Reason #50 Not to Fear: Simply Trust in His Wisdom

"Have I not commanded you? Be strong and of good courage; do not be afraid, nor be dismayed, for the LORD your God is with you wherever you go."
Joshua 1:9

A person learns to trust the Lord one day at a time. I look back and wonder how I've managed for thirteen years, caring for my husband. In the beginning of this ordeal, I could hardly think or talk clearly. My children made most of the decisions. I was fearful, apprehensive, and scared.

One day the Lord made me face all my fears, and I finally learned to trust Him completely. Bob was in rehab and took a turn for the worse. This happened when I was all alone and the doctors wanted to know my decision about his care. I excused myself, got on my knees, and turned to Him for guidance. I said, "I trust that You will tell me what to do, Lord. Thank You." I went back to those tending Bob and said, "Do nothing." They wanted to call the ambulance to take him back to the trauma center, but I said no, because I knew in the ambulance they would shock his heart if it stopped beating, and I didn't want that again.

Eventually the ambulance was called, but I made sure the men understood my wishes regarding bringing Bob back to life. Complete peace swept over my soul, and that was the beginning of my trust day by day in the Lord's guidance and help. He has never failed me or forsaken me since.

God told Joshua not to be afraid. Feelings of fear can overtake you when you have to step into a new adventure. The very next day Joshua would lead the Israelites into the promise land as they crossed the Jordan River. When they took this step of faith into this new adventure, they would be met with opposition. And again they would be challenged to trust God. Fear and discouragement could overtake them. God knew about all their fears and that is why he spoke to Joshua. Fear hinders us from moving forward. It restricts us and it keeps us from doing our best for Him.

Where is God leading you? Are you afraid to follow? Is fear cutting you off from doing your best? God cares about your fearful heart. Just as Joshua was not alone, you are not, either. Joshua moved ahead despite his fears and so should you. Take on the new ground. Move forward. Take a big step and remember the Lord your God is with you.

February 20
Reason #51 Not to Fear: God Is Faithful to Save

*"For the LORD your God dried up the waters of the Jordan before you until
you had crossed over, as the LORD your God did to the Red Sea, which He
dried up before us until we had crossed over,* [24] *that all the peoples of the earth
may know the hand of the LORD, that it is mighty, that you may fear the LORD
your God forever."* Joshua 4:24

As I write this, it will be Veterans Day in a couple days. On that day, we remember all those who gave their lives in military service, those who once served, and those who are presently serving. We have parades, flags and speeches to remind us of the value of our freedom.

When I grew up in Wisconsin, my grandparents and parents would take me to the cemetery on that day. There we would place a wreath next to the flag on my other grandfather's grave who served in the war. Now my father has died and my family will do the same on his grave. Memorials are important, recalling the times God has worked in your life

What are the memorable events you remember? We mark birth dates and wedding dates; we celebrate Thanksgiving, Christmas, Easter and the Fourth of July with our families; we remember Christ's death at communion in church; we celebrate our children's graduations; we honor our mothers and fathers and grandparents on their special days. Why do we do this? Why do we have a Memorial Day and a Veterans' Day?

In this passage, we are told that Joshua was instructed by the Lord to build a stone memorial of their crossing of the Jordan River, and He gives two reasons for them to do this. One was so that future generations would know and understand that it was by the Lord's might, faithfulness and protection that they crossed the river to start their new life in the Promised Land.

The second reason was for a testimony and witness to all the nations of the earth that God is mighty, that He is able to save His own people, and that all mankind should fear Him.

These are the reasons we, too, should celebrate. We should remind our children and grandchildren of the faithfulness and love of the Lord in our lives, and we should be a witness to the world of God's might, love and protection. Next time you gather to celebrate, think of these things and give God the glory for what He has done in your life.

February 21

Reason #52 Not to Fear: I Depend on God's Word and Will

"So they answered Joshua and said, "Because your servants were clearly told that the LORD your God commanded His servant Moses to give you all the land, and to destroy all the inhabitants of the land from before you; therefore we were very much afraid for our lives because of you, and have done this thing. Joshua 9:24

The people of Israel were fighting battles and winning them. You can imagine the euphoria when the soldiers returned to Shiloh and reported that this town, this village, or that great coalition of armies had been defeated.

One day a travel-worn caravan appeared in the camp. The men wore ragged, dusty clothing. Their bread was moldy and almost gone. Their camels or donkey were caked with mud and were exhausted. Everything about these men shouted: "Long journey." They declared they had come from a far country and wanted to make a peace treaty with the Israelites.

This must have caused quite a stir! I can see the heads of the people being lifted up in pride: *we are known far and wide! Look, this delegation came from a far country!* Without consulting God, Joshua and the other leaders made the treaty with them. Only after the oaths were said did they discover that these people were Gibeonites who lived just over the hill. The Israelites had been scammed; they'd actually made a peace treaty with God's enemies!

When asked why they did this, the Gibeonites said they *feared greatly.* They knew the instructions God gave to Moses about elimination. Self-preservation was at the top of their *to do* list, and pride caused Joshua and the leaders of Israel to believe the scam.

God dealt me a mighty blow to my pride when Bob was taken ill. To this day, I am cast upon God for many of the simple tasks and decisions that come my way. Yet it is so easy to allow myself the luxury of pride and self-preservation. These attitudes are powerful. Pride oozes down through the cracks in our defenses like molasses on a hot day.

What motivates you to do the things you do? Be careful when you make decisions. Base all your decisions on the Word of God and the will of God. Seek His advice above all other things. Ask for godly wisdom from those you trust, and ask God for guidance and wisdom. Don't be the victim of a scam. It can be costly to you, too.

February 22

Reason #53 Not to Fear: Love Conquers Hate

"That they feared greatly, because Gibeon was a great city, like one of the royal cities, and because it was greater than Ai, and all its men were mighty.
Joshua 10:2

Fear is the father of war. Why? Fear makes us distrust one another. It builds walls. It rears up armies. It makes us the enemy of our brother or sister. Suddenly it is "them" or "they" as opposed to "me" and "us." Taken to the extreme, we then feel justified to fight them and kill them.

After Joshua and the Israelite nation entered the Promised Land, they utterly destroyed Jericho and Ai, and now they are getting ready to conquer the other city-states of the Canaanites. Remember that the land of Israel is no larger than the state of New Jersey. Distances are not wide and spacious as we know them in America. Just to the south, southwest of Ai (maybe a radius of 50 miles) lie the cities of Jerusalem, Hebron, Jarmuth, Lachish and Eglon. The king of Jerusalem became very fearful of the Israelites. Notice he did not want to change his religion or the way he did things, nor did he inquire after the Lord Jehovah to seek God's forgiveness for his sins and the sins of his people.

Instead he formed a coalition with other city states and marched on Gibeon, which had come under the protection of the Israelites. *If they want war, they will get it,* he reasoned, confident he would be victorious.

Think with me about this issue of fear and hatred. We find it in our nation, in our churches, in our families, in our own hearts. God says, "I have not given you the spirit of fear, but of power, and love and a sound mind." II Tim. 1:9 (KJV) Yet we disregard this verse and fear others. Then we begin to hate them. They become the enemy and we are the virtuous, righteous ones. This divides our families and our churches; it divides the people who live in our great nation.

Who do you fear? Who is your enemy? Who are you struggling with today? Set aside your fear and take a good long look at the hatred and anger you have for these people. Ask God's forgiveness. Now ask Him to fill your heart with love instead of hate. Pray for these people each day and discover how God can change them from being your enemy to being your dearly beloved friends and brothers and sisters in Christ. It *is* possible. Try it.

February 23

Reason #54 Not to Fear: He Is Able to Accomplish His Purpose

"The Lord said to Joshua, 'Do not fear them, for I have given them into your hands; not a man of them shall stand before you." Joshua 10:8

The other day, one of my grandchildren said to me, "Menzie, you are very tall. You are very big." You know, from her point of view, I am tall and I am big. In her view, I can do almost anything! (Little does she know how weak I am!)

The Gibeonites were threatened and they asked the Israelites to help them as they saw a huge army approaching their city. In their view, the Israelites stood tall and were very big. In reality, the Israelite army was probably small compared to the coalition that joined together to fight the Gibeonites.

In the verse we are looking at today, the Lord assured Joshua that he did not need to be afraid or fear this battle. God said He would be with them and that the Canaanites and Amorites would not stand before them to fight. God would give them the victory.

Have you ever felt small when looking at a big project or a big problem caused by others? Have you felt under attack or opposed? Are there those in your life who call upon their friends to join with them in their fight? What should you do?

For a large part of our lives we served the Lord in two missions. One was in Chicago; and one was in Chambersburg, PA. During those years, I learned four very important truths.

#1-Expect opposition when you work for the Lord.

#2-No matter what, do not dishonor your obligation and the Lord.

#3-Do not fear your enemies.

#4-God will always prevail in the end.

The end of this story brings us hope. God defeated the coalition, brought victory to Joshua and the Gibeonites, and the people of Israel went on to conquer most of the southern part of Israel for God.

"Now to Him who is able to do far more abundantly beyond all that we ask or think according to the power that works within us." Eph. 3:20

Take this promise to your battle today.

February 24

Reason #55 Not to Fear: God Gives Us Victory

"Then Joshua said to them, "Do not be afraid, nor be dismayed; be strong and of good courage, for thus the LORD will do to all your enemies against whom you fight." Joshua 10:25

It is an awesome thing to see God bring about a great victory. But the danger is that we might rest on our laurels and become lax in our spiritual life as if the victory was our doing and not God's. It seems for every victory, there is another battle to fight.

You know what I mean. You finally master one job, and your boss gives you a more difficult one. You rejoice over the fact that you got one lesson finished, and encounter another one that is harder. You finally win the argument with your teen-ager, only to discover they've dodged you and another battle looms on the horizon that is even tougher to overcome.

The children of Israel had come into the land and fought God's enemies, obeying His commands to utterly wipe them out. God gave them success in every battle, as He promised. What reward does Joshua get for this? His enemies band together and come at him again -- this time in greater numbers than ever before.

Once again God gives them the victory. Now they held the five kings as captives. The kings are brought before Joshua and the assembled mass of people watch with bated breath to see what he would do. Joshua commanded the people not to fear reprisal, not to fear doing the will of God, and he had the five kings executed.

In our spiritual lives, we have enemies that we want to drive out and defeat. Maybe there was some area of your life that the enemy controlled for a great length of time, but you determined by the power of God to drive him out. So you put on the armor and engaged your enemy. You won that huge battle and now you have victory.

However, here is the warning: *with each success, there is another area of your life your enemy wants to control.* His campaign of opposition against you will intensify. When you start to attack enemy territory, you can write it in red that your enemy will not give up without a fight, and that means you must exercise more faith and be vigilant to keep close to God.

He will give you the victory. Walk in that victory today.

February 25

Reason #56 Not to Fear: I Pin My Hope in Christ Alone

"Then the Lord said to Joshua, 'Do not be afraid because of them, for tomorrow about this time, I will deliver all of them slain before Israel..."
Joshua 11:6

After his victories in the south, Joshua suddenly faced a bigger, more dangerous coalition. This one came from the kings of the north, from Hazor, Madon, Shimron and Achshaph. We do not know these cities today, yet at the time they were large with powerful armed forces. It would be like a tribe of untrained soldiers coming down out of the hills to threaten San Diego, a city that bristles with armed forces, a navy installment, and millions of people.

The Israelites were outnumbered, outmanned, outmaneuvered. They went forward, only by faith in their living God. How far would you get in such a battle?

It only took you a few seconds to read this verse from Joshua, and it only takes a few minutes to read the whole eleventh chapter. We need to remember it took a long time for all of these events in this chapter to take place. Joshua made an extensive war with the northern kings. In fact, it would take the Israelites seven years to occupy the Promised Land. During those seven years, Joshua faced more kings and armies, but he also had the Lord telling him, "Do not be afraid of them."

Throughout his lifetime, Joshua learned how important it was to move in the Lord's timing. He was not reluctant to accept any challenge. He faced unexpected forces with courage and fearless faith.

We would do well to follow his example. When faced with a challenge, instead of drawing back, we should advance, knowing the Lord goes before us, that the Lord prepares the way for us. We would remember the Lord overcomes any and all opposition, and He tells us, "do not be afraid," too.

Joshua accomplishments were possible because he trusted the Lord. What about you? Do you trust Him? If you are facing a hopeless situation, this is the time for your faith to take over and your fear to flee. Don't pin your hope on anything or anyone else, except only the Lord. Trust in Him no matter what.

February 26

Reason #58 Not to Fear: We Don't Fear People

" 'But in fact we have done it for fear, for a reason, saying, 'In time to come your descendants may speak to our descendants, saying, 'What have you to do with the LORD God of Israel? For the LORD has made the Jordan a border between you and us, you children of Reuben and children of Gad. You have no part in the LORD.' So your descendants would make our descendants cease fearing the LORD.' " Joshua 22:24, 25

When we lived in Pennsylvania, I taught a large Bible study, but after several years, was asked to stop teaching. I sought the advice of two pastors. One said to *leave immediately*, and the other said to *finish the year*. I followed the second advice and finished the year. But it was the worst year of my life and in the life of the class. I was afraid of the talk that would go around and figured if I stayed until the class ended, the talk might die down. It was a decision fueled by fear and I regret it to this day.

Joshua successfully invaded Canaan and set up his headquarters at Shiloh. It was then that the soldiers from the two and a half tribes across the Jordan River returned home to rejoin their families. These men built an altar on the far bank of the Jordan as a memorial that would remind future generations of their allegiance to the Israelites on the other side of the river, and to insure that their children would be welcome in Israel when they went to worship Yahweh.

The trouble began when the leaders of the tribes on the west side of the river mistook their intent and thought they were building it as an idol. They planned to declare war on their brothers who helped them claim their land, but a calm voice, that of Phineas the high priest, prevailed. He suggested that they find out the reason for the memorial. When the truth was discovered, the western tribes allowed the altar to stand. Fear almost caused a civil war in Israel.

Fear can creep in so craftily, even along with good motives. Beware of what motivates you and guard against fear. It might cause you to make a decision you will long regret. And above all, pray about it and be obedient to what God tells you to do.

February 27

Reason #57 Not to Fear: We Serve Him Faithfully in the Long Run

"Now therefore, fear the LORD, serve Him in sincerity and in truth, and put away the gods which your fathers served on the other side of the River and in Egypt. Serve the LORD! And if it seems evil to you to serve the LORD, choose for yourselves this day whom you will serve..... But as for me and my house, we will serve the LORD." Joshua 24:14

I've never run a marathon, but I admire those who do. Trudging up the mountain and down into the valleys, they experience sweat burning their eyes, legs like rubber, stomach heaving. Yet the prize is ahead and they keep going. One step at a time, praying so hard they think God is tired of hearing their voice. The long run involves keeping your promises to God and others. There have been other times when I reneged on a promise. I have done that with my family and even the Lord, and I want to tell you that this is not good.

In this chapter, Joshua calls upon the people to fear the Lord and serve Him in sincerity and trust. They enthusiastically promised to do this, yet they failed to do it in the long run. While Joshua and his generation were alive, they obeyed and feared God. But it did not take long for them to become apathetic in their faith after Joshua and his generation was gone. During the days of the Judges, they fell into such apostasy that God had to judge them over and over by allowing their enemies to have victory over them.

Making a commitment to the Lord is not easy. We like to choose things that are stress-free, uncomplicated and comfortable. So making a commitment to the Lord often requires a covenant or promise. We need to think of serving God with all our hearts, our time, our devotion and our love. For the long run.

As soon as the Israelites made their pledge, Joshua confronted them with getting rid of their foreign gods and worshipping the only true God. Would they do it? Would you? For those people, and for you, there has to be a sincere commitment to God.

If you make a promise to worship the Lord, it will mean you also have to prioritize your way of life, your values, your goals, and your dreams. Will you put away some idols that are creeping into your life? Will you worship and fear God *alone*? Stay true to your word. Keep your promise. Uphold your pledge. For the long run.

February 28

Reason #59 Not to Fear: Worship Yahweh God Alone

"Also I said to you, 'I am the LORD your God; do not fear the gods of the Amorites, in whose land you dwell.' But you have not obeyed My voice."'
Judges 6:10

My brother-in-law accepted Christ before he married my sister and started out well in his Christian walk, becoming an avid learner and a teacher of a men's Bible study. But then he moved up the corporate ladder in his career and became a successful businessman, making a lot of money. Money, travel, late night dinners, and the high life became the norm for his life.

The enticements from the world took over his life. He became a stranger to his family. His walk with the Lord diminished and then eventually dried up. The pride of life, the lust of the flesh and the pleasures of the world ensnared him. My sister did not know how to cope with the situation. She learned that confrontation only brought bigger conflicts.

But God's grace is wide, and He is good. I am thrilled to report that after many years he returned to the path of righteousness. He repented and changed the way his life was headed. Today he is once again teaching and hosting a men's Bible study, and is active in his church.

The Israelites also began with good intentions, high hopes and steadfast obedience when they left Egypt. However, during their journey they encountered many unexpected fears. Their enemies were giants in the land and they became very fearful. God wanted to grant His people deliverance, but in order to do that, He first had to convict them of the sin of fear. They were not only to obey His voice, but they also must repent of their sin.

Be careful not to get caught up in worshipping or serving the gods of this world. Unbelievers can worship whatever god they want, but God's people cannot. Believers are to allow nothing and no one to distract them from complete alliance to the Lord. Lamenting your troubles will not lead to forsaking them. Only true repentance will. Remember who is the Lord your God and don't allow other things to creep into your life and get ahead of Him.

Remember: drifting leads to doubting and doubting leads to defying God. Don't drift into the way of the world as my sister's husband did. Confess your sin today and start living a new kind of life, one that has Jesus Christ at the very center.

February 29

Reason #60 Not to Fear: God Is Bigger Than Our Problems

*"Then the LORD said to him, "Peace be with you; do not fear, you shall not die." So Gideon built an altar there to the LORD, and called it The-LORD-Is-Peace. "*Judges 6:23

Gideon was not a fool. His family was starving, the harvest of wheat needed to be threshed, and the Midianites prowled the countryside looking for stacks of grain to steal. So he hid in the winepress and busily beat out the kernels of grain. Smart man!

To his great surprise, a large person appeared, looking at him intently. This alarmed Gideon, who thought initially he'd been discovered by his enemies. I can imagine he began groping around for that staff he kept handy. But of course he couldn't hope to knock this man on the head; he was much too big and tall.

More surprising than the creature's appearance, though, were his first words. "The Lord is with you, O valiant warrior!"

I think Gideon must have looked over his shoulder nervously. Was the big, strong stranger speaking to someone else? Who in all his life had ever addressed him as a valiant warrior? No one. As the last of a large family, Gideon was a shrimpy little guy, always given the least appealing jobs.

Ah! The light dawned on him. He dropped the sheaf of wheat he was going to use to beat the guy's brains out, and began a conversation with the angel of the Lord, which led Gideon to become the valiant warrior the Lord saw him to be.

The Lord can see into your heart and He knows what kind of person you can become if you will only lay aside your fears and believe His Word. What mighty deeds of valor and faith could you accomplish if you let go and allowed God to have full control of your life?

Will you remain in the wine press like Gideon, always peering over your shoulder, fearful of every breath you take? I pity you if you are like this.

"You will not die," the angel assured Gideon. And neither will you. But if you do, ah, then! What glory! What honor and praise you can bring to your King!

God may not have a great deed of valor for you to accomplish, but He might want you to do a small deed of faith. What is it? Ask Him and He will show you. Be a Gideon today!

March 1

Reason #61 Not to Fear: Confession of Sin Brings Blessings

"Now therefore, proclaim in the hearing of the people, saying, 'Whoever is fearful and afraid, let him turn and depart at once from Mount Gilead.' And twenty-two thousand of the people returned, and ten thousand remained."
Judges 7:3

When I began thinking and praying about teaching a Bible study, the group I was associated with interceded with God for sixty-five or more people to attend. Month after month we would hold registrations and ask people to sign up, but we never secured sixty-five people. On our knees we would form a circle and ask the Lord to bring people to us. We asked ourselves, *why won't God answer?* One day we were challenged to confess our sins privately.

For quite a long time we all remained on our knees. I cannot begin to tell you what a different atmosphere there was when we got up. God honored our request after that and soon we had more people than the room could hold!

Gideon was called by God to lead Israel as a judge and a military captain. He began by tearing down the idols in his home town and incurring the wrath of his neighbors. The Midianites came to fight the Israelites and the valley was filled with multitudes of soldiers. Gideon rallied the soldiers in Israel, but he could only gather thirty-two thousand men.

Gideon announced to the men that if anyone was timid or afraid, they could go home. Twenty-two thousand left, leaving only ten thousand. Next God gave them another test: anyone who lapped water from their hands could stay and fight; anyone one who leaned over and drank had to go home. Twenty-one thousand, seven hundred men had to go home that day! That left only three hundred men to fight the innumerable army of the Midianites!

It took a great deal of faith to go ahead with the campaign at this point. I can imagine that each one of those three hundred men got down on their knees, confessed their sins, and cried out to God for help! Which group of people would you have been in? Would you have chosen to go home or to fight? Is your faith in God, or in yourself and your own abilities? What sins are you hiding today that hinder God working through you?

If you can, get down on your knees and confess any known sin. Thank God for His forgiveness. Now return to the tasks of your day, knowing that He is with you and He will help you in everything you do.

March 2

Reason #62 Not to Fear: We Listen to Advice

*"Now it happened at midnight that the man was startled, and turned
himself; and there, a woman was lying at his feet. And he said, "Who are you?"
So she answered, "I am Ruth, your maidservant. Take your maidservant under
your wing, for you are a close relative."* Ruth 3:8.9

Naomi Cole is an older woman who had a huge impact on my life. When
we lived in Chicago, I would often drive to her house and sit and talk to her.
Her words, advice, and counsel were priceless. Through the years, she
counseled me about everything in my life. One piece of advice she gave me was
to make my spiritual walk with the Lord top priority in my life. She said that no
price can be put on the value and privilege of knowing and serving Christ.

Naomi's words encouraged me to grow in my spiritual life, praying more,
reading and studying the Bible more, and reading spiritual books. When
tragedy struck our lives, I had a good foundation of faith and trust in the Lord
on which to fall back. Hard days were ahead for me. I am so grateful for the
advice of this godly woman.

One of the greatest friendships in the Bible was between Naomi and Ruth.
It is a very unlikely love story, one between a mother-in-law and her daughter-
in-law, but these two became real friends. It was through Naomi that Ruth came
to know and believe in Yahweh God. When Ruth and Naomi returned to
Bethlehem, Ruth found safety and employment in the fields of Boaz, a kinsman
of Naomi. When Naomi told Ruth to go and sleep at the feet of Boaz, Ruth
followed her advice and fulfilled her request.

Boaz, a godly man in an ungodly society, was afraid, but his fears were laid
to rest when he recognized the woman was Ruth. The rest, as they say, is
history. He wed Ruth who became the great-grandmother of David, and
eventually, Jesus Christ. Imagine what Ruth's life would have been like if she
had not obeyed her mother-in-law!

Are you confused over what God is doing in your life? Why not consider
speaking to an older friend? Over a cup of coffee or tea, seek this person's
counsel for your problems. If you truly trust this woman, do what she says. It's
one thing to unload on another person and hear their advice -- it's another thing
to follow what they say.

March 3

Reason #63 Not to Fear: God Does Not Live in A Box

"So the Philistines were afraid, for they said, "God has come into the camp!" And they said, "Woe to us! For such a thing has never happened before." I Samuel 4:7

Religious symbols are in great evidence in today's secular society. Many people have figures of saints or angels in their homes or on the dash of their cars. Some people might treasure an old family Bible, thinking that by its very presence they are safe from harm. In many religions, figures or pictures of gods are prominently displayed. Many people carry good luck charms and think they will be protected from harm or from evil by these amulets.

In the Old Testament, Yahweh God inhabited the Ark of the Covenant. The Philistines were at war with Israel, and before the battle is enjoined one day, they heard a great commotion over in the Israelite camp. They discovered that the Israelites brought the Ark of the Covenant into the camp and their joy was so great that the earth shook and the air was rent with the sound of it.

This caused alarm in the camp of the Philistines. They thought of the Ark as a talisman, an object that would guarantee the Israelites victory in the war. And so they armed themselves, gathered their courage and marched out against God's people.

Sadly, the Israelites put their trust in the Ark as if it was a talisman, too. They had lost their heart for God and had waned in their obedience to Him. As they met the Philistines that day, their confidence was in a gold-covered box, not in the Yahweh God of their forefathers. And so they were defeated. Terribly defeated. The army was slaughtered and scattered, Saul and his sons were killed, and the Ark of the Covenant was taken.

Both the Philistines and the Israelites were wrong: the Ark was not a magical talisman, nor did its presence ensure a victory when God's people were not right with Him.

How is your heart today? Are you trusting in something or someone besides the power and grace of God? As you face difficult experiences, you will flounder and fail if you trust anything but Jesus Christ. Remember His faithfulness to you in the past. Place your trust in Him. He is able. He can meet your needs.

March 4

Reason #64 Not to Fear: We Trust in Christ Alone

"Now when the Philistines heard that the sons of Israel had gathered
together at Mizpah, the lords of the Philistines went up against Israel. And
when the sons of Israel heard it, they were afraid of the Philistines."
I Samuel 7:7

What are you afraid of? The Israelites feared the great army of the Philistines who marched up to Mizpah and camped in the valley. If an army came and attacked your city, would you feel a shiver of fear flutter down your spine?

What does it take for you to let go of your pride and cry out to God for help? Is it a child that lies at death's door? Or the loss of a job that you felt was secure? Is it the loss of your health? An accident that changes the whole tenure of your life? We trust in so many things in our society that God is often left out of the picture. What is it that you are trusting in today? Your money? The government? Your job? The people in your life? Your electronic gadgets?

The Israelites had a great deal of pride. They had come into the land but had not kept God's commands to overcome their enemies and claim the territory. They were disobedient and followed the Baal gods instead of giving their heart and love to Yahweh God.

Their waywardness continued for many years, and so God allowed enemy nations to defeat them. During these years, Samuel challenged the Israelites to worship and obey the Lord. He said that if they repented of their sin, the Lord would deliver them from the oppression of the Philistines.

Israel listened to him. They repented, and despite the fact that the Philistines brought fear throughout the nation, they believed God would grant them victory in this battle. Read the rest of the chapter and find out what happened.

If you want to be like Jesus in this world of ours, you must learn to obey Him and walk in His fellowship and light. Turn to Christ alone for your hope, your life, your future. Listen to good deep teaching and determine to obey His Word. If you do this day by day, He will give you the victory over sin and fear, as surely as He gave the victory to those trembling people in Samuel's day. Try it and find out for yourself.

March 5

Reason #65 Not to Fear: God Knows What Is Best

"If you fear the LORD and serve Him and obey His voice, and do not rebel against the commandment of the LORD, then both you and the king who reigns over you will continue following the LORD your God." I Samuel 12:14

Have you ever made a request of God for something that was just for you -- something that you wanted and maybe even craved, but that you felt was a little selfish?

Caring for someone like Bob full time is not easy. My days are mostly spent answering the questions that Bob repeats over and over, meeting his needs, seeing that he is fed, rested and comfortable. My service is accomplished privately and alone. I get worn out -- mentally, physically and spiritually. And so I told the Lord I needed time to get refreshed so my spirit would be renewed and my perspective changed.

A little later some of my friends planned to go on a retreat together. We talked about it and made plans for months to reunite, but at the last minute, the person I had gotten to look after Bob for the weekend could not come. So one of my dear friends stayed home from the retreat and filled the obligation so I could go. I needed to get refreshed and could not have done it without her kindness. God had answered even this simple request I had made.

The Israelites requested a king from the Lord, something that Samuel warned them against. But they insisted. They were tired of judges and prophets. They wanted a king like all the other countries around them had. So finally God accepted their request and gave them a king. In this verse they are told that by asking to have a human king, they had rejected the Lord as their King. Yet God is gracious. Even when we pray silly or selfish prayers, He answers us.

The Lord through Samuel told them that if they and their King were obedient to His commands, if they would listen to His voice, then all would be well. God would continue to be their Guide, Leader, Provider, and Protector. God would not forsake them as they did to Him.

Don't be foolish like the Israelites and insist on your own way. The kings of Israel brought untold suffering and harm to the people. How much better if they'd chosen God as their king! Make your requests to Christ, but leave the final answer to Him, trusting that he knows what is best for you.

March 6

Reason #66 Not to Fear: When We Repent, God Is Gracious

Then Samuel said to the people, "Do not fear. You have done all this wickedness; yet do not turn aside from following the LORD, but serve the LORD with all your heart." I Samuel 12:20

Samuel literally poured out his life for his people, the Israelites. At the last of his life, they rebelled against the God-given scheme of things and demanded a king. The nation up to this time was ruled by a theocracy, God being the king and the judges being those who prayed for the people, taught the people, and judged the law cases for them.

Now the people clamored for a king so they could be like the other nations. Samuel warned them what having a king was going to be like. He would take their best land, their best sons and daughters and their money in taxes, and he would use all this for his own pleasure. They thought having a king would give them security and powerful. But if a king did not follow God's leadership, he became a heavy weight around the necks of the people.

After hearing all this, they still wanted a king. Samuel, acting as God's spokesman, brought down a hail storm that destroyed the wheat harvest. This was to teach them a lesson on the power and sovereignty of God. They fell on their faces and repented of their wickedness and rebellion.

Samuel prayed for them and pled with them to continue to follow the Lord, even though they were shortly to get the king they wanted so much. "Fear the Lord," he says, "obey His commandments and entrust your lives to Him."

So many times we look to other things to satisfy our longings. We might look to a strong government, to our financial portfolios, to our careers or education, to our families, or to our pastor and church. All of these things can fail us. The advice that Samuel gave to the people so long ago echoes down through the centuries to us.

Trust only in God for your security, your power, your strength. Fear God. Obey His Word. Do not merely give Him a nod in the morning when you spend fifteen minutes in your daily devotions, then go and live the rest of your day in your own wisdom and strength. He needs to be a part of your every moment. He longs to invade your life that every thought, every conversation, every desire and every action is an extension of Him living in you.

March 7

Reason #67 Not to Fear: We Remember What Great Things God Has Done

"Only fear the LORD, and serve Him in truth with all your heart; for consider what great things He has done for you. But if you still do wickedly, you shall be swept away, both you and your king." I Samuel 12:24

God did something wonderful for us back in Chambersburg, Pennsylvania when Bob first began working in the mission, ministering to street people.

We did not receive a salary and had to raise our own support. The pastors and laymen who formed the board suggested a certain amount of money before Bob left his job to establish a mission. However, my husband could not wait. He believed that the Lord would be faithful and supply the support.

Our first year was a lean one, but we never did without. Remember we had children to care for and other financial commitments to keep. We were dependent on God to meet our *daily* needs. I remember going to Him in prayer many times for bills that needed to be paid or for medical treatment that was needed or for clothes for the children. God was faithful; He was our support, our caregiver and provider.

Bob moved out on faith, and I believe the Lord honored his unwavering commitment. In this day when the bottom line is financial gain or loss, when real estate values and the stock markets are declining, when people are losing their investments and retirements, it is good to remind ourselves from time to time: *God is bigger than all of this.*

Samuel exhorted the children of God to serious godliness. Your great duty is "to be sure to you fear the Lord." This type of fear is to know, respect and reverence Him. Consider God your Lord and Master and consider yourself His servant.

It is good to every once in a while to review what great and wonderful things God has done for you. Recall what mercy, goodness, and kindness God has allowed to touch your life. Every day, month after month, year after year, God has allowed your life to receive His wonderful riches. Out of a sense of fear and reverence for Him, be honest, sincere and pure.

Allow the fear of God to become more than a concept to you. Let it become a guiding principle that affects the way you live and make decisions.

March 8

Reason #68 Not to Fear: God Is Greater Than Our Giants

"And the Philistine (Goliath) said, "I defy the armies of Israel this day;
give me a man, that we may fight together." When Saul and all Israel heard
these words of the Philistine, they were dismayed and greatly afraid."
I Samuel 17:10, 11

Each of us has Goliaths in our lives. They come in the form of problems, people, or sins that we give into and fear. Some Goliaths are worry, doubts, fears, anxiety, depression or insecurity. Goliaths are intimidating, and they can cause major difficulties in our lives.

The story of David and Goliath is familiar to us, yet we need to take a closer look at it today. The Philistines were ready to do battle with Israel. Therefore, they sent out a man named Goliath who was their champion soldier. Israel, on the other hand, could find no one to fight with this giant.

David heard the voice of Goliath as he delivered supplies to his older brothers. Goliath taunted Israel and Yahweh. David was appalled at Goliath's ridicule and the cowardly reaction of the soldiers of Israel. David could not understand this fear that gripped the whole Israeli army.

Goliath's threats caused great fear throughout the Israelite army. Not one man wanted to compete with the giant. The clattering of their armor as they shook must have reached the Philistines, and how the enemies of God must have jeered, hooted and laughed! But David responded to Goliath's words with faith. The victory was won that day by a youngster fresh from the sheepfold, one who could not even wear armor or carry the king's sword.

The victory was won that day by a young boy and a sling shot, yet held in the hands of a person who trusted God, this meager weapon became deadly. David taught the Philistines something that day about the power of God. He also taught the soldiers in the army of the Israelites something about fear.

Confront, challenge and conquer your Goliath today. Pray about your anxieties. God will provide His strength to confront them. Remember that God is greater, stronger, and bigger than your Goliath. Daily use His strength and get ready to enjoy your life like never before. Do not be intimated by negative words and attitudes around you.

By faith claim your victory in God and march out to face your giants today. Without fear.

March 9

Reason #69 Not to Fear: Faith Is the Victory

"When all the men of Israel saw the man, they fled from him and were dreadfully afraid." I Samuel 17:24

I remember when my daughter called me from Indonesia to tell me her husband had died. Every part of my body trembled. I could hardly get any words to come out of my mouth to talk to her.

Her words were abrupt and short. "Mom…are you there? Mom, listen to me….James has just died. Mom….did you hear what I just said? James is dead."

No mother ever expects a phone call like that to come from their children. My mind could not wrap itself around what she told me. Not James. He is superman. He is God's worker. He is a father of three children. He has to write the Bible for the DaAn people. The more I let this awful, terrifying, interfering news sink in, the more I trembled. Young people don't die, do they?

There would many more phone conversations until my daughter arrived home. Each time the phone rang, my emotions became uncontrollable. This sad, heavy news allowed an uncommon fear to enter my life.

In the two months since James died (as I write this), my family and I have seen God provide, sustain, and support us. His peace and joy has continued to engulf us daily. We have fought against this giant of fear and worry each day. But instead of giving into it, we choose to cling to our God.

Giants come in all shapes and sizes. They come in the form of guilt, temptation, anger, failure, loneliness, worry, resentment, and jealousy. Fear may come sharply as it does when you are sliding off the road on an icy highway, or in the form of a dull ache of grief when faced with living the rest of your life without your loved one.

Do you have a giant in your life causing you grief and fear? Whatever it is, God is bigger. He will be with you and empower you to defeat your giant.

He will provide you with the strength you need every day. Do not allow the giants in your life to shackle you. Like David, trust God. Put on your spiritual armor and go out today without fear, without worry, without dread. God will help you. Believe in Him and find the victory today.

March 10

Reason #70 Not to Fear: We Refuse to Allow Fear to Mar Our Relationships

"Now Saul was afraid of David, because the LORD was with him, but had departed from Saul. Therefore Saul removed him from his presence, and made him his captain over a thousand; and he went out and came in before the people. And David behaved wisely in all his ways, and the LORD was with him. Therefore, when Saul saw that he behaved very wisely, he was afraid of him."
I Samuel 18:12-15

Fear and jealousy aid and support one another.

Two men from English history stand as examples of these destructive forces. King Henry II and Thomas 'a Becket were once friends, yet they became fierce enemies when Thomas, the son of a tradesman, skyrocketed to a position of power in the kingdom when he became not only Chancellor of the realm but the Archbishop of Canterbury. He was recognized as a man of importance, second only to the king, and in some eyes, higher than the king.

Now Becket's power rivaled the king's, especially in matters of the church. These two former friends engaged in bitter warfare of animosity and distrust that ended with the death of Thomas at the hands of King Henry's soldiers. He was murdered at the very altar where he served God.

King Saul was fearful and jealous of David. The young man who defeated Goliath now brought fear to Saul's heart. His jealousy grew stronger as the people began to love and praise David more than him. Because of his disobedience, the Spirit of God departed from Saul, never to return. Jealousy, fear, and disobedience were Saul's downfall, and can be our downfall, too.

Have you allowed yourself to be jealous of the attention, praise and importance heaped on another's head and not your own? Have you jealously guarded your friendships to the exclusion of others? Has fear motivated you to become bitter and angry?

What is the cure for such evil? Recognize this attitude as wrong. Repent of it. Release that person to God and take your hands off the situation. Stop comparing yourself to others. Pray for them. Encourage them. Only by doing these things can you find freedom from the awful power of jealousy and fear.

March 11

Reason #71 Not to Fear: We Refuse Jealousy

"Thus Saul saw and knew that the LORD was with David, and that Michal, Saul's daughter, loved him; and Saul was still more afraid of David. So Saul became David's enemy continually. I Samuel 18:28, 29

It is a sad state of affairs when we become so jealous for the friendship and affection of a person that we allow bitterness and rivalry to enter into our relationships. Yet it happens all the time and is the one of the major causes for the breakdown of friendships and marriages.

Jealously among Christian women is a cancer. It is awful and should not be allowed to grow or exist in our hearts. James says, "But if you have bitter jealousy and selfish ambition in your heart, do not be arrogant and so lie against the truth. This wisdom is not from above, but is earthly, natural, demonic. For where jealousy and selfish ambition exist, there is disorder and every evil thing." James 3:14-16 (NASB)

Over the years, I have an many wonderful friends. In different seasons of my life the Lord provided just the type of friend I needed. However, one particular friend wanted one hundred percent of me.

When my obligations caused to me to have to have interaction with other women she became upset. When I would have to travel and speak somewhere else, she became offended. What it boiled down to was a spirit of jealousy. My friend did not like being ignored or replaced.

Soon resentment grew between us. Eventually we had to distance ourselves from each other. Jealously cannot be allowed. It destroys. It is damaging. It will cause the best of relationships to die. Therefore jealousy is worth giving up.

The more successful and blessed David became, the more Saul feared and hated him. He was so jealous of David that he sinned against God by seeking to put him to death. Jealousy soured his heart and brought him darkness and death.

What do you do when you are tempted to feel jealousy toward another person? Do not allow jealousy into your life. Turn it over to God. Confess your sin and give it up. God will bless your life and give you peace.

March 12

Reason #72 Not to Fear: We Do Not Wallow in Self Pity

"Stay with me; do not fear. For he who seeks my life seeks your life, but with me you shall be safe." I Samuel 22:23

How can things go from bad to worse so quickly? Have you ever encountered a difficult situation, and as you set out to fix it, only made it worse? Oftentimes in church settings, feelings can be hurt. Things are said and sides are drawn up, and before you know it, the pastor has resigned and half the church goes with him. Sometimes life simply is not fair. In your family, you try your hardest to do what is right, and instead of a pat on the back or a reward, or even a word of thanks, you are dealt with injustice and cruelty.

In this passage, we find David in such a time. He fled from Saul and went to the only refuge he knew -- the tabernacle of God at the village of Nob. There he deceived the priest into thinking he was on an errand for the king, but he got the help he needed.

David was experiencing one of the most difficult times of his life. Saul's envy and hatred of him grew to the point of wanting to kill him, so he had to flee Jerusalem. He lost his wife, his friends, his job, his prestige, his self worth, his dreams, and his confidence. He is homeless. He is on the run.

When Abiathar, a young man of the priestly family, arrived and told David that Saul killed all the priests and the people of the village, David took the blame on himself, for he was wrong to deceive the priest. Yet I believe that David never truly forgave himself for the mistakes he made while he ran from Saul, mistakes made from fear and not from faith.

When you are hopeless, when you have come to the end of your rope, what is your response to life's difficulties? Fear or faith? If you give into fear, you will commit error. Your sin will haunt you the rest of your life. If you follow God no matter what the cost, you will come out blessed by God.

Some of you have had difficult things happen to you recently. Are those things going to drag you into fear and self pity? Do not allow it! Turn to God in faith and commit your ways to Him. Remember the Lord has a future for you and that He is for you, not against you. Like David, become a person of faith.

March 13

Reason #73 Not to Fear: We Love Our Friends

"Then Jonathan, Saul's son, arose and went to David in the woods and strengthened his hand in God. And he said to him, "Do not fear, for the hand of Saul my father shall not find you. You shall be king over Israel, and I shall be next to you. Even my father Saul knows that."
I Samuel 23:17

Friends are gifts of God. They are given to us to compliment our strengths and weaknesses, encourage us when we lag on the way, exhort us when we stray, and touch our hearts by their steadfast love.

I have had a few people like that in my life. Most of them live far away and I rarely see them, yet when we meet, it is like we've never left each other. Our hearts, minds and souls are so close that we pick up right where we left off and there is no awkward time of getting to know each other again.

The friendship between David and Jonathan was unique. These two men loved each other, committed themselves to each other, and protected each other. They were openly honest with each other. Therefore, David could tell his friend that he feared King Saul (Jonathan's father) would kill him. Jonathan, being the loyal friend he was, gave David wonderful advice. "Stay strong in the Lord and do not be afraid."

I think the very presence of Jonathan brought comfort to David. Despite being a strong man, David needed his friend. Jonathan reminded David of his calling from the Lord and his anointing to be king. Jonathan strengthened the hands and heart of his friend.

Jonathan was a true, honest friend. He was self-denying and took pleasure in David's advancement over his own. Once again these men renewed their God-given friendship.

I wrote down some questions to ask myself pertaining to what type of friend I am. What type of people am I drawn to? What are the essential elements in a godly friendship? How have I invested myself in a friend?

How about you? Are you displaying steadfast love to your friends? Are you *there* for them despite the circumstances? Can they depend on you for counsel, encouragement and prayer? You do not need a lot of friends. You need only one or two. Take a good look at your relationships today and decide to make them more like David and Jonathan's friendship.

March 14

Reason #74 Not to Fear: God Answers Prayer

*"So David made haste to get away (*for fear of, KJV*) from Saul, for Saul and his men were encircling David and his men to take them."* I Samuel 23:26

There was quite a lot of drama behind these simple words. David was an outlaw, a wanted man, a man on the run. He had collected other fugitives to fight with him, men who had disagreements and were disgruntled about the current leadership of Israel. They were camped in the Judean wilderness, fleeing Saul's soldiers.

Remember that the wilderness of Judea is not like the wildernesses in our country. It is a barren desert sprinkled here and there with oases and wadis where water flows in the rainy season only, and a few gnarled tamarisk or broom trees grow. Only a seasoned desert traveler or shepherd would know where to find water and shelter.

Saul, acting on information from spies, thought he had David trapped. The whole Israeli army was on one side of the mountain while David and his men were on the other. David cried out to God for help because he was afraid for his life. At this particular point he was at his best in listening to God while Saul was at his worst.

When David asked the Lord for protection, things seem to only get worse. He and his men were outnumbered. It seemed like Saul would achieve his evil intent and capture him. However, at just the right moment, like a cliffhanger in a movie or book, a messenger came to Saul and told him that the Philistines had invaded the land. Saul was needed somewhere else -- urgently, and so he leaves David and goes to fight with the Philistines.

How marvelously and amazingly is God's timing! God delivered David's life and the lives of his men from death. I can imagine the rejoicing that went on that night in the camp on the far side of the mountain!

Have you made any urgent cries to God for help recently? Remember Heb. 4:16, "Therefore let us draw near with confidence to the throne of grace, so that we may receive mercy and find grace to help in time of need." Draw near to God. Depend on His grace. Thank Him ahead of time for His answers. On the far side of the mountain, at wit's end, at the end of your rope, call out to God.

March 15

Reason #75 Not to Fear: I'm Staying Close to God

"When Saul saw the army of the Philistines, he was afraid, and his heart trembled greatly." I Samuel 28:5

It has been my goal to finish well and I am saddened by those who do not -- who refuse God and all the blessings He offers to His children.

It has been my goal to finish my life well. It has also been my goal not to wander from the Lord and listen to what He instructs me.

I spent many summers working at Lake Geneva Camp in Wisconsin when I was in my teens. Over the summers, I made some close friends, and we were always sad to tell each other good-bye. However, there was one girl I visited in her home in Illinois during the year. I loved going to church with her family and interacting with her siblings.

Over the years, our friendship stayed intact, yet I learned to my distress that she no longer went to church. I made one last trip to see her. It was disturbing, for she told me that she no longer believed in God and that He was not real to her. No matter how much I pleaded with her, she would not change her mind. Several years later I learned of her death. As far as I know, she never repented or changed her ways.

Saul, too, refused to repent. During his lifetime, he showed contempt toward the prophet Samuel, he murdered the priests and their families, and he maliciously persecuted David. He had cut himself off from God and now he'd come to the end of his career -- and his life. When he saw a large army of the Philistines, fear overtook him. He had no faith to call out to God for help. Because he was not in communion with God, he had no resource of faith or encouragement.

In his fear and panic, he asked a woman who was a witch to summon Samuel from the grave. What happened next not only frightened the king, but also the woman! Samuel appeared that night and his message was not comforting. He said that Saul and his sons would die and that Israel would be scattered like chaff on the mountainsides. Saul knew he would die, but he still would not repent.

There is a way to ensure that you will finish well. Commit your life to Jesus Christ and walk in obedience to Him. Stay in the Word. Listen for His voice. Spend time in prayer. You will find not only a good ending to your life but a better day for today.

March 16

Reason #76 Not to Fear: We Forgive Others

"Then David said to the young man who told him, "Where are you from?"
And he answered, "I am the son of an alien, an Amalekite." So David said to
him, "How was it you were not afraid to put forth your hand to destroy the
LORD'S anointed?" II Samuel 1:13, 14

Forgiveness is the key ingredient to a peaceful life. The only person you harm when you hold a grudge is yourself. It is the most freeing thing in the world to release those hurts to the Lord. Yet some people cannot do this. The feeling of grief and anger that fester in your heart leads to hatred and hatred spirals into bitterness.

In stark contrast to this attitude is the one of *agape* love, grace and forgiveness.

A wealthy Japanese businessman had only one son. While he was away on an extended trip, a man broke into his home, stole many of his possessions and killed his son. Upon returning home, he visited the criminal who was now in jail. Every day this Christian businessman visited the young man, who was tried, convicted and sentenced to death. When the trail came, the businessman spoke up and pled with the judge for his life to be spared. The judge said he needed someone who would take him into custody. The man took the convict who had killed his son into his home and eventually made him his son! That, my friend, is what forgiveness and grace is all about!

When news reached David about the death of Saul and Jonathan, David sincerely mourned for the king and his son without any malice in his heart even though he had suffered at the hands of the king for the long period of time. Does this tell you that he had forgiven, that his own heart was free of carrying the baggage of grief, hurt and hatred that might have been there?

Only through forgiveness can you find that kind of freedom. What kind of baggage are you carrying around with you today? Think of those who have harmed or wronged you, then *forgive them*. You may have to do this many times, but each time you bring them to the Lord, God will heal your heart and give you a measure of freedom. Do not rejoice in the revenge game when it comes to other Christians, or even to those outside the faith. Forgive, forgive, and forgive again. It is the way of the Cross.

March 17

Reason #77 Not to Fear: We Know and Obey God's Word

"David was now afraid of the Lord and asked, "How can the ark of the LORD come to me?" II Samuel 6:9

The Ark of the Lord had been captured by the Philistines and when they sent it back to Israel, it eventually came to rest in the home of Abinadab for twenty years. When David became king, he longed to bring it back to Jerusalem. David planned that day with meticulous care. He took thirty thousand men to move the Ark, along with Abinadab and his sons, Uzzah and Ahio.

However, in his excitement he made a dreadful mistake. He placed the Ark on a cart and disregarded the written instructions of the Lord on how to carry it. It should have been carried on the shoulders of the priests by the means of long poles. It was never to be touched or seen uncovered. On the journey, the oxen stumbled and the Ark toppled. When Uzzah touched it to steady it, God struck him immediately and killed him for his irreverence.

David went from joy to fear in an instant. He wept beside Uzzah's body, remorse filling his whole being. What had begun as a victory celebration ended in a dirge, a funeral for a boy who was only trying to help. David suddenly feared God and he was very angry -- not at God, but at himself for his disobedience. He had neglected one very important step: follow the law. Go back to the Instruction Book and heed it carefully. He wanted to move the Ark his way, not God's. Therefore, his efforts failed, and worse, someone died because of his disobedience.

Thankfully, most of the time, our disobedience does not end in such a tragedy. Yet so often we miss the blessing of God, the joy of the Holy Spirit, and the unity of believers because we want to do it our way and not God's way. Or maybe the issue is one of timing. David's timing was all right, but his method was wrong. A good intent failed because he hadn't done his homework.

The same is true for you. All your efforts will fail if they do not line up with the Word of God. Do you know the Word? Are you studying it daily? Honor His Word. Obey His Word. It is your life, your joy, your handbook on how to live.

David was afraid of the Lord in the right way. He got himself back into the Word of God and obeyed God's Word. Do that today in your own life.

March 18

Reason #78 Not to Fear: We Keep Our Promises

"So David said to him, "Do not fear, for I will surely show you kindness for Jonathan your father's sake, and will restore to you all the land of Saul your grandfather; and you shall eat bread at my table continually."
II Samuel 9:7

It is a common occurrence for politicians to not keep their campaign promises; so much so that this has become a standing joke in America. Who can believe their promises? How many people, from local officials to the office of the president, have reneged on their promises? What does it do to us when our leaders do not keep their promises?

Yet we suffer more from personal infidelity and dishonesty that we see around us all the time. There was a time when a hand-shake would suffice to close a business deal. Today we sign scores of contracts for something as simple as the purchase of a vehicle, and we know even as we sign, we could get out of these contracts if we really wanted to.

David and Jonathan were friends who made covenant promises to each other. They promised that they would show kindness to each other and to the others' descendants, as well.

After David became king and had settled the affairs of his kingdom, he recalled the promise he had made with Jonathan. Instead of brushing it aside as if it no longer mattered, he carefully investigated and discovered that Jonathan did, indeed, have a living son, Methphibosheth. David invited the young man to come to Jerusalem and meet him.

You can imagine the fear Methphibosheth felt as he prostrated himself before the king that day. He was a cripple, and more importantly, was the only man who could claim the throne as a descendant from Saul. David lifted him to his feet, and I believe, with tears in his eyes, elevated this man to be his friend and companion, offering to keep and feed him for the rest of his life at his own table. David was a leader who kept his promise.

What are some promises you have made? Are you keeping them? Think about this soberly. Undo the wrongs you might have done and resolve today to keep your promises, even if they are hard to keep. God will bless you in ways you cannot imagine.

March 19

Reason #79 Not to Fear: We Trust God

"When the waves of death surrounded me, the floods of ungodliness made me afraid." II Samuel 22:5

Have you ever been totally, mortally afraid for your life?

A missionary family served in a country on the African continent. At one point in their ministry, an opposing army overtook the city where they lived. They had to flee the country, but the roads were blocked and roving bands of terrorists shut down the city. They arrived at one checkpoint only to be ordered into a building. On the floor, they waited. Outside they heard gunfire, screams, sounds of violence and mayhem. They cowered on the floor, sure that in any instant gunmen would burst into their sanctuary and kill them.

The man recalled that moment later and said, "We had nothing except our faith in God. He came through for us. I prayed out loud and God seemed to fill the room. His presence gave us peace. We remained on the floor for several hours and finally we were allowed to get in our car and resume our journey." They escaped because of the hand of God protected them.

David magnified the Lord for delivering mercies -- he should know, because time and time again he was exposed to many physical and spiritual enemies. He compares his enemies to waves of death, to an angry sea. Destruction seemed certain and he was afraid.

Saul, Abner, and Absalom tried to destroy David. So fierce were their threats, attacks, and force that David admits they made him afraid. Charles Spurgeon said, "The most courageous man, who as a rule hopes for the best, may sometimes fear the worst."

Strong as his faith was, occasionally David feared that Saul would eventually kill him. The threats were from the outside, but they caused David to be afraid on the inside. You may not face the extreme fear of losing your life, yet you may be tempted to fear when things are not good in your life.

If you experience the torment of fear from without, it may cause you to be afraid within. Confront your external fears. You cannot wish fear away, but you can pray that it will flee. Use the power that is available today and you will find peace.

March 20

Reason # Not to Fear 80: We Treat Those Under Us with Kindness

"The God of Israel said, The Rock of Israel spoke to me: 'He who rules over men must be just, Ruling in the fear of God. And he shall be like the light of the morning when the sun rises, A morning without clouds, Like the tender grass springing out of the earth, By clear shining after rain.'"
II Samuel 23:3, 4

King David, the sweet psalmist of Israel and her greatest king, penned these words at the end of his life. He recognized that even kings must bow their knee to God, fear Him and submit to His authority.

In America, we have a good example of a godly man who ruled our country in the fear of God. Abraham Lincoln was a humble man, one who cared for his people.

It was said that after the war many soldiers came to petition the president for help. They filled his anteroom and waited patiently until he could see them.

One young man had lost both legs and came to ask the president to find help and care for his mother. He waited all day and yet there were many before him. A young boy approached the soldier toward the end of the day, and listened to his story. The soldier said he did not suppose he would get in to see the President. The boy replied, "Oh, yes, you will, sir!" Just like that, the boy ran into the President's office. In a short time, he returned and said, "Come on in, sir!"

To the soldier's great delight, he was taken to see the president. The boy turned out to be Tad, Lincoln's son, and the President did, indeed, give the soldier aid for his mother.

As sunshine comes through a clear morning, or as tender grass sprouts after rain, so is a ruler who fears the Lord and deals justly with his subjects. This kind of man is tender, compassionate and gentle to the infirmities of those he rules.

How about you? Who are those under your authority? Do you rule them with kindness, humility, graciousness and the fear of God? Or are you full of pride and haughtiness? Check your heart and make sure you are humble and sweet to those who live under your rule.

March 21

Reason #81 Not to Fear: We Teach Our Children to Fear God

"Then hear in heaven Your dwelling place, and forgive, and act, and give to everyone according to all his ways, whose heart You know (for You alone know the hearts of all the sons of men), that they may fear You all the days that they live in the land which You gave to our fathers." I Kings 8:39, 40

The human heart enjoys grand ceremonies and pageantry. The priests of the pagan gods in ancient Israel knew this and played to the people's desires. Even though they did not have our modern technology, they could produce quite a show.

We love a good show, too. Millions of people watched the royal weddings in England in all their glory, opulence and romance. Thousands of people like to attend live concerts, enjoy a fireworks show, spend hours watching TV in all the myriad offerings it gives to please the eye and feed our pleasure-mad society. Well, my friend, you have never seen *anything* compared to the service Solomon put on to dedicate the brand new temple to God! This verse is part of Solomon's prayer of dedication at the temple he built for the Lord.

Solomon realized several things about this temple. He realized in this temple people would pray to God and he also realized that it would be the place where God dwelt on earth. What a thought! Solomon himself marveled that the God of all the universe would live in this temple he had a part in building.

The king looked into the future in his dedication and wanted those who heard about this temple to fear and honor the name of the Lord and to walk in His ways as long as they lived. Even beyond his own nation, he wanted *all people in the earth* to know and fear the name of the Israel's God.

Isn't that what each of us wants for the generations that follow us? Most certainly I want each of my grandchildren to reverence the Lord and to walk in His ways. When the time of your life is over, how will you be remembered? What is the legacy you are passing onto your children and grandchildren?

How can you insure that the next generation will follow, revere, and obey God? What do you need to change in your life to do this? Put Him first in your life so your children will also love and obey Him.

March 22

Reason #82 Not to Fear: We Give God Glory and Praise

"Then hear in heaven Your dwelling place, and do according to all for which the foreigner calls to You, that all peoples of the earth may know Your name and fear You, as do Your people Israel, and that they may know that this temple which I have built is called by Your name." I Kings 8:43

In this verse, Solomon included the foreigner and the stranger in their midst. He prayed that if even this person comes to the temple and prays to Yahweh God, that God would hear his prayers so that all the nations of the earth would know that God is God alone and there is no other One so high and lifted up as He. God's intention from the beginning was that all peoples of the earth would know Him, worship Him, and be in fellowship with Him.

When you read the news of horrific events happening in an African nation, does your heart cry for these oppressed people? Do you pray for justice and mercy for the ones who still live with the horror of death and genocide? Or do you flip on over to some favorite mindless show? Take a moment and pray for the persecuted church around the world.

In your prayer time there should always be a time when you give glory to God, a time when the fresh experiences of God's promises call for praise from your lips and heart. Knowing God's promises should encourage you to depend on Him more and more. Solomon praised God for this brand new temple, and he also prayed for his people who would worship there.

The Israelites knew both the mercy and forgiveness of God. They knew God heard and answered their prayer, forgave their sin and displayed His favor on them. From their experiences many might be led to fear the Lord and receive His goodness as Israel did.

It is not about a place. It was not the temple that brought about God's favor and blessing, although He designated Jerusalem and the temple as the place to bring sacrifices in the Old Testament. For us today, the Spirit of God dwells within each one of those who have put their faith in Christ. What is it, then, that we proclaim to the nations?

Lord, in my life please shine consistently. May those I come in contact with today sense Your aroma and fragrance. Grant me the privilege of guiding people to You in a world that is filled with darkness. You have put me here for Your purposes, may I fulfill them. Please go ahead of me in all I do and say. Allow me to honor Your name as I live for You.

March 23

Reason #83 Not to Fear: We Obey by Faith

"Then Elijah said to her, 'Do not fear; go, do as you have said, but make me a little bread cake from it first and bring it out to me, and afterward you make some for yourself and your son." I Kings 17:13

Elijah went to Zarephath on the word of the Lord. While there, he asked a widow for a drink of water. As she was going to grant his request, he also added that he would like a piece of bread. That was no small request. He was asking her to make a significant sacrifice. There had been no rain, which meant there were no crops and no food. This widow lived in extreme poverty. She had only enough flour and oil for one last meal for herself and her son.

What would you do if you were that widow from Zarephath? Submit? Believe that God was speaking to you through this situation? Believe that the flour and oil would not run out like Elijah said? We must remember she was a heathen, not Jew, not a believer in Yahweh. Yet she must have heard about Israel's God and she recognized this man who stood before her as a prophet of Yahweh.

She was asked to make the biggest decision of her life. Would it be faith or unbelief? Yet what did she have to lose? She was sure both she and her son would soon die. Now that Elijah had spoken, she would have to respond with an act of faith, or an act of unbelief. The Word of the Lord would either cause her to repent or harden her heart.

I have never been in such an extreme situation, and I do not suppose you have, either, but I can imagine the despair, sorrow, exhaustion and fear she lived with daily. We do not know what prompted this woman to respond to Elijah the way she did, but she acted on her faith, not on her fears. She gave Elijah one last, long look and did what he asked her to do.

This woman made a total and complete sacrifice. She gave everything she had to Elijah and the Lord rewarded her act of faith. What caused this woman to take this action? Her extraordinary faith. She submitted and acted on her faith to feed the Lord's servant. She overcame her fear through her faith.

Do you have that kind of faith? It is a faith that stops at nothing short of giving God your all. When you face life's difficult circumstances, remember to put aside your fears and respond with this kind of faith. If a widow from Zarephath can do it, so can you.

March 24

Reason #84 Not to Fear: God Is More Powerful Than Evil

"And it shall come to pass, as soon as I am gone from you, that the Spirit of the LORD will carry you to a place I do not know; so when I go and tell Ahab, and he cannot find you, he will kill me. But I your servant have feared the LORD from my youth." I Kings 18:12

Christians in China have been tested to the utmost for their faith for the last fifty years since the Communists took control of the government and outlawed Christianity. Just recently a home church, unlicensed by the government, was kicked out of the building in which they met. The government officials thought they could destroy the church in this way.

The leaders of the church decided that if they were not allowed to meet in the building, they would meet outside. They chose a park and quietly met there. Each Sunday morning, the police arrived and took many of the leaders and people to prison. However, more and more people came to fill their shoes. It was like trying to empty a bucket into which flows a living stream of water!

These people, and especially those in leadership, are godly individuals who are standing for their faith in spite of the wickedness all around them.

After the long drought on the land, Elijah was sent by the Lord to speak to King Ahab and his wife, Jezebel. But just before Elijah's arrival, Ahab summoned Obadiah. He confessed to the king that he was only a servant and one who had feared the Lord from his youth. He is not boasting, but stating the truth. This simple declaration revealed his faith. He was a righteous man in a wicked place.

Even though America claims to be a Christian country, it is still filled with evil. Often Christians are good people in a bad place. Therefore, when you decide to follow the Lord you will have to make your way through the meshwork of wickedness. You will be faced with innumerable temptations which will tear at your beliefs.

We live in a very selfish, materialistic world. Distrust and deceit are all around us and piercing it with the principles of God is difficult. A godly person must make it clear where he stands. You must stand up and show your true loyalty. Count for righteousness. Let your light shine for Christ. Be radiant. Good people in bad places can demonstrate their belief and reap the benefits.

March 25

Reason #85 Not to Fear: There Are More With Us Than With Them

"So he answered, "Do not fear, for those who are with us are more than those who are with them."And Elisha prayed, and said, "LORD, I pray, open his eyes that he may see." Then the LORD opened the eyes of the young man, and he saw. And behold, the mountain was full of horses and chariots of fire all around Elisha." II Kings 6:16

When my daughter and son-in-law invited me to visit them for an extended length of time recently (at the time of this writing), I was very glad to say "yes" and plan for the trip. They were missionaries in Borneo, Indonesia, with New Tribes Mission, living in the jungle. While in the jungle, I had many fears. My greatest fear was contacting malaria. My daughter's whole family has had malaria at one time or another and when I heard how terrible it was, I was afraid of this disease. So I prayed that God would protect me, and He did just that! I brought home the pills I took with me in case I contracted the disease! God rescued me from the fear of a very small thing.

Gehazi, Elisha's servant, feared the armies of the Syrians. Early one sunny morning, he walked out on the rooftop and caught the glint of sunlight against a shield. And, *yes!* There was a horseman perched on the hillside just a stone's throw away! His eyes swept the entire countryside, and he saw a *whole army* of enemy soldiers! He was instantly so afraid he could hardly speak. Quickly he awoke Elisha and told him the horrible news. But Elisha only chuckled and came up on the roof to see for himself.

"Do you see?" Gehazi said, sweeping his arm in a wide arc. "The whole army is here! There is no escape! Alas, my master, what shall we do?" Elisha was not anxious. "Do not fear, Gehazi, for those who are with us are more than those who are with them." After Elisha prayed for his servant, his eyes were opened and he saw an angelic host of heaven outside the ring of human enemy soldiers! What a sight that must have been.

What are you afraid of today? Big things or small things? Bring all your fears to God and let Him illuminate your spiritual eyes to know by faith that angelic beings are protecting you and helping you. Your soul will be comforted, I can assure you. You will be able to face whatever it is that is causing you fear – whether it is a mosquito or a whole army of enemies!

March 26

Reason #86 Not to Fear: We Do Not Worship Idols

"For so it was that the children of Israel had sinned against the LORD their God, who had brought them up out of the land of Egypt, from under the hand of Pharaoh king of Egypt; and they had feared other gods."
II Kings 17:7

In the Da'An Tribe in Indonesia, many of the tribal people believe in evil spirits, which leads them into many strange practices. The witch doctor teaches the people that evil spirits can harm them, are all around them, and need to be warded off and appeased. After a woman gives birth in the tribe, she wears a red rope around her stomach for a length of time. She believes that this rope will fend off the evil spirits from her and her newborn baby.

While I was visiting in the tribe, a woman gave birth across the path from my daughter's home. Several days later, when my daughter saw the woman, she noticed the red rope tied around the girl's stomach. Like all of her people who have not come to salvation in Jesus Christ, she lived in constant torment and fear of evil spirits, a bondage that shapes her whole life.

In 722 B.C. Shalmaneser, the captain of the Assyrian army under Sargon II, captured the capitol city of Israel, Samaria, and carried off most of the people and brought them to Assyria as slaves. The existence of the northern kingdom ended. Why did this happen? Because the Israelites failed to obey the Lord God of Israel, Yahweh Elohim. They refused to listen to the message of repentance from the prophets. While they claimed to worship Yahweh, they had given their allegiance to false gods.

A similar attitude prevails today in America. Many people claim to believe and trust in Christ, but they refuse to give up their heathen customs. They say that they believe in God, but they participate in activities and amusements that He forbids.

Do not copy the evil conduct of those around you, or be shaped by the world. Do not worship the false gods of pleasure, money, fame, or possessions. Remember the serious consequences God brought upon His people.

What are the idols you have allowed into your life that come before God and His service? Search your heart and reset your priorities today.

March 27

Reason #87 Not to Fear: We Worship God With our Whole Hearts

"Then one of the priests whom they had carried away into exile from Samaria came and dwelt in Bethel and taught them how they should fear the Lord." II Kings 17:28

Today is Sunday and like millions of other people, I attended church with the intent of worshipping the Lord. Yet as I look out on the congregation, I see some people yawning, some dozing, some people with far-away looks in their eyes, maybe wondering how the football game is going, maybe others are thinking about what to do after church. Many people come to church just as a ritual, as a show. They have not come to worship God; in fact, God is the last thing they want to think about, even in His house of worship.

The Assyrian nation had conquered and taken the Israelites into captivity. Then, because the land needed people to farm it, they brought foreigners into the land. These people worshipped idols, yet they were afraid because lions and other wild beasts roved the land and killed many of them. Therefore they petitioned the king of Assyria to send a Jewish priest to them so they could learn how to worship Yahweh. It was Yahweh's land and they surmised if they had a form of Jewish religion that would solve the lion problem. The king complied with their wishes and sent a priest who set up a form of sacrifices and worship system. They attended these pseudo-Israeli services and did what they were instructed to do.

Yet they did not fear Yahweh or worship Him from their hearts. The result of this was a religion that was a mixture of Yahweh worship and idol worship. Yet why did they do this? Did they think that Yahweh was like their own gods, and that the system worked like charms and superstition like we see in pagan countries today? They were missing the point of it all.

We can, too. We can attend church and go through all the motions, even take part in some of the activities, yet still miss the point.

You see, dear friend, you must worship God with your whole heart and fear Him above everything else. He will not take second place to other gods in your life. Confess your sin of putting God into second, third or last place in your life, and begin today to worship Him and fear Him with your whole heart, soul and mind.

March 28

Reason #88 Not to Fear: We Get Rid of Our Idols

"But the LORD, who brought you up from the land of Egypt with great power and with an outstretched arm, Him you shall fear, Him you shall worship, and to Him you shall offer sacrifice." II Kings 17:36

In II Kings, chapter 17, we find a sad chapter in the life of the nation of Israel. Since the days of Jeroboam, who made the golden calves and told the people to worship them, they had resisted the Word of God and gone their own ways, worshipping idols and adopting the practices of the heathen people in the land. Hoshea was the last king to reign over the ten tribes of Israel, the northern kingdom. He was a puppet king set up by the Assyrians, but he rebelled against his masters and fought against them for three years. They defeated Israel and took most of the people as captives to Babylon.

We shake our heads and wonder how those Israelites could have been so stupid and stubborn. Yet are we any different? Many of us sit on our soft couches and eat the delicacies of the nations brought to our supermarkets by trucks, trains and airplanes; we enjoy every pleasure and comfort that comes to mind, living like kings and queens.

We worship the little TV gods of our world, the stars and idols, the sports heroes, the media figures who sit behind their little desks and comment at length with worldly wisdom. We complain and throw a temper tantrum if we don't get a good parking space. We think our life is over if we run out of chips and the store down the way is closed. We can become spoiled rotten, and loose lost touch with the real God who loves us, desires our fellowship and yearns over us as a husband whose wife has been unfaithful.

Idols? We have them by the score. Our society encourages the worship of people, places and things. We are no better than those people so long ago. People deny the existence of God, yet He is real and He alone is to be worshipped. He is the everlasting God to all generations.

Ask yourself: what do I worship today? Get up and move off your couch and if you are able, get on your knees. Spend time in prayer, asking God to reveal to you where you need to change and what you need to do. When you get up, look at the world and your life like He does. Worship Him in fear and trembling. Love Him with all your heart, soul and mind.

March 29

Reason #89 Not to Fear: God Alone Is My Strength and Shield

"But the Lord your God you shall fear, for He will deliver you from the hands of all your enemies. II Kings 17:39

When I was nineteen, I unexpectedly ended up in the hospital. It was one week before Christmas and I was scheduled for surgery in a couple of days. My blood count was very low and I was given several transfusions. The doctor believed that I was bleeding somewhere inside of my stomach area and wanted to do exploratory surgery to find the cause of this.

I was fearful, totally frightened and extremely worried. My Bible was by my bedside and I read and re-read the books of I & II Peter. I asked God to close the door regarding the surgery set for the next morning, because I had no peace about it. My doctors and parents decided that the surgery was important and they would not change their minds.

Morning arrived. My doctor came to see me and to my surprise he told me that he was going to delay the surgery. I was so relieved, and I never did have the surgery. I have never forgotten this lesson where God encouraged my faith. God can always be trusted.

A dramatic struggle was ensuing between the Assyrians and those in Israel -- a struggle between confidence in the military, or faith in God alone. For many years, spiritual inconsistencies existed in the Lord's people. God's prophets had warned them to turn from idols to fear and worship Yahweh. They had not listened. God allowed a foreign nation to invade their land, killing and enslaving the people. Now God is reminding the people who are left in the land that they should fear Him and worship Him. If they would, He would deliver them from their enemies.

Is there some fear holding you back in life? Are you struggling with some specific fear today? It is okay to feel fear, but you must move beyond fear to faith. Fear is a tool of the Satan to keep you frozen and stationary in your walk with God.

When fear rears its ugly head, say these exact words to yourself. Repeat them out loud if you have to. *"I will not be afraid."* In whom do you trust? Who do you fear and worship? If your confidence is not in God, you will make the same mistakes the Israelites did. Replace your fear with trust in God today.

March 30

Reason #90 Not to Fear: I Trust in God's Promises

"And Gedaliah took an oath before them and their men, and said to them, 'Do not be afraid of the servants of the Chaldeans. Dwell in the land and serve the king of Babylon, and it shall be well with you.'" II Kings 25:24

Jeremiah gives us further insight into this story (Jer. 42). The Babylonians had conquered Judah and set up certain men to govern those who stayed in the land. Gedaliah was the governor of the province. He was a man who feared God and was going to lead them in worship of Yahweh God. These men, the leaders of the people, appealed to Jeremiah as to what they should do. Should they stay in the land or should they flee and go somewhere else?

Can you imagine how they felt? They had witnessed the most horrific scenes imaginable. Their nation lay in shambles. Most of the people were gone. They did the right thing in asking Jeremiah. Both he and Gedeliah counseled the people to stay in the land and not to fear the Babylonians. Sadly, they did not listen. Evil men came and killed Gedaliah and the people fled to Egypt, taking Jeremiah with them. There they continued to worship the Egyptian idols, particularly Ishtar, the goddess of the heavens.

It is always sad when we give in to our fears instead of heeding and obeying God's Word. Sometimes we begin the day with the greatest hopes, dreams and plans. We are moving forward with joy. But before the day ends, fear disrupts our thoughts.

More days than I can count fear has dominated my life, and this derailed the Lord's blessings in my life. It may not be as dramatic as what Jeremiah experienced, but I end the day thinking, *if only I had not listened to my fears*. Fear distorts your view and robs you of the right perspective. Fear brings out the worst in us and tempts us to get our eyes off God and onto ourselves. We forget to trust Him, honor Him and acknowledge Him.

Take a deep breath and refuse those fears in your life that will cause you to make the wrong decisions, disobey the Word of God and take matters into your own hands. The outcome of that is tragedy.

Trust God for your future. For today. As for me, fear will not drain me, at least not today. I will believe in God's promises and Word. Will you?

March 31

Reason #91 Not to Fear: We Don't Make Choices Based On Fear

"And all the people, small and great, and the captains of the armies, arose and went to Egypt; for they were afraid of the Chaldeans."
II Kings 25:26

Fear causes you to make foolish choices, choices you regret later.

One of the saddest examples of this is in regard to my mother-in-law. When my husband became a Christian, he was still living at home. The change that occurred in him did not set well with anyone in his family, particularly with his mother. She hated and mocked his decision to accept Christ as his Savior and the reason for all this hatred was me. When I told Bob about Christ and he decided to accept this truth, her hatred intensified.

Perhaps her fear was that her son found someone in his life more important than her. Slowly her fears became realities. Bob's decision to follow Christ *did* lead him away from her, and he followed a career that was totally opposite everything she wanted for him. This caused a huge division between them. For quite awhile, they did not even speak to each other. She always resented the fact that her favorite son found Christ.

This story, like the one recorded in II Kings 25, does not have a happy ending.

Jeremiah was forced to flee with the Jews to Egypt where they continued their worship of the "queen of heaven" and disobey God. Jeremiah prophesied to them, urging them to repent, but they would not. Jeremiah died in a foreign land because the people were afraid and refused to trust God.

Fear is aggressive and has to be defeated by you, personally. The key is to pray about what is causing you to live in apprehension, and as you isolate the things that cause you to dread, and turn them over to God. He will provide you with the strength to confront each one.

When you feel terror controlling your emotions and thinking, pray about it immediately. Do not wait to see how bad things are going to get. Do not make choices based on fear. Do not let your trepidation of people, places, or things consume you. Face these issues. Release them to God. Become grounded in the Word; it will help you tackle those concerns that cause you to tremble. *Fear not, God is with you.*

April 1

Reason #92 Not to Fear: We Worship According to God's Word

"David was afraid of God that day, saying, 'How can I bring the ark of God home to me?'" I Chronicles 13:12

My children, Nicky and James Poarch, lived (at the time I wrote this) in the jungle on the island of Boreno, Indonesia. Tribal living can be unusual for those of us not accustomed to it. The first time I went to visit them in the tribe, I was welcomed with open arms by the people. However, when I went to church in the tribe, it certainly was not like going to church in Phoenix, AZ. There were no guitars, piano, drums, or worship team. The people simply sang, off and on tune. If anyone from a Caucasian, modern church had come to these services, they might have thought the worship was all wrong.

Worship is important in our lives. Jesus said to the woman at the well, "God is spirit and those who worship Him must worship in spirit and in truth." (John 4:24) He was trying to get this woman to see beyond the customs of her people. We may not all worship the same way. The elements of our worship service may vary in regards to the songs we sing, the order of service, the length of the sermon. But the most important thing is our hearts. Are we worshipping God in spirit and in truth?

The greatest worshipper in the Bible was probably David. However, he made a serious mistake when he brought the Ark of the Covenant into Jerusalem. He was wrong because he used this occasion as a performance instead of a worship time, and he consulted with the leaders how to return the ark to Israel, not with the Lord. He had the priests carry the Ark on a cart, not with long poles on their shoulders as the Law said to do. Consequently, a young man died.

When this happened, he was angry at himself and fearful of God. The good news is that he went back to the Book and did it right the second time.

How many churches employ the wrong methods and principles in their worship of a holy God? How many churches have a performance on Sunday morning instead of a time to glorify God? Do you worship in spirit and in truth? Search your heart and cleanse your motives. You cannot copy the ways of the world when it comes to worship.

April 2

Reason #93 Not to Fear: The Battle Is the Lord's

"Then the fame of David went out into all the lands; and the Lord brought the fear of him upon all nations." I Chronicles 14:17

I love teaching God's Word. I love to see how it impacts people's lives and changes them. For a number of years while we lived in Pennsylvania, I taught a very large Bible study and loved every moment of it. After several years, those in authority over me did not like my way of teaching any longer and told me I could no longer teach.

Rumors surfaced everywhere. I was the talk of the town and defending myself did no good. There were a lot of meetings, a lot of discussions, a lot of hurt feelings. I tried to explain that teaching was my gift and many people were blessed through it, yet it did no good. I struggled with this situation, praying desperately and questioning why the Lord would allow it.

Despite all I did, I was dismissed as teacher of the Bible study. As I endured this painful trial, I learned the hard way to rely on the Lord to win the battle for me. It is now over ten years since that incident happened. Over the years God has renewed my gift of teaching and given me many opportunities to exercise that gift. It was His battle and He won it for me in the long run.

King David was definitely blessed by God. When he was just a boy, God saw that his heart was faithful to Him. Even though he failed at times, David became the greatest king Israel ever had and became the ancestor of Jesus Christ. How was it that David's fame spread everywhere? It all started with *the spirit of the Lord came upon David*. God choose David to be king and David fulfilled God's assignment with joy, proving to be faithful and obedient.

In every battle that David faced, he always remembered the battle is the Lord's. It was a battle for God's glory, not his own. David believed he would be victorious because the Lord was with him and that caused many nations to fear him.

Are you in a battle? Are you facing a giant? If you are in a fight, you will definitely be defeated if you have self-doubt, timidity, negative attitudes, uncontrolled anger, fear, worry and lack of focus. In every conflict, remember that the battle is the Lords, not yours. Turn it over to Him and trust in Him alone. He will not fail you.

April 3

Reason #94 Not to Fear: We Ascribe Glory to God

"Give to the LORD, O families of the peoples, Give to the LORD glory and strength. Give to the LORD the glory due His name; Bring an offering, and come before Him. Oh, worship the LORD in the beauty of holiness! Tremble before Him, all the earth. The world also is firmly established, It shall not be moved." I Chronicles 16:28-30

The NASB (New American Standard Bible) translates the word "give" as "ascribe". *Ascribe* is an interesting word. In our English dictionary, it means to believe or say that something was caused by a particular thing; to believe that something belongs to or characterizes a person or group. Synonyms are: to assign, credit or attribute. We ascribe to the fact that the sky is blue; we as Christians ascribe to the fact that God created the world and so He is the cause of the blue sky.

We often misjudge in our ascribing, don't we? We ascribe to someone what we think they did and find out later we did not know all the facts and so jumped to the wrong conclusion. Sometimes we ascribe bad things to the wrong people, or good things to the wrong people. We have to be careful in judging, for we don't know the heart and we don't know all the facts.

I have eight grandchildren. The youngest is three (at this writing), a little girl I call Boo. We often sing together, and lately I've teaching her old Sunday school songs, like, "This Little Light of Mine" or "Jesus Loves the Little Ones Like Me, Me, Me." Recently I taught her "God is So Good". As I was teaching it to Boo, once again the words impacted my heart. God is really so good to me. It is true. God is good ... all the time. All the time ... God is good!

We can ascribe goodness, praise, glory and honor to Him, knowing we have ascribed it to the right Person! Look at the verse at the top and read how many attributes the psalmist mentions about God. Verse 27 of this passage says, "Splendor and majesty are before Him, strength and joy are in His place."

Does your heart thrill with the knowledge that God is majestic, splendid, glorified, strong, and good? Do you fear Him, love Him, and honor Him with every breath you take?

Why not sing about God's goodness today?

April 4

Reason #95 Not to Fear: Just Get Up and Do It

"And David said to his son Solomon, "Be strong and of good courage, and do it; do not fear nor be dismayed, for the LORD God--my God--will be with you. He will not leave you nor forsake you, until you have finished all the work for the service of the house of the LORD." I Chronicles 28:20

When Bob was approached to begin a mission to troubled teens on the streets of Chambersburg, Pennsylvania, my heart sank. I knew how difficult, demanding, and complicated birthing a work can be. I never anticipated the Lord would call us to begin a mission, and I felt overwhelmed at the challenge. Would Bob be successful? How would we buy a building? Who would support the work? How does it even begin?

We did not have any of those answers, but the Lord did. Slowly the Lord Himself birthed NETWork Ministries in the inner city. It is still in existence, reaching troubled youth and people for almost twenty years. God put within Bob the gifts of wisdom, joy and a deep love to launch this work. Every day that he worked at the mission, I can say he loved it. Every person he met, he wanted to help.

God did not tell Bob to build a temple, but He told him to build a mission.

Solomon might have felt overwhelmed when David approached him and told him his task was to build the temple. Even though David had prepared many things for it, as Solomon thought about the enormity of the task, I am sure his knees quaked.

David wanted to build a temple for the Lord, but God had other ideas, and the job was given to Solomon. This was an awesome responsibility. He had to follow all of his father's carefully laid plans and the pattern for the temple that was given in the law. Each detail had to be done in the most meticulous manner possible.

David wanted his son to be totally dedicated to this work. It may not have been easy or popular, but it was the right thing to do. It cost Solomon a great deal to accomplish this task in terms of time, money and labor. But he did it.

God probably has not directed you or me to build a temple in Jerusalem, but He has told us to reach out to our community, to witness and serve. He is faithful to give us what we need if we are willing to do it. Ask the Holy Spirit to give you strength and courage to carry on your duties. Get up and do it.

April 5

Reason #96 Not to Fear: God's Presence is With Us

"That they may fear You, to walk in Your ways as long as they live in the land which You have given to our fathers." II Chronicles 6:31

I read the other day how modern Jews are divided about the Temple Mount. Some see it as only a pile of rocks or a historical site. They ask: are we falling into the same trap as other nations who fight over "sacred" ground and sacrifice lives over something trivial?

The other camp sees the Temple Mount area as sacred, blessed by God, and the only place on earth that the Third Temple could be built. Aside from the deep historical and spiritual heritage the place brings to mind, they see this piece of earth as terrifically important to preserve, to die for, and to regain as their own prized possession for God's glory.

Solomon built a magnificent structure on this site around the year of 959 BC. Using our present US currency, this temple cost 58 billion dollars. Solomon stood with his hands spread out before the altar of the Lord in front of the entire community of Israel and prayed a prayer of dedication regarding the temple of the Lord. When he finished praying, fire flashed down from heaven and burned up all the sacrifices and God's holy presence filled the temple. The people fell on their faces and worshipped the Lord.

Solomon wanted the people to walk in the ways of the Lord and fear Him, to reverence and honor Him. He also desired that others from the nations around them would be attracted to Israel's God. He wanted the temple to draw and point people to the Lord God. Know what? It did, at least for some people.

For many years this temple stood as a lighthouse, pointing the way to God. Solomon realized that this was more than a building and the land it was on was more than a pile of rocks. God's presence dwelt there. It became a symbol to the whole world of the person and work of God in redeeming lost mankind and reaching out to them to dwell in their midst.

The reason you and I are in this world today is to reveal God to those around us. God's Holy Spirit dwells within each of us and we are His lighthouse to a lost world. How is your light doing today? Is it shining brightly? Or does it need trimming, refueling or fixing? Do what you need to do today and use it for His glory.

April 6

Reason #97 Not to Fear: We Turn Praise Back to God

"Then hear from heaven Your dwelling place, and do according to all for which the foreigner calls to You, that all peoples of the earth may know Your name and fear You, as do Your people Israel, and that they may know that this temple which I have built is called by Your name." II Chronicles 6:33

Oh, how the crowd cheered!

It was not the dedication of Solomon's temple, but a U2 concert. The stadium in Salt Lake City was filled to bursting with young people, children, and even older couples. Joy, excitement and anticipation characterized those who waited for the band to appear. The show itself was everything the audience desired -- multi-colored lights, a revolving tower, many special effects and excellent music.

This band, as talented and as dedicated as they are to their craft and to the Lord, are just men. How do they deal with the adulation of the world? Recently George Beverly Shea, at 104 years old, went to be with the Lord he loved so much. When he was 102, he appeared on a Bill Gaither video and sang *The Love of God* in his deep bass voice. When the audience cheered, he waved away the applause. Here is a godly man who does not desire the spotlight or the praise of men.

The crowning achievement of Solomon was the temple he built for the Lord his God. When the temple was complete, Solomon inaugurated it with prayer.

The temple in Jerusalem was built to draw people from all over the world to come and worship the Lord as Israel did. Many were attracted to it and became proselytes to the Jewish faith. Solomon asked God to honor and hear the prayers of these people so that all the earth would come to know and fear Him. It was Solomon's longing that the entire world would come to know the Lord.

Your worship to God may not be as elaborate as those who came to the temple. Worship certainly can be simple and spontaneous. What matters is not the setting, the program, the building, lights, or huge audiences. What matters is your heart attitude. When God gives you success, turn the glory back to Him. Make that moment an occasion to worship and praise God and you will lead others to Him.

April 7

Reason #98 Not to Fear: Fear God and All Else Will Fall into Place

"So they taught in Judah, having the Book of the Law of the LORD with them; and they went throughout all the cities of Judah and taught the people. And the fear of the LORD fell on all the kingdoms of the lands which were around Judah, so that they did not make war against Jehoshaphat."
II Chronicles 17:10

The revival started in Judah under the godly king Asa in 911 BC. He removed the "high places" of idolatrous worship, and all the foreign altars, sacred pillars and cut down the Asherim poles (places where the goddess was worshipped). He built fortified cities and commanded the people to seek the Lord God and observe the law and commandments of their forefathers. Asa faced a great challenge to his faith some years later when the Ethiopians, under the mercenary general Zerah, came against them between Gaza and Jerusalem with a million men and 300 chariots.

In that battle (II Chron. 14:11-12), Asa depended solely upon the Lord for victory. Asa was Jehoshaphat's father, and this young man learned his lessons well when he became king in 873 BC. His father taught him to rely on the Lord and to immerse himself and his people in the Word of God. Jehoshaphat did the same thing his father did. Verse 3 of this chapter tells us he followed the example of his father and his great ancestor, David, in removing the Baal gods, seeking Jehovah, and teaching his people to do the same.

King Jehoshaphat sought the Lord and earnestly desired to follow God and obey God in every detail of his life. He used his influence to cause people to worship God in the right way. The result was that all the nations surrounding Judah feared them. Therefore the Lord and did not make war against them and there was peace in the land.

There can be no revival without turned back to the Word of God. We live in a society that is increasingly leaving God out, marginalizing Him much like the Israelites did. Are you looking for the Lord's favor to rest on your life today? Get back to the Word. Drink it in. Hunger for it. Seek Him and yearn for Him to control more and more of you.

Allow a godly reverence to infuse your life, then use your influence to bring that same desire to those around you, to your family, your church, your friends. God will bless you for it. It is a promise!

April 8
Reason #99 Not to Fear: God Is a Just God

"Now therefore, let the fear of the LORD be upon you; take care and do it, for there is no iniquity with the LORD our God, no partiality, nor taking of bribes." II Chronicles 19:7

As a general rule, life is not fair for those who try to live life God's way.

Today is my son-in-law James' birthday. He would have been 37. He is not on earth any longer, he is in heaven. The unfairness of being a widow has touched my daughter. The unfairness of being without a father has touched my three grandchildren. I have read that it takes about two years to become emotionally stable after the death of a spouse. Sometimes it may even take longer.

My daughter wonders if her life will ever be happy and fulfilled again. I hear my grandchildren say that they would like to tell their dad about a certain thing they are doing at school, or wish that he could come to their baseball game, or go for a bike ride with them.

This is what one of my grandchildren wrote, "I am thankful that I can be with my family. God, please help me and my family because of my dad."

From my point of view, the ache in each of their hearts is unfair. Yet we have learned to trust in a loving God even when we cannot understand or see.

King Jehoshaphat, one of the best kings of Israel, began making reforms after he became king. He appointed judges who feared and honored the Lord. Numerous times he encouraged the officials to listen and reverence God in all their decisions, and not to take bribes. He knew that justice is important in the land and brings peace and security.

The judges were accountable to God; they needed to serve Him in fear and with undivided hearts, faithfully and wholly. When a nation has these types of God-fearing leaders, the moral fiber of a country is affected for good. Justice in the land is a powerful incentive to fear God. The lack of justice leads to every kind of anxiety, oppression, greed, and anger you can imagine.

How do you react in the face of injustice? Our natural response is anger and bitterness. When you are in a situation like this, turn it over to God, because He is able to heal your heart and bring you peace. Don't demand your own way. Trust in God and fear Him. He will right all wrongs and bring justice to all when they stand before Him at the Throne of God. For today, commit your way to God and turn all your issues over to Him.

April 9

Reason #100: We Have Faithful Hearts for God and His Word

"And he commanded them, saying, "Thus you shall act in the fear of the LORD, faithfully and with a loyal heart." II Chronicles 19:9

In the movie, *A Few Good Men*, a young naval lawyer, played by Tom Cruise in a stellar performance, defends two Marines when one of their regiment died after being razed by the two soldiers. The plot deals not only with justice, but with honor, loyalty, and the duty each man feels to defend his country. These issues are explored in a dynamic way in the courtroom. Were the two men justified in disciplining this man? If all servicemen were allowed to slack off, where would our armed services be? Who would defend our country? While murder is wrong, and should be judged so, where does justice fall when one man dies for the good of his whole country?

Where do we find justice and equity in this world? You know as well as I do that most judges can be corrupted, as can most jurors. Where is the fine line between justice and mercy? Between loyalty and love? Between right and wrong? Who is to say that a certain behavior is wrong and must be punished by death?

This is a dilemma we face in our society today. Having been taught in the public schools that we are nothing more than animals, and that there are no morals, no rights or wrongs, people have begun to act like animals. What is the cure for the social problems that we see prevalent in America today?

The only source of justice is God. The only basis for right and wrong is found in His Word. King Jehoshaphat knew that truth. He knew that the most effective way to bring reform to his country was to teach the people the laws of God and to install judges who would use the Word to decide each case. Jehoshaphat felt that judges were to take their jobs seriously, to be accountable to the king and to God, and to decide cases fairly according to the law.

What can we do to bring about change in our society? Don't look to the government or to the president. Look to God. Pray consistently for those in leadership and do what you can on the local level to bring about revival -- a revival centered on the Word of God and His standards. Pray today for that purpose and goal.

April 10

Reason #101: We Give the Battle to God

"And he said, "Listen, all you of Judah and you inhabitants of Jerusalem, and you, King Jehoshaphat! Thus says the LORD to you: 'Do not be afraid nor dismayed because of this great multitude, for the battle is not yours, but God's. " II Chronicles 20:15

King Jehoshaphat was confronted with a dire situation: war was on his front borders, a coalition of armies amassed in great multitudes to wipe Israel off the map. His kingdom was not large, yet he was a godly king and he believed the promises of God. It was recorded in Moses' writings that if a nation feared and obeyed Yahweh, Jehovah God, they would be protected from their enemies, that a handful of them could chase a multitude of enemies.

But the king had a choice to make. Should he send fast couriers to ride to other nations, like Egypt, to ask for help? Should he make sacrifices to the other gods of the land, hoping these gods could help him? Should he strategize and build up his army?

He did none of the above. Because he believed in God, he declared a fast, gathered the people together, and went to prayer. Read all of chapter 20. His prayer is amazing in its humility, focus, and grasp of the promises of God. Jehoshaphat realized he had an insufficient force to meet the enemy. They were outnumbered and outclassed, and he realized that only as he turned to God, and God alone, would he have hope to survive.

God answered his prayer. He said, "This battle is not yours. It is Mine."

There have been many times when I've wanted to fight the battles that are in front of me. Maybe it is someone who is opposing me or my ministry. Or maybe it is an illness. Or maybe it is a lack of finances, wisdom or courage to complete the task ahead. Often we find ourselves in situations where we want to do the fighting. We forget whose battle it really is. Each time God kindly whispers, "Give it to Me. I will take care of you."

What is your battle today? No matter what it is, turn it over to God, and He will fight it for you. Take yourself out of the equation. Focus on God and forgive those who have harmed you.

Do it right now. Remember Jehoshaphat. Someday you will shake his hand and thank him for the wonderful example he gave us to walk this life of faith.

April 11

Reason #102: We Find Courage and Strength in Our God

"'You will not need to fight in this battle. Position yourselves, stand still and see the salvation of the LORD, who is with you, O Judah and Jerusalem!' Do not fear or be dismayed; tomorrow go out against them, for the LORD is with you.'" II Chronicles 20:17

My sister-in-law and her four children desperately needed a place to live. I was afraid to open my home to her and her children, because in the past she had used, abused, and manipulated us. She never exhibited any concern or kindness to us, so why should I be kind to her?

My husband wanted to give assistance to them, and so they lived with us for quite a while. I had no one to talk to about it except God. Day by day, I relied on Him for strength and patience, and He heard my cries and helped me. In myself, I could have never ever done it. Yet God changed my heart, and I found I could live with her in my home. When I allowed God to work, He brought about a miracle of love and grace!

Thousands of Israelites assembled in and around the temple precincts that day to hear the king's prayer. They were very afraid, eyeing the horizon to see if the vast army of the Assyrians would appear to wipe them from the face of the earth. "Station yourselves," the prophet said. "Go out tomorrow and face them and don't be afraid."

Jehoshaphat did not know *how* God was going to work in winning the battle, but he knew he must be obedient. The priests were to go ahead of them, singing praises. An amazing thing happened as they did this: all the enemy soldiers began fighting each other in great confusion and they were destroyed while the king and his army watched from a safe distance!

God can take all situations of your life and deliver you. He is able to destroy, demolish, and defeat any mighty army in your life. When God tells you don't be afraid, don't! He delights to undertake for His children. When He does that, no matter how powerful or prominent your foe, God will give you the victory.

When you face peril, pray that your conduct will reflect God's character, then in the deepest sense, a victory is won. A marvelous triumph takes place. Praise Him today for His wisdom, strength, and grace.

April 12

Reason #103: God Has Provided People to Help Me

"Be strong and courageous; do not be afraid nor dismayed before the king of Assyria, nor before all the multitude that is with him; for there are more with us than with him." II Chronicles 32:7

Eighty-eight years later, we read about another king of Judah who faced something similar to Jehoshaphat's problem. King Hezekiah was one of the most righteous kings of Israel, and he, like Jehoshaphat, faced a great army of Assyrians who came to besiege Jerusalem. King Sennacherib sent his army to Jerusalem against Hezekiah. Besides going to God in prayer, Hezekiah also dug tunnels and water chambers under the walls to provide fresh water for the people in the city. He used wisdom and intelligence in a practical sense, and he also used spiritual wisdom to cry out to God for help.

Perhaps he was influenced by stories of his predecessor, King Jehoshaphat, to trust in the Lord and turn the battle over to Him.

I have been greatly influenced by a godly woman, one who has become a unique and special friend to me over the years. Florence Littauer, the author of over forty books and a wonderful speaker and teacher of God's Word, became my mentor a number of years ago.

Our paths crossed in Maryland when she was the keynote speaker at a ladies retreat, and I was one of the seminar teachers. She and I have spent much time together, and I view Florence as a blessing from the Lord in my life. She supports me, prompts me to do better, and prays for me. Her words often provide me with confidence at just the right time. I always want to make sure I give glory to the Lord for bringing Florence Littauer into my life.

Hezekiah laid the letter from Sennacherib on the floor of the temple and bowed to the ground over it. He enlisted the help of Isaiah, the great prophet of God, to pray. That night God sent an angel who killed the enemy army of 185,000 men! What a wonderful ending to the story!

Do you have a Florence Littauer, an Isaiah, or a Jehoshaphat in your life? Look around. Find a woman who is spiritual and deep in her walk with God. Spend some time with her. Learn from her, and spend time with her. Like Hezekiah, learn from the *greats,* the *greats* in the faith.

April 13

Reason #104: We Move Out In Faith

"Though fear had come upon them because of the people of those countries, they set the altar on its bases; and they offered burnt offerings on it to the LORD, both the morning and evening burnt offerings." Ezra 3:3

I am a bit disappointed today. I just found out that the sale of my home here in Arizona has fallen through, and my home is back on the market.

Everyone knows disappointment. People we trust break their word, marriages end, children get mixed up in questionable behavior, friends betray us, we get laid off, doctors give us bad news regarding our health, investments vanish, our dreams disappear, and even our churches disappoint and discourage us.

The Jews had been in captivity in Babylon for seventy years, but now they were given permission by the Persian king, Cyrus, to return to their land and rebuild their nation. In 538 BC, Zerubbabel led a group of fifty thousand Jews back to Israel. When they arrived, they set up the altar on the old foundation stones of the temple and celebrated the Feast of Booths.

Zerubbabel was a good leader. He knew it was important to continue worshipping the Lord God during the time they were rebuilding the temple and the walls. He knew that the altar was the focal point of their national faith in God, a place where their sins were forgiven and they could come into a right relationship with Yahweh God once again. So despite the unfriendly disposition of the local residents, the altar was erected and the people were joyful as they worshipped God once more in their own land.

Fear of the future or of being hurt by people should not stop you from worshipping God. You may have enemies, but then your need of God as your friend is great. When we are afraid, we can lie awake at night, thinking about the "what ifs" and imagining all the things that could happen. This mental frenzy keeps us awake, depletes our energy, and allows Satan an entrance into our minds. Instead, talk with God about your fears.

Name your fears. Watch them shrink as you begin to realize the protection of a great and loving God. Despite the obstacles, move out in faith, not fear. Build an altar to God in your heart and worship Him. God will bless and provide. *Build that altar!*

April 14

Reason #105: We Chose to Fear God Above All Else

"'O Lord, I pray, please let Your ear be attentive to the prayer of Your servant, and to the prayer of Your servants who desire to fear Your name; and let Your servant prosper this day, I pray, and grant him mercy in the sight of this man.' For I was the king's cupbearer." Nehemiah 1:11

We often fear the wrong things.

We tend to fear people, circumstances, events, or times when we are called upon to stand up for our faith. We fear sharing our faith with others. We fear the opinion of others. We fear looking foolish or being embarrassed. We fear losing control of our lives. We fear sickness, loss of jobs, loss of money. These things we fear above the fear of the Lord.

John and Betty Stam were missionaries in China during the Boxer Rebellion of the 1900's when the government began massacring all foreigners, including missionaries. The Stams felt led of God to stay in the country. After several years of house arrest, during which time Betty gave birth to a beautiful little girl, they were arrested and led through the streets of the city. Then they were beheaded. Chinese Christians rescued the little girl and by a series of miracles were able to take her out to freedom. When she grew up, she returned to China as a missionary.

Many people saw the Stams' actions as foolish, yet they feared God.

Nehemiah was the king's cupbearer, a high position of trust. Nehemiah learned of the desperate straits in which the Jews in Palestine found themselves. Without walls, they were open to attack from enemies. And so he prays. Notice in verses 8-11 how he prayed. It is not long, lengthy, or liturgical. It is a brief petition. Prayers of urgency do not have to be long.

Nehemiah truly desired to fear the Lord, even above an earthly king or his own safety.

If that is your desire, too, God will graciously give you opportunities to live out your desire. Favor with people springs from the mercy of God. Meeting and speaking to people in all walks of life is an opportunity God can give you. But make sure your desire is to fear His name, and just like the king showed his favor to Nehemiah, who knows what will come when you speak to someone about the God that you fear?

Turn away from your other fears and fear God alone. It will mean blessing and courage as you live your life in this world.

April 15

Reason Not to Fear #106: We Don't Fear Our Enemies

"And I looked, and arose and said to the nobles, to the leaders, and to the rest of the people, "Do not be afraid of them. Remember the Lord, great and awesome, and fight for your brethren, your sons, your daughters, your wives, and your houses." Nehemiah 4:14

My family and I returned to our homeland after a long time of slavery. I built a home for my wife and children in the shattered city of Jerusalem, yet there was no wall around the city for protection, and our enemies lurked everywhere. My family worked to grow the crops necessary for our livelihood, but every day I wondered how long it would be before our enemies captured us and enslaved us again.

Then one day Nehemiah came to Jerusalem. He stirred up the people with talk about rebuilding the walls. I was proud to help, and as the work progressed, I felt a deep surge of joy and thanksgiving to God for allowing me to return to Israel and to have a part in building the walls.

Yet there were many enemies who wanted to stop the work, and they used many tactics to defeat us. My hopes faltered. On the street corners, the people said with downcast faces, "The strength of the burden bearers is failing, yet there is much rubbish, and we ourselves are unable to rebuild the walls. We can't fight the Ammonites and the Ashdodites. Who are we trying to fool? We might as well give up." The work was halted.

But Nehemiah called us together. We stood on the temple mount and he jumped up on a pillar and lifted his voice. "Do not be afraid of them!" he shouted. "Remember the Lord who is great and awesome!" He called upon us to fight for our families and our homes. We cheered and threw our hats into the air. We *will* continue the task! It was a choice, you see, of fearing our enemies or fearing God. Nehemiah gave us a plan. The work went on, and the walls went up, despite the wickedness of our enemies. Praise God!

What do you fear today? There are many who would tear down the work of God. Will we stop working? No way. Turn your focus, as the people of Israel did, to the fearful and awesome God of your faith and walk out of your home this morning with strength and joy.

April 16

Reason Not to Fear #107: We Are Kind to the Poor

"Then I said, "What you are doing is not good. Should you not walk in the fear of our God because of the reproach of the nations, our enemies?"
Nehemiah 5:9

Money, wealth and power go hand in hand.

When we worked in the inner city of Chicago for a mission, the board was composed of several wealthy men who did not live in the inner city. They only came into the inner city when they had a board meeting or other obligations at the mission. Therefore, they had no understanding as to how those living in this area were treated, what their needs were, or how they thought or lived.

The decisions they made that controlled the ministry was sometimes flawed. My husband would try to correct their thinking in these areas. This is a difficult situation to find one's self in, for they literally paid our salary and sought to control how the ministry was run.

There was one man in particular who considered himself above the people who lived in the ghetto. His attitude toward those he served was not right according to the Bible because he did not have a servant's heart.

It is a sad but true fact that often those poor in this world are misused and abused by the rich. In Nehemiah's day, wealthy people were defrauding the poor, taking their wives and children as slaves, and exacting high interest rates on loans. They were violating the command of "doing to others as you wish others to do to you." Nehemiah declares in this verse, "What you are doing is not right!" Most certainly it was not. He went on to say that they were bringing reproach and dishonor to the name of the Lord in the hearts of their enemies.

Never forget that those in the world are watching you. They want to see if you are going to live up to your profession of faith. Inconsistent behavior hurts the body of Christ and harms the church of God. Do not let your enemies mock you. Walk in the fear of God and treat all people fairly and honestly. If you are wealthy, be kind to the poor and help them. If you are poor, trust in God to meet your needs. In everything you do, do it all for the glory of God. Then God's name will be honored in your life.

April 17

Reason Not to Fear #108: We Are Faithful To God With All Our Resources

"But the former governors who were before me laid burdens on the people, and took from them bread and wine, besides forty shekels of silver. Yes, even their servants bore rule over the people, but I did not do so, because of the fear of God." Nehemiah 5:15

TV evangelist, Jim Bakker and his wife, Tammy, appeared on their show wearing high priced clothing, watches and make up. When federal agents arrested Mr. Bakker for tax evasion, and their house and belongings were confiscated, they discovered gold faucets in the bathrooms, expensive jewelry, pricey fur coats and many other luxuries in their mansion. The Bakkers lived a high lifestyle on the donations that had been given to them by supporters, many of them poor people with little money.

In contrast, R. G. LeTourneau was a man who had great wealth, yet it did not turn his head. He made his fortune inventing and producing large equipment. He began LeTourneau University and by the end of his life, he was giving ninety percent of his income to the Lord's work. His contributions and ministry did much for the cause of missions around the world.

Nehemiah was another man who obeyed God and was careful not to live above the people he served because he feared God. Former governors taxed the people to support their high living, taking both bread and silver for their own personal gain. But Nehemiah refused to act with such cruelty. His concern was the welfare of the people. He had an awe of God and feared displeasing Him. Therefore he did nothing cruel or harsh. During the rebuilding of the walls in Jerusalem, Nehemiah was an example of generosity, justice, and hospitality.

While you may not be a governor, a CEO of a company, or the head of a large para-church organization, how do you show generosity and compassion to the poor who live around you?

Take a moment to consider your life and decide today to do one act of kindness to a stranger, a visitor, or a person you meet in a place of business. Kindness begins at home, and so does God's love. Be sure you're not living above people and defrauding them of the same kind of mercy you enjoy from God on a daily basis.

April 18

Reason Not to Fear #109: God Provides Strength for the Journey

"For they all were trying to make us afraid, saying, "Their hands will be weakened in the work, and it will not be done." Nehemiah 6:9

"O God, strengthen my hands." I have prayed this prayer so many times! Instead of becoming fearful and turning away from the work He has given us, we would do well to mimic Nehemiah's prayer and trust in God to provide us with the strength, wisdom and perseverance necessary to complete the task.

Ministry can be demanding, dirty and disillusioning. We begin oftentimes with an exalted opinion of ourselves and a visionary's dream-like assessment of the job to be done. Many missionaries go to the field thinking the mission field is going to be almost like heaven, with a romantic feeling about it all. Yet within a year, they are ready to call it quits.

After my children spent several years in Indonesia, I could tell from talking to them and then visiting with them, that something was wrong. In the beginning, their work was hard, but they found it exciting and rewarding. Now they were criticized by their fellow missionaries and felt rejected and discouraged. They began to wonder if they were where they should be.

This resulted in the fact that they had lost their confidence in their abilities to do the job and also many doubts, uncertainties, and hesitations in the ministry. Finally the superintendent came, sat down with Nicky and James and reassured them they were doing a good work and not to be distracted from it.

Nehemiah resisted distraction too. He flatly refused to be sidetracked by fear. Do not get detoured. Do not let opportunities or criticism or fear derail your pursuit of God's vision for your life. Keep your eyes focused on the finish line.

What are you facing? What causes your heart to quake and your flesh to shrink back in fear? Don't give in. Hang on. Call on God, like Nehemiah did, and you will find He will raise you up with new strength for the journey. Renew your strength today in the Lord through His Word.

April 19

Reason Not to Fear #111: We Don't Come Down Off the Walls

"My God, remember Tobiah and Sanballat, according to these their works, and the prophetess Noadiah and the rest of the prophets who would have made me afraid." Nehemiah 6:14

The Bible provides us with many examples of exceptional leadership. Nehemiah is an excellent role model of fully devoted leadership. He not only was humble and lived on about the same level as the people he served, he was a man of God who knew the Word and kept his eyes fixed on God.

The enemies of Israel, Sanballat the Horonite and Tobiah the Ammonite (and others), had thrown everything they had to stop the work Nehemiah was doing. They used mocking scorn (2:19); gossip and criticism (4:1-3); they called their friends together to stop the work (4:8); they conspired to kill the workman on the walls, which amounted to open war (4:11); they tried to get Nehemiah to meet with them on the plains of Ono (6:2); they tried to frighten Nehemiah and the leaders with nasty letters (6:5-7); they tried to get Nehemiah to go into the inner rooms of the Temple to hide (6:10-12), they threatened to send letters to the king of the Medes and Persian.

But Nehemiah doggedly kept at his task, trusting that God would take care of those who opposed him. He didn't have time to come down off the walls to answer their accusations!

Despite heavy opposition to his goal of rebuilding the walls of Jerusalem, he motivated and encouraged the people to complete the project in just fifty-two days! The enemy's smear tactics didn't intimidate or cause Nehemiah to fear because he faced each opposition with faith and prayer. In spite of everything, Nehemiah kept on working, and he motivated the people to do the task, as well.

If you are in a position of leadership, how do you respond to conflict? Do you respond like Nehemiah with faith, prayer and resistance? Or do you run from adversity? Perhaps it is time to recommit yourself and build the walls. Even if you don't hold a position of authority, how do you respond when people criticize you or gossip about you?

The best possible response is what Nehemiah did: pray for your accusers, keep at your task, and commit it all to God. Refuse fear. Trust God.

April 20

Reason Not to Fear #110: We Step Out in Faith

"Also they reported his good deeds before me, and reported my words to him. Tobiah sent letters to frighten me." Nehemiah 6:19

Have you ever been afraid to tackle a new assignment? Have you ever declined a good work to do for the Lord? Boy, I sure have.

One of the things I love to do most is teach the Word of God, and I have had many opportunities to do just that. I have spoken at women's retreats, seminars, and weekly Bible studies. However, when we moved to Arizona, I was afraid to teach or speak again -- ever. So I declined invitations and opportunities and continued to do that for almost ten years. Do you know why I declined invites and opportunities to teach? Because of the world, the flesh and the devil. I allowed fear to develop in my heart. I was afraid to open my heart and let the grace of God flow from it. I feared what others would say or think of me.

When a new year dawned, I decided it could hold some exciting challenges for me and I did not want to miss what God had planned for me anymore. The greatest mischief our enemies can do to us is to frighten us so that we say *no* when we should say *yes*. When I began to say *yes*, my passion for teaching revived and God opened up the doors for me. Now I not only speak numerous times to ladies groups across the country, God has allowed me to teach three women's Bible studies.

Nehemiah's task was daunting and he could have said, "I am not doing this. I am afraid of the people, my life is in danger, and the pay is not very good, either."

He did not do that. Instead, he trusted God to give him wisdom to deal with all the problems and threats. Tobiah was well spoken of by the people who passed on to him some of the things Nehemiah had said. Then Tobiah, speaking from a position of power and wealth, wrote letters to Nehemiah, trying to frighten him. Praise God, it didn't work!

Despite what the *Tobiahs* or the *Sanballats* in your life say or do to you, do not let them frighten you any longer. Go for the new assignment. Do not be afraid of the people. He can touch your mouth, your arms, your body and give you strength for the task. He can move your spirit, direct your mind and use you today if you will commit yourself to Him.

April 21

Reason Not to Fear #112: Courage is Born on the Wings of Faith

"And Esther said, "The adversary and enemy is this wicked Haman!" So Haman was terrified before the king and queen." Esther 7:6

We often wonder where is God in our lives, what He is doing, and if He is with us at all. Yet God is involved in the smallest details for our lives; His presence and power is at work in our lives even if we do not detect it.

Haman became Esther's enemy. When she discovered his evil plot to kill off the Jews, she feared for her life and did not want to speak up about it. Yet when she was confronted by Mordecai, her cousin and the man who raised her, she had to consider completing her "mission impossible" assignment from the Lord. She decided to trust God and went into the king's presence without his permission, risking her life.

When Haman was revealed as the Queen's enemy, he was frightened and fell to the floor, a shuddering, trembling heap of quivering flesh. He was executed and the Jews survived his plot. The victory that Esther brought to her people through God's help is still celebrated today, and she is held in honor as one of the great heroes of the faith.

There are two types of people in life -- righteous and wicked; people for God and people against God. Ultimately, the righteous will win and the wicked will be destroyed.

Never forget God skillfully manipulates the strands of time and the threads of human life and history to carefully weave His purposes and goals in your life. It is not always easy to see His hand at work in our lives. Stress and the pace of life cause His ways hard to comprehend. But if you want to see God at work in your life, you have to begin by looking to Him instead of your fears. You have to develop eyes of faith.

God is looking for people who will stand up for Him today. In the midst of a crisis, when you have to stand alone, that God is ready, willing, and able to empower you as you stand against evil. Where did Esther get her courage to confront the fearful Haman? Was she born with it? No. She got her courage from God. And so will you.

April 22

Reason Not to Fear #113: We Speak Up for God

"The Jews gathered together in their cities throughout all the provinces of King Ahasuerus to lay hands on those who sought their harm. And no one could withstand them, because fear of them fell upon all people." Esther 9:2

There are many unsung heroes in the pages of history; people who have stood close to leadership, giving advice to kings and presidents.

Winston Churchill was a man who served as Prime Minister of England at the beginning of World War II. When he began his political career, many people looked down on him because he was outspoken, common in appearance, and had not come through the proper channels. Yet he was God's man to turn the tide against Hitler, an aggressive dictator who sought to take over England.

"Let us therefore brace ourselves to our duties, and so bear ourselves that if the British Empire and Commonwealth last for a thousand years, men will still say, 'This was their finest hour.'" (Speech delivered to the House of Commons on June 18, 1940 following the collapse of France.) Knowing that after France capitulated to the Germans, England would be next on the agenda, Churchill led the English nation to fight for their homeland.

Today some men fear that women are becoming too aggressive and assertive. Many do not like women having independence. However, the book of Esther illustrates the fact that God uses women as well as men to do His will. Had Esther been unwilling to step forward and make her voice heard in the court of the Persian Empire, God would have delivered His people some other way, but it would not have been His perfect will.

Esther secured from the king permission for every Jew to fight their enemies who sought to destroy them. The plot for the first Jewish holocaust failed. Esther interceded for her people and lives were spared. God demonstrated His sovereignty over His people.

As you think about Esther, why not speak up and act for God when given the opportunity? God put you in the place you are for a specific purpose. Find His will and do it. Because you belong to God, you should not fear what people think, say, or do to you. You should be confident that God will take care of you in everything you do.

April 23

Reason Not to Fear #114: We Dare to Stand For What Is Right

"And all the officials of the provinces, the satraps, the governors, and all those doing the king's work, helped the Jews, because the fear of Mordecai fell upon them." Esther 9:3

Mordecai, Esther's cousin, sat at the King's Gate. This was a position of high importance, probably a judicial position. As he sat there, he could continue his guardianship of his beautiful ward, Esther. He also heard many conversations. Mordecai overheard a plot to assassinate the king and reported it. Later on, this played a powerful part in defeating the Haman's plan to kill off the Jews.

Mordecai was elevated to the second highest position in the nation. As such, he commanded great respect and fear from all the people. Yet he did not use his power, wealth and fame to forward his own career, but to please God and follow Him. Twenty years after the story of Esther, the priest Ezra left for Jerusalem. I believe it was Mordecai who wrote the letters that secured the pilgrims' safety as they journeyed. It was Mordecai's influence that protected the Jews throughout the days of Ezra as the temple was rebuilt.

Mordecai proved to be God's man in the right place at the right time. He could have protected his own interests and folded under pressure, going along with everyone to worship Haman as a god. But he did not. He remained true to God's Word and God's will and became a good leader.

Because of his influence, when it came time to slaughter the Jews, not a hand was raised against them across the vast empire. How different was the story when Hitler began his systematic genocide of the Jewish nation across Europe! What would have happened if there had been a Mordecai and an Esther to stand up for what was right? What would have happened if all the godly people in Germany, Poland and other nations had risen against Hitler instead of letting him have his way out of fear?

Where has God put you today? Think about it: one man made a huge difference in 479 B.C. What can God do with you if you are wholly dedicated to Him? Try it out for one day. Lay aside your own agenda and seek to do God's will. Stand up for what is right. You can make a difference in the circle where God has put you. Be a Mordecai and an Esther today.

April 24

Reason Not to Fear #115: We Commit Our Ways to God

"Then the LORD said to Satan, "Have you considered My servant Job, that there is none like him on the earth, a blameless and upright man, one who fears God and shuns evil?" So Satan answered the LORD and said, 'Does Job fear God for nothing?'" Job 1: 8, 9

Few of us have faced the deep levels of suffering that Job did. Yet God said he was the finest man on the face of the earth! Think about the implications of that.

When my husband had a cardiac arrest and subsequent brain damage, I could make no sense of it. Here was a man who served God with every fiber of his being, who trusted God in every dangerous situation you could imagine, who loved God, his family and the people he ministered to. Why had God allowed this awful thing to come into our lives? Was it some kind of punishment? Were we being slapped down, disciplined, put aside? Were we displeasing to our heavenly Father in some mysterious way?

There are some Christians who teach a "health and welfare" gospel, that if we have enough faith, we will suffer no lack or difficulty. I wonder if these people have ever read Job.

Remember Job had no inkling what was transpiring in heaven. He only got this insight after his trial was ended. He did not know that God had been bragging him up to the angels; that Satan had taunted God, and accused God that He had bought his man; that they had made a deal, and he was the guinea pig for the big experiment.

Satan accused God of buying Job's loyalty, and concluded that Job was only devoted to God because he was rewarded with wealth and prosperity. But he was wrong. Despite being stripped of his possessions and family, Job continued to bless the name of the Lord.

We oftentimes struggle like Job and try to make sense with our finite minds why and how long this trouble will occupy our lives. Why do you follow the Lord? For a reward? Or is your commitment to the Lord out of simple authentic faith? Search your heart today.

Commit yourself anew to Him and to His will. Then walk out of your house with joy in your heart, knowing God will take care of you and you have no reason to fear.

April 25

Reason Not to Fear #116: God Is Full of Mercy and Grace

"For the thing I greatly feared has come upon me, and what I dreaded has happened to me. I am not at ease, nor am I quiet; I have no rest, for trouble comes." Job 3:25, 26

There are many people who have a lot of this world's possessions. They have money in the bank and investment portfolios, large homes, nice cars, boats, clothes, and many other things. Taking a walk through their homes is like touring a museum. You would think that all this wealth would ease their minds and help them to be free of worry, cares or fears.

But the very opposite is true. It seems the more we have, the more things we have to worry about. We might be fearful that the stock market will go down and we will lose some of our invested money. There might be the gnawing tension that real estate will plunge in prices and the lands and houses we own will lose their value and we will not be able to sell them or recoup our investment.

Luke 6:24-26 says, "But woe to you who are rich, for you are receiving your comfort in full. Woe to you who are well-fed now, for you shall be hungry. Woe to you who laugh now, for you shall mourn and weep. Woe to you when all men speak well of you, for their fathers used to treat the false prophets in the same way." These are words of Jesus that we need to take to heart in our culture of over-abundance of food, possessions and pleasures.

Job was very prosperous, yet in his financial successes, he was full of fears. He worried about the loss of his family and property. Job knew that his abundance came from the hand of God and that it could be taken away. What he dreaded took place. He lost his family and material possessions. His friends concluded that God was punishing him for his hypocrisy. Yet he clung to his faith in God with both hands despite the trials that beset him.

God is sovereign over our lives. He sends poverty or wealth, sickness or health. It is God who humbles and exalts. James 4:10 says, "Humble yourself in the presence of the Lord and He will exalt you."

Do you have pride in your heart? Do sickness, trials, difficulties and set-backs knock your faith about a bit? Are you tied to the things of this world? Yield to His will and pray for peace, grace, and a thankful heart. It might be a good idea to do it right now!

April 26

Reason Not to Fear #117: Even In Sorrow, We Can Find Peace

"Is not your reverence your confidence? And the integrity of your ways your hope?" Job 4:6

In the space of a couple of days, you receive news that all ten of your children have been killed in a storm that collapsed the house they were in; all your business is gone, including your portfolios, your bank accounts, your savings, your pensions, your investments; all your servants except one have been killed; and to top things off, your health is destroyed due to a terrible wasting disease that disfigures your looks and causes you to itch and stink. Even your spouse urges you to curse God and die.

This actually happened to Job. As he sat in the ashes outside his house, his three friends arrived for a visit. They dismounted from their camels and didn't say a word. They sat in a circle around him and didn't say a word. This goes on for seven days. At that point, the grief and sorrow that was mounting in his heart like Mt. Everest exploded. After pouring out his heart with tears running down his cheeks, he paused and lifted his head, waiting for his friends to speak.

Eliphaz, possibly the oldest, spoke first. His arguments were based solely on personal experience, and his words blistered Job's already battered soul. He assumed that Job was being punished by an angry God and that the solution to his problem was to repent of the sin and everything would be okay. I am always amazed that Job's sufferings did not touch his three friends! Instead they judged him harshly.

Sooner or later that will happen to many of us -- we will run into someone who challenges our motives, methods and morals, especially when we are in a trial or difficulty. Elihpaz reminded Job that his fear of God should give him comfort during this trying time of his life, and in this he was right, yet he was not right to condemn Job and judge him.

How would you respond to such criticism in the face of personal loss and grief? Whether you are comforting someone today who is hurting, or receiving comfort yourself, remember this: God loves you and He does not condemn you if you have found refuge in Him.

Put your trust solely in Him and not in other people. Pray for those who criticize you and go about your day with peace and joy in your heart!

April 27

Reason Not to Fear #118: We Don't Give Up

*"Behold, happy is the man whom God corrects; Therefore do not despise
the chastening of the Almighty.... You shall laugh at destruction and famine,
and you shall not be afraid of the beasts of the earth.* Job 5:17, 22

Several years ago, Israel and the Hezbollah terrorists who occupied
Lebanon were engaged in a war. Destruction and death touched each country.
Rockets sailed back and forth, and the residents fled into bomb shelters. They
feared the destruction that the bombs would do, and truly, there was much
bloodshed and grief as a result of that war. People suffer when there is war.

Eliphaz continued to instruct Job on how he should feel and act in the face
of his adversity. What he said is true, and is repeated in the New Testament. In
Heb. 12:4-11, for instance, we are told that God disciplines and corrects His
children, and that this correction leads to righteousness and peace.

When going through my husband's ordeal, many of my friends heard about
Bob's damaging cardiac arrest, and each offered countless kind words. In fact,
scores of them quoted Bible verses to me. The verse I heard over and over
again was Romans 8:28. "All things work together for good...to those who love
the Lord."

I came to the point where I told the Lord if one more person quoted
Romans 8:28 to me, I was going to punch them in the nose! I simply wanted
them to weep with me, or to sit quietly with me. I was struggling with what
God had allowed to enter my life. I needed comfort, sympathy, and empathy
from my friends. I am so thankful that numerous people provided that for me
day after day.

Being corrected by God may cause you to want to run from Him, however
your only true comfort is in running *to* Him. When you do that you can find
joy, and you also will be able to give joy to others as they suffer. Be a joy-giver
today. Do not be like Job's so-called friends who simply added to his distress.

If you are suffering, hang on. Hang on to God and to His promises. It may
take awhile, but do not give up. It may be heavy-going, but do not give up.
Eventually you will have a new vision, a new purpose, and a changed heart
towards God.

April 28

Reason Not to Fear #119: We Comfort Our Friends in Their Distress

"For now you are nothing; you see terror and are afraid." Job 6:21

You have all seen and experienced the shock of it.

I am talking about pictures on TV and other media that shows children with large stomachs, bald heads, and arms and legs the size of toothpicks who are three or four years of age and are dying of starvation. I have heard some well-fed Christians express disgust over these images. They turn the TV to another channel and watch a football game or a sitcom. Disaster relief organizations have learned not to portray these stark pictures of suffering humanity in their literature because people do not want to see them.

We lack compassion for those a world away who struggle for every breath, for those who have to watch their children wither and die from malnutrition. It is true: America has been the forerunner of relief to the third world countries, yet the tide is turning and as the economy fails in this country, fewer dollars are going overseas to help needy people.

If you had seen Job sitting on the ash heap, covered with boils, possibly bald, would you have turned away in disgust? On top of everything else Job was called on to bear, he had to deal with the loss of true friendship. The men who came to comfort him were poor comforters, indeed! To Job's dismay, they became fearful over his calamity and despised him for it. When he was down, they jumped on him and trampled his heart into the ground. He had been rich, powerful, and godly, yet now he is stripped of everything, and they lectured him when they should have shown kindness and love.

When you are down, do not depend on humans to be the solution to your problems. People will disappoint you and the very ones that you turn to will often thrust the knife in deeper.

How do you react when calamity touches your friends? Do you pull away from them in disgust and horror, as if the curse of tragedy can be caught like a disease? Do not fall into that way of thinking! Reach out to those who are hurting. Do not condemn them. The truth of the matter is: you might experience difficulty yourself. *Love your neighbor as yourself* is the royal law of Christ. He wants us to show unselfish love to others each and every day.

April 29

Reason #120: We Hang On One More Day

"I am afraid of all my sorrows; I know that You will not hold me innocent."
Job 9:28

*When you are going through something hard and wonder where God is --
remember the teacher is always quiet during a test.* Unknown

Some troubles are deeper than others. Some problems hold more worry and concern. I feel my daughter is in a very heavy suffering time in her life. The death of her young husband has proven to be a immense difficulty. People have sent flowers, notes, and food. Many prayers have been spoken to the Lord on her behalf. Some have even visited, coming to console Nicky.

One particular friend came and all she did was sit next to Nicky. Nothing more. Just sitting. No talking. They wept together, experiencing grief without words. This young friend gave Nicky exactly what she needed. No long sermons. No lectures about how "God works all things together for good." (He does this, Romans 8:28, but Nicky did not need to be reminded of this at the time!) No speeches on how she should behave and get her life together.

Nicky simply needed someone with a tissue and a quiet presence to sit next to her who loved her.

Who has experienced the level of Job's suffering? Who can make sense of Job's suffering, or even their own? Job felt that God had resolved to destroy him; he felt hopeless, and that there was no possibility of him ever returning to his former life. He was dismayed, discouraged and despondent. His physical and spiritual strength were depleted.

Yet in this verse, Job acknowledged that even if all of his sorrow and grief were withheld for awhile, his fear of God would remain. His reverence and honor for God would continue despite the pain he was experiencing.

In life's hardships, can you do as Job did and trust God? You may not be able to see into the future, and that scares you. But trust Him for today. Lean on Him. Get a 3x5 card and write out one verse that gives you courage and strength. Carry that verse with you throughout the day.

Thank Him for the friends who are there for you -- who hand you a hankie when you need one.

April 30

Reason #121: God Is Sovereign and He Is Love

"Will not His excellence make you afraid? And the dread of Him fall upon you?" Job 13:11

Zophar, who was more blunt and harsh than Eliphaz, argued from the position of common sense -- the ultimate authority, according to him, was *himself*. He strikes me as a very proud person. These people are full of themselves and their so-called wisdom. They tend to give out advice like candy, but it is as bitter as wormwood to a suffering soul. Job replies (verse 2), "I am not inferior to you." And a little later he says, "Oh, that you would be quiet and that your silence would become your wisdom!"

Job tried to remind him that God is sovereign and His power is dreadful.

When tragedy strikes your life, as it has mine, a person struggles to make sense of it. We try to use our finite reasoning to understand what God is doing in our lives. The truth is, not one of us is able to comprehend misfortune, and that is because we do not have all the facts.

Our heartbreaks should drive us to God and cause a reverent fear to well up in us because of His wisdom. There is no shame in wondering why sudden calamities touch your life. When my husband had a cardiac arrest so long ago, I was not prepared for it, had no inkling that my life was about to change forever. As he lay in the hospital, I struggled with the implications of this tragedy, but I still had little idea what it would mean to me. I didn't know that he would be like a seven-year-old boy, and that I would be called upon to take care of his needs as a mother and not a wife.

In an instant of time, the normal that was our lives vanished and we entered an unknown, unexpected world of suffering and tragedy. You can bet your bottom dollar that over these thirteen years, I have wondered, inquired, and even questioned God. Why *us?* Why *this?* Why *now?* However, over the years I have learned that His Excellency, His Sovereignty, makes me fearful to inquire about issues I am not supposed to understand. I am encouraged to trust His love which is beyond anything I can imagine.

I cannot say why you are going through what you are going through. We must cling to the good judgment of God and to His love. *We will understand it better by and by*, as the song says. In the meantime, we need to obey Him, love Him, and follow wherever He leads.

May 1

Reason Not to Fear #122: God Is In Control

"Only two things do not do to me, then I will not hide myself from You: withdraw Your hand far from me, and let not the dread of You make me afraid." Job 13:20, 21

"Just leave me alone!" or "Get your hands off me!"

We have all heard these and similar comments made by children and teens. Why do people say these kinds of things? They might be angry, hurt, bewildered, or rebellious. They want to go somewhere away from everyone and sulk. They want to nurse their pain in solitude.

Is God unfair? Is God silent? Is God hidden? Have you ever struggled with these questions? I think every person at some junction of their life wrestles with them.

Despite the questions, despite the fact that he didn't understand what was going on, Job continued to trust God. Job had perseverance. He refused to renounce God. He would go through poverty, hunger, sickness and near death, believing that God is still worthy to be trusted. Job had commitment, and his commitment set aside his deepest fears.

In the extremity of his pain, Job cried out to the Lord his God for strength and support. He knew that God is all-powerful, that God *allowed* what happened to him, and that God could very well be the *cause* of what happened to him. He was in stark terror of God, for he saw Him as wrathful and harsh. Job felt very restricted and hedged in by this trial. When you experience something like this, you know that your options are limited. You feel put in a box or on a shelf.

"Oh, Lord, please remove Your hand from me!" Job asked. "Don't let me fall into the dread of the Lord." Job thought that God's presence was a thing of dismay. Little did he understand the greater good that God was working through his circumstances because of His heart of love and mercy.

Can you trust God if your circumstances do not change? We may not always be able to see it, but in every situation in our life, God is bringing Himself glory and working out our good. Let His presence bring you comfort. Don't fear His gentle hand as He reaches into your life and brings healing. Give Him your worries and fears. Allow Him to ease your burdens, and He will.

May 2

Reason Not to Fear #123: We Speak Words of Grace

"Yes, you cast off fear, and restrain prayer before God." Job 15:4

Sorry comforters came to Job that day; the best thing they did was to sit with him for seven days without saying a word. When they opened their mouths, they spouted out such foolishness, heresy, and judgmental condemnation that God Himself must have trembled! You would think that for someone as beat down and trampled upon by trouble as Job was that God could have provided some really nice, wise and righteous men to comfort him in his grief and sorrow.

But these three so-called friends of Job only added to his burdens.

I have had my share of disagreements with my family, friends, and even complete strangers! When I feel strongly about some issues that matter to me and when I meet up with someone who has another point of view, I can get fired up. Most of us have strong opinions, and some of us need to share those with others. However, there are times to speak and times to be silent.

Job needed encouragement, but all his friends offered was judgment and blame. They were trying to play God in his life.

I can imagine them sitting around Job, keeping their beautiful, immaculately clean robes well away from him and the ashes, their noses in the air, arguing with him that he needed to repent of his sins. Eliphaz tells Job that God is angry at him. Bildad tells him that his misfortunes are his own fault, and Zophar tells him that he is being punished. All of them conclude that Job has no fear or reverence for God. All of them were definitely wrong in their assessment.

What about you, dear friend? Do your friends back away because you jump to the wrong conclusions? When you are talking to someone, what is your motivation? To get them to agree with you or to listen to what they are saying? Read Prov. 15:1, 2.

Reevaluate your words today and make sure they are sweet and gentle. Make sure when you speak of God, you are representing Him correctly in His love and mercy.

May 3

Reason Not to Fear #124: We Can Lean on God in Our Need

"As for me, is my complaint against man? And if it were, why should I not be impatient? Look at me and be astonished; Put your hand over your mouth. Even when I remember I am terrified, And trembling takes hold of my flesh."
Job 21:4-6

When the phone rings in the middle of the night, we often shudder before we answer it. The news that is shared at that time is usually bad news. We have all received calls of this nature that are hard to take, that bring trouble and bad tidings, and that change our lives.

Can you imagine how Job felt as he tried to deal with the loss of ten children? Do you think he might have remembered each child, whispered their name, recalled some funny incident from their lives? Do you think he recalled how they laughed, how their eyes twinkled with mischief, how they rallied around him the time he was sick? He didn't have photographs, Facebook, recorded messages or home movie shots, yet he could bring back each happy moment of his children's lives with such clarity that it broke his heart.

As Job remembered the past, he was filled with dread and horror for the future. How could he exist and live with such pain wracking his soul? C.S. Lewis, who lost his beloved wife, Joy, wrote, "No one told me grief felt so much like fear."

These thoughts are not happy ones. Unexpected difficulties in your life can cause you to change your perspective. Life here on earth is not forever. It is a gift and should be treasured. Yet many times we "walk wounded" through life. Where can we find ease and comfort for our souls when life ends, when disaster strikes, when that phone call comes late at night?

Only God, the creator of life, the giver of joy, the hope of the ages, the rock of our faith can give us strength to go through these difficult and unexpected circumstances of life.

Look to Him in your hour of need, and He will comfort, heal and bring great peace.

May 4

Reason Not to Fear #125: The Morning Comes

"But He is unique, and who can make Him change? And whatever His soul desires, that He does. For He performs what is appointed for me, And many such things are with Him. Therefore I am terrified at His presence; When I consider this, I am afraid of Him." Job 23:13-15

Recently I heard that the economic structure in our nation would collapse in three months, that the Chinese would call in our enormous debt and take over the country, that there would be no more Social Security, Medicare or Medicaid, welfare, or help in any form for the elderly, the handicapped or the poor. It is true that we need to be diligent, proactive, and aware of what is going on in politics and the government and to stand up for what is right.

But to be afraid? To tremble? To live in fear? Is this where you live today?

These kinds of doomsday predictions are as old as the human race. While they may contain a kernel of truth, what emotions do they cause in you? Do you fear the future? Are you fearful that you may suffer hardship or persecution? What does God say about this kind of fear?

Job was unsettled and frustrated over his impending future. He had endured an enormous amount of pain and suffering. He did not see an end to his afflictions and when he considered that, it made him afraid of God. God has overwhelmed Job with calamities, and he was in the dark as to what may come next. As he thought on the future, fear invaded his heart.

Why was Job terrified of God's presence? Is this the godly fear that drives us to worship our creator and king? I don't think so. While we should fear God above all, He does not want us to be trembling poor souls that grovel on the ground. He wants us to stand before His presence with praise and joy in our hearts.

Does the thought of an all-powerful God strike terror and fear into your heart? You may feel like you are in the dark and you are uncertain of what is coming next. Turn to Him today. Confess your fears and ask God to remove them. Declare that you will trust Him no matter what He takes you through. The night passes and morning comes. He will see you through the dark valleys. Commit your way to Him and then sit back in His peace and watch the morning dawn. Close this devotional time by reading I Timothy 1:7 and think about what it says.

May 5

Reason Not to Fear #126: Find Something Funny in the Situation

"Dominion and fear belong to Him. He makes peace in His high places."
Job 25:2

Can you picture the scene? Job is sitting in the ashes, covered from head to toe with painful boils. His hair is uncombed, he stinks, he is bleary-eyed and his clothes are dirty, torn and ragged. Surrounding him are his three friends. Did they sit on the ground beside him, or were they perched on low stools, their robes carefully drawn away from the soil of the ashes and from Job's offensive body odor?

They hear Job's complaints, but they are not truly listening. They are forming their next arguments to convince him that he is a sinner, that he must confess, that he must agree with their arguments that they are right about God and about life. Their monstrous pride keeps them stiff-lipped and solemn. Looking down their long noses, they proceed to set him straight.

Laughter has its way of creeping into the direst of circumstances and is God's gift to us to lighten the burden of our day. Caring for Bob has brought those moments. Recently Bob's sister from Florida came to visit. She smokes, and so I told her she had to smoke on the patio. When I returned from my walk one morning, I asked Bob where he sister was. He said, "I don't know, but there's a strange woman smoking a cigarette on the patio!"

Bildad told Job that fear belonged to God and that He establishes peace on the high places. I believe Bildad was trying to sound deeply theological and wise. What he said, though, was true. Even though God may afflict a just person, He is still to be revered and reverenced, and we can find peace in Him despite our trials.

God is an absolute sovereign being. He has power over all persons and things, and those who have trouble with this attribute of God should learn to fear Him. Truthfully, it is foolishness to quarrel with the Lord regarding His methods of dealing with you. Why not simply let God be God in your life?

Why not find the humor in the situation, even if you have to laugh at yourself? To find peace today, commit your way to Him and leave your worries at the Cross. Then find something funny about your situation and laugh at it and at the absurdities of life.

May 6

Reason Not to Fear #127: God Gives Us Wisdom

"And to man He said, 'Behold, the fear of the Lord, that is wisdom, And to depart from evil is understanding.'" Job 28:28

The wisdom of children never ceases to delight me. The story is told of a little boy who came home from Sunday School and looked under his bed. Wondering what he was doing, his mother asked him to explain his actions. Standing up, he said, "Well, in Sunday School they said that God created man out of the dust and that someday we're all going back to dust. Mom, there's a lot of people coming and going under that bed!"

What is true wisdom? In the book of James we are instructed that there are two types of wisdom: that from God, which is good, kind, gentle, reasonable, unwavering and without hypocrisy; and that from below, which is evil, sensual, demonic and selfish. (James 3:13-18) From which wisdom source do you draw from -- from God and the Word of God, or from your sinful nature and the devil?

Job declared that the fear of the Lord is true wisdom. Is God fair? If anyone could ask that question, it would certainly be Job. Calamity struck him as he went about his day in worship and praise to God. He was not a bad person; in fact, God said he was righteous and hated evil!

Truth be told, if we received what we "fairly" deserved, we would all end up in hell! It was God's love and mercy that redeemed the world by the death of His Son on the cross. In all fairness, Jesus shouldn't have had to die. But He did, and He paid for the sins of all who would come to Him by His sacrifice.

If you acknowledge your dependence on God, you will accept His providential will and find peace -- the peace of God. You will find a rock to stand on when the strange, horrific or tragic circumstances befall you as you make your way through this dark world.

Periodically you should examine yourself and see how much of your wisdom is really of yourself and how much of it is of God. We can only find true wisdom from God: from His Word and from His Holy Spirit. James 1:5 says that if we ask God for wisdom, He is delighted to give it to us. Pray for wisdom today.

May 7

Reason Not to Fear #128: We Wait for the Right Time to Speak

"So Elihu the son of Barachel the Buzite spoke out and said, 'I am young in years and you are old; therefore I was afraid, and dared not declare my opinion to you." Job 32:6

Have you ever sat in or witnessed a debate in which several older more spiritual people were talking about God and things of the Word? How would you have felt if they had turned to you and said, "What do *you* think about this?"

I can imagine what I would have said, had I been young in years and in my faith. I would have been tongue tied and probably would have refused to answer! That is exactly how Elihu, Abraham's relative, felt when he sat and listened to the long conversation and argument between Job and his three friends. I wonder what went through his mind as he sat there day after day, listening.

As I'm getting older, I have noticed numerous things that are different in my body, mind, and soul. One thing that has happened to me as I have entered my sixties is that most of the time I speak my mind when it is appropriate. I am more willing to take a chance and a risk. I figure time is not on my side, so why side step the issue?

Elihu was one of Job's friends who came to comfort him. After listening day after day, Elihu was gnawing at his fingernails and jiggling his feet in his desire to speak what was in his heart and mind. Yet even as strongly as he wanted to speak, he waited for the right time. He allowed those older to speak first.

When he did speak, what he said was worth listening to! I am sure Job was surprised and truly directed toward God as he heard what this younger man had to say. What truth this man declared! He revealed that God is a gracious redeemer to someone who is suffering. Now let me tell you, as a young man, I do not know if Elihu understood all he was sharing with Job, but I do know that God was able to use him.

God is able to speak His heart through you when you speak at the proper time and in the proper way. Wait for it, then don't be afraid to speak out what God has put in your heart. Even if you are young -- or old. God used Elihu; He can use you, too.

May 8

Reason Not to Fear #129: We Are Transformed by the Word of God

"Therefore men fear Him; He shows no partiality to any who are wise of heart." Job 37:24

Do you have a wise heart? We don't hear people talking much about wisdom today. When you watch TV or read the newspaper or magazines, count the number of times you see the word *wisdom*. Our society does not count it important anymore to fear God and to have a wise heart, and sadly, even Christians have lost this focus.

Take a look at Romans 12:1, 2. This passage gives us the recipe for godly wisdom. "Therefore I urge you, brethren, to present your bodies a living and holy sacrifice, acceptable to God, which is your spiritual service of worship. And do not be conformed to this world, but be transformed by the renewing of your mind, so that you may prove what the will of God is, that which is good and acceptable and perfect."

Offer God your body as a spiritual sacrifice. We are to commit to God our mind, wills and soul continually. We are to be transformed into His likeness on a daily basis. How is this accomplished? By the washing and regeneration of the Word of God (Titus 3:5). Washing yourself in His Word sets your mind on the right track and washes it of the earthly, sensual and demonic wisdom that is from below. This takes more than a five-minute dip by reading one or two verses from the Bible. This involves time, study, and memorization of God's Word.

Elihu (the youngest of Job's friends) ended his argument by saying that God is to be feared above all. His words are correct, impressive and inspiring. The excellency of God confounds one's mind and reasoning.

I believe there is no greater thing for you to do today than to fear and reverence God. The more you put this into practice, the less your life will be frustrated. Tell Him today that you will cooperate with His plan and ask Him to give you a heart of wisdom. To fear God properly, you must be convinced in your soul that He is worthy.

Let God make and mold you into the person He created you to be as you practice fearing Him.

May 9

Reason Not to Fear #130: We Do Homage to the Son, the King

"Serve the Lord with fear and rejoice with trembling." Psalm 2:11

This royal psalm, designated because the theme is the King of kings and Lord of lords, tells us what the nations think of God -- they hold Him in derision; they mock Him and want to cast aside the fetters of His law and His Word.

We see disrespect for God and Christians all around us today, especially in the media and TV shows. I read about a new primetime ABC sitcom called GCB, an acronym for Good Christian Belles. It was originally the letters for Good Christian Bitches. It depicted a group of "Christian" women who are scantily dressed and exceedingly foul-mouthed. The basic plot is that one woman is plotting to ruin another woman's life through her evil speaking. This is a direct attack against God and the morals found in His Word.

What is the meaning of godly fear? Our verse today describes it very well. Worship the Lord. Come before Him with fear and trembling. Be fearful lest you anger Him. Do homage to Him. Trust in Him and love Him with all your heart.

We make a big deal of the fact that the fear of God doesn't involve terror, yet here it says that we should *tremble* before Him lest He become angry and we perish on the earth! Do you come before Him with trembling? Do you honor Him and give Him your heart worship?

He is a loving God; a God of mercy and grace. David ends the song by stating, "How blessed are all who take refuge in Him!" Why? Because He is the King of kings and Lord of lords. Because He controls all things and has the power to do His will on this earth.

God loves to save people. He does not delight in judging them. God would rather have humans live in peace with Him rather than rebellion. As you serve the Lord with reverent fear, you will become a happy, contented person. Let honor mingle with your obedience. Let this joy overwhelm you. Don't follow along with the world and be entertained by wickedness. Instead, turn to God and focus on Him.

Give Him your life, your mind, your emotions, your will. This is what it means to have godly fear in your heart toward God.

May 10

Reason Not to Fear #131: God Lifts Up My Head

"I am not afraid of ten thousands of people who have set themselves against me all around." Psalm 3:6

Richard Wurmbrand, in his book *Tortured for Christ*, tells of his experiences in Romania as a pastor of a Christian church during the days of communism. When the Russians arrested him for his faith, he endured years of torment and imprisonment. During the days of his interrogation, they tried to get him to recant his faith. At one point, they forced him to stand eighteen inches from a blank wall and stare at it. He had to maintain this position for several days while he received no food or drink. A guard slurped water near Richard's face, all to no avail. They took him to where they executed prisoners and held a gun to his head. He said pure joy flooded his heart in that moment, for he knew he would soon be out of his pain and misery.

He said to the guard, "You can kill my body, but you can't kill my soul. I will live on in heaven. What about you, my friend? How is your soul before God?" Wurmbrand related that the guard held his position for a moment or two, then dropped the gun and returned him to his cell.

David faced many adversaries. He mentions ten thousand who set themselves around him and attacked him. Yet he remained confident of God's protection. "But You, O LORD, are a shield about me, my glory, and the One who lifts up my head." (v. 3)

There are Christians all over the world who are facing persecution, torture, the loss of their belongings and homes, and death for their faith in Christ. They remain fixed on God and have peace in their hearts in spite of the awful trials they are going through.

David's feet were planted firmly on the foundation of a sweeping confidence in God's presence which dispelled his fears. He could relax despite a multitude of enemies and troubles. He knew God was his protection, his glory, and the lifter of his head.

Whatever your need, whatever your situation, God will watch over you. God never sleeps. He takes care of you each moment. The One who grieves when a bird falls to the ground is your protector. If you are struggling with some fears today, your best action is to turn your fears over to the Lord. Even in days of persecution and trial, you can be at peace. Rest in Him today!

May 11

Reason Not to Fear #132: We Enter the House of God to Worship Him

"But as for me, I will come into Your house in the multitude of Your mercy. In fear of You I will worship toward Your holy temple." Psalm 5:7

The persecution of Christians in China continues. Just recently, a group of Christians had been meeting in a hall, but then authorities kicked them out of the hall. Here is an excerpt of the letter written by the pastor, Wang Dao, in a plea for help for his congregation, the Liangren Church. "In the past two years, the Liangren Church has had to move several dozens of times. The latest development has pushed the church into a very difficult situation where they continue to meet on the streets and face constant harassment by Chinese authorities. Due to the harsh reality of our circumstances, we again find ourselves in a dilemma where we are unable to find a place where we can gather! However, we still firmly believe in God's precious promises."

It doesn't matter *where* you go to worship God, the Bible says we must fellowship with other believers to find strength, help, and comfort. (Heb. 13:16) If the fear of God is deeply etched on your heart, then true worship and reverence will follow. How much would you sacrifice to attend church? To honor God by giving Him a couple hours on Sunday morning?

David had great honor and respect for the Lord and what transpired was devout worship. He loved to worship the Lord and counted it a privilege. He went habitually to the house of the Lord. God invites you to come into His holy house. He does not want you to stand at a distance. Approach Him boldly because of the abundance of His mercy.

This Psalm is a morning song, written, most believe, before David went out to meet his adversaries. This day for David would be filled with numerous dangers; therefore, before it begins he bows his heart and mind before God.

Someone said, "If the fear of God is deeply engraved on your heart, there is no doubt that it will make a suitable impression on the duties you perform."

As you face your day, it may be filled with unexpected dangers, risks, or threats. Why not begin your day, like David, bowing your heart to God and asking for His protection and guidance? And, oh, yes -- make it a priority to fellowship with other Christians this Sunday.

May 12

Reason Not to Fear #133: We Still Need God

"Put them in fear, O Lord; that the nations may know themselves to be but men." Psalm 9:20

There have been many predictions concerning when the end of the world will take place. Many have forecasted dates, circled them in red, and waited. To their surprise, Christ did not return on that specific date. People predicted that the end of the world would come on December 21st, 2012 because of the Mayan calendar, and that, too, has failed.

In Psalm 9, David references the end times. If you read the whole Psalm, you will notice seven times there is a reference to the *lawless one,* or *the wicked one.* The lawless one is the man of sin or the devil's messiah in the days of the Great Tribulation. Yet we see wicked people doing evil deeds all around us. Just recently there was a man who entered an elementary school in Connecticut and killed twenty kindergarten-aged children and five adults. We see these lawless deeds in our society and no one can stop them.

In this wonderful psalm, David praises the Lord for being the righteous judge and for destroying the wicked (v. 1-10). In verses 11-12, he exhorts the people to praise Him, and calls upon God to judge the wicked so that the righteous may be delivered (v. 13-20).

This psalm also points out that one day all our trials and tribulations will be swallowed up in victory when Christ returns. Until He comes, we are to reverence and honor Him. We can take comfort in this thought even when we see things around us falling apart and God's judgments are coming to our own nation against the wicked acts of men.

Are you cast down today in your spirit and soul because of the way our society is going? Take courage, my dear friend, and stay true to God. He has promised to deliver those who trust in Him. He may allow you to suffer times of trouble, sickness, or lack of things you might think you need, but He will never forsake you.

Today we are a highly developed society in which technology has taken over nearly everything. Yet despite that, we still need God. David prayed that all people would learn that they are mere humans, created beings. The nations need to fear God.

You need to fear God. Ask God to teach you to fear Him today.

May 13

Reason Not to Fear #134: We Acknowledge God

"They are in great fear, for God is with the generation of the righteous."
Psalm 14:5

When the shooting at the Columbine High School in Colorado occurred, we saw people standing in groups with heads bowed in prayer. When the attacks on the Twin Towers in New York City happened and the horrendous details of the killers of American people began to explode on TV, internet and radio, we saw people on their knees, people with their heads bowed, people who were not afraid to talk about God. God was first and foremost for a couple of weeks in America. People have a deep consciousness of God, even the wicked people of our day.

David, in this Psalm, mourns the moral foolishness and corruption of the whole human race and longs for the establishment of the righteous kingdom of God.

The Canaanites, who lived in the city of Jericho, were struck with fear as they observed that God was with the children of Israel. (Josh. 2:11) Catch it: they experienced fear and alarm because they knew God Almighty was with the Israelites. People may ignore and even act like God does not exist, but deep in their consciousness is the knowledge of the Most High God.

Even Richard Dawkins, the sneering atheist, must know deep in his heart and soul that God exists. Imagine the shock and terror people like this man will experience when they die and actually see Him whom they have so long hated and despised! Let me clue you into a secret: the basis of all atheism and agnosticism is the rejection of moral law and a higher authority. It is rebellion against God.

God sees everything. His watchfulness should cause a holy fear in us knowing that He is Omnipresent. What does that truth mean to you today? Do you go about your day as if God does not exist? Or do you give Him honor and reverent awe by praying to Him about everything? (Phil. 4:6,7)

God is with the *generation of the righteous*. He shows His favor on righteous people. We are righteous before God by faith (II Cor. 5:21), and so if you have been redeemed by the blood of the Lamb, you can claim this verse! Never forget God pays attention to what you are doing in this world.

May 14

Reason Not to Fear #135: We Stand in Total Amazement of God

"In whose eyes a vile person is despised, but he honors those who fear the LORD." Psalm 15:4

David knew what it meant to live in humility. He was the youngest of eight boys born to Jesse, a man of the tribe of Judah who lived in Bethlehem. As the youngest, David was often overlooked and given the least desirable tasks, like tending sheep. I can imagine that his older brothers mocked him, and reminded him often of his lowly position. He would not inherit the farm or the land and would probably end up as he began -- a lowly servant, working for the eldest, never amounting to much.

Even when he was elevated to Saul's court and life took a turn for the better, with Jonathan's friendship and his marriage to the king's daughter, David was beset with many troubles. He had to flee from Saul's persecution, live and hide in the desert, and find a safe home for his parents.

During all those years, God was "growing him up" spiritually. His faith was tested in many ways and he became a man after God's own heart because he feared God, was humble in his own sight, and developed the attitude of a servant. His deep everlasting respect for God formed the basis for his godly character, and he became one of the greatest kings Israel ever knew and the ancestor of the Messiah, Jesus Christ.

Do you desire to be a godly person? If you do, you must know and sense the fear of God in a deeper manner. You will need to come to the level of fearing God in such a fashion that it compels, constrains and controls you. If you desire to be a godly person, then obviously you will have to move beyond simply being afraid of Him. Respect, admiration and amazement need to become your daily companions.

Emotional feelings of awe, reverence and admiration can stimulate you to great thoughts about fearing God. Make it a practice to think great thoughts about God. Develop an attitude of reverential fear. Properly fearing God can change your life. Remember what this verse says, "he honors those who fear the Lord."

May 15

Reason Not to Fear #136: God Never Changes

"The pangs of death surrounded me, and the floods of ungodliness made me afraid." Psalms 18:4

Saul was dead. At long last, David was able to ascend to the throne for which he had been aiming and preparing for so many years. It was a time of rejoicing, victory and celebration. It might have been a time when David took his eyes from God and put them on himself. Many men are able to handle defeat, trouble and conflict but fail utterly when it comes to success.

David passed the test. His eyes remained firmly on the Lord God who had made all this possible. He wrote this Psalm in honor of God's help and mercy and love toward him, the one who was once a little shepherd boy out on the hills taking care of a herd of sheep.

In this wonderful song, David remembered the times when he was in dire straits, away from Jerusalem, out in the desert or holed up in a dank, cold cave somewhere down by the Dead Sea, hiding, running and afraid of King Saul's army. Whatever situation David recalled, he records for us the solution to his fear in verse six: "In my distress I called upon the Lord, and cried to my God for help; He heard my voice out of His temple, and my cry for help before Him came into His ears." God answered his cry!

Like a storm that thundered and moved across the sky, God came to David when he cried to Him and saved him from the horrible situation he was in. The key to David's greatness lay in the fact that he knew where his source of power and strength lay; it was in God.

Oh, dear friend, have you been there? Are you there today? Are you despairing of life itself? Have you taken your eyes off Almighty God and put them on yourself, on your circumstances, on other people, on your dwindling bank account? Read all of Psalm 18 to refocus your eyes on the One who can move into your situation, like He did for David, and bring the answer to you.

When we look at our situations with our earthly eyes, the ungodly can cause us to lose sight of God's presence and protection. No matter what is going on in your home, your church, your city, your state, or your world, believe God and trust in the power of His plan. God never changes. Nothing is impossible with Him. He is more than able to handle your problem.

May 16

Reason Not to Fear #137: God Cleanses Our Hearts

"The fear of the Lord is clean, enduring forever. The judgments of the Lord are true and righteous altogether." Psalm 19:9

Small children are about the only group of people in our society who are not concerned about cleanliness. I still can picture the mud pies that our children made, glorying in the lovely, warm squishy mud between their toes and not worrying a bit about the brown goo that covered their bodies from head to toe.

We live in a society that is obsessed with making everything clean. But what about our souls? Our hearts? Our minds? What can clean away the filth of sin, the muck of pride, the foul stink of lust?

In this glorious hymn of praise, David writes about the glory of God seen in creation, and also about the wonder and majesty of His special revelation seen in the Word of God. He begins this section with the words, "The law of the Lord is perfect, restoring the soul," and he continues to expound on the marvelous benefits of knowing God and keeping His Word. Not only will His Word restore your life, it will make you wise, make your heart sing, enlighten your eyes and your mind, and it will lead you into righteous behavior.

You can't go to the grocery store and buy a product from the shelves that will clean your soul. Only the fear of the Lord will do that. Why is that? Why does the fear of the Lord make you clean?

Because when we revere the Lord and His Word, we will do as He says. We will come to Him on His terms, asking forgiveness for our sin and committing our lives to Him. The blood of Jesus cleanses us from all sin. The fear of the Lord sanctifies our hearts. It cleans every nook and cranny.

There should be in each of us a fear of offending God. Do you have the fear of God and His Word in your life? This will shield you from disobedience, sin and defeat. It will keep you clean and it will enable you to accept all of God's Word. If you don't have it, pray and ask God to give you this kind of reverence and honor for Him and for His Word today.

May 17

Reason Not to Fear #138: God Is Bigger Than Our Troubles

"You who fear the LORD, praise Him! All you descendants of Jacob, glorify Him, and fear Him, all you offspring of Israel!" Psalm 22:23

Even when you think you are doing the right thing, sometimes trouble comes knocking at your door. In 1986, my husband and I made a decision to leave Sunshine Gospel Mission in Chicago and go work at a camp in Wisconsin. What a shock awaited us when we arrived, for we learned that the board knew nothing about us coming to camp, much less that we were hired by the director!

We felt alone, frightened, and extremely discouraged. The elders of our church came to visit us and were a great encouragement. Yet we had to live through this time and were often perplexed about why we should have gone there. A year later, God answered our prayers and lead us to a home and ministry in Pennsylvania that lasted for thirteen wonderful years.

The persecution that was directed at David by Saul was severe and fierce. Perhaps David may have thought God abandoned him. David wrote this song at a time when he was feeling down, depressed, alone and forsaken.

In this Psalm, we see many references to the suffering Messiah. He cried out from the cross, "My God, my God, why have You forsaken Me?" None of us can imagine or experience what He went through in that moment. Yet there are times when we despair of hope. We may feel exactly like Jesus did: forsaken of God and doubting the faith that has sustained us for so many years.

Sometimes we get ourselves into such a mess that we feel we are in way over our heads and we pray, "God, I feel like you have deserted in me. I feel like I'm all by myself." And God gently lifts your burdens, gives you strength for the journey, and leads you on to praise and serve Him another day. The more we praise God, the more reverently we will fear Him. Jesus values your praise. Holy fear should always cause us to praise our God.

The fear of the Lord will give you the right perspective in everything you do. Find God in your negative circumstances. He will bring something good from the trouble you are experiencing today. There is joy to be found in fearing God! Trust Him. Praise Him. Fear Him. It will get you past many moments of despair.

May 18

Reason Not to Fear #139: We Honor God and Keep Our Promises

"My praise shall be of You In the great assembly. I will pay my vows before those who fear Him." Psalm 22:25

The images of despair, grief and pain that David pens in this Messianic psalm are startling and clear, speaking directly to my soul. *Far from my deliverance are the words of my groaning; I cry day by day and You do not answer; trouble is near and there is none to help; I am like water poured out, all my bones are out of joint, my heart is like wax; my strength is dried up like a potsherd, my tongue cleaves to my jaws; they pierced my hands and my feet; they divide my garments among them, and for my clothing they cast lots.*

It is the picture of extreme suffering, physically, emotionally and spiritually. As David wrote this song, please note that nothing changed while he wrote it. His circumstances stayed the same, yet when he gets to v. 23, he writes confidently that he will praise the Lord. In the midst of his horrible situation, he determined that he would praise the Lord.

Hebrews 13:15 states, "Through Him, then, let us continually offer up a sacrifice of praise to God, that is, the fruit of lips that give thanks to His name."

What circumstance are you facing today? It is one that causes your knees to shake and your heart to tremble and your mouth to go dry? How can you face some of the extreme issues that people meet every day in the areas of health, careers, home foreclosures, and natural disasters?

Can you praise God even during these times? Can you praise Him in the assembly of His people? This is truly a sacrifice, for we put our own agendas aside and accept what God has for us.

God has one great assembly, and He receives praise from all His people. True praise is of heavenly origin. See Revelation 4:4, 5 for a sneak peek into heavenly worship. Our Lord Jesus loves the adoration of His people, and giving praise to Him is the best thing you can do when life beats you down. You may not be able to change your circumstance, but you can change your heart attitude and that makes all the difference in the world.

Instead of giving in to fear, exercise praise today. Let it ring out privately, or in corporate worship. God will be pleased. He will bless you with peace, comfort, hope and joy when you praise Him with your lips and your heart.

May 19

Reason Not to Fear #140: God Walks Close Beside Us

"Yea, though I walk through the valley of death, I will fear no evil; for You are with me; Your rod and Your staff, they comfort me." Psalms 23:4

David Livingstone said at his death, "Build me a hut. I am going home."

Charles Dickens said just before he died, "I commit my soul to the mercy of God through our Lord and Savior Jesus Christ, and I exhort my dear children humbly to try and guide themselves by the teaching of the New Testament."

Andrew Jackson's last words were, "My dear children, do not grieve for me ... I am my God's. I belong to Him. I go but a short time before you, and ... I hope and trust to meet you all in heaven."

Many people may not fear death but the process of death: the pain, the hospital stay, the medicine and discomfort, the loss of control, or the debilitating effects of old age and disease. We know that on the other side of death lies heaven and our Lord and Savior, Jesus Christ.

David likens God to a Good Shepherd and he assures himself of the Shepherd's presence when he comes face to face with death. Notice in this verse it does not say walking *in* the valley, rather, it is walking *through* the valley. A redeemed person goes through the tunnel of death and wakes up in heaven. We do not die; we awake in glory. Death, then, is the passage to heaven.

Notice again, it is not the valley of *death*; rather it is the valley of the *shadow of death.* David says, *"I will fear no evil."* Why? Because God was with him. God will be with us, too. It is the Christian's joy to fear no evil. For the child of God, there is nothing in death to harm you or cause you to fear.

Though you walk through the blackest valley, in the darkest of night, exposed to all sorts of evil, you should not fear if you are under the guidance and protective care of your Shepherd. He knows all about what dangers lie ahead and He will guide you through them.

If you have God at your side, you need fear no danger or evil. Don't fear death, or even the process of death. God will take care of you, as He does for all of His own. My prayer is that you will rest in this assurance today despite your circumstances. *God will take care of you!*

May 20

Reason Not to Fear #141: God Is My Light

"The Lord is my light and my salvation; whom shall I fear? The Lord is the strength of my life; of whom shall I be afraid?" Psalm 27:1

When you walk alone in the dark through a forest, you need a flashlight to illumine your way. This tiny beam of light is all you will need to take the next step. It will bring you comfort, guidance and the hope that you will arrive safely at your destination, even though wild animals might be lurking in the shadows or evil people might attack.

Pick up any newspaper, watch the television or listen the radio news, and you will soon discover that this world of ours is full of people facing giant problems, and they have no answer for them. They live in the darkness and stumble about with little hope, no solutions, and unending, gut-wrenching fear deep in their soul. No wonder people are full of anxieties, worries, and uneasiness. Everyone wants a solution for the fear problem.

Some people would be very grateful if someone would develop a pill to relieve them of their fears. We want peace in our hearts, yet we do not know where to get it. Our experience has taught us that no amount of money, success, or person can offer relief from fear. So the question is, "How can I defeat the fear that invades my life and torments me so much?"

This Psalm has the answer. In the very first verse, David states his personal faith in God. Catch the word "my." He also uses the word "light." The Lord, he says, is the light of his life.

When I walk into a dark room, I am uncomfortable until the light goes on. It is that way in my life as well. When I am walking in the dark, fear increases. When I am walking in the light, fear is gone. I have comfort, hope and assurance that I will arrive safe and sound in my eternal destination, heaven.

David's confidence in God was no passing fad -- it was rock solid. His relationship with the Lord was based on the Word of God and his own experiences. Over the years of his life, David put God to the test and found Him to be more than faithful.

What about you? What world are you walking in? Darkness or light? If you want to defeat your fears, turn on the light. Trust God. Read His Word. It's just that simple.

May 21

Reason Not to Fear #141: God Has Stored Up Blessings For Us

"Oh, how great is Your goodness which You have laid up for those who fear You, which You have prepared for those who trust in You in the presence of the sons of men!" Psalm 31:19

Three Hills, Alberta is called the Bread Box of Canada. If you were to visit this area in the spring, you would see luxuriant crops of wheat, barley, canola and other crops. Granaries, round, tower-like structures made of metal, stand at each farm and hold the grain. During harvest, the combines, while they are still moving, fill the trucks with the grain. Then the trucks unload into the bins. When the price is good to sell, the farmers unload from the bins and take their crops to market.

In this passage, David says that God has a storage bin, too. In it He stores up the goodness and mercy that He has for those who fear Him. When the time is right, when you are desperate and call out to Him, He unloads into His trucks and sends it down to you.

Life has its ups and downs, and maybe you feel like it has more downs than ups right now. We all have had to face adverse circumstances and accept them. Maybe you have felt like misery was going to overtake you, and then unexpectedly God's mercy reached down and enabled you beyond your expectations.

The Lord is able to take our brokenness and use it for His purpose and glory. I have come to realize that God is not cruel. Rather, He allows certain things to happen for a reason. Romans 8:28 stands true for us today, if we will only believe what it says. Oswald Chambers was right when he said, "If we are ever going to be made into wine, we will have to be crushed—you cannot drink grapes. Grapes become wine only when they have been squeezed."

As you encounter the ups and downs of life, remember God's storage bins. Learn to fear the Lord. Learn to trust Him through every trial. Hope is on the horizon, for your God has an inexhaustible treasure stored up for those who fear Him.

May 22

Reason Not to Fear #143: We Trust in God Completely

"Behold, the eye of the Lord is on those who fear Him, on those who hope in His mercy." Psalm 33:18

Trust and fear go hand in hand. They seem to be at odds with each other, yet the fear of the Lord is to respect Him, acknowledge Him, love Him, and trust Him.

Consider the trust a child has in its parents. Of my eight grandchildren I think my seventh grandchild is most trusting. Her name is Samantha, and we call her Sami. She is eight years old. This little girl trusts her mom, and that trust causes her to obey. As she matures, her trust in her mother will increase, and so will her trust in the Lord.

Sami loves to read her Bible and talk about heaven since that is where her dad is now. She trusts the words she reads and understands they are from the Lord to her. She trusts God. Oh, the value of child-like trust.

The Scriptures use the word *trust* quite frequently. Trust is a must in the Christian's life -- trust in God and His sovereign authority and love. Allow me to share a few truths about trust. You cannot be worried about circumstances and trust God at the same time. You cannot be angry at people and trust in God at the same time. You cannot be depressed, despondent or discouraged and trust God at the same time.

However, if you do trust in the Lord, you will experience hope, and you will have peace in your heart, and even in times of trouble, you will not be moved. You will think clearly, exercise self control, and look forward to what unfolds day by day in your life. Like Chris's granddaughter, you can rest secure knowing your heavenly Father will take care of all your needs.

This verse reminds us that the Lord's eye sees all who reverence and fear Him. He cares for His children and protects them at all times.

You see, world affairs are not in the hands of those who are behind the desks or on the thrones of the wealthy and powerful. God is on His throne, and His eye is on you with lovingkindness (mercy and love). Like a baby's devoted parents, He is aware and watching out for you. As we trust God more and more, we find security and peace.

What is your attitude to life today? Are you trusting in yourself, or in God? Renew your commitment to the King of kings and Lord of lords. Like a small child, trust Him today.

May 23

Reason Not to Fear #144: God Guards, Guides and Protects His Own

"The angel of the Lord encamps around those who fear Him, and delivers them." Psalm 34:7

Goliath was a monster of a man. He stood over ten and a half feet tall. His strength was extraordinary. For forty days he terrified Israel, roaring out his challenges and curses. You know the rest of the story. David killed the giant.

In this verse, David was remembering his ordeal with Goliath. When he looked back over that dreadful experience, he came to some full and fresh truths, and he wrote them down as a song of praise.

The Lord encamps around those who fear Him and He delivers them. David was living proof of this statement. Countless hosts of shinning ones, the mighty angels of God, preserve and protect the saints of God, and over them is the protection of the Lord Himself.

For some people, every day is full of fear. Maybe it is the fear of losing their job, or health, or money, or even their mate. It could be that you are afraid of growing older or what the future holds for your children and grandchildren. Our list of fears could go on and on.

David, when he escaped from the Philistine king at Gath, rejoiced in the Lord for His protection, love and care. God guards, defends, and looks after those who fear Him. You see, in order to realize that truth, you need to face your fears. You must eliminate them through faith in God. The closer you get to fear, the further you move from trusting the Lord. It is one or the other. Fear and trust cannot coexist.

List your fears. Then turn them over to the Lord and refuse to be frightened. Remind yourself that God's angels are on duty over your life. Then move confidently into your day with praise on your lips to God.

Remember the victory David had over the giant. Trust God and He will protect you today.

May 24

Reason Not to Fear #145: We Take Refuge in God

"O taste and see that the Lord is good; blessed is the man who trusts in Him! O fear the Lord, you His saints; There is no want to those who fear Him."
Psalm 34:8, 9

Sometimes the goodness of the Lord falls upon our lives even when we don't deserve it.

David, in desperation and fear, fled from Saul and ran to the Philistines, the enemies of the Israelites, to find refuge. Perhaps his faith was at low ebb when he did this. Perhaps he was tired of running and not ever knowing the security and comforts of a stable home. Perhaps he was tired of trying to provide for his men and their wives as they were cooped up in a dank cave somewhere in the desert country of Judah.

Whatever the reason, he suddenly found himself a captive, a wanted man, a man known for killing Goliath (who was from Gath!). To save his life, David feigned madness and the king in disgust expelled him from the city. After he fled the city, he ran back to the cave and sat down with his harp. After searching his heart, he realized that God's unmerited favor had fallen upon his life, and he composed this beautiful song for all of us sinners who often do exactly as he did.

Have you tasted the Lord's goodness on your life? Have you praised Him for His grace and love? Most of us know from first hand experiences that the Lord our God is good. His grace is as constant and plentiful as a rushing river. Stand by the bank of a creek or river and contemplate Lamentations 3:21-25. *The Lord's mercies are new every morning.* As you stand there, you see that it is not the same old water passing by, it is new water every moment. This is like God's mercies. They are new, ready to be used, fresh and sufficient every moment of your life if you will only trust Him.

David reminded all of us to honor and reverence the Lord. If we seek Him, our needs will be met, too. Read the verse again. Catch the words, "There is no want to them who fear Him." What is it that you want? Have you talked to God about it? Have you acknowledged God and trusted Him to meet your needs?

Meditate on that. When you are tempted to fear and run away, as David did, let God into your life. He will give you what you need today.

May 25

Reason Not to Fear #146: We Teach Our Children the Fear of the Lord

"Come, you children, listen to me; I will teach you the fear of the Lord."
Psalm 34:11

I love it when all eight of my grandchildren stay over at my house. They play Monopoly or Barbie Dolls or Uno. Then when it comes time to find places for them to sleep, the front room becomes a dorm room. Every pillow and blanket in the house is sought after. When they finally lie down (after I remind them to brush their teeth and get that last drink of water), I gather them around me and tell them a Bible story.

It is our moment. Our special time together, where I as their *Menzie* (Grandma) tell them something about the Lord that I trust they will remember over the course of their lives. They listen with rapt attention; and their childlike questions and comments stir my heart, and as they go to sleep, I can see the peace of God on those dear faces.

I think it must have been like that for David. He grew up as the youngest of his family, a position hardly of any renown or importance. To him had been relegated the lowliest of all tasks -- taking care of Dad's sheep. Maybe as he sat out there in the pasture, he remembered the stories his great-grandma Ruth would tell as she gathered her little ones around her. Maybe some of the songs he sang he learned at Ruth's knee.

David wanted to gather his children and the young men of his household around him and tell them about his God. All of them loved and admired David.

And so he did. He shared with his family, friends, servants and soldiers, telling them what he learned in his own life. He wanted to pass on to them the *fear of the Lord*, what it means to hold Yahweh God in high honor and respect.

It is the fear of the Lord that will influence your journey of faith more than anything else. David knew and understood the fear of God, and he wanted to pass that understanding on to those who followed after him.

Who should you gather around you? Who should you share what the Lord is doing in your life? Don't let the opportunity slip through your hands.

Go for it.

May 26

Reason Not to Fear #147: We Confess Our Sin to God

"An oracle within my heart concerning the transgression of the wicked: there is no fear of God before his eyes." Psalm 36:1

In our society today, we have become a people who airbrush the word *sin* right out of our vocabulary. People do not call an immoral lifestyle like what is portrayed on TV sitcoms as *sin*? They look at the immoral lives of Hollywood movie stars and would not think of it as *sin*.

Yet sin is all around us, and so are those who do not fear God. Read verses 1-4 in this chapter and take note of the results of not acknowledging sin.

Just recently a man entered an elementary school in Connecticut and killed twenty-four people, most of them kindergarten-aged children. Yet I have not heard anyone except a pastor label that deed as evil or sinful. No one from CNN, Fox, ABC, NBC or any of the other news media called it sin. This man listened to the wickedness in his own heart, picked up the gun, and committed a horrific transgression of God's law because he did not fear God.

Sin hardens, hinders, and hurts your relationship with the Lord. It prevents you from experiencing God's power and plan for your life. It causes you to be fearful, worried, angry, hateful, and rebellious. Do not shrug sin off, rather acknowledge it, hate it, confess it to God and resist it. Most of all, don't be entertained by it!

This verse describes a sinful man who has no fear of God, because he does not hate or detect sin in his life. A person who sins constantly and continuously really has no fear of God, and he will produce the fruit of wickedness. But the children of God, those who are truly Christians, should have a different view of sin.

We believe God is everywhere. How can we sin in His presence if we fear Him? Those who have no fear of God now may one day regret that foolish choice.

Do you need to acknowledge the gravity of sin? Do you need to confess your sin to God? Why not begin today with a clean slate, trusting and fearing God as you should?

May 27

Reason Not to Fear #148: God Is Bigger Than the Biggest Army

"God is our refuge and strength, a very present help in trouble. Therefore we will not fear, even though the earth should be removed, and though the mountains be carried into the midst of the sea." Psalm 46:1, 2

A ferocious army advanced south from Assyria, down along the Fertile Crescent, and came into Damascus, and then to Judah, wiping out villages and walled cities. It was like a heavy stone, rolling relentlessly along, leaving death and destruction in its wake.

The year was 701 B.C. and the godly king Hezekiah was on the throne of Judah. Sennacherib, the Assyrian king, marched with his army right up to the walls of Jerusalem. As they prepared to lay siege to the city of Jerusalem, they taunted the God of the Israelites by saying, "How is your god any different from the gods of the people whom we have conquered?"

Terrified, Hezekiah threw himself on the mercy and grace of God, going to the temple and laying the letter before God. (Read this account and his wonderful prayer in II Kings 18:13-19:37.) That night, God sent an angel to deal with the besieging army -- one angel, and 185,000 soldiers lay dead! There was no more Assyrian army. Jerusalem was saved. The very men who mocked God were killed. Sennacherib returned home and several years later, he was slain by some of his own men.

This Psalm celebrates and commemorates that day of victory for King Hezekiah and the Israelites who trusted God. Someone has said, "When hope is fading and almost gone, turn to Psalm 46."

Just as there was Someone to help the Israelites, there is Someone to help you in your battles, so fear does not have to overtake you. Read it again: *fear does not have to overwhelm you, even if the earth shakes and the mountains move into the sea.* Put your trust solely in God. He is able to help. He will guide you, comfort you and give you strength for your journey.

If your hope is fading, growing weak, find a quiet place and read this whole Psalm in a new light. Then bow your head and commit your problem, your life, your heart to God. He is able. Trust Him.

May 28

Reason Not to Fear #149: It Is God's Strength I Must Rely On

"God will hear and afflict them, even He who abides of old. Because they do not change, therefore they do not fear God." Psalm 55:19

Over the fourteen years I have cared for my husband, there have been many times I have been tempted to give up and run away from all my responsibilities. I have felt these negative feelings creep into my mind these last few months. Today I am extremely weary of this lifestyle. I wish I had some fairy dust to sprinkle throughout my home and change things instantly.

The long term pressures we face every day tend to wear us down. But God calls us to serve Him and to be faithful to Him in the extended haul, for the time-consuming distance, up the tedious climb, in the daily grind. How can we do this? What strength buoys us up when the undertows of doubt, self-pity and exhaustion threaten to pull us under? Consider this from Psalm 55:22, "Cast your burden upon the LORD and He will sustain you, He will never allow the righteous to be shaken."

When you are hard pressed by your circumstances, when things are beyond your control, it is the time to plunk yourself down and have a good talk with your soul. Have you been trying to do it in your own strength? Are you trying to fight this battle with your own wisdom, your own resources, your own patience?

If so, you are setting yourself up for failure. The only thing I can do when I begin to feel low is fling myself into the arms of the Lord. That is exactly what David did in this song. He refers to his enemies as those who do not fear the Lord. People like his favorite son, Absalom. They were not God fearing people and had no intention of changing their ways. David left those kinds of people in God's hands and found comfort in the Lord. He realized only God can change people.

David never gave up. He continued to be a man after God's own heart. Life is worthwhile because God sees your situation. When you ask Him, He will provide you with the strength to take the next step up the long, long path toward Home.

I don't want to give up, and I hope you don't, either.

May 29

Reason Not to Fear #150: God Is Able to Help Even in the Worst Situations

"Whenever I am afraid, I will trust in You; in God I have put my trust; I will not fear. What can flesh do to me?" Psalm 56:3

Fear. Terror. Dread.

David wrote this song when he fled to Gath. He was afraid of King Saul, for Saul had sought to kill him and brought an army out to do just that. David went south into enemy territory. In fact, Gath was the hometown of the giant Goliath that David had killed.

While following his fears, he ran to the least desirable place of all -- the very headquarters of his enemies who would have liked to put him to death. When they brought him to the king, he pretended to be insane.

What a picture he is with spit dribbling down his beard, scrabbling senselessly at the walls, screaming gibberish. While following his fears, David does not look like the godly, confident king he would one day become. In disgust, the king of the Philistines told them to release David as he had enough crazy people in his kingdom already!

I am sure David learned a lesson that day that stood him in good stead for the rest of his life. *Don't listen to your fears.* Trust God, and He will protect you, fight for you, honor you, and watch out for you every day of your life.

When David returned to Israel, he sat down and wrote this song. Out of his stress and fear, he encouraged himself in the mercy, memory, and might of the Lord. Wow. Isn't that a refreshing way to face the pressures of life?

When my fears get the best of me, I want to steal away. I want to get under the covers and not see anyone. I find it hard to keep my hope alive. When that happens, I have to make a conscious decision to turn away from fear and re-focus my eyes on God, trusting in Him to keep His promises.

Have you ever felt you are in a hopeless situation? If all is going smooth, we can usually coast along and try to cope on our own. But when life becomes hard, we cry out to God and learn to trust and fear Him..

We must remind ourselves that we only have limited power to control issues, but God is able to help us when fear tries to overtake us. Remember David. Be like him and trust in God today.

May 30

Reason Not to Fear #151: God Comforts Me When Tears Fall

"In God I have put my trust, I will not be afraid. What can man do to me?"
Psalm 56:11

As I usually do, I awoke at 5:30 A.M., made my coffee, got my Bible and other devotionals, and began my quiet hour with the Lord. However, after a short time, my husband awoke. I walked into the bedroom and told him that it was only 6 A.M., and he should go back to bed and sleep a little more. He did not respond well to me. I was upset and tried to find peace as I read my Bible and prayed. Yet the more I read, the more I wept.

Crying and shedding tears are a part of life. I am comforted to know that the Lord says He places my tears in a bottle. He knows about my hard, difficult morning. He understands why I was crying, and He cares about my circumstances.

Once I was reminded of this transformational truth, I could return to my Bible study, prayer and worship of the Lord with a peaceful heart. The first thing we need to do when we are in a bad time is to turn the control of the situation over to God. Trust Him verbally. Say something like, "I don't know why this is happening, God, but You do and I know that You love me and care for me. So please take charge here, Lord, because I'm lost without You."

What can man do to you? People can't steal your joy, ruin your peace, or destroy your faith if you are planted solidly on the firm foundation of His love. Yes, the tears may come, but they won't stay for long when you remember that God loves you.

Trusting Him in your fearful, tearful moments leads you to a stronger and steadier Christian life. Most likely, I will have many more upsetting mornings with my husband. But this I have come to know: I must simply trust God and leave it with Him. This is the only remedy to my distress.

Trusting God is serious business. *Thank you, Lord, that I can trust You with my tears, my life, my fears.* When the tears start to roll down your cheeks like a river, know that God sees and records them. He is there to comfort you, just like He was for me today.

May 31

Reason Not to Fear #152: We Leave Our Burdens With the Lord

"All men shall fear, and shall declare the work of God; for they shall wisely consider His doing. The righteous shall be glad in the LORD, and trust in Him. And all the upright in heart will glory." Psalm 64:9, 10

Psalm 64 is a "lament" or a song of complaint. David was experiencing a lot of grief from his enemies, so much so that in v. 1-3, he says, "Preserve my life...hide me from the secret counsel of evildoers...those who have sharpened their tongue like a sword and aimed bitter speech as their arrow."

Have you ever been the brunt of vicious gossip?

While living in Pennsylvania, my position as the Teaching Leader of the Bible Study Fellowship class was terminated. I held the position for almost ten years. The class had grown from sixty-five women to over three hundred during those years. It was a delightful class.

When the decision was made to close the class, I had to stand in front of my friends and share the miserable news. The announcement brought complaints, divisions, and arguments, as well as gossip. A huge division occurred between those for the decision and those against it.

Rumors abounded. Many people found fault with me, and there was no way I could go around and defend myself. Over the years, I have heard how many people spoke maliciously, hatefully, and spitefully about me. Even to this day, the memory of that causes hurt and damage in my heart.

David was facing opposition that was much more serious. Once again he poured out his heart to the Lord over falsehoods being spread about him. Was King Saul behind these lies and rumors? Possibly. I can imagine that he would relish in them and spread them with delight. One by one, those lies blackened David's name.

Have you been talked about and maligned? Have you been the brunt of gossip, rumors and lies? Don't be afraid. Do what David did -- take it to the Lord and leave it there. He is able to defeat your enemies, bring you peace of mind, and lift your heart. Then all people will see your righteousness and the fear of the Lord will enter their hearts. Take refuge in Him today. "Cast all your anxiety on Him because He cares for you." I Peter 5:7

June 1

Reason Not to Fear #153: We Step Out in Faith to Serve Him

"God shall bless us, and all the ends of the earth shall fear Him."
Psalm 67:7

Visionary people challenge me. They are the ones in our churches who see a need and have the vision to implement a program to meet that need. When more and more children come to church, they are the ones who say we need a Sunday School or a mid-week Bible club. When they begin seeing teens filling our pews, these dear folks are the first to suggest a youth group program. Are there some older folks who cannot hear the sermon? Visionary people will put up the funds to buy listening devices for them. They are the ones who will say, "We have to step out in faith and begin a building program." And they do!

I think David was a visionary. He not only saw the need for godly leadership in Israel, he stepped forward to take on that responsibility.

This psalm is a vision into the future; it is about the rule of Christ, which will one day occur. When the rule of Christ begins, there will not be a hint of dissatisfaction. He will reign justly and perfectly. Apostasy, rebellion, and defiance will all come to an end and Christ Jesus, our great King, will bless us.

This verse also points out that *all the ends of the earth will fear Him.* Missionaries in third world countries work hard to spread the Gospel with people who live at the ends of the earth. Many of these tribal people presently have no fear of the Lord, despite the missionary work going on there. They offer the Lord no obedience and still worship their false gods.

But all people, no matter where they live, will one day fear the Lord, serve Him, and worship Him. This day has not come yet, but it is getting closer. Many need to hear the gospel message and place their belief in Christ.

Visionaries want all people from the ends of the earth to fear the Lord.

Are you like this? In this day when money is tight and getting tighter, it is easy to cling all the harder to our bank accounts and our tidy little nest eggs. If we fear the future, we might not want to give or work toward spreading the Gospel with those around us. We need to let go of our fears and step out in faith for God. What can you do that will spread the news of the Gospel to the world in which you move? Think about it and do it today.

June 2

Reason Not to Fear #154: God Will Bless Those Who Fear Him

"They shall fear You as long as the sun and moon endure, throughout all generations." Psalm 72:5

When my husband attended Moody Bible Institute, his favorite course was the Psalms. The other day, in one of his study books, I found his notes on this particular Psalm.

These notes, written in his handwriting, brought tears to my eyes, and for just a few moments, I found myself drifting back into a time when our lives were so full of activities and fun. As I write this page, I am looking at my husband's notes and perhaps will write a few of his thoughts along with mine.

Most believe this may be the last psalm David wrote and that he wrote it for his son, Solomon, who was a handsome man, one in whom he could take pride. Read the whole psalm; it is beautiful, full of praise to God. The language lifts you above the ordinary occurrences of the day. Perhaps it was sung at the occasion of Solomon's coronation.

Picture David who is aged and his young son, Solomon, standing there with joy and fervent faith in his eyes as the ceremony takes place. What would you say to your child if he were to take on such an awesome responsibility? David's desire for Solomon was that he would fear the Lord Almighty *as long as the sun and moon endured.* Wow, is that ever needed today!!

People need to not only need to love the Lord, they need to fear Him. They do not need more theological discussions about Him, or arguments about the finer points of doctrine, they need to experience Him and reverence Him. Why? Because the fear of the Lord, a healthy respect, honor and worship of God, will keep you from evil, will make your feet stay on the right path, and will guard you against presumptuous sins.

We are destined to be conformed to His image and that process can only take place when you honor and worship the Lord out of your great fear for Him. He will bless you if you fear Him. Stand in awe of Him and do that as long as the sun and moon endure.

June 3

Reason Not to Fear #155: God Is Mighty

"You, Yourself, are to be feared; And who may stand in Your presence When once You are angry? You caused judgment to be heard from heaven; The earth feared and was still." Psalm 76:7-8

Have you ever been caught in a situation where there is no deliverance, no help and no solution? Does the trouble you are facing loom closer and closer like the headlight of a speeding locomotive? In II Kings 18-19 or Isaiah 36-37, we read the story when godly King Hezekiah faced such a circumstance.

Against God's Word and Isaiah's wise counsel, Hezekiah had joined an alliance of nations that rebelled against the powerful Assyrian nation. King Sennacherib was furious at Hezekiah's rebellion and marched with his great army into the region, decimating and plundering nations as he went. He swept through Judea, taking forty-six fortified cities and all the smaller cities.

Hezekiah realized his mistake too late. After he emptied the treasuries of his kingdom to appease King Sennacherib, he saw the armies approaching and knew they would soon lay siege to Jerusalem. At that point, his only resource was to cry out to God for help. Isaiah 37 records his amazing prayer for help, and at the end of the chapter, we read how God responded.

In one night, God's angel killed 185,000 Assyrian troops. Sennacherib limped home and was killed by his own sons. This psalm is thought to have been written in praise to God for His deliverance, help and mercy. Notice the song writer says that even the earth feared God! Who may stand before God when He is angry? Answer: no one.

What trouble are you facing today? It may be of your own making, as was Hezekiah's. It may be something totally out of your control, as sickness. It may be someone in your life who is terrorizing you and making your life impossible.

Whatever it is, you do not need to stand in fear of them. You only need to fear and trust God. Turn to Him when you see those fearful headlights of the oncoming train drawing close. Draw close to Him and relinquish your fears. He is able. If He can destroy a whole army with one angel, what can He do for you?

June 4

Reason Not to Fear #156: We Remember God's Goodness

"But He made His own people go forth like sheep, And guided them in the wilderness like a flock; And He led them on safely, so that they did not fear; But the sea overwhelmed their enemies." Psalm 78:52-53

We can learn many lessons from our past experiences. In Psalm 78, David recalls the redemption of the nation of Israel from the Egyptians. He remembers their history and God's faithfulness. It was God who brought the Israelites out of bondage and into blessings.

This whole Psalm seems to sea saw back and forth with remembering what Israel did to God and what God did for Israel. Over and over, the Israelites were reminded of God's mercies.

Remember means to keep in mind. Each of us who have walked with the Lord a number of years, should commit to memory His compassion, kindness, and unselfishness. Do not forget the times God kept and protected you. Share with your children, grandchildren, and friends those precious memories.

I remember how the Lord once provided an unexpected vacation for us in Amsterdam. The Billy Graham Association invited Bob to come to their conference, but I wrote back and said that Bob could not go because he would not like leaving his wife behind. A few days later the Billy Graham Association called our home and invited both of us to attend the conference all expenses paid! I love remembering that story.

In recounting the history of Israel, the psalmist brings back to memory the awesome acts of God in delivering the nation of Israel from Egypt with a strong arm and mighty deeds. This event, the Exodus, and the defeat of Pharaoh's army in the Red Sea, was such an amazing miracle of deliverance that for years afterward, even the heathen nations in the area referred to it.

It is good to remember how God has helped us in times past. As you look back on your life, you can praise God anew for His help, mercy and love in your life. Share these stories with your children and grandchildren. Remind them that if God can do it in the past, He is able to do it now.

You will be surprised at how encouraged you will be as you keep walking this road in faith. These reminders will keep your eyes on the goal, your heart steadfast, and your hope alive.

June 5

Reason Not to Fear #157: The Angels Call Him Holy

"For who in the heavens can be compared to the LORD? Who among the sons of the might can be likened to the LORD? God is greatly to be feared in the assembly of the saints, and to be held in reverence by all those around Him."
Psalm 89:7-8

Angels were, for a time in our society, a topic of great interest and popularity. Everywhere you went, you saw angels. Today, the topic of vampires, demons and zombies, is capturing the imagination of writers of books and movies and our society. There are even groups of people who are arming themselves to kill the zombie invasion that they believe will come.

Our culture in America today has made the paranormal a cult. If you were to walk through any book store, you will see shelves and shelves stacked high with the topic of the occult -- books about witches, demons, spirits, curses and omens, fairies, vampires and zombies.

Vampires are evil fantasy creatures, however, they are portrayed as innocent and good in the recent spurt of books and movies about these mythical beings. A whole generation of young people has been indoctrinated about witchcraft, sorcery and spiritism by the Harry Potter books. These things are strictly forbidden in the Word of God for Christians. (See Deut. 18:9-14)

The difference between miracles and magic is the *source of power*. Where does the power come from -- God or the devil? If it is from God, it will conform to the Word of God and lead one to worship, fear of the Lord, holiness, and obedience to Him. If it is of the devil, it will lead deeper and deeper into darkness, sin, terror, conflict and torment.

In heaven, as this Psalm states, God is feared, respected and honored as the highest of all. He is the great creator God who is loving, holy, and mighty. The angels and all created beings who gather around the throne proclaim Him to be the one and only true God.

Are you dabbling in the occult? Do you enjoy watching movies about demons and witches? Cleanse your life of these false gods today. Get rid of all the books and movies that elevate witchcraft, spiritism and the paranormal. Then get out your Bible and spend time in it, and you will renew your relationship with the one and only true God.

June 6

Reason Not to Fear #158: We Use Our Days Wisely

"The days of our lives are seventy years; and if by reason of strength they are eighty years, Yet their boast is only labor and sorrow; for it is soon cut off, and we fly away. Who knows the power of Your anger? For as the fear of You, so is Your wrath. So teach us to number our days, That we may gain a heart of wisdom." Psalm 90:10-12

At times I cannot believe I am sixty-six! Where did the years go? The older I get though the more I long for heaven and all it holds. Perhaps you are like me and have come to realize that the years are flying by too quickly.

This psalm of Moses was about growing old. I am reminded of my age every time I have to kneel down on the floor. A friend of mine said, "At my age, when I get down here, I look around to see if there's anything else I can do!"

This is a wonderful song of Moses, who wrote it as he grew older and wiser. Notice he emphasizes the sovereignty of God over all creation, and over our individual lives. He notes the short span of life we are each allotted.

We hope that we will become wiser as we age, but this is not always the case. God's wisdom is more about obeying and fearing God than it is about the grey in our hair or the aches and pains of our bodies. Moses lived his life in the fear of the Lord. He learned some very tough lessons, and through those, became a man of great wisdom.

Moses came to realize that dwelling in the presence of God and fearing Him is the best place to be. Do you know that even if hard times, unexpected times, horrible times, or confusing times come, God will continue to be your only true refuge? It is a wise person who remains in the fear of the Lord all his days, who find their shelter and care in the Lord regardless of the situations of life.

Never forget that God is your safe place in the hard times of life. This verse reminds us that God is awesome and knows all about your life and how quickly life passes. We are to use our days as God would ordain them to be used. Become wise as you age. Set your sights on the living hope of eternal glory!

June 7

Reason Not to Fear #159: God's Love Is Greater Than My Sin

"For as high as the heavens are high above the earth, so great is His mercy toward those who fear Him." Psalm 103:11

I have to confess: this Psalm is one of my favorite Bible passages, one that I turn to frequently when I need a "pick-me-upper." It is definitely one that takes your breath away. There is nothing in the world that cheers your heart, brings peace to your mind, or makes a complaining spirit disappear than to tick off the blessings of the Lord in your life.

This is what David did in this song. First he began by stating, "Bless the Lord, O my soul, and all that is within me, bless His holy name." v. 1 We bless the Lord by adoring and thanking Him for all the things He has done for us. Read through the next eight verses and write down how God has blessed your life over the years.

The word lovingkindness is a word that my computer doesn't like. It underlines it in red every time I use it. But I like it. It combines the thought of God's patient, loyal love and His mercy and grace. David says in this verse, "As high as the heavens are above the earth, so great is His love towards us."

This reminds me of a New Testament verse on the love of God. In Paul's great prayer for the believers in Phillipi, he wrote, "and that you, being rooted and grounded in love, may be able to comprehend with all the saints what is the breadth and length and height and depth, and to know the love of Christ which surpasses knowledge, that you may be filled up to all the fullness of God." (Ephesians 3:17-19)

When was the last time you sat down to think about the magnitude of God's love for you? Sure, you and I stumble into sin. We constantly struggle with it, but God's love is far greater, deeper, and wider than your sin. This verse points out that His love is unfailing. Therefore, when God loves, He loves unrelentingly, devotedly, completely.

God says to the weak, needy, guilty, and frail who are His children, *"Come and rest in My divine love."* Do you want this today? Make Him your Rock today. Enjoy His mercy and wrap yourself in His abiding love. Who can understand the height, length, and depth of this divine love? As you grow in grace, may you comprehend His love more and more each day.

June 8

Reason Not to Fear #160: We Get Rid of Guilt and Doubt

"As a father pities his children, so the LORD pities those who fear Him."
Psalm 103:13

I love it when David talks to himself in song. In this wonderful song (read it entirely), he tells his soul to bless the Lord and then recounts the many ways God has blessed him. God pardons his sins, heals his diseases, redeems his life from the pit, crowns him with lovingkindness and compassion, satisfies his years with good things as long as he lives, and renews his strength day by day.

I owe the bank money when it comes to the mortgage of my home. I owe my credit card money when it comes to some items I recently purchased. I owe some money on my car. However, none of that compares to what I owe the Lord. How can I number all His benefits and blessings? Perhaps that is why David begins and ends this psalm with these words, "Bless the Lord, O my soul."

There are times in our lives where we feel we are not good enough to receive God's blessings. Please listen: no matter what you are or what you have done, you are good enough to be loved and forgiven by Christ.

Did you notice the order of the words I just wrote? Loved, forgiven. Always remember that Christ loved you first and is willing to forgive. This verse makes it clear the Lord has compassion on those who fear Him. I love hearing the word *compassion*. It touches my heart because it speaks to me concerning God's unexpected, undeserved mercy. Lovingkindness brings it all together -- His love, His mercy, and His grace toward me.

Do not allow the walls of your heart to be layered with guilt. Do not allow your mind to be filled with unbelief. Do not allow your spirit to be untouchable. Rather take seriously the Lord's compassion and care for you. And then permit your lips to "count your blessings and name them one by one, count your many blessings, see what God has done."

Spend some time right now to count your blessings. Write down a list. Keep adding to it. You will find it lifts your spirits, gives you a sparkle in your eyes and a spring to your step.

Bless the Lord, O my soul!

June 9

Reason Not to Fear #161: We Praise God and He Gives Us Joy

"But the mercy of the LORD is from everlasting to everlasting on those who fear Him, and His righteousness to children's children, to such as keep His covenant, and to those who remember His commandments to do them."
Psalm 103:17-18

Who should bless the Lord? How should you bless the Lord? Why should you bless God's name? At what age should you begin to bless the Lord?

Do you teach your children and grandchildren to praise the Lord? Are you counted among those who keep His Word and obey His voice? Are you counted as one of the righteous who will stand in the day of judgment (Psalm 1)? If the answer is yes, then you should praise the Lord and bless His name. This verse points out that from *everlasting to everlasting,* the Lord's love is with those who reverence and honor Him.

Therefore, I think we should *all* praise Him *all* the time.

Young men should praise the Lord with their strength, ambition and stamina. Young girls should praise Him with their charm, values and innocence. Little children should praise Him with their laughter, curiosity, and interests. Young men who are seeking to make their mark in life should praise Him with their strength and vitality. Older women who understand life and have served the Lord for a length of time should praise him with their kindness, wisdom and comfort. Older men who are wise should praise Him with their love, kindliness, and gentleness.

It boils down to this: from *everlasting to everlasting* we should praise and bless His name. We do not do this out of fear or terror of Him, instead, our fear takes on the terms of goodness, gratefulness, and gratitude.

In Romans, chapter one, verse 21 states, "For even though they knew God, they did not honor Him as God or give thanks...." People did not give God thanks; they did not praise Him, and so they became darkened in their thoughts and went their own way into sin.

Do you want the joy of the Lord? Then praise Him! While we are here on this earth, we need to fear the Lord and bless His name. Make it your number one priority on your list of things to do today.

June 10

Reason Not to Fear #162: We Are Wise When We Fear God

"The fear of the LORD is the beginning of wisdom; a good understanding have all those who do His commandments. His praise endures forever."
Psalm 111:10

As we go through the book of Proverbs, we will see the theme of godly wisdom often highlighted. What is wisdom? How can we attain it? Who is wise among you? How can you tell a fool from a wise person?

Many people in our society drink. We all know what alcohol can do to a person. Some people can limit their intake while others cannot. Those who make the choice to drink too much lose the ability to speak clearly, walk steady, and think clearly. They embarrass not only themselves but those who are with them. Their foolish behavior spoils the whole evening. Do you know why? Because the whole event revolved around themselves. God and other people were not important, therefore whatever came to their minds, they said or yelled it.

This is a picture of a fool. Wisdom is a matter of a moral choice to obey God and put Him first in your life. A fool is a person who denies God and lives as if there is no tomorrow. (Psalm 14:1-3) Many people today claim to be wise. In fact, we give awards to people who are supposedly wise: inventors, scientists, and politicians. People may talk with knowledge and may even be very eloquent in speech, but that is not how real wisdom is displayed.

James 3:17-18 says, "But wisdom from above is first peaceable, gentle reasonable, full of mercy and good fruits, unwavering, without hypocrisy. And the seed whose fruit is righteousness is sown in peace by those who make peace." Do these qualities dwell in your life, in your speech, in your thoughts and attitudes, in your actions? If not, then you might need to change some things.

A wise person in God's eyes is the one who fears Him. The fruit of fearing God is wisdom. Holy reverence for God comes in the form of fearing and worshipping Him. Why should the Lord not be obeyed? Only a person who is unwise would not obey Him.

The wise person praises the Lord. The praise of the Lord will endure forever and His praise will outshine the wisdom of the world.

So breathe out His praise as one who fears His holy name.

June 11

Reason Not to Fear #163: We Put God First in our Lives

"Praise the Lord! Blessed is the man who fears the LORD, delights greatly in His commandments." Psalm 112:1

I know people who greatly delight in sports; in fact, you can hardly peel them away from their large flat-screen TV while a football game is on, or while a golf tournament is being played. There are people who delight in playing computer and video games, in texting and spending time with their gadgets, in shopping -- whether it is online, through TV, or in the stores.

The list could go on and on. We all have passions into which we are tempted to pour our entire time, money, affection and attention. For me, I have to admit I love to read, walk, spend time with my grandchildren, teach the Bible, and study.

But how many of us *greatly delight* in the commandments of the Lord?

If you were given a whole day to do whatever you wished, how would you spend it? Would the reading, studying and memorizing of God's Word have any part in that day? Do you consider reading and studying the Bible and going to church to hear a sermon a chore and a duty? Are these activities pretty low on your priority list? Do you have the attitude of, "Well, if nothing else more interesting comes along, I'll attend that church activity?"

This psalm challenges us to look deeply into our hearts to see the place where we have put God and His Word in our daily lives and in our affections. Read the rest of the chapter. The song writer describes a person who fears the Lord and *greatly delights* in His Word: his descendants will be mighty on the earth, he will be blessed with riches and wealth (spiritual wealth), his righteousness will endure forever, light arises for him out of darkness, he is gracious and compassionate, he will win his cases in court, he will never be shaken.

That is quite a list! Would you like some of these blessings on your life? Then put aside the computer, the phone and texts, the TV, the sports, the shopping, the extra hours at work, the money -- and concentrate on God and on His Word. Put Him first in your life; not just for today, but for each and every day the rest of your life. Attend a Bible class. Go to a Bible seminar. Make church a priority.

Get serious with God, and He will bless you.

June 12

Reason Not to Fear #164: We Are Not Fearful When Bad News Arrives

"He will not be afraid of evil tidings; his heart is steadfast, trusting in the LORD." Psalm 112:7

The phone rings in the middle of the night and your heart drops as you answer it. Usually a call that comes at that time is not good news. Or you are sitting in the doctor's office and with a very sober face, he tells you the tests came back, and it is not good news.

One night the phone rang. It's two in the morning. *Who could be calling?* Certainly the news cannot be good, not at that hour. It was my Grandma. Her wobbly voice came over the line, "Christine, come over. I need you to take me to the hospital. Grandpa is not doing good."

During the first five years of my marriage, I lived five houses away from my Grandma. I loved the fact that we saw each other every day. We ate, walked to the grocery store, and cooked together. I threw on my clothes and ran down to my Grandma's home. She was frantic and in her broken English, she told me she did not understand what the hospital had told her. Within a few minutes, my aunt and uncle arrived, and we learned that my Grandfather had died.

Bad news can shake us, shatter us, and if it is really bad news, smash us. It is hard to swallow, unless you are a child of God.

The verse in this song is describing the person who fears the Lord, and the ways that God blesses such a person. A person who greatly desires the Word of God will not fear bad tidings. Why? Because their feet are firmly planted in the promises of God. See Hebrews 6:17, 18

When ill tidings come, they do not bring about total fear because our hearts remain fixed and trusting in the Lord. God does not exempt us from disasters. He offers rest, endurance, and joy to those who trust in Him in the midst of difficult circumstances when bad news comes.

If you are one who fears the Lord and greatly desires His Word, bad news does not need to cause you to be fearful. It causes you to trust in Him all the more as you trust Him to bring about His perfect will through your yielded life.

June 13

Reason Not to Fear #165: Our Security is in God

"You who fear the LORD, trust in the LORD; He is their help and their shield." Psalm 115:11

Previously in this chapter, the song writer denounces the false gods that Israel has adopted and worshipped. Some of these they had brought from Egypt (the calf god), some they picked up from the surrounding nations (the Baal gods, the Asherim, Molech, and Chemosh). The psalmist says, "Their idols are silver and gold, the work of man's hands. They have mouths, but they cannot speak; they have eyes, but they cannot see.... Those who make them will become like them, everyone who trusts in them." Psalm 115: 4-8

He begins the passage by saying, "But our God is in the heavens, He does whatever He pleases." v. 3

Their false gods were made of wood or stone and covered with gold or silver. They had to be carried around, fed (they brought sacrifices of food to them), and cared for. What kind of a god has to be tended? These gods could not do anything; they could not even feed themselves!

We shake our heads and deplore the sinful, immoral practices that surrounded the worship of these pagan gods. Yet don't we as Americans do the same? We worship our cars that have been made by human hands. We worship our houses and the things we put in them. We worship our jewelry, electronics, our sports teams, we worship actors and actresses and talk show gurus on TV. These gods need tending, painting, fixing, watering and feeding.

We insure everything we own. We spend more money on maintaining our possessions than we care to admit. The more "stuff" we own, the more time we spend in fixing it, using it, cleaning it, protecting it and running it. How many of you have become totally upset and angry when your computer/ipod, iphone, ipad, or whatever you have does not work? How many of you become depressed and angry when your favorite sports' team doesn't win the big game? How many of us are dejected when we cannot watch our favorite TV show?

Where does our help and our security come from? Not from these false gods we love to accumulate! Only God Almighty, the Jehovah of the Jews, and His Son, Jesus Christ, can fill that empty place in your life. Turn to Him today. Worship Him alone. Give Him your love, fear and respect.

June 14

Reason Not to Fear #166: Blessed Are Those Who Fear the Lord

He will bless those who fear the LORD, the small together with the great. "
Psalm 115:13

Do you feel small today? Over my life, I have felt small and insignificant.

Several years ago, I was at Sandy Cove Bible Camp in Maryland as a seminar speaker. The main speaker for this large women's conference was Florence Littauer, who has written over forty books. She speaks all over the world. I stood beside this lady, feeling very small as she interacted with the other seminar speakers. She knew most of them by name. There I was, feeling even smaller. No one knew me or even heard of me. Florence was cordial and tried to interact with me, but really we were worlds apart. Florence lived in Palm Springs, CA. while I lived in Mennonite country Pennsylvania.

Through that weekend, though, Florence paid extra attention to me. She would made an effort to seek me out and talk. Finally, the afternoon came for my seminar presentation. I thought I was prepared until Florence herself opened the door and sat in my seminar! Every word in my head disappeared. By the end of that weekend, Florence and I became friends, and she extended an invitation to come to her home in Palm Springs. What a week it was! I will never forget it. It was a dream come true.

God assures all will be blessed who fear Him, who respect Him, acknowledge Him, and live their lives in obedience to His Word. The word *bless* means to be straight, to be level or right, to be happy, to go forward or prosper in your way, to go, guide, lead and relieve. I was tremendously blessed by Florence's friendship and the invitation to visit her in her home, even though I still feel small compared to her accomplishments.

Whatever your circumstances are, no matter if you are great or small, prince or pauper, it makes no difference to the Lord. He is able to bless you. Whatever may be the situation in your life, He is your all in all. As long as you fear, reverence, and honor the Lord, assuredly He will bless you. He is the supplier of your every need. He does not forget the godly, no matter how small or great their position. God has an equal interest in **all** His children.

God has reserved for you an uninterrupted stream of blessing. Never forget that truth. He will *bless those who fear Him*, and that means you.

June 15

Reason Not to Fear #167: The Lord's Love Endures Forever

"Let those who fear the LORD now say, "His mercy endures forever." Psalm 118:4

There are not many things in this world that last forever, yet we make heroes out of make-believe characters and imbue them with godlike characteristics. These fake superheroes are ones like Superman, Batman, Spiderman, Agent 007. We might even add in Santa Claus and the Easter Bunny. How good or effective are these superheroes in solving your daily problems, in giving you peace of mind, or forgiving your sin? What are we teaching our children when we hold up these fake superheroes to worship instead of God?

If I had a choice, I would want God on my side, not some fictitious person. Only the Lord can help you face life without fear. Only He can make you feel loved, worthy and wanted. Only God Almighty can give you love. He is fully in love with you and His love endures forever. This verse specifically states that if we fear the Lord, if we reverence and honor Him, we should be saying and thinking, "His love (for me) endures forever."

There is no shortage in regard to His mercy, grace, power, salvation, ability, healing, and of course, love. His love lasts forever. In our culture, our young people worship nihilism, the philosophy that nothing matters, that death is the ultimate experience. These people are "walking dead". They have no hope, peace, joy or love. They deny the existence of God and of any kind or moral rules, laws, or standards. This is sweeping through our nation today.

So let us put this verse in some everyday language. It does not matter what happens today; the Lord's love endures forever. It does not matter how bad your circumstances are; the Lord's love endures forever. It does not matter how hopeless things look; the Lord's love endures forever. It does not matter if the conditions are bigger than you; the Lord love endures forever.

We know that our bodies do not last forever. Our houses, cars, books, electronics and possessions will be gone someday. Even the cities, mountains, rivers and hills in our world will pass away. Nothing lasts forever. Only God, our souls, and the Word of God are eternal. Write down ways He has blessed your soul and tell others about this today.

The possessions and cares of this world will fade away; instead, focus on the eternal.

June 16

Reason Not to Fear #168: The Lord Is on Our Side

"The LORD is on my side; I will not fear; what can man do to me?"
Psalm 118:6

That verse is quite a mouthful. Think about it. Martin Luther said regarding this psalm, "It is my favorite. It has helped me out of many great troubles and fears, when neither emperor nor kings, nor wise men, nor saints could help me."

There are many Christians today who face persecution, loss of jobs, loss of homes, and loss of life because of their faith in Christ. While an evangelical pastor was preaching in Pakistan recently, a large group of armed men entered the church and ordered the people out. They fled, but the men detained the pastor. In a small room in the back, they beat this poor man up, shouting at him and demanding that he recant his faith. When he did not, they continued the torture until he was dead.

Here was a man who could have entertained the fear of man. But he did not. He did not fear what man could do to him. He feared the Lord.

All who are true believers in Christ are on a journey home to heaven. This psalm can help us on the journey, just like it helped Martin Luther. As I grow older, I realize more and more that the Lord is on my side. I can confidently say, "I will not fear what man (or woman) can do to me."

The opposite is also true. When I do not remember to fear the Lord and trust Him, I am usually full of all types of fear. I fear what people might say about me, think about me, and believe about me. However, what really matters is not what man can do to me, but instead what God can do!

Jesus set the example for us. During His lifetime, while He ministered, He was confident no one could touch Him or harm Him. Yes, there were times He eluded the masses and their murderous intentions; however, he had no fear of what man could do to Him.

Yes, sometimes we are afraid, and that is okay. The point is not to allow your fear to block your movement on your spiritual journey. Your enemy wants to prevent you from moving forward, from enjoying life and from any kind of spiritual progress.

Move forward and have no fear of what man can do to you.

June 17

Reason Not to Fear #169: We Learn the Fear of the Lord Through His Word

"Establish Your word to Your servant, who is devoted to fearing You. Turn away my reproach which I dread, for Your judgments are good."
Psalm 119:38, 39

How can we learn to fear the Lord in the proper way? And what will it bring into our lives when we do? Consider these questions in light of the verse we are looking at today.

Faith is a hot topic in America today; however, it is not a faith based on the Bible or on traditional church experiences. The faith people are adhering to today consists of many other kinds of faiths, like Buddhism or Islam or any other "brands" of religion. Barna's surveys have found people today view being a Christian or associating with the Christian faith is not as attractive as it used to be. They want to pick and choose their doctrines, and they want to find their own "plate of teachings" that most pleases them, whether is it Buddhism, Muslim, spiritism, Catholicism, or mainline Protestant religions.

Barna goes on to say that according to the studies done among evangelical Christians, Bible reading has become the religious equivalent of sound-bite journalism. The "devotional time" for most Christians is to read maybe one or two verses from the Bible, quickly scan someone's written thoughts about that verse, pray briefly, and go on about their day.

They do not want to spend time and energy studying the Word. Barna observes that there is shocking little growth evident in people's lives in their understanding of the main themes, doctrines and truths of the Bible. Just half of all Christians firmly believe the Bible is totally accurate, and barely one-fourth are confident that Satan exists.

David was so wise when he said that the Word of God would bring us the fear of the Lord. Through the consistent, diligent and extensive study of the Word, we can learn what it means to be in reverence, awe and fear of God. David wanted to live a life that would please God.

How are you when it comes to the study of God's Word? It is my prayer that you are doing more than a five-minute perusal of the material presented in this book. Get a good study guide on a book of the Bible. Write down what God is saying to you. Spend some time really studying the Word this week and see what a difference it can make in your life.

June 18

Reason Not to Fear #170: We Choose Our Friends Wisely

"I am a companion to all who fear You, and of those who keep Your precepts." Psalm 119:63

"A true friend is someone who thinks that you are a good egg even though he knows that you are slightly cracked." (Bernard Meltzer) "A real friend is someone who walks in when the rest of the world walks out." (A Proverb)

"Associate with men of good quality if you esteem your own reputation; for it is better to be alone than in bad company." (George Washington) "It is easier to pull someone off the wagon than to lift him up. Choose your friends carefully, for they may pull you down." (A Proverb)

You have probably heard all of these familiar quotes on the value of having not only good friends, but friends who will influence you to a deeper walk with God. David writes that he associated with people who fear the Lord, those who walk in obedience to God. We have the definitive word on it in I Cor. 15:33, "Do not be deceived: Bad company corrupts good morals."

I am not saying to avoid the people who are not spiritually mature or strong Christians. I am saying that you should not make them one of your "constant companions", or your inner circle of tried and true friends of your heart. Why? Because people who do not have your same interests, morals, or priorities will pull you down to their level.

We see this all the time with young people and their peer groups. They have formed close friendships with others who do not share their faith or their basic moral foundations in the Word, and they are sucked into sin very easily. Trouble comes knocking when they associate with those who drink alcohol irresponsibly, use drugs and practice immorality. The Bible is very clear that we should chose our friends carefully.

You may need to spend less time with some friends and more with others. Starting today, decide with whom you will spend your time, and choose your friends wisely.

June 19

Reason Not to Fear #171: We Have Hope in Jesus Christ

"Those who fear You will be glad to see me, because I have hoped in Your word." Psalm 119:74

Most of us realize that Psalm 119 is a very long psalm, and it is to be read in portions. This portion of the psalm has to do with God's hand, help, and heart. In this particular verse David sees God's hand as motivating him to have hope and security in God's Word.

Hope is a very powerful word. It causes people to be lighthearted and happy. Over the fourteen years after my husband's heart and brain damage, I wish I could tell you I have always been hopeful, but that would not be true. Many times I have not had a positive attitude and have lost my hope. During those times, life is not positive and enjoyable. But when hard circumstances touch our lives, we must maintain our hope in the Lord.

The Bible is filled of hope-filled promises for each of us. Some of my favorites are: "For the grace of God has appeared, bringing salvation to all men, instructing us to deny ungodliness and worldly desires and to lie sensibly, righteously, and godly in this present age, looking for the blessed hope and the appearing of the glory of our great God and Savior, Christ Jesus." Titus 2:11-13

Or this: "So that by two unchangeable things in which it is impossible for God to lie, we who have taken refuge would have strong encouragement to take hold of the hope set before us. This hope we have as an anchor of the soul, a hope both sure and steadfast and one which enters within the veil." Hebrews 6:18, 19

Consider this: "Blessed be the God and Father of our Lord Jesus Christ, who according to His great mercy has caused us to be born again to a living hope through the resurrection of Jesus Christ from the dead." I Peter 1:3 A *blessed* hope, a *sure* hope, a *living* hope.

Notice what David says about himself in Psalm 119:74. When people came around him he wanted to be a source of joy to them because of his hope which was in the Word of God. When he came through the door, he brought joy into the room. People felt good to just have him around. What a challenge for us. When you enter a room what do you bring to it? Gloom or glory? Focus on God and His Word and you will have great hope and joy.

June 20

Reason Not to Fear #172: We Live in the Light of His Fellowship

"Let those who fear You turn to me, those who understand your testimonies." Psalm 119:79

What kind of friends do you gather about yourself? David was like all of us -- he needed and appreciated friendship with people. He valued their counsel and stood on their shoulders, so to speak, as the king and leader of Israel. He wanted to accumulate godly people around him who would give him support, pray for him, and help him make wise decisions.

Most of us know of David's sin with Bathsheba, of David's murder of her husband, Uriah, and the death of their son. We know that this grieved God, but do we know that this sin also may very well have alienated some of the godly friends David had?

This verse may be referring to those who have turned away from David because of his sinful actions. Therefore, he begs God to turn to him and then to turn these friends back to him. It seems David craved their love, companionship, and friendship.

Losing friends can be devastating, especially if it is due to sin. We may have to pray hard to have them forgive us and re-enter our life.

Remember David was God's leader. His heart became wounded when he realized that those who feared the Lord were not kind or considerate to him anymore. They were not thrilled to see him, like they once were. They did not want or desire his company, nor did they want to have conversations with him. This was a high price to pay for foolish sin.

Have you ever been where David is? I can recall times in my life where my wrong choices have cost me the friendship of those for whom I cared. Once we lose the trust of people, it is hard to get it back. David faced the heartache of Absalom's rebellion and death, and the near-collapse of the nation in civil warfare. He was never the same after he faced some of these heart-rending circumstances that arose from his sin.

Perhaps this verse will make us think seriously about our actions and how our sin affects those close to us. Confess your sin, ask those you have hurt to forgive you, and live in the light of His fellowship today. You might not regain the friendship of those you have wronged, but you will find peace of mind with God and with others.

June 21

Reason Not to Fear #173: We Fear Offending Our God

"My flesh trembles for fear of You, and I am in dread of Your judgments."
Psalm 119:120

In today's society, we have gotten away from the truth of God's judgments against sin. People question God's dealings with mankind and say, "If He is a God of love, why does He allow suffering in the world?" They reject His Word, refuse to bow before Him in repentance and faith, and shun and mock those who do. They jeer at His Word as a bundle of myths and lies. They kick Him out of their schools, government, entertainment, pocketbooks and lives.

They do not want to talk about sin. They don't want to call something evil. In fact, they call evil good and good evil! Yet God is still sovereign, and He is not to be mocked. There are consequences to sin. He judges the wicked and rewards the righteous. It is not right to question God. He has given us His Word which is a revelation of His heart, His purpose and the final state of all things. One day Jesus Christ will reign on this earth and all sin, death and suffering will be put away forever.

God's words about judgment are solemn and they may bring fear into your life. You should have a holy fear of God. There should be dread at the thought of offending the One who is holy, pure, and righteous. Each heart contains unclean thoughts and motives, yet God's piercing eye sees it all.

I pray that your fear of the Lord will lead you to obedience and reverence of Him. This is true worship. God is not asking you to have a slavish type fear of Him. Rather, this fear is one of awe and reverence. "None reverence the Lord more than they who know Him best and are most familiar with Him," wrote William Cowper.

Understand that there should be a proper mixture of fear of God and hope in His mercy. Is it not an insult to our God that we do not fear and reverence Him properly? When these two things are balanced rightly in our lives, you will give Him the honor and respect due His name.

Notice that is exactly what this Psalm is encouraging you to do. Have spiritual fear, a reverential awe of God, and a richer, greater understanding of God's Word will be yours.

June 22

Reason Not to Fear #174: We Find Peace When We Fear the Lord

"Blessed is everyone who fears the LORD, Who walks in His ways. When you eat the labor of your hands, you shall be happy, and it shall be well with you. Your wife shall be like a fruitful vine in the very heart of your house, your children like olive plants all around your table. Behold, thus shall the man be blessed who fears the LORD." Psalm 128:1-4

The picture painted for us here is something like a Norman Rockwell painting. A family is seated around the table. They all join hands. Their heads are bowed. The youngest, a little boy with a mischievous twinkle in his eye, is peeking from under his hand, hungrily eyeing the steaming plates of fried chicken and mashed potatoes. There's a sort of glow over their heads as if God Himself is smiling at the scene.

What strikes me most about this painting is the peace that emanates from it. Yes, the children might fuss about the delay. The oldest may have something to say about going out that night and the fact that he's old enough to stay out longer than his parents think he should. The young daughter might be concerned over what she is going to wear to a special function at school. Mom might mention the fact that Dad has not fixed the plumbing on the toilet that was leaking earlier that day, and Dad might be thinking about going fishing.

Yet overall, they have peace, and they are happy. In Israel, the word picture for peace and prosperity was "every man sits under his fig tree." In this verse, it is the olive tree. The olive tree is an amazing plant. They say olive trees never die. They send out new shoots and keep growing. The olive trees that Jesus prayed under in the Garden of Gethsemane are still there. To have many olive shoots would be a sign of great prosperity.

Blessed are all those who fear the Lord. Are you afraid? Worried? Concerned? Stressed? Burdened? Full of doubts, conflicts or trouble? This is not the way God wants you to live. He wants you to live in peace. Seek peace. Simplify your life so that you will find peace. A wise man once said, a butterfly lands on you only when you are quiet.

To those who fear, love and obey God, He gives His peace. Find it today.

June 23

Reason Not to Fear #175: We Offer the Sacrifice of Praise

*"Bless the LORD, O house of Levi! You who fear the LORD, bless the LORD!
Blessed be the LORD out of Zion, Who dwells in Jerusalem! Praise the LORD!"*
Psalm 135:20-21

How can you bless the Lord? How can you enrich the life of the One who created you and owns the whole universe? Have you ever thought of this before? How can we give back anything to a God who possesses all things?

Talk about the person who has everything! The only thing He does not own is the human heart. He gave humans a free will, and by doing that, He ceded over to mankind the choice to love Him -- or not to love Him. We can keep this treasure, or we can give it back to Him. This is the supreme gift we can give to the Lord.

God is blessed by our praise, our adulation, our love for Him. Somehow we can enrich His existence by our praise. I love the verse in Psalm 22:3, "Yet You are holy, O You who are enthroned upon the praises of Israel." Hebrews 13:15 says, "Through Him, then, let us continually offer up a sacrifice of praise to God, that is, the fruit of lips that give thanks to His name."

When Noah came out of the ark, he sacrificed to the Lord there on Mt. Ararat. "The Lord smelled the soothing aroma; and the Lord said to Himself, 'I will never again curse the ground on account of man, for the intent of man's heart is evil from his you; and I will never again destroy every living thing, as I have done."

In Lev. 29:18, "You shall offer up in smoke the whole ram on the altar; it is a burnt offering to the Lord: it is a soothing aroma, an offering by fire to the Lord."

What is a *soothing aroma* to the Lord? Is it a particular smell? I don't think so. I think it is a person who fears God, gives Him reverence, and gives Him praise and obedience with all their heart. It is this that pleases God and that blesses His heart.

Every morning we should yield our bodies, our hearts, our minds and our souls to God; we should acknowledge Him in all things and give Him praise. In this way, we who fear the Lord will bless His heart. We not only give Him our obedience, but we praise Him and thank Him even when things are not as we want them.

Begin right now to do that. What a privilege it is!

June 24

Reason Not to Fear #176: Your King Hears You and Will Rescue You

"He will fulfill the desire of those who fear Him; He also will hear their cry save them." Psalm 145:19

I remember my first Christmas in Arizona. How different it was from my Christmas' in Illinois and Pennsylvania. In Arizona, it is warm, sunny, and even celebrated outdoors! Because it is so warm, people decorate elaborately. You will see many people in my neighborhood wearing shorts and flip flops as they spruce up their homes. They bring out their plastic Santa Clauses, Rudolphs, and balloons filled with elves. What a sight.

My question is, where are the manger scenes? Where are the images that point to Jesus? Have we lost the ability to worship Jesus in the season in which we celebrate His birth?

We might label Santa as the visible form of the money gods of our time, and with him, the Elf on the Shelf has appeared. How many people actually worship this god, the lord of all material things, who will bring them whatever they desire? Materialism, money and pleasures are the gods of our day, yet these cannot truly satisfy hearts and souls.

The world often portrays God, the Christians' God, as unapproachable or unreachable. Yet when Jesus was on earth, He was very approachable. God extends an invitation to come boldly into His presence and meet Him at His throne of grace (Heb. 4:16).

If you will reverence His name and His decrees, God will hear you and He will develop in you a holy heart. Remind yourself that Jesus heard Mary Magdalene and saved her. Jesus heard the cry of the two blind men and restored their sight. He also heard the pleas from the lepers and cleansed them. Jesus heard the cry of the thief on the cross and promised him that they would be together in paradise that very day.

Your King hears you and will rescue you, too. Do not trust in a Santa-god, or in anything of this world. Place your trust in Jesus Christ and He will fulfill His purpose for you.

June 25

Reason Not to Fear #177: We Place Our Hope in His Unfailing Love

"The Lord takes pleasure in those who fear Him, in those who hope in His mercy." Psalm 147:11

God's unfailing love and mercy is a topic I love. While we can never completely understand it or comprehend the depths of it, God's love is the undergirding foundation for my very life and breath.

Whitney Houston, in an interview with Diane Sawyer in 2002, discussed the pain and frustration she experienced in her failed comeback attempt. At one point in the interview she turned to Ms. Sawyer and asked, "Have you ever heard the sound of 10,000 people disappointed in you?"

Hailed as perhaps the greatest vocalist of all time, Whitney Houston once stood atop the music industry as the unchallenged queen of pop. The greatness of her talent was met by an equally magnanimous outpouring of love from millions of fans the world over. But when her abuse of drugs and other related habits finally robbed her of that "golden voice," the cheers turned to jeers.

In that same interview, Ms. Houston declared emphatically, "I know this—*Jesus* loves me!" It was a declaration she would assert repeatedly, even at the occasion of her final public appearance the night before she died. Despite her flaws and self-doubt, there was one thing she did not question: the love of Jesus. What a critical realization, one which highlights the important distinction between the love of the world and the love of God. The former is fickle and fleeting; the latter is sure and eternal.

God's love is unconditional and unfailing for all His children. He delights in those who fear Him, in those who obey and love Him, in those who walk in His ways and have put their hope and faith in Him.

Do you hope in God's mercy? Does His love comfort you on bad days? Can you find others to share God's love with? Or are you bitter, cold and clinging to a loveless lifestyle? Find your joy and praise in the love of Jesus.

The Lord finds pleasure in those who fear Him and praise His name.

June 26

Reason Not to Fear #178: Godly Wisdom Comes From the Fear of the Lord

"The fear of the Lord is the beginning of knowledge; fools despise wisdom and instruction." Proverbs 1:7

The story is told about a person who was at the airport, checking in at the gate when an airport employee asked, "Has anyone put anything in your baggage without your knowledge?" To which he replied, "If it was without my knowledge, how would I know?" She smiled condescendingly and nodded. "That's why we ask."

When a man and his wife arrived at an automobile dealership to pick up their car, they were told the keys had been locked in it. They went to the service department and found a mechanic working feverishly to unlock the driver's side door. As the man watched from the passenger side, he instinctively tried the door handle and discovered that it was unlocked.

"Hey," he announced to the technician, "It's open!" To which he replied, "I know - I already got that side."

Are these people foolish, stupid or merely just clueless? According to the book of Proverbs, a fool is a person who is *morally irresponsible and bankrupt.* The difference between a wise person and a fool is the relationship they have with God. It has nothing to do with low mental acuity or lack of social skills. It has everything to do with the fear of the Lord.

This verse teaches us that the fear of the Lord is the beginning, the basic ingredient, to wisdom. God's wisdom is applying the knowledge of the Lord and His Word to our everyday lives. It is the practical working out of our faith. It is choosing the right way, making good decisions, being able to discern good from evil, acting in such a way that your life gives glory to God and brings peace, joy and harmony to all your relationships.

How do we get this kind of wisdom? We do not get it in our genes. You cannot buy it. You cannot attain to it by studying school books and learning facts. You can only get it one way: by fearing God; by giving Him respect, honor and obedience. God's wisdom leads us in paths of righteousness, stability, peace and joy. Yet we are told that fools despise wisdom and instruction.

Which do you want for your life? If you want God's type of wisdom, then apply your heart and mind to fearing God and to the study of His Word.

June 27

Reason Not to Fear #179: We Do Not Marginalize God

"When your terror comes like a storm, and your destruction comes like a whirlwind, when distress and anguish come upon you. Then they will call on me, but I will not answer; they will seek me diligently, but they will not find me. Because they hated knowledge and did not choose the fear of the LORD."
Proverbs 1:27-29

Foxhole prayers amount to very little. When 9-11 struck our nation, we witnessed people praying on every street corner. Even bars and strip-tease joints had signs on the windows that read *God Bless America*. It was a popular thing in those days to call upon God for help, to praise Him, and to shout His name from the rooftops and in public.

Today it is a different matter. A hurricane battered Louisiana and the east coast, and do we see people praying or hear them speak of God? The most common thing we see on the TV news about the people in those hard-hit areas are complaints that the government did not help them soon enough. I have little doubt that there are people who prayed and who talked about God in those states, but it didn't get on the evening news.

Why? Because it is not popular these days to talk about God. To even to mention the name of Jesus in our national or state capitols, to pray before a football game, to carry a Bible to school is an offense. What is God's response to the fact that America has marginalized Him?

"They will call on Me, but I will not answer." To a people who have left Him out of their schools, out of their government, out of their very lives, God says, "You left Me out, now I am leaving you out."

Fools disrespect God. They ignore Him, hate Him, fight against Him and rebel against Him. This verse says it very succinctly: *they did not choose to fear the Lord.*

Where do you stand today on this issue? Will you be numbered with those who choose not to fear the Lord, or will you stand in the congregation of the righteous and be numbered among those who fear Him, love Him and obey Him? Make your choice and stand on it today.

June 28

Reason Not to Fear #180: We Do Not Remain Naive or Foolish

"For the turning away of the simple will slay them, and the complacency of fools will destroy them; but whoever listens to me will dwell safely, and will be secure, without fear of evil." Proverbs 1:32, 33

The book of Proverbs highlights several less than desirable character traits. We meet **The Fool**, v. 7 (one who despises God's Word and chooses to go his own way); **Mr. Sinner,** v. 10 (a person who loves to sin and entices others to do it); **Ms. Scoffer,** v. 22 (those who mock God and His Word); and **Miss Naive Simple** (those who chose to be ignorant of God and His Word) in v. 32.

I think of myself as a simple person. In fact, when I have been asked to describe myself, I always say, "I am a simple woman." However, being simple has often caused people to mock and make fun of me. People have called me naïve because I rarely wear fingernail polish, make- up or lipstick. I am not into the glitz and glitter scene.

People think of "simple" in terms of a being a fool. In our society today, that means a person with less mental abilities or social graces than the normal person. The dictionary describes this person as "lacking intelligence or common sense; easy and not involved or complicated; childlike, wide-eyed, round-eyed; lacking mental capacity and subtlety; humble, lowly, undistinguished."

This passage teaches us that God views the simple or naive person as one who *willfully disregards wise counsel and chooses to be rebellious against Him and His Word.*

It is a serious thing to remain naive, disregarding God and His Word, for your lifetime, for it will lead to death and destruction. How many young people are taught that God is not relevant, that He does not exist, that humans came from a single-cell organism floating in the water? This is being naive.

How many people disregard God in their daily lives? This is being simple.

However, verse 33 gives us hope. "But He who listens to me shall live securely and shall be at ease from the dread of evil." Are you at ease today? Are you resting in the goodness and love of God despite your circumstances? If you are, then you are not simple or naive. You are wise.

June 29

Reason Not to Fear #181: We Dig for Hidden Treasure

"So that you incline your ear to wisdom, and apply your heart to understanding; yes, if you cry out for discernment, and lift up your voice for understanding, if you seek her as silver, and search for her as for hidden treasures; then you will understand the fear of the LORD, and find the knowledge of God." Proverbs 2:2-5

The story is told of a man who tried to make a living from a small piece of land in the south many years ago. He was discouraged about his lot in life and after thinking about it, decided he would sell his land and use the money to go find treasure. Someone told him there was a great treasure to be found somewhere else. So he sold his land and moved away.

It was not many years later that the new owner of his property decided to dig into the soil, search the streams that flowed through it, and explore it thoroughly. To his great surprise and delight, he found a treasure in the soil -- diamonds! Today there is still a diamond mine on that property.

This passage tells us that we should also dig for treasure, the treasure of God's Word. We should dig for it as we would for silver and gold. The promise? We will discern and understand the fear of the Lord. We will discover the knowledge of God.

Is this worth the effort?

Many people would say *no*. Oh, they might acknowledge the importance of God's Word and the knowledge of the fear of the Lord just to sound spiritual. Yet by their actions, they shout a different story. When faced with decisions about priorities and time schedules, what is most important to you? Is it studying God's Word, praying, meeting with other Christians? Or when you are asked to teach a Sunday School class or work in VBS, or help out with the youth group or visit in the nursing home, do you automatically say, "I don't have the time." Do you spend the hours of your day texting, talking on the phone, Facebooking, watching CNN, gossiping with your friends, shopping, playing your favorite computer games or watching your favorite sport on TV? What is most important to you?

It is time to get serious about knowing God and His Word. It is time to fear the Lord above all other things and people. It is time to seek for wisdom, search for understanding, unearth the treasures of God's Word through diligent study. Start today. Take time for God.

June 30

Reason Not to Fear #182: We Acknowledge God in Our Daily Lives

"In all your ways acknowledge Him, and He shall direct your path. Do not be wise in your own eyes; fear the LORD and depart from evil."
Proverbs 3:6, 7

Is God interested in finding you a parking space? In finding your wallet or phone? In trying to decide what to fix for dinner? Or what to wear today? I know there are many Christians who would answer *no* to that question.

They say that the God of the universe should not be bothered with the ordinary details of our day. We go about our days with self-centered confidence in our own abilities, strengths, skills, intelligence and finances until something happens that knocks us down.

Then we cry to God for help. But God might say, "Why should I help you now? You weren't interested in Me during all those hours, days and years of your life. Why not go to your gods of money, skill, intelligence, knowledge, computer, sports, or materialism? Where are these gods when you need help?"

Most of the time, God is so gracious that He does answer our cries for help even when we do not deserve it. Yet wouldn't it be better to have God's input into our lives on a daily basis? What does it mean to *acknowledge God in all your ways?*

When we acknowledge Him and invite Him into every moment of our days and lives, this verse states that He will guide us faithfully, He will make our paths straight or direct, we will know what to do and what His will is for our lives and we will not fear evil. Read verses 8-10 and see how God longs to bless you when you acknowledge Him.

We can *acknowledge* so many other things and give our trust to them. We might trust in insurance policies, our bank account or financial portfolio, our lands and possessions and electronics, our knowledge, careers, position, social standing, or appearance. Yet all of these can disappear in a matter of moments. When these things are gone, in what will you trust?

Trust in God first. Acknowledge Him by bringing Him into your daily life. How can we do this? II Thessalonians 5:17 tells us to pray without ceasing and to give thanks continually. Bring all your cares to Him.

Don't worry about things, but pray about them. Begin to practice acknowledging God today. Bring every concern, problem and situation to Him. God will bless you if you do!

July 1

Reason Not to Fear #183: We Hate Evil and Refuse It

"The fear of the LORD is to hate evil; pride and arrogance and the evil way and the perverted mouth I hate. Proverbs 8:13

Do you hate evil? Can you recognize evil? When you see lewd, foolish, and unrighteous behavior on TV, on your favorite sitcom show, do you turn away you turn off the TV? Or do you sit through the immoral parts and justify it in your mind? Remember *Seinfeld*? It was an extremely funny show, yet the scripts had the performers acting out the most evil behavior I have ever witnessed, flaunting God's laws and making a laughing joke of the Ten Commandments. *Will and Grace* and *Friends* were even worse. These are small potatoes compared to what they air today, which includes every kind of sexual sin, nudity, violence, and profanity.

You are not being wise if you tolerate evil and bring it into your living room, being entertained by it. When many people begin home schooling their children, they are told that this will damage the children forever. These critics say that children need to be around wickedness to learn to avoid it and that a person should be exposed to evil to learn to hate it.

This is worldly thinking, and the very opposite is true! There are two wrong thoughts in this statement. The first is that children must be out in the world to identify evil, yet the Bible tells us that evil is in our hearts. We face it every day, whether we live in a monastery or on skid row. We confront evil from the inside out and must learn to overcome it.

The second erroneous statement is that children should be "inoculated" by evil to be able to resist it. The thinking is that we must see evil and practice a little bit of evil to be able to identify it and overcome it. This is not true. To learn to identify evil and to hate evil, we must focus on the Word of God. When we learn what is right, what is holy, what is truly righteous behavior, *then* we can identify and turn away from evil. We learn to hate evil by loving what is good.

No child is ever harmed by studying God's Word or by keeping their lives free from sin and evil. What about you? Clean up your life today. Determine to focus on His Word and on Him rather than those smutty TV shows or computer apps. You will learn to hate evil and love what is good.

July 2

Reason Not to Fear #184: We Cry Out Against Evil

"The fear of the Lord is the beginning of wisdom, and the knowledge of the Holy One is understanding. Proverbs 9:10

The fear of the Lord is the beginning of knowledge. What is the fear of the Lord? It is to choose God. It is to seek God diligently and search for His truths above all else. It is to acknowledge Him in all your ways. Here we learn that the fear of the Lord is to hate evil. Do you hate evil?

In these days, we hardly know what evil is. The lines have been blurred. Now young people say something is *bad* or *evil* or *wicked* if they mean it is extremely good. Now we have movies in which the hero or heroine is doing evil deeds, and people think this is good. No one talks about evil these days, except God's remnant alive on this earth.

In fact, the worst evil, according to our world and culture today, is to label something evil that the world wants to participate in. It is to mention the name of Jesus on the floor of our U.S. Congress. It is to pray publicly before a school's football game. It is to display the Ten Commandments on the wall of City Hall. It is to speak out against homosexual activity.

Do you hate evil? Do you cry out against evil?

"I don't want to be radical," I hear some of you saying. It's comfortable to sit in your chair in your living room and watch the horrors of prostitution, slavery, murder and war that are displayed on the evening news on your large screen TV. Yet what are you doing about it?

Have you hated evil enough to get out of your chair, pray for wisdom to know what God wants you to do, and do it?

On the streets of Bangkok, there are thousands of young girls who are enslaved to evil. But also on the streets of that city, there are ministries who are seeking to rescue women and children from the sex trade. Those who have visited this area say that the evil is so prevalent, you can feel it and taste it.

The Christians who minister there are the streets are courageous in the face of this great evil. They hate it so much they are willing to do something about it, and they regularly rescue young women from this life style.

What about you? What can you do today? Pray about it. Then do it.

July 3

Reason Not to Fear #185: The Fear of the Lord Will Prolong Your Life

"The fear of the Lord prolongs days, but the years of the wicked will be shortened." Proverbs 10:27

Have you ever seen someone who has been on meth for any period of time? They may be young, but they look very old. Their skin is brittle and wrinkled, their teeth have fallen out, they walk stooped and in pain, they look out upon the world with reddened, bleary eyes, and their hair is falling out in clumps. They are walking skeletons, because this drug is a lethal combination of chemicals that is designed to kill. And kill it does.

One of my dearest friends in Pennsylvania has three daughters. Each of them are a delight. They have looks, personality, and intelligence. However, one of the three became involved in drugs during her high school years, and the desire for drugs grew as she matured. When she graduated, she moved in with her boyfriend who also used drugs, and their drug use and dependency continued.

My friend strongly suggested to her daughter that she enter a rehab center. She did, yet it was only a temporary fix. Back to the drugs she went. As the years went on, she checked into one facility after another. None of the programs permanently broke her addiction. For many years, this young woman has been in prison, given birth to a child, and still she uses drugs. Her lifestyle has not changed, and this addiction will shorten her life.

This is true of many young people who have chosen to substitute drugs, alcohol, or other chemical substances instead of putting their faith and trust in God. The fear of the Lord has no part in their lives.

When you chose to honor God and obey Him and give Him your life, He will lead you in His path which provides safety, security, and shelter. The length of your life will be lengthened because you are walking according to God's Word. The fear of the Lord will prolong your days is a true statement.

Do you believe it? When you chose to honor God, obey Him and give Him your life, He will lead you in the path of safety and peace. Your life will be prolonged. Fear Him today. It is your only hope.

July 4

Reason Not to Fear #185: We Walk in Righteousness and Honor Before the Lord

"He who walks in his uprightness fears the Lord, but he who is perverse in his ways despises Him." Proverbs 14:2

Devious. Lying. Scheming. Tricksters. Scammers. We all know people who can be put in this category, or we have heard of them. Perhaps someone you know has fallen prey to a scam. What is the pay-off for scammers? Money. Prestige. Power.

The movie, *Catch Me If You Can*, based on the real-life story of Frank W. Abagenale, Jr., tells the story of a young man who had all that the world could offer because he was a good scam artist. It also tells of the FBI undercover agent who finally caught him. Frank, whose father taught him all he knew about scamming people for gain, impersonated a pilot, a doctor and a lawyer -- all before his 21st birthday!

What was his pay-off? Money, esteem, and the "high life" of girls, booze, fine clothes, and the *I'm smarter than they are* attitude toward life. Incredibly intelligent, he accomplished his goals until he was caught as he was printing thousands of dollars of counterfeit money in France. In portraying someone he was not, he was ensnared in a world of unreality. To survive, he had to come up with more and more lies. The lies hurt the very people he wanted to love.

Thankfully, the story has a happy ending. While serving time in prison, the FBI agent recruited him to spot and track down criminals who were doing the same things he had been doing. Eventually he married, became a Christian, and continues to serve in this way as a law abiding, God-fearing man.

Do you walk in uprightness? Are all your dealings honest and above-board? Or do you fudge a bit when it comes time to paying taxes, to giving your tithe? Do you tell little white lies to get a better business deal? Will you work on Sunday or any other day if it gets you a little more money? Do you ignore your family to pursue your career?

This gets to the heart of who you truly are. Do you fear the Lord, trust Him and walk in His ways? If you can answer *yes*, then continue on! If you answer *no*, change your lifestyle today. Clean up those little messy, dishonest issues and come clean before God and men.

Like Frank B. Abagenale, you will be glad you did!

July 5

Reason Not to Fear #187: We Have Strong Confidence in the Lord

"In the fear of the Lord there is strong confidence, and His children will have refuge." Proverbs 14:26

Another proverb along this line is Proverbs 18:10, "The name of the Lord is a strong tower; the righteous runs into it and is safe." It brings to mind the battles that were fought in the old days. When the city was besieged and the walls were broken, the people fled to a strong tower, the *keep*. They barred the doors and were safe.

Christians can live with strong confidence in the Lord. We have many Scriptures that promise us God's help in time of need, His comfort in time of grief, His strength when we are weak, and His peace when everything around us is falling apart. Anyone who does not avail himself of these promises is like a rich man who owns millions of dollars but lives like a beggar because he hoards his great treasure.

This does not mean that all people who fear the Lord and live righteously will suffer no harm. Christians all over the world are experiencing persecution and facing deprivation, imprisonment, suffering, hunger and death. Then can this statement be true? How can the writer of this proverb state with such conviction that those who fear the Lord will find refuge? Refuge from what? Is there is there another kind of refuge that has nothing at all to do with our physical life on this earth?

Another verse I like is Isaiah 33:6, "And He shall be the stability of your times, a wealth of salvation, wisdom, and knowledge; the fear of the Lord is his treasure."

The old song goes, "This world is not my home, I'm just a'passin' through." We can live with strong confidence that God will help us through this life, no matter what we face, and our children and grandchildren will benefit from our faith, for they, too, will have a refuge in times of trouble. This world may not be nice to us, but praise God this world is not our home!

We have a great future ahead of us. Our refuge is Jesus Christ Himself, and our *living hope* (I Peter 1:3) is that we will be in heaven one day with our Savior. Don't despair about how the world is going. Praise God and live in our great hope!

July 6

Reason Not to Fear #188: In Christ We Have the Fountain of Life

"The fear of the Lord is a fountain of life, to turn one away from the snares of death." Proverbs 14:27

During his twilight years, American author Mark Twain noted that "life would be infinitely happier if we could only be born at the age of 80 and gradually approach 18." We smile at that, but how many of us hate growing old? I would say all of us do! The ancient Greek poet, Homer, called old age "loathsome." William Shakespeare termed it a "hideous winter."

It is not hard to understand why there have always been hopes and rumors that something exists that could prolong our lives, like water from a magical fountain, the Fountain of Youth.

The name linked most closely to the search for the fountain of youth is 16th-century Spanish explorer Juan Ponce de Leon, who thought it would be found in Florida. In St. Augustine, the oldest city in the U.S., there's a tourist attraction that purports to be the fountain of youth that Ponce de Leon discovered soon after he arrived in 1513.

There are a couple of problems with labeling St. Augustine's natural spring as Ponce de Leon's fountain of youth. Elderly visitors who drink the spring's sulfur-smelling water don't turn into teenagers. And Ponce de Leon probably wasn't looking for such a fountain and may not have set foot near present-day St. Augustine. The closest he may have gotten to it was 140 miles south.

In this verse, we see that the fear of the Lord is actually the true "fountain of life". Why? Because giving honor and reverence to our eternal King leads us to eternal life found in Jesus Christ. Jesus said, "If anyone is thirsty, let him come to Me and drink. He who believes in me, as the Scripture said, 'From his innermost being will flow rivers of living water'." John 7:37-38. When we fear the Lord, we drink from the true fountain of life.

Do you have this "living water" in your life? Come to Jesus. Through reading His Word and through His Holy Spirit, eternal life from God Himself will flow in you. And you won't have to go to Florida to find it! Fear God. Trust in Jesus. Find your peace, love, life and joy in Him. Then share it with someone else. Let the water flow to others.

July 7

Reason Not to Fear #189: We Live Simply

"Better is a little with the fear of the Lord than great treasure with trouble." Proverbs 15:16

How many of us really believe this to be true? Our culture spells success like this: M-O-N-E-Y. We are often tempted to fall for the thinking that more equals satisfaction, but more is not *ever* enough. When asked who is more content, the man who has a million dollars or one who has ten children, the answer is the man with ten kids because the man with the million dollars wants more!

We can always find a person who has a bigger house, a better car, a larger TV screen and more electronic gadgets than we do. But if we buy into the scam, work two jobs and dedicate our lives to getting all that stuff, what do we get in the end? We might have a big bank account, lots of money, a fat investment portfolio, IRAs, CDs, possessions coming out of our ears, and numerous properties. Yet have all these things increased our happiness? Our satisfaction? I don't think so.

Imagine with me for just a moment how it was to live sixty years ago in a rural setting in this country. You lived on a farm. You worked hard, slept hard and lived simply. Women stayed home and took care of the kids. Everyone in the family helped out with the farm and did chores. You had a big garden, and from the produce of that, you preserved vegetables and fruits. Your whole family worked together. You built fences, hunted and fished, made your own clothes, and spent most of your days as a family working and playing together.

I'm not saying these people did not have problems. They had a lot of challenges and difficulties. Yet they found satisfaction in simple things like a picnic, a ball game with the neighbors, a hoe-down dance, a game of croquet on the lawn, visits with their neighbors.

How long has it been since you found pleasure in taking a walk with your family? In playing a game of Monopoly with your kids? In singing around a campfire on a starry night?

"I don't have time," you might say. Are you too busy amassing money and possessions to stop and enjoy what you have with those you love? Stop for a moment. Reassess your life and begin to live more simply. You will be glad you did -- and so will your family!

July 8

Reason Not to Fear #190: Pride God Before A Fall

"The fear of the Lord is the instruction for wisdom, and before honor comes humility." Proverbs 15:33

Muhammed Ali, whose real name was Cassius Clay, fought Sonny Liston for the heavyweight championship. Even at the beginning of his career, Clay was a braggart, but it got worse as the years and victories went on. Before his 1971 fight with Joe Frazier, Muhammed Ali said, "There seems to be some confusion. We're gonna clear this confusion up on March 8th. We're gonna decide once and for all who is the king! There's not a man alive who can whup me. I'm too smart. I'm too pretty. I am the greatest. I am the king! I should be a postage stamp cause that's the only way I could get licked!" *Ali lost to Frazier!*

In another incident when Ali was in his prime, as he was about to take off on an airplane flight, the flight attendant reminded him to fasten his seat belt. He replied brashly, "Superman don't need no seat belt." The attendant replied, "Superman don't need no airplane, either." Ali fastened his belt.

This man needed to read this Scripture and others like it! Pride goes before a fall (Prov. 29:23). God resists the proud, but gives grace to the humble (James 5:5). We can't overstate this obvious truth, but so many times we miss it if we are not careful. Pride brings a downfall; humility gains the grace of God.

And there is something here beyond that -- humility and fear go together. Why is that? Because a truly humble person recognizes their need of God, His grace and His help. People who fear the Lord are humble people.

Would you describe yourself as someone who fears the Lord? A lack of fear of God indicates that you don't know Him very well. God is worthy of your fear, your respect, and your reverence. Contemplate the fact that God holds your next breath in His hand, that He is omnipotent, omnipresent and omniscient. Know Him. Fear Him and He will instruct you more and more, because fearing the Lord God is the beginning of wisdom.

It is the beginning of instruction. Think about it and apply it to your humbling circumstances today.

July 9

Reason Not to Fear #191: We Turn Away from Evil

"In mercy and truth atonement is provided for iniquity; and by the fear of the Lord one departs from evil." Proverbs 16:6

Love, kindness, mercy and truth paint a picture that stirs my soul. It is a Roman cross set up at the busy crossroads outside the ancient city of Jerusalem. There were three crosses there that day. Maybe a lot of folks just hurried by, urging their children not to look at the pathetic, naked forms that suffered there before they died.

Yet on one of the crosses, a man hung. While he did not seem unusual in any way, save for the fact that he still lived after several hours of torture, he still drew quite a crowd. It was the third hour. The sun suddenly became dark and an earthquake shook the earth.

There *was* something unusual about that central figure hanging there so humbly and pathetically. Just as He died, He cried out these words, the greatest three words in all human history. "It is finished!" Then he bowed his head and died.

You and I know that the figure on the cross that day was our Savior, Jesus Christ, the God/Man who came to die for our sins. Love, kindness, mercy and truth atoned for my iniquity that day. Jesus Christ not only died, but He rose from the dead three days later.

When we trust in Him, we fear the Lord. We ask God to forgive our sins and find His life flowing into our bodies. By the fear of the Lord we can keep away from evil.

No one talks about evil these days. What is evil?

It is to walk in disobedience to God. When evil comes on your large flat-screen TV, do you turn it off, or do you continue to listen and watch? Do you invite wicked people and evil situations into your living room? Do you *enjoy* bloodshed, murder, gore and mayhem? Do you *enjoy* seeing sexual acts displayed on your TV screen? I pray to God that you do not.

If you fear God, you will turn away from evil. God protects His people from evil if they trust in Him. But if they run after other gods, He will not help us. What gods are you running after today? Jesus died to save you from sin and evil. Don't allow them into your life.

Shut out the evil of this world and walk in purity today.

July 10

Reason Not to Fear #192: Evil Cannot Touch Our Souls

"The fear of the Lord leads to life, and he who has it will abide in satisfaction; he will not be visited with evil." Proverbs 19:23

Corrie ten Boom and her sister, Bessie, lived through some of the most horrendous times that can be imagined. Who would have thought that the German war machine, led by the demon possessed madman, Adolph Hitler and his minions, would conquer the Netherlands and bring horror to that land and other European countries? Who would have thought that a humble clockmaker, shopkeeper and Christian man and his family would be brave enough to hide Jews in their home and eventually be caught by the evil that spread like cancer?

They did what they could for the Jewish people who were being exterminated like rats. They opened their home and helped operate one link in an underground railroad that aided these people in escaping Holland. And they paid for it. Their father died in a prison when they were first taken. Corrie and Bessie were shipped by railroad in a cattle car to a prison camp. There, with thousands of others prisoners, they endured conditions that were like an unspeakable, horrible nightmare.

They who fear the Lord will sleep satisfied, untouched by evil. Were they untouched by this great evil that overtook their land? They were imprisoned, forced to perform hard labor, fed little, compelled to sleep in rat and lice infested buildings and treated like the scum of the earth.

How could you say that this verse was true for them? But it was.

Evil never touched their souls. They were able to rise above it, even in those surroundings and in those horrendous circumstances. It was the guards, prison leaders, army, and German rulers from Hitler on down that were in slavery and bondage to sin. Bessie died in that prison and was released to heaven. Corrie lived to tell her story and spread the message of God's love and faithfulness to His children in the deepest, darkest pit.

Where are you today? If you fear the Lord, this path will lead you to a life that is eternal and full of joy and purpose. It gets better as it goes along. Can you fall asleep feeling satisfied and peaceful? If not, your fear and trust may be placed somewhere besides God.

Ask God to show you where evil is touching your soul and mind. How is it making you like the world? Ask Him for forgiveness. Sweet dreams tonight!

July 11

Reason Not to Fear #193: We Are Bold in Speaking out Against Sin

"By humility and the fear of the LORD are riches and honor and life."
Proverbs 22:4

"Come out of the closet! Gay marriage is now legalized!" This cry echoes across our land. One of the problems with this statement is the word *gay*. There is nothing further from the truth than to label such a relationship, which is strictly forbidden by God in Scriptures, as gay.

This group of people, as well as all who rebel against God and His Word, exist in their own private hell, and they have ruined a perfectly good word!

The second problem with the above quote is that it combines *gay* with *marriage*. If we were to redefine the meaning of marriage to include homosexual people, then we have left behind the meaning of the word. Yet these people, who are not married and are not gay, are preaching from the rooftops that their choice in flaunting God's Word is the best way to live. I heard someone say recently that he could now marry his dog!

Consequently, there seems to be among many no genuine fear of the Lord.

How are we doing to proclaim the Good News of Jesus Christ to our generation? Today, we have to become bold, brash, and brave when it comes to sin. We explain it simply by saying, "This is the God's Word, like it or not."

Billy Sunday lived in the early 1900's. He boldly preached against all types of sin. He named wickedness, and after his sermon, people would often advise him to tone it down. They didn't him want offending so many people. Nonetheless, Billy Sunday continued to challenge people to fear the Lord. He did not walk on eggshells, nor did he sidestep any issues. He gave out the message of God in a fiery delivery.

This verse says that if we fear the Lord, we will benefit by it. Our lives will be better, we will be truly *gay* (*ie. happy and carefree*), and we will have the blessing of God on our lives.

Billy Sunday, D.L. Moody and Billy Graham and others have preached the Gospel boldly. They and many others have called people to live in fear of the Lord so they would live pure, humble, and authentic lives.

The fear of the Lord starts with you. Get on your knees and beg the Lord to refresh you in godly fear. Don't leave your knees until He does.

July 12

Reason Not to Fear #194: Look Up and Give God the Glory

"Do not let your heart envy sinners, but be zealous for the fear of the Lord all the day." Proverbs 23:17

Envy it is not a nice word. It has been labeled the "green-eyed monster." It is a topic that we do not like to talk about or admit we have. The Bible contains a lot of stories about envy. Cain envied his brother, Abel. Haman was envious of Mordecai. King Saul envied David. Jacob's son's envied their brother, Joseph. Envy has been around a long time.

As much as I hate to admit it, I have fallen into its trap. I have found myself envious of other writers and speakers, of women who have normal husbands. Envy has crept into my life when I've seen people living in bigger and better houses than mine and who can afford to take dream vacations with their whole family. My list could go on and on.

Envy is not worth the energy that we use to indulge in it, and it cancels out gratitude and kindness. Envy is a deadly, unseen disease. It can eat at your heart, decay your soul and sour everything that you touch.

Who hasn't been tempted to be envious of someone who has wealth, position, good looks, a great physical body, possessions and personality? Maybe you are tempted to be envious of someone who has been promoted while you have been left behind.

A wise man, James the Apostle, wrote, "What is the source of quarrels and conflicts among you? Is not the source your pleasures that wage war in your members? You lust and do not have; so you commit murder. You are envious and cannot obtain; so you fight and quarrel. You do not have because you do not ask." James. 4:1-2 Envy is a kind of lusting. It leads to quarrels, fights and conflicts in your home, in your family and with your friends.

How are you going to deal with this disease? Thankfully, there is a definitive answer. Jesus Christ died to save you from all kinds of sin. The verse for today says that we should not be envious, but we should fear the Lord.

Confess envy or jealousy you have in your heart toward your brother or sister. Instead of looking around and comparing yourself to one another, look up and give God praise and glory for all He has done in your life.

Live your life free from envy. Live your life in the fear of the Lord.

July 13

Reason Not to Fear #195: We Obey God

"My son, fear the Lord and the king; do not associate with those who are given to change, for their calamity will rise suddenly, and who knows the ruins those two can bring?" Proverbs 24:21-22

There have been many civil disobedience movements in human history; in fact, our nation is an example of civil disobedience. In that case, the leaders of the colonies and the people rose up against British rule. The Boston Tea Party was probably the highest act of civil disobedience anyone had ever seen. It sparked the Revolutionary War and the birth of our nation.

Is civil disobedience good or bad? In the proverbs quoted above, the wise man counsels his son not to rise up against the Lord or the king, for both (the king and the Lord) can bring ruin on people who rebel against them. In the general sense, this advice is true. Yet when the government is evil and goes against the Word of God, we are encouraged to fight against it. Daniel disobeyed the king's law and was thrown into the lion's den.

On March 12, 1930, Mohandas Gandhi, in India, began a defiant march to the sea in protest of the British monopoly on salt. Britain prohibited the Indians from collecting or selling salt, and the people were forced to buy it from the British who exerted heavy taxes on it. Gandhi led a peaceful group of people across the country to the coastal town of Dandi on the Arabian Sea.

By the time they reached the town, the crowd had grown to tens of thousands. Even though the British police arrested them, beat them, and tried to keep them from the beach, Gandhi reached down and picked up a piece of raw salt. This led to the formation in 1947 of the independent nation of India.

We have to be careful when we participate in acts of civil disobedience. Fear God first. Give Him your allegiance, loyalty and service. Then live in obedience to the governing officials over you (Romans 13:1-7) and to the law of the land. God has put these people in authority over you for your safety, your peace, and your security.

By being obedient to the laws, you show your fear of the governing powers over you and also of your fear of God. Above all, obey God. If the government goes against God's Word, don't fear man, but fear God. Have courage and do what you can to change your society.

If Daniel could do it, so can you.

July 14

Reason Not to Fear #196: God Is Bigger Than People

"The fear of the man brings a snare, but whoever trusts in the Lord shall be safe." Proverbs 29:25

King Saul was afraid. He and the Israeli army had been facing the Philistines across the Elah valley for several days. When a champion of the Philistines came out and challenged the Israelites to single combat, the king's fear increased. He didn't want to fight the giant, and had no one in his army who was willing to fight him either. Then David came along. While Saul was afraid of a man, David wasn't. David feared God. God gave the victory to this young shepherd boy who trusted in Him.

What we call peer pressure, people-pleasing, or co-dependency is what the Bible calls the *fear of man*. In a nutshell, the fear of man can either be a fear of what others think of us or what they will do to us. It means that we crave approval from others and fear their rejection. This kind of fear indicates that we are thinking about ourselves and about the people around us, rather than about God. We want to please people more than we want to please God.

Here are eight consequences of fearing man. **1) Idolatry--** you make an idol of people. **2) Ineffective service--** your service is tainted by your self-absorption and desire to please. **3) Lack of love--** your love dims as you strive to please others and cannot do it. **4) Insincerity--** you will say and do what you think others want. **5) Apathy--** you stop trying and stop caring because you can't please everyone. **6) Dishonesty--** you will always say what you think others want to hear instead of the truth in love. **7) Isolation and Micro-Managing--** you cannot delegate jobs because people might do it wrong and this would be a reflection on you. **8) Inability to make decisions--** you might make the wrong one and displease someone.

The most radical solution for the fear of man is the fear of the Lord. God must be bigger to you than people are. The task God sets for us is to *need them less and love them more*. If you have been caught in the trap of fearing man, stop and examine your heart today.

Confess your sin of idolatry and co-dependency and turn to God. Seek to please Him alone. Then see how much this frees you to love, to serve and to enjoy others around you!

July 15

Reason Not to Fear #197: Submit to the Authority of God

"I know that whatever God does, it shall be forever. Nothing can be added to it, and nothing taken from it. God does it, that men should fear before Him."
Ecclesiastes 3:14

Here is an insightful commentary on this verse by Matthew Henry: "Everything is as God made it; not as it appears to us. We have the world so much in our hearts, are so taken up with thoughts and cares of worldly things, that we have neither time nor spirit to see God's hand in them. The world has not only gained possession of the heart, but has formed thoughts against the beauty of God's works." *Matthew Henry Concise Commentary*

People want a benign deity who makes no demands on their lives, their time, or their affections. They want a god who will pat them on the back, always give them good and provide them with every comfort and pleasure they desire. They ask Christians, "If God is good, why does He allow bad things to happen?"

This question shows where their hearts are. They do not want to recognize sin or the consequences of sin. They do not want to be punished if they disobey God's laws. They don't want to take responsibility for their wrong-doing, and they don't want a God who allows evil in the world, never thinking that it was humans who made the decision to turn away from God.

God has provided an answer to sin and evil, to disease, sickness and death. The answer is the cross of Christ. On the cross, Jesus paid for the sins of all mankind, if only they will turn to Him, repent of their wickedness, and follow Him. Whatever God does is final. His transactions are unchangeable and far above human control. All of God's counsels and decrees are eternal and fixed. Humans can do nothing to hinder His providence. In view of His supremacy, He should be feared. As you consider His sovereignty, you should learn to trust, submit, and fear Him.

The unchangeableness of God is designed to lead you to reverence and fear Him. Whatever God creates is a means of pressing into you a sense of His greatness, and when that truth dawns, God will receive the fear and reverence that is rightly His.

Your responsibility and duty today is to acknowledge Jesus Christ as Lord of your life and submit to His authority as you fear Him.

July 16

Reason Not to Fear #198: Love God, Love Others

"For in the multitude of dreams and many words there is also vanity. But fear God." Ecclesiastes 5:7

In Paul's letter to the Corinthian church, he addresses the topic of spiritual gifts in chapters 12-14. Sandwiched between two practical doctrinal passages on these *sign gifts* and their function in the church, we find the great chapter on God's love, chapter 13. This, Paul says, is the greatest gift. Love is what we should aspire to, strive for, focus on, and practice until our very last breath.

Instead of focusing on gifts that might puff us up in pride, Paul instructs us to love one another. "If there are gifts of prophecy, they will be done away; if there are tongues, they will cease; it there is knowledge, it will be done away... but now faith, hope and love abide, these three, but the greatest of these is love." I Corinthians 13:8, 13

Visions, gifts of prophecy and knowledge and speaking in tongues are showy gifts that mean little when it comes to the real issues of life and death, salvation and growth as a Christian. Talk is cheap, like daydreams and other useless activities. The New Living Translation reads, "Fear God instead."

The Preacher (Solomon) experienced it all. He had time, money, desire, intellect, and everything he desired. He had done it all and seen it all and came up with this conclusion: *it is all emptiness.* The only thing of value is to fear God.

What did he mean by this? Fear God means to trust Him, obey Him, give Him your total life. Acknowledge Him and He will direct your paths. Serve Him with all your heart. Don't go after other gods. Don't love the world.

How is your life before God? By that I mean, have you made a commitment to do something, but you haven't fulfilled it? God is eager to see you deliver on your words. He waits for you to fulfill what you spoke.

In our society, words are not always considered important or binding. Just consider the vows of matrimony. Did you really mean them, or were they words only of convenience? God is paying attention to what you say. Don't be a cheap talker. Your word is all you have, so keep it.

Love God. Love others.

July 17

Reason Not to Fear #199: All Is Emptiness Without God

"Though a sinner does evil a hundred times, and his days are prolonged, yet I surely know that it will be well with those who fear God, who fear before Him. But it will not be well with the wicked; nor will he prolong his days, which are as a shadow, because he does not fear before God." Ecclesiastes 8:12, 13

Hitler was an Austrian-born German politician who lived from 1889 to 1945. He became the leader of the Nazi Party and was chancellor of Germany from 1933 to the end of his life. He became dictator of Germany in 1934. This man became known as the wickedest person who ever lived.

He prospered for a time and conquered most of Europe, killing off those who opposed him. He also killed a large percentage of the Jewish population, proclaiming he was the Messiah and his reign would be the Third Reich. Yet his star of ascendancy did not last very long.

He thought he was prolonging the days of his life, but he was only 56 years old when he and his wife committed suicide. His kingdom, admirers, prison camps, armies, plans for the perfect race and the extermination of the Jews all lay in a smoldering heap somewhere in Germany. It did not go well for Hitler, nor will it go well for any other wicked person who raises themselves up to rebel against God and His Word.

Some may praise, admire, and applaud them, but this does not last long, and the reason is because the wicked do not fear the living God.

If you want life to go well with you, I strongly suggest you give God your reverence. Do not be insincere about your faith and worship. Worship is meaningless and an offense to God if we do not live what we talk. Live in the fear of God.

Personally, when I am just going through the motions of my faith, or when I am just pretending to obey God, things are out of sync in my life. My values get mixed up, and I find myself seeking self-gratifying pleasures. I am relying on my human efforts to achieve my happiness. It's all hollow and empty, just like the writer of Ecclesiastes said. Remember your life will only be of high quality if you reverently fear the Lord from your heart.

Do that today. Give Him glory, thanks and praise. You will benefit, and so will others around you.

July 18

Reason Not to Fear #200: The Only Reality Is to Fear God

"Let us hear the conclusion of the whole matter: Fear God and keep His commandments, for this is man's all." Ecclesiastes 12:13

If you were to read the whole book of Ecclesiastes, written by Solomon at the end of his life, you would discover his quest for the meaning of life. As a man who had riches and power, he tried everything: knowledge, passions and lusts of the flesh, pleasure, materialism, riches, power, and even religion. His conclusion at the end of it all?

Vanity, vanity, all is vanity. Everything under the sun was meaningless, a shadow, a wisp of smoke that evaporated even as he reached out and took it in his sweaty grasp. Once he is dead, every achievement a man makes in his life is gone. Even great riches stink like rotten food because his children fight over the money, and it is soon gone because they squander it.

In a short time, even the most godly and wise person is forgotten. Death takes us all and soon we are forgotten, lying cold under the soil, our corpses rotting away just like all the things we have attained.

Thankfully, the king comes at last to his great conclusive statement: *the only reality in life is to fear God and keep His commandments.* And this, he says, applies to every person. God brings all things to judgment, so every deed of our lives, every thought and every word takes on meaning because God judges the good from the evil and rewards us according to them.

When we come to Christ and ask Him to forgive us for our sins, His blood takes our sins away. We never have to stand in judgment for them again. Yet even Christians are judged for their deeds and actions in this life. Take a look at II Corinthians 5:10-13 and I Corinthians 3:10-15.

In the final analysis of life under the sun, we must take God into account. Without Him, we are like sticks drifting on a muddy river. This is not how a person who fears God looks at his life. We believe that every word, thought, action and deed in this life has meaning and purpose to forward God's kingdom on earth.

With that hope, with that purpose driving us on, we can live our lives in the assurance that God loves us, that He is in control and that He will take us home when our job here on earth is finished. With that assurance, we can confidently serve Him today.

July 19

Reason Not to Fear #201: God Will Judge Your Pride

"Enter into the rock and hide in the dust from the terror of the Lord and the glory of His majesty. The lofty looks of man shall be humbled, the haughtiness of men shall be bowed down, and the LORD alone shall be exalted in that day."
Isaiah 2:10, 11

The word **terror** used in verses 10, 19 and 21 of chapter 2 is *pachad*, which means *fear, dread, greatly (fear), dreadful.* It is different than the word we usually use when we read the *fear of the Lord.* It is exactly what it means: terror.

Have you ever experienced abject terror and dread? We all have had times when we thought something horrible was going to happen and it turned out to be a false alarm. We felt a little silly for becoming so frightened.

In the instance of our Bible passage, though, the terror that the Lord brings to people is real. Isaiah warned his people of Judah to turn from their wicked ways and return to their God, Jehovah. If you read the first part of this chapter, you would see many of the sins they were committing.

Isaiah begins by saying, "Come, house of Jacob, and let us walk in the light of the Lord," v. 5. The people were involved in sorceries and witchcraft. They made treaties and pacts with other nations instead of trusting in the Lord; they trusted in their hoarded silver and gold, horses and chariots (armies), idols and the things their hands had made.

If this doesn't sound like America in this age, you haven't been paying much attention!

"Enter the rock and hide in the dust," God counsels His people. They must run and hide from the anger of the Lord as He comes to discipline them in His anger.

How much pride do you have? You may think you are doing pretty well in that department, but consider how much you hate to ask for help when you need it and how few people you ask for prayer when you need it. Consider how much you love to show off your possessions, knowledge, career advancements, or connections.

We all have pride. I pray that you will not go down that path so much that God will need to discipline you. Hide in the Rock, Christ Jesus. Only He can forgive you and set your feet on the solid Rock. Come to Him today.

July 20

Reason Not to Fear #202: You Cannot Hide from God

"They shall go into the holes of the rocks, and into the caves of the earth, from the terror of the LORD and the glory of His majesty, when He arises to shake the earth mightily." Isaiah 2:19

Where would you go to run from the Lord? Adam and Eve hid behind some trees and made aprons for themselves from leaves. Hagar hid beside a stream. Lot and his daughters hid in caves. Jacob ran to Paddan-aram and hid by the river Jabbok. Jonah hid in a ship bound for Tarshish. Elijah hid on a mountaintop.

People hide from God when they are face to face with the splendor of His majesty and the terror of His righteous anger. In Revelation 6, we find the same thing. During the Great Tribulation, men will hide from the face of God. "Then the kings of the earth, and the great men and the commanders and the rich and the strong and every slave and free man hid themselves in the caves and among the rocks of the mountains; and they said to the mountains and to the rocks, Fall on us and hide us from the presence of Him who sits on the throne, and from the wrath of the Lamb, for the great day of their wrath has come, and who is able to stand?" Revelation 6:15, 16

What astounds me in these verses is that the people of that day knew God. They knew the judgments came from Him, they knew of the Lamb and they were so terrified they ran and hid in the caves of the mountains. Yet they would not bow their knees in obedience and faith to this God of all the earth! Even these great and awesome troubles that will fall on the earth during this coming judgment against sin did not break their hearts!

They are afraid, they are terrified, yet they are not repentant.

What does it take to bring you to your knees, to acknowledge God in every aspect of your life, to set aside your idols of football, TV shows, electronics, golf, buying and selling? What does it take to cause you to turn back to God?

Righteous people who love God will applaud His justice and righteousness when He comes to judge the sin of the people of this earth. Will you? When He arises to make the earth tremble, which side will you be on? I hope you are trusting in Christ, walking in obedience to Him, and watching for His appearing.

Get on your knees and praise Him today for the splendor of His majesty!

July 21

Reason Not to Fear #203: God Is Our Delight

"To go into the clefts of the rocks, And into the crags of the rugged rocks, From the terror of the LORD And the glory of His majesty, When He arises to shake the earth mightily." Isaiah 2:21

What words do you like to use when you describe God? What words do you like to hear that describe God? I like the words *majestic, awesome, holy, wise*, and *great*. I also like the phrase that is often found in the book of Isaiah, *the splendor of His majesty,* which is repeated several times. I think that phrase would make a wonderful book title.

When is the last time you heard some use the word *splendid*? It means something that is magnificent, impressive, excellent, and good. The synonyms are: gorgeous, magnificent, superb, grand, glorious. We don't use that descriptive word very often. My children would describe it as old fashioned.

My daughter and her family are missionaries in Indonesia. During their eleven months that they were home on furlough, many vacations were enjoyed by all of our family. My grandchildren particularly took pleasure in finally going to Disneyland in Florida. Several days were spent in that area doing what tourists enjoy. If you would ask my grandchildren what they thought of their time in Florida, I am sure the word "splendid" would be appropriate.

That word might mean something different to you. Maybe it is an excellent piece of chocolate. Maybe it is just the right pair of shoes to match your outfit. Maybe it is that Mustang you've always wanted to buy. Maybe it is a vacation in Hawaii.

But if you are a person living in disobedience and sin, separated from God and on the run from Him, like Jonah was, He is not splendid to you. You are always looking over your shoulder to see if He is going to "get" you. You hear the nagging voice of conscience in your heart and head urging you to get right with God. You get convicted when you sit and listen to a sermon, and so, of course, you don't go to church much.

But if you are in a right relationship to God through His Son Jesus Christ, He is splendid to you. He is a delight. You love to read His Word, pray and talk to Him, talk about Him, and fellowship with other Christians.

What an amazing thought that God would share some of His splendor with His people!

July 22

Reason Not to Fear #204: Stay Refreshed in Your Soul

"And say to him, 'Take heed and be quiet, do not fear or be fainthearted for these two stubs of smoking firebrands, for the fierce anger of Rezin and Syria and the son of Remaliah.'" Isaiah 7:4

I am exhausted, fatigued, worn out today. Ever have one of those kinds of mornings? Before the day even began, I was pooped. Most of us have encountered exhaustion. However, there is a weariness of heart that can go so deep that it puts your spiritual life in danger. There is a tiredness that can overtake us that affects our very souls.

The prophet Isaiah had an important message to convey to King Ahaz. He wanted to let Ahaz know that God did not want him to give into the pressure two other kings were putting on him to join them in an alliance in rebellion against Assyria. Isaiah met with Ahaz privately and told him God's message. Yet Ahaz was not prepared to receive it. Maybe he was exhausted. Maybe he was tired of hearing Isaiah's sermons. Maybe he just wanted a few moments to himself. Yet because he didn't trust Isaiah, or God, he became fearful.

Isaiah encouraged the king to pray, to ask God for a sign to show him what God could do for the nation of Israel. But Ahaz refused. Why would he not pray? Assyria was threatening his nation and things were looking bad. Yet because of his unbelief, he refused to believe God. He trusted in himself and his own wisdom, might, and wealth to find the way out of his difficulty. He just could not bring himself to let God handle the armies that were coming against him. He couldn't let go and let God control the outcome.

Exhaustion can cause an abnormal fear to grow in you.

Thirteen years ago, when I started this unexpected role of care-giver to my husband, one of the many doctors who helped us through the years, sat me down and looked me in the eyes. He said, "Don't become exhausted, Chris, in this new journey of yours. Don't become emotionally or physically depleted. Pace yourself. It is going to be a long journey." How I have valued his advice through the years.

Do not become used up, washed up, or beat up. Stay refreshed in the Lord and trust in Him with all your heart, soul and mind. He will give you the strength to face another day.

July 23

Reason Not to Fear #205: God Is Our Sanctuary

""Do not say, 'A conspiracy,' Concerning all that this people call a conspiracy, Nor be afraid of their threats, nor be troubled. [13] The LORD of hosts, Him you shall hallow; Let Him be your fear, And let Him be your dread." Isaiah 8:12, 13

Isaiah lived and preached in a dangerous, treacherous time in the history of his nation, much like we do today. His job was not an easy one. He was commissioned by God to preach and prophecy until no one listened to him, until their hearts had become so hard that God hardened them further and finally gave up on them. Wow. That is not a job I'd like to have!

Isaiah is preaching publicly to the nation, probably standing at one of the gates (main thoroughfares into the city). He's brought his little son, Maher-shalal-hash-baz along with him. Every time the people saw this little boy, they were reminded of the message inherent in his name: *swift is the booty, speedy is the prey.* If the nation did not turn back to God, they would very quickly be plundered, sacked and destroyed by an invading army.

But they would not listen to Isaiah. In fact, they mocked him and his small group of disciples and followers, saying they were seditious and were spreading traitorous lies among the people, and that they were conspiring against the king and the nation. Why did they say this? Because Isaiah said over and over again that the king and nation should not enter into an alliance with the Assyrians, which they thought would protect them from harm. It was like joining with the big bully down the street so he wouldn't beat up on you every night.

No! Isaiah shouted until his throat was sore. *Trust only in Jehovah and He will protect you! Don't call it a conspiracy!* And to his followers he said, "Do not fear what they fear or be in dread of what they dread. Fear only the Lord and He will become a sanctuary to you."

How about you today? What do you fear? Do you see financial loss coming down the pike in your direction? Was the result of your tests and the doctor's prognosis poor concerning your health? Are you afraid of where this great nation of America is headed?

Isaiah's message rings down the centuries to us today. *Fear God alone and put your trust in Him.* He is able to save; He is still on the throne. Have faith in Him. Do it today and set your other fears aside.

July 24

Reason Not to Fear #206: We Cast All Our Worry on God

"Therefore thus says the Lord GOD of hosts, O My people who dwell in Zion, do not be afraid of the Assyrian. He shall strike you with the rod and lift up his staff against you in the manner of Egypt." Isaiah 10:24

I have a friend who is Syrian. She lives in Chicago, and since we are both from ethnic backgrounds, we have a lot in common. We have been friends for over forty years. She has said that her people have a long history of being very brutal and causing a lot of fear in their enemies. Today we see the king of that nation committing genocide against his own people!

It is easy to understand why the people of Isaiah's day would be afraid of the Assyrians. Their favorite pursuits were war, conquering other nations, and subjugating them. Their armies were strong and ruthless. We are told they burned cities, raped women, killed the unborn and children, and beheaded people. They would then bring their own men into the country to mate with the women to produce half-breeds whose loyalty would be to their own nation.

In verse 24 of this passage, Isaiah (as God's mouthpiece) said, "Don't be afraid of the Assyrians anymore." In other words, he was saying don't be intimidated by them any longer. For such a long time the Assyrians were a problem for the children of Israel. Isaiah is now saying that no matter what you may face it is only temporary. If you were to read the rest of the chapter, you would see how complete God's judgment was on the nation of Assyria.

I may not understand your problems, but Jesus does. Whatever problems you face, they are only temporary. Difficult times are temporary; they can be changed. The "Assyrians" in your life will not be there forever. And just like God delivered the Israelites from their power of the Assyrians, He can do the same for you.

What is troubling you today? What fears do you face? Is it a doctor's appointment, a work day that you fear will be horrendous, a confrontation with your teenager, your parents, your spouse? Whatever it is, God can deliver you wholly from the fear of your problems.

What He said to the ancient Israeli people, He says to you. "Casting all your anxiety on Him, because He cares for you." I Peter 5:7. Though this problem may attack you every day, though it invades your life, it can no longer control your emotions if you turn it over to God.

July 25

Reason Not to Fear #207: The Water of Life Is Available to All

"Behold, God is my salvation, I will trust and not be afraid; for YAH, the LORD, is my strength and song; He also has become my salvation. Therefore with joy you will draw water from the wells of salvation." Isaiah 12:2, 3

How much fear is in your heart concerning the future? What exactly do you fear? Look at these issues squarely in the face. Write them down. The reason I am asking you to do this is because you lose your joy in direct proportion to the fears you harbor in your heart. Many of these issues involve control. If you feel you are losing control, your natural response is to be afraid.

In this portion of Scripture, Isaiah is looking forward to the day when God will turn from His judgment of His people for their sin and restore them to a right relationship with Himself. The prophet writes this song and it is for the Millennium, the 1,000 year reign of Christ on the earth when Israel will again enjoy all the blessings of God from Mt. Zion.

Since the death of my son-in-law, I have some new fears when it comes to the future of my daughter and her children. Who will my daughter, Nicky, grow old with? Who will be the father image these children desperately need? Will Nicky stay a widow all her life? How long will I be able to help her and the children?

Fear can take over my thoughts in an instant, and I find myself slipping into its clutches. Fear is not my friend. It brings doubts into my mind. It makes me question God. How much better it is to "trust and not be afraid."

In this song, Isaiah consoles the people by saying that the Lord God of Israel is their salvation both spiritually and physically, and they should not be afraid. He is like a well of water, a spring that erupts from dry ground and brings life, joy, peace and laughter to all who drink of it.

Have you come to that well of water? Does His Spirit bring that refreshment, hope and joy to your heart amidst your trial and troubles? Can you drink of it today and find His salvation, His comfort, His presence with you? O my dear friend, it is there, waiting for you.

Lift up your eyes and come to Jesus for all that troubles you. He loves you. He cares for you. He wants you to give Him your burdens today.

July 26

Reason Not to Fear #208: We Put Aside Our False Gods

"And the land of Judah will be a terror to Egypt; everyone who makes mention of it will be afraid in himself, because of the counsel of the LORD of hosts which He has determined against it." Isaiah 19:17

In this prophecy against Egypt, God is declaring His intention to strike the Egyptians with civil war (19:2), confusion and demoralization (v. 3), and slavery to another nation (v. 4), dry up the waters of the Nile (v. 5), which would lead to famine (v. 8), which would then lead to the fall of the economy, (v. 8-10) and the demise of the nation.

Why? Why would God come against the Egyptians in such a ferocious manner?

Verse one mentions the idols and false gods of the Egyptians. Even though they knew the truth, they refused to believe in Yahweh God and turn to Him. They had a spirit of pride, rebellion and disobedience to God and His Word. "In that day," from verse 16, indicates a future time even than when Isaiah was prophesying, a time during the Kingdom Age of Christ's reign here on earth.

We are told that Egypt will acknowledge the Lord in those days and come to Him with tribute in their hands. A great highway will be built from Egypt to Jerusalem to accommodate all those who want to go to Jerusalem to worship the king, Christ Jesus.

The Jews often went to Egypt for help when they should have trusted in the Lord. Egypt was always a place of disobedience and stepping out of the will of the Lord for them. It was a place of slavery, degradation and idol worship. Jeremiah was taken to Egypt in his old age after the Babylonians conquered Judah. There he witnessed the people (the women) baking cakes to the "Queen of Heaven," Ishtar, a filthy goddess of the Assyrians and Babylonians. He prophesied against this practice and eventually died in that land.

The Bible tells us that we can find help only from God Almighty, the Holy One of Israel, and Jesus Christ, His Son. What are you relying on today to get you through your difficult situations? Turn to God and trust in Christ alone.

He will give you wisdom, peace, joy and love for each day as you serve Him.

July 27

Reason Not to Fear #209: We Get A New Perspective on Our Problems

"Therefore the strong people will glorify You; the city of terrible nations will fear You. For You have been a strength to the poor, a strength to the needy in his distress, a refuge from the storm, a shade from the heat, for the blast of the terrible o nes is as a storm against the wall." Isaiah 25:3, 4

During a time of stress or distress, it is always a good idea to get the right perspective on your situation. Stuart Hamblen wrote his famous song, *Until Then*, after attending a funeral of a friend. He wrote, "The things of earth will dim and lose their value when we recall they're borrowed for a while. And things of earth that cause our hearts to tremble, remembered there will only bring a smile. But until then, my heart will go on singing. Until then, with joy I'll carry on. Until the day my eyes behold the city, until the day, God calls me home."

While predicting judgment and doom to the nation of Judah, Isaiah saw down the long centuries to a time when God was going to restore the nation to the land again and bring about the Kingdom of Jesus Christ to this earth. During this future time, he says that the nations of the earth will fear and honor the Israelites and come trembling before the King to bring offerings and tribute to the capitol, the center of the world, Jerusalem. What a day that will be!

What about the right perspective for the problems you are facing today? What hope does God give you to face each challenge and endure so many trials as you seek to serve Him and honor Him? Think about the positive things God has in store for you beyond this life.

Read Romans 8:28-22 right now.

If you are a believer, the glorious future that God has for you should so grip your soul and thrill your heart that you can face whatever this life throws at you with joy and confidence. He has purchased us, redeemed us, set us free from sin and Satan, brought us into the Kingdom of His dear Son, set our feet on the right path, and given us a wonderful hope of a future with Him forever.

If that doesn't set your heart singing, I don't know what will!

July 28

Reason Not to Fear #210: The Lord Is My Helper

"Fear not, for I am with you; Be not dismayed, for I am your God. I will strengthen you, Yes, I will help you, I will uphold you with My righteous right hand." Isaiah 41:10

Yesterday I taught on Matthew 19. This chapter contains some verses about divorce, which is an uncomfortable subject. After I taught, I went to lunch with one of the women in the class. She brought up the topic of divorce. On my hour and half drive home, I thought about divorce. The topic consumed me until I walked into my house and discovered the toilet had overflowed and was still running over! Water was everywhere and my husband was sitting in his chair, oblivious to it all.

Later that evening, when I was putting two of my grandchildren to bed, the conversation turned to how much they missed their father, James. Within moments, I gathered them into my arms as they sobbed. I tried to comfort them. We admitted we missed James and needed him. My heart ached for these young children.

When I thought about divorce, when the toilet overflowed, when I had to comfort my grandchildren, I felt alone and helpless. I needed someone to comfort *me* in their strong arms. I wanted someone to turn to and ask how do you handle life? But there is no one to turn to.

Or was there? That day I got on my knees and cried out to the Lord for guidance and strength. Through my tears, I begged Him to rescue me from wallowing in self-pity. How kind the Lord is to hear and answer me. His righteous right hand enveloped and sustained me.

For the people of Judah, Isaiah's message was one of comfort and encouragement. God was looking forward to the time when they would return from bondage in Babylon and reestablish their nation, their faith and their lives. They were few in number and living in unwalled villages. They struggled to maintain their identity in a hostile world. God said to them, "Do not fear, for I am with you." He will never leave you or forsake you. (Hebrews 13:5,6)

Claim this verse as your own. Look to the Lord for the help He has promised, and He will do it. Fear not!

July 29

Reason Not to Fear #211: We Faint Not, Fear Not and Forget Not

"'For I, the LORD your God, will hold your right hand, saying to you, 'Fear not, I will help you.'" Isaiah 41:13

No one needs to tell you that life is tough. The Lord did not promise us an easy passage through life -- we all know that, too. What someone might need to remind you is that God has some wonderful promises in His Word that will encourage you when you are ready to throw in the towel.

Today, I am a bit low because I am weary of taking care of my husband. One of my friends informed me of her upcoming vacation with her husband to Georgia, something that was on her bucket list. I came home a bit discouraged, because I have a bucket list, too, but I know none of the things on it will get fulfilled. I would love to enjoy a vacation with my husband, but that is not going to happen. So, here I am, discouraged.

Yet regardless of how tough life may get for any of us, or how bleak the future may seem, I am not ready to give up. God's message to us today is: don't throw in the towel.

In Israel's darkest days the Lord told them three things.

#1-Faint Not, Isa. 40, for He is the Almighty God, the creator of the universe, the One who rules the nations with His hand. He is the One who gives you strength, courage and wisdom.

#2-Fear Not, Isa. 41, for He is able to keep His promises concerning you. He is with you and will not forsake you. He is strong and mighty to save. He is greater than any false god or any of the idols people worship today.

#3-Forget Not, Isa. 42, for He has sent His Servant, the very Son of God, to meet your need of salvation from sin. This Servant was so meek and tender, He did not bruise a smoking reed or extinguish the dimly burning wick of a candle. He will be your Light, your praise, your new song. My plan for you, He says, is one of deliverance, joy and rejoicing.

God will uphold your right hand when it falters. He will give you light for your way, courage for the day and strength enough to help you stay the course. I challenge you to read the three chapters above and write down all the encouraging promises you find in them. I assure you, you will not be cast down when you finish.

Even if you have an incomplete bucket list!

July 30

Reason Not to Fear #212: We Surrender Our Lives to God

"'Fear not, you worm Jacob, You men of Israel! I will help you,' says the LORD and your Redeemer, the Holy One of Israel." Isaiah 41:14

This message was given to the nation of Judah long before it was overcome with the Babylonian army. God was looking down the long road, past the destruction and judgment He was planning for His people, to the day when He would comfort them, restore them and bring them back to Himself. As the weary Israelites returned to their land after Cyrus the Persian king released them in 538 BC, they probably recalled these words of Isaiah. This was an encouragement to their hearts in a difficult time.

Israel is called a worm in this passage because she was despised, feeble and stepped on by the nations of the world. Yet God had great plans for Israel, plans that reach beyond our own day and time. The partial fulfillment of this prophecy occurred during the time of Ezra, Zerubbabel, and Nehemiah. These men led their people back to the land and rebuilt the city, the temple and the nation.

The complete fulfillment of this prophecy will occur much later, during the time immediately following Christ's second return to the earth to set up His kingdom. "I will help you," God declares, "for I am your Redeemer." No longer will the people and the kings look to foreign countries for help. No longer will they pray to strange, false gods, the idols of the nations around them. No longer will they put their hope and assurance in their own abilities, machinations, strength or power. They were cured of all that when they suffered for seventy years as captives in Assyria and Babylon.

What does it take for you to give up and surrender to God? Pride is the major reason most people do not want to believe in God or accept Him as their Redeemer and Savior. Jesus, God's Son, died on the cross to save us from our sin, revealing God's love for us. Yet people today shake their fists in His face and claim He is unjust, cruel and powerless to save.

God holds out His arms to us and wants to comfort us. He is our Redeemer. Come to Him. Come *back* to Him. Turn your whole life over to Him today.

You will find salvation, joy, hope and peace.

July 31

Reason Not to Fear #213: He Is With Me Every Moment

"Fear not, for I am with you; I will bring your descendants from the east, and gather you from the west." Isaiah 43:5

Have you noticed the headlines of the news these days? They are not comforting. The magnitude of this loss is almost overwhelming and it causes many people to fear. There are scandals, a bomb explosion in Afghanistan that killed ten girls, people calling for gun control laws, war escalating in Syria, Egypt in disarray, riots in many countries and financial ruin for major companies. It all adds up to a world on the brink of total disaster.

And you say that we should not be afraid? Not to fear? Hello. I am a real person, living in precarious times. The world I live in is a far cry from the world my grandmother and mother grew up in.

Catastrophic changes have taken place. I am not sure my grandmother would even recognize this world. And yet, with all of these modern changes, there is not one person who does not experience fear at various times in their lives.

Many people fear what is in the future for the United States. Others fear what lies ahead for the whole world. We might as well be real and confess that even though we are born again children of God, we still have fears!

Your fear concerning unsettling issues should cause you to grab tighter to the Lord. When anxiety attacks, when your calm is disturbed, remember the Lord's words: *I am with you.* This is not an illusion, it is a fact.

We will never be exempt from pain, suffering or trouble. Fear will haunt our very souls until the day we die. Yet if we fear the Lord above all other things, we can live in peace despite the morning news reports. You are God's child and that means you are not alone.

Whatever uncertainty may darken your day, you do not have to face them alone. Your wise and loving Father is with you. Take comfort in that, then go out and serve Him with joy.

August 1

Reason Not to Fear #214: We Allow God to Comfort Us

"Thus says the Lord who made you and formed you from the womb, who will help you, 'Fear not, O Jacob, My servant; and you Jeshurun, whom I have chosen.'" Isaiah 44:2

Did you know that God formed you in your mother's womb? That He loves you with the tender love of a mother for her child? That He wants you to be happy, fulfilled, and close to Him? I challenge you to read Psalm 139 in connection with our devotional today and write down how much the Lord God loves you and has demonstrated that love to you. He calls His people *Jeshurun*, meaning "upright one", an affectionate name God gave them.

Yet we often face troubling circumstances that cause us to fear.

When my first grandson was born, it was a very happy day. However, within a few weeks, we learned that Tyler, who was six weeks old, needed open heart surgery. My son and his wife were thrust into making major decisions. The surgery was performed, but not without some complications. In fact, Tyler would need several more surgeries. Just four years ago, Tyler had another open heart surgery, and he seems to be doing much better.

How does a person react when you hear the doctor say, "your child needs open heart surgery immediately?" When my son called me, he was crying, and so was his wife. I am so thankful that they know the Lord and have been able to turn to Him all along this journey with Tyler. In a quiet, positive manner, they have lived out their faith in front of doctors, nurses, therapists, and other patients in the hospital.

Some of the trials that come upon us are ordained by God to strengthen our faith. Some trials are allowed to discipline us and bring us to renewal of our faith and cleansing from sin. Some we experience so we can glorify God and be a testimony to others through our pain.

Yet there are times when we bring our sorrows upon ourselves. When we drift from God and fall into sin, we experience doubt, fear, worry, and torment. God did not plan this for us. God gently woos us back to Himself with words of comfort and love.

If you are facing difficulties today, reach out to God and allow Him to comfort you. Do not fear. Do not become bitter. Trust God and seek ways to glorify Him.

August 2

Reason Not to Fear #215: There Is No Other God but Jehovah

"Do not fear, nor be afraid; have I not told you from that time, and declared it? You are My witnesses. Is there a God besides Me? Indeed there is no other Rock; I know not one." Isaiah 44:8

Have you watched these television shows: American Idol, Dancing With the Stars, or America's Got Talent? Millions of people watch these shows and others like them faithfully every week, and then they vote and the winner is announced. The winner becomes the new American Idol and some of them go on to become very famous.

But what kind of people are they? Should we worship these people? The obvious answer is *no*, yet many do. We worship Hollywood movie and TV stars, we worship those who excel in sports and make heroes and idols out of them. We worship those in the music industry.

Idol is a strong word. In the Bible, idols were absolutely forbidden. So was the construction of any image. The reason for this was that those who have idols would worship them rather than the Lord Almighty. Israel's calling, and yours, is to worship the one true God always.

This verse in Isaiah makes it clear that there is only one Holy One to be worshipped. All other forms and types of worship are empty, and they will fill your life with emptiness if you chase after them.

Now, I am sure you do not have a carved image of Baal on your fireplace mantle, or an Asherah pole in your backyard, but you may have other types of idols. What is it that draws you away from God and the worship of God? What do you spend your time, money and affections on? It may be pleasure or the accumulation of money and possessions. It may be family, food, clothes, movies, sports. If these things are above God in your life, they are your idols.

When you participate in things that are dearer to you than the Lord, then an unhealthy fear begins to reside in you. Slowly the idols of materialism, love of leisure and pleasure, and worship of yourself grows. What is the object of your affections today?

Pray about it and read the verse again. Is there any other Rock than Christ Jesus? Renounce false gods and begin to worship Him alone sincerely from your heart. Give Him priority; give Him honor; give Him your life.

August 3

Reason Not to Fear #216: Putting God First Means We Fear Him

"Surely all his companions would be ashamed; and the workmen, they are mere men. Let them all be gathered together, Let them stand up; yet they shall fear, they shall be ashamed together." Isaiah 44:11

In verse 9 of this chapter, Isaiah writes, "Those who fashion a graven image are all of them futile, and their precious things are of no profit." There was plenty of profit for those who made idols in Judah! In fact, it was quite a booming business. Yet Isaiah goes on to say (read the rest of the chapter) how foolish and stupid it is to worship these things made of wood and covered with gold or bronze. You take a tree and with part of it, you burn for fuel and with the rest of it, you carve a god. You have to carry this god around with you. You feed it and tend it. This chunk of wood then becomes your god.

We shake our heads over this. Yet we do the same things. We take a chunk of metal and form a car. We buy the car, polish the car, feed the car, purchase things for the car, admire the car, and actually worship the car. Are we any better than the Israelites in the 7th century BC?

Maybe it's not a car that you worship. You might adore hats (I know a woman who has several hundred hats!), jewelry, shoes, clothes, TVs, or purses. It might be your house, your properties, your boats, your financial portfolios, your education, your social standing. The second of the Ten Commandments states, "You shall not make for yourself an idol."

The commandment against idol worship is at the top of the list because the Lord knew people would always yearn after the fake gods of their day. Idols separate you from Him. Remember the children of Israel were saved out of idol worship to a relationship with the Lord. And so were you.

Worshipping anyone or anything before the Lord God is idolatry.

We live in a society and age when people do not want to make commitments to teach a Sunday School class or help with the youth group or serve in any capacity. Why? Because they want to be "free" to run to every activity that might come on the horizon. Are you like this?

Don't make God less than God. He is to be reverenced, feared, and honored as the Highest. Worship Him and stay devoted to Him and to your local church.

August 4

Reason Not to Fear #217: We Are Not Ashamed of Jesus Christ

"Do not fear, for you will not be ashamed; Neither be disgraced, for you will not be put to shame; For you will forget the shame of your youth, And will not remember the reproach of your widowhood anymore. For your Maker is your husband, The LORD of hosts is His name; And your Redeemer is the Holy One of Israel; He is called the God of the whole earth." Isaiah 54:4, 5

Judah had been in bondage and slavery in Babylon for seventy years. While there, she was viewed as a wife of God, separated from her Husband, but eventually, it was prophesied, restored to a right relationship with Him again.

God uses many word pictures in the Bible to convey relationships. The Israelites were called "children" many times, denoting their total dependence upon God while they wandered in the wilderness and came into the promised land of Canaan. They were called the "wife" of God in Ezekiel 16, denoting God's tender love for His people, how He rescued her as a baby, raised her and then married her. Yet in Hosea, we find that His dearly beloved wife turned away from Him and pursued other lovers (idols), committing unspeakably evil and lewd acts. She was eventually sold into slavery.

While the Israelites were in slavery, they felt shame and humiliation. Nowadays, people don't feel shame. They have forgotten how to blush over their sins. We are much like the people of Israel in Isaiah's day. But the destruction of their nation, the slaughter of thousands and the enforced march across the desert -- all of this humbled the Israelites and made them ashamed.

Now God is saying to His beloved, "Don't fear. Don't be ashamed. I am going to bring you back and you will be greater and more favored than you ever were before."

Jeremiah has this wonderful verse, "For I know the plans I have for you, declares the Lord, plans for welfare and not for calamity to give you a future and a hope.'" Jer. 29:11

For those of you who have come back to the Lord and feel shame for your past deeds, take comfort in these words. For those of you who have come out of a trial, trouble or tribulation, take joy in these words. God is there for you, ready to comfort and heal. He will heal and restore you and you *do not have to fear*. Only fear Him and all else will fall into place in your life.

August 5

Reason Not to Fear #218: Fearing God Helps Us Make Right Choices

"And of whom have you been afraid, or feared, That you have lied And not remembered Me, Nor taken it to your heart? Is it not because I have held My peace from of old That you do not fear Me?" Isaiah 57:11

We all remember the date of September 11, 2001 when a hijacked jetliner struck the south tower of the World Trade Center in New York City, another jet crashed into the Pentagon, and a third one was brought down in a field in Pennsylvania. Only four people survived above the 78th floor of the World Trade Center. Two of those who survived were on the 84th floor with four other people.

Six men ran to the stairwell and started down the stairs. On the 81st floor, they met a woman who told them that the floors below were all in flames. She said they had to get above the smoke and fire. Everyone in the buildings was confused, terrified and disoriented, and so it was a hard decision to make. Now they could not see, and their brains were overloaded and beginning to shut down. Which way to go? They had to go up or down.

Four of the men decided to climb up, thinking they would be rescued by a helicopter. What they did not know was that the rooftop doors were locked, and even if they could break through, the passageways, corridors and stairwells were dense with smoke.

The other two men continued down the stairs. They, too, struggled to breathe. They came upon many during that long journey down the stairs, and someone has said that they began singing Amazing Grace. The smoke only lasted for a floor or two, and the two men were the last to get out of the south tower alive. Their friends did not make it.

Going the wrong way can be tragic, and yet this is what people are doing every day. Spiritual smoke prevents them from finding and discovering Jesus.

What are the smoke screens Satan has put over your eyes to keep you from Jesus? If you have given Him your heart and life, what keeps you from trusting Him more? Are you choosing the wrong stairwell? The Word of God and His Spirit can clear away the smoke. Come to Him today. Turn to God and spend time in the Word and in prayer. His Spirit will direct your paths as you choose the right way.

August 6

Reason Not to Fear #219: We Read the End of the Book

"So they shall fear the name of the Lord from the west, and His glory from the rising of the sun, when the enemy comes in like a flood, the Spirit of the LORD will lift up a standard against him. The Redeemer will come to Zion, and to those who turn from transgression in Jacob,' says the LORD."
Isaiah 59:19, 20

Some people love to read the end of the book first. Generally, this is not a good practice, yet in one Book there is an ending that everyone should read. It is the book of Revelation in the Bible. Isn't it amazing that God allows us to know the end of the story?

Many people veer away from Revelation because they think they cannot understand it. Yes, Revelation is full of symbolic language and it reveals God's judgments on the earth and on sinful mankind. With a good commentary, you can study this book, learn valuable lessons from it, and find out it is not scary but very interesting and exciting as we see God moving onto the human landscape in astounding ways to bring about His will and His plan to the earth.

Rev. 19:6-8 reads, "Then I heard something like the voice of a great multitude and like the sound of many waters and like the sound of mighty peals of thunder, saying, 'Hallelujah! For the Lord our God, the Almighty reigns. Let us rejoice and give the glory to Him...'"

Isaiah saw this happening when he wrote the above verses. I find great joy and comfort in these uncertain days when I read, "For He will come like a rushing stream ... A Redeemer will come to Zion." What a day that will be!

As you face the humdrum issues of your life today, or even if they aren't so humdrum, consider the end of the story of human history. God is victorious over sin, Satan and all evil. No more will people kill a roomful of children. No more will tears, sadness and grief stain our eyes. We will live forever with our loved ones and with our great God and Savior, Jesus Christ.

Did you weep this morning? Is your heart heavy over a wayward child? Are you facing tests, surgeries, sickness and maybe even death? Do you grieve for loved ones gone ahead of you? Are you lonely, scared, worried or frustrated? Read the end of the Book, my friend.

Lift up your head and rejoice in God's love, glory, power and grace. Then tell Satan to get behind you, strap on your shoes of the gospel of peace and do God's will with a glad heart.

August 7

Reason Not to Fear #220: Turn from Your Sin to God

"O Lord, why have You made us to stray from Your ways and hardened our hearts from Your fear? Return for Your servants' sake, the tribes of Your inheritance." Isaiah 63:17

In this song, beginning chapter 63:7, Isaiah joins several other great prophets of the Old Testament to become a voice for his people before God, praying a heartfelt prayer of remorse and repentance for their sins. See also Daniel 9:3-19, Ezra 9, and Nehemiah 9. Here, Isaiah is praying to God to forgive the nation of Israel for their sins and praising God for His lovingkindness (loyal love and grace).

It seems in this verse that he is blaming God for the evil that befell them for their sins, yet look closer at what he is truly saying. In James 1:13, we see that God does not tempt humans to sin, and He Himself cannot be tempted by evil, for He is holy and totally separated from sin and impurity. Can God cause us to stray from Him and harden our hearts so we cannot obey?

He hardened Pharaoh's heart (Ex. 7:3), but that was only after Pharaoh hardened his own heart five times! Read Isaiah 29:13, for it gives a little more light on this situation. The people continued a form of religion, but their hearts were far from God, and God lets them go.

At a certain point, God turns people over to their own sin and hardness of heart. It is not that He will not hear them if they repent, but he uses their own disobedience and rebellion to bring glory to His name.

Sobering thoughts! Only in repentance and humility do we find forgiveness and a right relationship with God. As long as we stubbornly go our own ways, resisting the call of God on our lives and living in pride, disdain and hardness of heart, God will let us go. He will allow us to continue in our sin, and we will reap the consequences of it.

This prayer of Isaiah is simply, "Don't do that, Lord! Forgive our sin and come back to us! We need You. Please help us."

Where are you in your walk with the Lord? Are you rebelling in some way against His Word? Are you walking in pride, refusing to ask Him for help? Search your heart, my friend. Seek His forgiveness and help. Turn from your ways of sin back to God. He will restore you.

He will forgive you. He will bless you.

August 8

Reason Not to Fear #221: God Will Punish Sin and Evil

"So I will choose their delusions, and bring their fears on them; because, when I spoke they did not hear; but they did evil before My eyes, and chose that in which I do not delight." Isaiah 66:4

Can you see God's hand in the events of our nation and world? Do you believe that He is calling unrepentant sinners to Himself through the catastrophes that are coming closer together and with greater intensity? Just recently the Boston Marathon was interrupted at the finish line by a bomb explosion that killed four people and injured many. The two young men who perpetrated this crime are evil murderers. Yet, even in this, we know that God allowed it to bring people to Himself.

In the midst of prophesying the coming Kingdom Age of Jesus Christ on this earth, Isaiah had to stop, almost mid-sentence and mid-breath to remind them that they were dangerously close to incurring the wrath of Almighty God on their nation and lives. "This is the one I esteem: he who is humble and contrite in spirit, and trembles at My word", verse 2. Also, in verse 3, "They have chosen their own ways, and their souls delight in their abominations."

The Israelites learned that painful lesson the hard way. They were warned over and over again about God's judgment coming upon them because of their sin, but they turned a deaf ear to God's messengers, persecuted them and killed them.

Finally God did just what He said. He had to bring in the cruel Assyrian army to conquer and take captive the northern kingdom of Israel. Later on, He brought the Babylonian army to conquer and take captive the southern kingdom of Judah. These people stayed in captivity for seventy years. Their nation was no more. They had no religion, priests, temple, cities, farms or homes. Their land lay desolate and barren for seventy years.

When we walk contrary to God's Word and follow our hearts' desires, not heeding the Word of God or obeying His commands, we must pay the price. God is not mocked. His judgment will fall. Is this where we are headed today in the nation of America? Is God calling people back to Himself today? Is this call largely unheeded, ridiculed and ignored?

Check your own heart today. Make it right with God, and then go out to serve Him.

August 9

Reason Not to Fear #222: When the Path is Too Hard, He Is There

"Do not be afraid of their faces, for I am with you to deliver you, says the Lord." Jeremiah 1:8

Has the Lord asked you to walk a path that was terrifically difficult? Even as you view it from its beginning, you know it will be something beyond your strength. Your heart quails before it, whimpering and afraid, bowed down with imagined or real fears that claw at you like a monster from the deep.

I have been there. When my husband suffered his cardiac arrest and subsequent brain damage, I knew this would be a hard path, one I had not chosen, did not want, and could not accomplish in my own strength. Yet day by day, step by step, God has proven Himself faithful to meet my every need.

But once in a while I am reduced again to that cringing lump of flesh that cowered before the awful weight of what I would have to bear. Today was one of those days. I am disheartened, weary and exhausted. For two cents, I would throw in the towel when it comes to my responsibilities of caring for my husband. Yes, I am more than willing to give up today.

Jeremiah was a young man when God first spoke to Him and commissioned him to be a prophet to His people of Judah during the 6th century BC. Jeremiah was not too excited over the prospect, but God assured him that He would be with His prophet, would protect him from the people, and would give him the strength for the hard path.

The Lord touched his mouth and gave him the message, the Word of God. This is the same comfort, strength, and joy we can find when life beats us down. The Word of God can lift you up, restore your faith, lighten your load and give you hope. You can either read it or sing it. You most certainly should memorize it and study it. Listen to Christian music and this will uplift you, too.

So today I will remember, like Jeremiah, that God has called me to take care of my husband and He intends to be with me, not only to guide me, but to empower me. He can do the same for you, too, my friend. Reach out to Him and find Him ready to help you in whatever circumstance you face this day. He is there for you. Do not be afraid of their faces.

August 10

Reason Not to Fear #223: God Is A God of Justice

"Then I saw that for all the causes for which backsliding Israel had committed adultery, I had put her away and given her a certificate of divorce; yet her treacherous sister Judah did not fear, but went and played the harlot also." Jeremiah 3:8

Israel (the northern ten tribes) and Judah (the southern two tribes) are likened to sisters. Israel was taken into captivity by the Assyrian nation in 722 BC as a judgment of God because of her sins. The prophets delineated these sins very clearly so there was no doubt in the people's minds why this was happening to them. Of course, they did not want to be reminded about the fact that they had persecuted and killed the prophets while they continued with their idol worship. They did not want to hear about their wanton sexual practices, their pride and disobedience of God's Word.

You would think that Judah (the younger sister) would have returned to God when they saw Israel go into captivity. As the Assyrian army marched into Judah during the days of good King Hezekiah, they destroyed everything in their path. Hezekiah led the people in a great spiritual revival, but it did not last. But by the time his son, wicked Manesseh, came on the throne, they went right back to their evil practices.

America is following this same disastrous path today. Our society and culture has steadily gone away from God. The decline into the pit of wickedness has sharpened drastically in recent years. Our godless government wants to do away with any religious connotation for Christmas.

Isaiah says that Judah did not fear. What did the nation **not** fear? They lost their fear of the Lord and this led them into debauchery, sin and destruction. When you fear the Lord, you respect Him, honor Him, glorify Him and seek to obey Him.

The Israelites had forgotten He had brought them out of Egypt, provided for them to conquer the land, and given them everything they needed. Yet they turned from Him to worship other gods; the idols of sex, money, lands, power, possessions, pride and position.

Americans have enjoyed over two hundred years of freedom, prosperity and all the good things of life. We, too, are in danger of following in the footsteps of these two sisters. Guard against false gods in your life. Keep close to God. Fear Him. You will be glad you did.

August 11

Reason Not to Fear #224: God Will Judge the Unrighteous

"They do not say in their heart, 'Let us fear the Lord our God who gives rain, both the former and the latter, in its season. He reserves for us the appointed weeks of the harvest.'" Jeremiah 5:24

California and Arizona are in a drought. In Arizona, we have not had any rain for more than one hundred and sixty days! People are being told to use the water wisely. We are told not to waste water, too.

Arizona is a desert and parts of this state is totally barren. How anything grows here is beyond my comprehension. Why God brought me to this state I will never understand! I would much rather live where there is green beauty all around, but here I am in Arizona.

Israel is partly desert land, too. The only thing that keeps it green is the goodness of God as He sends the early and latter rains when the people are obedient to Him.

Jeremiah is known as the weeping prophet and that is because he understood God's coming judgment on Jerusalem. His message caused him to have many enemies and few friends. In fact, he spent a lot of time in prison for preaching the Word of God. When he was older, he was cast into a pit half filled with mud and left there to die.

It was a foreigner who finally rescued Jeremiah from this plight. Yet even this did not deter Jeremiah from preaching the messages God gave him. He witnessed the siege of the city by the Babylonian army, the cruel effects of starvation in the city, and the final conquest and fall of Jerusalem.

He wept copiously from a broken heart because he deeply loved his people.

God stripped away crops, protection, and wealth from the children of Israel in order that they would fear Him. *Perhaps,* God reasoned, *if they do not have these things, they will turn and reverence Me again.* But that did not happen. They had no desire to follow His commands and therefore they had no proper fear of Him or of their upcoming judgment.

Do not wait for God to do that in your life. What does God have to take away from you before you truly fear and worship Him? Before He has to do that, turn back to Him one hundred percent. Give Him your life and put Him at the top of your priority list.

Confess your sin, get rid of your false gods, and commit your life to Him. Do it right now.

August 12

Reason Not to Fear #225: God Makes A Way When The Path is Dark

"Do not go out into the field nor walk by the way, because of the sword of the enemy, fear is on every side." Jeremiah 6:25

We hear so much that God is love that we often forget that He is also holy and just. He will bring into judgment those who despise Him and His Word. Jeremiah warned the people of Judah that the judgment of God was coming on the nation because of their sins. Verse 16 of this chapter is a good one to contemplate.

"Thus says the Lord, 'Stand by the ways and see and ask for the ancient paths, where the good way is, and walk in it; and you shall find rest for your souls.' But they said, 'We will not walk in it.'"

At what point does God withdraw His mercy and love and become a God of wrath and judgment? It is only after He has warned people through His prophets, after He has died for the sins of the world, after He has exhausted every means to reach people. He does not delight in the death of the wicked. Yet He will come as a God of wrath if we do not obey Him and fear Him.

As God's child, you will never experience the wrath of God on your life for your sin, yet you will face challenges that provide you with the opportunity for spiritual maturity. However, your enemy wants to stop that growth, so he puts fear in front of you so that you will doubt God. Remember, your enemy is out to create fear and confusion in your life.

God's Word assures us that God wants to guide, lead, and teach us His ways. If you are walking with Christ, He will give you confidence. Depend on God, not your enemy.

Once your heart connects and attaches itself to God, all doubt and fear will melt away. Do not wander away from God when you are confused about your circumstances. God is leading you in ways you cannot figure out and in areas you would not choose.

Do not drift away from Him, for He is on your every side. He will make a way even when there seems to be no way. Receive by faith what God has planned for your life, and walk out in joy today.

August 13

Reason Not to Fear #226: God Is the Only True God

"They are upright, like a palm tree, and they cannot speak; they must be carried, because they cannot go by themselves. Do not be afraid of them, for they cannot do evil, nor can they do any good." Jeremiah 10:5

It's always dangerous business to attack the gods of the people. Gideon found that out when he pulled down the Baal god and almost lost his life for it. People love their gods.

When my daughter lived in the DaAn tribe in Indonesia, they learned of the many ways the tribal people worshipped their gods. During a funeral, the people would dress up in their proper funeral clothing and then dance around a pole which is craved with faces and images of their gods. They believed this pole made of wood was their link to their gods. On one of my visits to the tribe, I saw this pole which is right in the middle of the village. People see it all day long and are reminded to pray to their gods.

Why would a person kneel down and worship a god made of wood or stone? Or one of metal and rubber? Why worship a god who cannot speak, walk, talk or act? Some people worship "saints" and carry images of them in their cars and have them on their shelves at home. Why would they pray to these mini-gods when they could pray to Jesus Christ?

Tongue in cheek, Jeremiah denounced these false gods that his people loved so much. The nation of Judah had fallen into the practice of worshipping idols, drunkenness, sexual impurity, moral corruption and many other abusive sins. Jeremiah warned them repeatedly that God would severely punish them if this continued. However, they ignored his words and warnings. They simply did not care. The fact is, the more he warned, the more they refused to repent, and they persecuted him very much.

What are the gods you love? Is it sports? Traveling? Shopping? Is it money in the bank, your investment portfolio, your career, your education? What do you depend upon to get you through your day? Coffee? What would you find the hardest to lose? What occupies your thoughts, time and energies? What keeps you from worshipping in church?

It is only when you stop and examine in your life that you can repent. God wants your whole life, devotion, love and honor. Don't ignore His warning. Listen to what He says. He is our sovereign Lord and God. Yield to Him today.

August 14

Reason Not to Fear #227: We Get Rid of False Gods

"Who would not fear You, O King of the nations? For this is Your rightful due. For among all the wise men of the nations, and in all their kingdoms, there is none like You. But they are altogether dull-hearted and foolish; a wooden idol is a worthless doctrine."
Jeremiah 10:7, 8

In verse two of this chapter, Jeremiah warns the people against the practice of idolatry, which includes the worship, study and fascination with the stars, such as we have today in the horoscopes. This is the message he gives in the name of the Lord, "Do not learn the way of the nations, and do not be terrified by the signs of the heavens although the nations are terrified by them."

My grandchildren like to watch movies, but lately I have been rather shocked as to what is appropriate for them. It seems the movie industry wants to push the limit when it comes to films for children. Truthfully, some of the films rated PG are shocking. Today young children are enamored with witchcraft, spiritism, and vampires. They connect with the power these images provide for them. Today we have waves of movies and books about demons, evil spirits, and the devil himself.

These are the idols of our day and age. They are the created images of hearts far from God. These images have been given faces and personalities for our young children to connect to. They have become an overwhelming obsession. The kingdom of darkness has impacted many a young mind.

Can these gods help us? Save us from sin? Give us hope, peace or joy?

Where does idol worship take us? It takes us away from the true God, our Lord and Savior, Jesus Christ, and it puts us in a position where God must exercise His judgment and wrath against our sin and sinful ways. The people of Israel and Judah found out about God's wrath when they sinned against Him.

Where do you want to be? Do you want to enjoy a loving and fulfilling relationship with the Creator of the Universe and Redeemer of our souls, or do you want to live in fear of His judgment? Consider your ways carefully, my dear friends. Please: choose God and His Son, Jesus Christ today. Walk in His joy and love, and never look back.

August 15

Reason Not to Fear #228: God Is My Dread Champion!

"For I heard many mocking: 'Fear on every side!' 'Report,' they say, 'and we will report it!' All my acquaintances watched for my stumbling, saying, 'Perhaps he can be induced; then we will prevail against him, and we will take our revenge on him.'" Jeremiah 20:10

Have you ever been mocked, endured gossip and lies about your character by those you considered your friends? I know that you probably have. CS Lewis wrote that his idea of hell is an office! People who work together in the small confines of an office space usually indulge in a lot of gossip and back-stabbing. In fact, they say that you don't ever want to be the first person to leave a gossip session, because they will then talk about you.

Churches, sadly, are also places where people can gossip and malign each other. Jeremiah's friends whispered behind his back. They mocked him for saying that fear and terror would come upon the nation from every side. They denounced him. They wished and probably even prayed that he would be found in error in his predictions. If they could prove this, they could stone him according to their laws.

These were his "trusted friends", his relatives and neighbors! Can you imagine how much this hurt? Yet Jeremiah loved his people. Because they had broken so many of God's laws and sinned over and over again, his heart was broken. Numerous times he tried to warn them of God's coming judgment, but they would not listen.

In verse 11 of this chapter, Jeremiah records his thoughts concerning his faith in the face of these persecutions. "But the Lord is with me like a dread champion, therefore my persecutors will stumble and not prevail."

I love that. Instead of being cast down and quitting the task God gave him to do, Jeremiah renewed his faith and trust in God. His heart bursts into a song of praise to God in verse 13. "Sing to the Lord, praise the Lord! For He has delivered the soul of the needy one from the hand of the evildoers."

When you are tempted to give up because someone mocks you or makes your life difficult because of your faith, remember how Jeremiah handled this problem. His enemies could not stop or destroy his passion to serve God. May that be said of you and me today!

August 16

Reason Not to Fear #229: He Is My Good Shepherd

*"I will set up shepherds over them who will feed them; and they shall fear
no more, nor be dismayed, nor shall they be lacking," says the LORD."*
Jeremiah 23:4

When we lived in Pennsylvania, I had a friend who raised sheep. Since we moved to Pennsylvania from the inner city of Chicago, I was totally unacquainted with sheep and their life. I loved learning about them. I came to understand that sheep are very interesting animals.

When it came time for the sheep to give birth to their babies, I wanted to be there. My friend and I made a nice little space for our bodies in the hay as we waited for the birth. Then it happened. A lamb was born. Instantly my friend took the baby lamb and attached it to the mother to nurse. She wanted to make sure the mother knew this was her baby. She wanted them to bond immediately.

Over the next few months, I would visit this mother and her baby, and there they would be, walking side by side. They knew each other. They connected. She knew for certain which was her baby and the baby as well knew which was his mother.

During the days of Jeremiah, the priests and teachers of the law had become people who were out solely for what they could get out of the sheep. They were truly "fleecing" their own flocks! These cruel and evil shepherds did no good in helping the sheep stay close to God, and God had to judge them very severely.

Yet what a relief and blessing it is to have a shepherd who really cares for you! The Lord assured the people of Judah that during the last days, when the nation would one day be re-gathered into their own land again, God would provide them with shepherds who would seek their good, give their lives for the sheep, and help them stay close to God.

Jesus said He is the good shepherd (John 10). He takes constant care over us. We can trust His love. "I am the good shepherd ... and I lay down my life for the sheep." Are you helping others to stay close to God? Do you guide them into the truth of God's Word? Are you faithful to correct them when they go astray? All of us can function in this way.

Make sure you are following in the steps of Jesus. Are you a good shepherd to those under your care? Do not be like foolish sheep who do not know their own offspring. Trust in God and do His will today.

August 17

Reason Not to Fear #230: We Speak Out about Our Faith

"Did Hezekiah king of Judah and all Judah ever put him to death? Did he not fear the LORD and seek the LORD's favor, and the Lord relented concerning the doom He had pronounced against them. But we are doing great evil against ourselves." Jeremiah 26:19

Jeremiah was facing the death squad as he stood before the assembly of the priests and the false prophets. He had delivered a message to the people of Judah, and more specifically, to King Jehoiakim, warning that they were sinning against the God of Israel and they needed to repent and come back to Him.

The priests and prophets seized him and dragged him into the court, screaming, "You must die! Why have you prophesied in the name of the Lord saying, 'This house will be like Shiloh and this city will be desolate without inhabitant?'" (v. 8-9)

Shiloh was a city to the north in the nation of Israel that held the Tabernacle for a time. It was completely destroyed by the Assyrian army in 722 BC. These prominent religious and political leaders were infuriated that Jeremiah predicted the same thing would happen to Judah.

At that moment, a company of men, both officials and common people, arose and defended Jeremiah. They brought to mind that in the days of Hezekiah, the prophet Micah had predicted a similar thing when the Assyrians came. "He was not put to death because he feared the Lord ... and the Lord changed His mind concerning the pronouncement of doom. So we would be committing a great evil if we put this man to death."

These words saved Jeremiah's life. As God promised, he was rescued from these evil men and given the chance to continue his ministry where God placed him.

How about you? While you may not face down an angry king or a violent mob that is bent on destroying your life, you may face opposition and hatred as you live your faith in these last days. Are you faithful to God even when things go from bad to worse?

Are you courageous enough to talk about your faith to a dying patient even if that means your job? Consider the cost today and follow Him according to His leading in your life.

Be another Jeremiah who did not back down even when he faced certain death.

August 18

Reason Not to Fear #231: When We Repent, the Joy Returns

"Fear not, O Jacob My servant, declares the Lord, and do not be dismayed, O Israel; for behold, I will save you from afar and your offspring from the land of their captivity. And Jacob will return and be quiet and at ease, and no one will make him afraid." Jeremiah 30:10

Does joy and discipline go together?

The Word of God says, "Now no chastening seems to be joyful for the present, but painful; nevertheless, afterward it yields the peaceable fruit of righteousness to those who have been trained by it." Hebrews 12:11

Discipline is not a pleasant thing to go through. It is painful. Its purpose, when applied correctly, is to cause enough pain to bring about a sorrowful repentance for the sin that was committed and to train a child to walk in the way of righteousness. This passage in Hebrews says that all good fathers discipline their children because they love them. Susanna Wesley, who raised ten children, believed firmly in the biblical concept that if you "spare the rod, you spoil the child". She was said to have had a rod handy at all times and had a sign over it that read, "I Need Thee Every Hour".

This godly woman, the mother of John and Charles Wesley, has been much criticized in our society where it is taught that a parent must never spank a child or correct a child for misbehavior. Yet the fact that at least two of her children went on to make a big impact on the world speaks for itself. Discipline is important.

Jeremiah lived through the horrendous siege of Jerusalem and the destruction of his nation and people, and he trusted God through it all. In chapter 30, he begins a series of prophecies that look beyond the time of judgment to a time of restoration when God would bring them back into the land and they would again enjoy the blessings of a redeemed, forgiven people. The joy would return.

Have you been there? Have you wandered away from God, felt ashamed of what you've done, and then been gently reassured that you need not fear? God is now comforting you and helping you as He did before. Yes, discipline and joy can go together when we repent of our sin and turn to God. If you've been wandering, come home. Let the joy return.

August 19

Reason Not to Fear #232: God Keeps His Promises

"And I will make an everlasting covenant with them, that I will not turn away from doing them good, but I will put my fear in their hearts so that they will not depart from Me. Yes, I will rejoice over them to do them good and I will assuredly plant them in this land with all My heart and with all My soul."
Jeremiah 32:40, 41

God asked Jeremiah to do a very strange thing. The situation was that the Babylonian army surrounded the city of Jerusalem and doom was certain. After two and a half years of a siege, during which the people starved to death, the gates were finally opened to the fierce army who destroyed the population and the city.

Before this happened, Jeremiah was in the city when a word of the Lord came to him. In our language, the Lord said, "Jeremiah, your cousin is going to come to you and he will ask you to purchase a piece of land from him that is in your family. I want you to buy this land."

"But wait, Lord," Jeremiah replied. "That land has been taken by the Babylonians, unless You haven't noticed. Why should I buy the land? It won't do me any good."

The Lord's reply was interesting. "Just obey Me. Nothing is impossible for Me."

God went on to explain why he wanted Jeremiah to buy the land. He said that someday, He would bring His people back to their land, and someday Jeremiah would be there, too. During the Kingdom Age, the Israeli nation would rule the world, and Jeremiah would have his property.

So Jeremiah purchased property he could not possess or even see because he feared, trusted and obeyed God.

God wants you to trust Him. He wants to make an everlasting promise to you that He will not turn away from you. In fact, He will put His fear, His reverence in your heart so that you will no longer desire to depart from Him.

The respect you have for God should be the foundation of your life. As God's child, He has instilled in your heart wonder and adoration for Himself. Every day God wants to inspire you to fear and adore Him more. So fan the flame of the fear of the Lord. Kindle the spark so it grows.

Ask Him to unite your heart to respect and honor His name, then watch the growth in the fear of God begin in your life.

August 20

Reason Not to Fear #233: God Will See You Through

"Then it shall be to Me a name of joy, a praise, and an honor before all nations of the earth, who shall hear all the good that I do to them; they shall fear and tremble for all the goodness and all the prosperity that I provide for it." Jeremiah 33:9

Jocelyn Green tells the story on her blog of her experiences in Washington DC on the morning of September 11, 2001. She worked in an office just eight blocks from the Capitol building. She describes the shock, horror, pain and confusion that reigned in the city during the attack by terrorists. The staff she worked with met to pray and a woman shared Psalm 30:5, "Weeping remains for the night, but joy comes in the morning." She remembers wondering how long their night would last and when joy would return to her.

In the days following the attack, she descended into a time of gloomy despair and nothing seemed to help to get her out of it. She did not doubt God; her faith held steady, yet she could not shake the dark cloud of grief and fear that settled over her soul. Then one day as she attended a church service, she saw a woman she'd known in college. The woman was laughing. They met and Jocelyn began showing this other lady around the city, going to concerts, tourist attractions, historic places and museums. Gradually the cloud began to lift and Jocelyn could laugh again.

Joy came in the morning.

She writes, "The terrorist attacks were intended to cause a crippling fear to take root in our country. But you know what? I saw Bible studies pop up in the offices of senators and congressmen where God's name was not mentioned before. I saw people reaching out to each other. We prayed more. Terrorism was met with heroism. And what man intended for evil, God used for good."

In this verse, Jeremiah again comforts his people about the good that God intended to bring to them once they were disciplined and judged for their sins.

Are you going through a tough time right now that tests your faith? Are you in the darkness, wondering when the morning and the joy will come? Don't lose hope. Cling to God and He will see you through, just as He did for Jocelyn, and just as He did for His people of Judah.

August 21

Reason Not to Fear #234: God Will Deliver Us from Our Fears

"But I will deliver you in that day,' says the Lord, 'and you will not be given into the hand of the men of whom you are afraid. For I will surely deliver you, and you shall not fall by the sword; but your life shall be as a prize to you, because you have put your trust in Me,' says the Lord." Jeremiah 39:17, 18

The city had fallen to the Babylonians. The king and his sons tried to flee through the garden gate, but they were captured. The victors, the army and officers of the Babylonians, sat in the gate to judge those captured and decide their fate. King Zedekiah's sons were killed before his eyes, along with all the nobles and officials of his kingdom. Then they put out Zedekiah's eyes, bound him with chains and took him with the rest of the captives to Babylon where he later died. He had rejected God's Word and the message from Jeremiah for many years, now he paid for his rebellion against God.

Jeremiah had been taken into the guardhouse where he was protected, fed and clothed while the Babylonians razed the city. Finally King Nebuchadnezzar gave orders about Jeremiah. "Take him and look after him, and do nothing harmful to him, but rather deal with him just as he tells you."

Jeremiah emerged from the bloodbath unscathed, and was given into the care of Gedeliah, the governor of the province. God had a message for Jeremiah to send to a man who had previously saved his life: Ebel-melech the Ethiopian. This man had rescued Jeremiah from a miry pit a few months before, and now he hid from the Babylonians, sure that he would soon lose his life. Yet the message was one of comfort. "Do not fear, I will deliver you," said the Lord. "You will not fall by the sword...because you have trusted in Me, declares the Lord."

God is able to do all that He has promised us. He has promised that He will never leave us or forsake us. He has promised to take us Home to His house in glory. He has promised to give us courage, wisdom, peace and joy as we face life's challenges.

I think we underestimate the God we serve. God will rescue you from those you fear. He does not want you to face your alarms alone. In fact, He will not only go before you, He will go behind you and beside you. He will walk with you and rescue you from those you fear. Never forget: God plans to redeem you from all evil. Trust Him today.

August 22

Reason Not to Fear #235: We Obey God Even When It Seems Strange

"And Gedaliah son of Ahikam, the son of Shapan, took an oath before them and their men, saying, 'Do not be afraid to serve the Chaldeans. Dwell in the land and serve the king of Babylon, and it shall be well with you.'"
Jeremiah 40:9

Has the Lord ever spoken to you and asked you to do something that seemed rather strange? And did you pause for a moment and wonder if you heard Him correctly?

I can vividly remember many incidents in my life just like that. One in particular was when He led my husband and me to move away from my family in Milwaukee, Wisconsin to live in Chicago. The reason it was so unusual is because Armenians stay close to each other. We raise our families together. We interact in all aspects of life together. We live near each other, or at least down the block.

In this verse, Gedeliah, the governor the Babylonians put over the Jews who remained in the land, said that they should not fear the Babylonians, but they should get busy and harvest the produce of the land. You can imagine that the people were fearful. You would be, too, if you witnessed the total destruction of your nation, your religion and your cities. You would be fearful if you had seen your fellow citizens carried away to captivity.

Jeremiah might have thought this was a strange message, too. Yet he nodded in agreement and encouraged the people to follow this advice. The people would be protected. They would not have to fear if they got busy with the tasks they had to do before winter.

Our beginning months in Chicago were lonely for me. My husband was busy attending Moody Bible Institute while I stayed home and cared for our young son. However, hard as those early years were, they were years that caused me to be extremely dependent on the Lord for companionship. Slowly, over time, every fear I faced He replaced with peace.

Can you trust in what God tells you to do and not be afraid? He will give you peace when you do, just as He did for me. You may face something that seems strange. God may speak to your heart and tell you to do something that seems a little bizarre. Yet if you obey Him, He will give you joy and peace.

August 23

Reason Not to Fear #236: We Don't Ignore God or His Word

"Then it shall be that the sword which you feared shall overtake you there in the land of Egypt; the famine of which you were afraid shall follow close after you there in Egypt, and there you shall die." Jeremiah 42:16

The people left in the land after the Babylonians conquered the nation were frightened out of their wits. There were just a few of them, and they could find no safe place to hide or to find shelter. There were empty houses by the score, but they did not feel safe anywhere. The enemy soldiers could come again and kill them all.

Gedeliah was appointed to be governor. Ishmael, a man who was in the royal line and might have felt jealous of Gedeliah, came to Mizpah and murdered Gedeliah and all his men. Now the people feared that the Babylonians would return and kill them all. Can you see what fear does to people when they turn away from God?

The people wanted to go to Egypt because they worshipped the female goddess Ishtar from that land, and there they could freely continue their idolatrous worship. They implored Jeremiah to ask God for direction. In reply, God said that they should not go down to Egypt! If they did, God said, they would be killed by the sword that they feared in Judah. Furthermore, they would die of famine and sickness if they went to Egypt.

Yet they would not listen. Isn't that just like we are today? We ask for counsel, and we might even pray about a situation, but if it is not the answer we want, we go our own way.

All the Israelites' difficulties, struggles, and losses had not taught them anything about what is truly important in life! They were still bent on running after their own desires away from God, away from the Word, away from the protection God was willing to give them in the land. And it came about as Jeremiah said. They were killed in the land of Egypt. Even Jeremiah himself died there. How sad.

How about you? Are you running away from God, pursuing your own desires? You'd better get back on track with Him. It is a dangerous thing to ignore God. Just ask the Israelites who went down to Egypt! Confess your sin and get right with Him today.

August 24

Reason Not to Fear #237: Acknowledge God in All You Do

"They have not been humbled, to this day, nor have they feared; they have not walked in My law or in My statutes that I set before you and your fathers."
Jeremiah 44:10

How could it be possible to witness the death, destruction, mayhem, misery and devastation the Babylonian army brought about and not repent of your sins? How could these people, the poorest of the poor, not cry out to the God of heaven and seek Him again with their whole hearts?

They traveled south to the land of Egypt in direct disobedience against the Word of the Lord that came to Jeremiah. They fled there for safety. But their hearts were already in Egypt, for they worshipped the gods of Egypt. They thought, perhaps, that Jeremiah would die on the way and they wouldn't have to listen to his sermons anymore. But God had a message for them, one that we would do well to listen to today in 2013 America.

God said He would cut them off, and they would meet their end in the country of Egypt. Instead of a place of refuge, this land would become their doom because they rejected the true and living God. We may shake our heads in amazement at the stupidity of these people. Yet are we not committing the same kinds of errors in our country today?

We have gone through many national disasters: 9/11, the hurricane Katrina, flooding and hurricanes throughout the south, and hurricane Sandy in the east. In the west, we have seen wildfires consume much of our national forests and many homes. We have seen flooding, shootings, drought, crime and trouble multiplied as we have wandered further and further away from the God who brought us to this land and provided us with so many blessings.

While there was an immediate turning of hearts toward God when the terrorist attacks first occurred, it wasn't long before God was again shoved out of our schools, our government, our media, our homes and hearts.

Yes, we are in the same kind of danger that these people faced. We have sinned. We love and worship other gods, and we need to turn back to the God of Israel before it is too late.

Search your own heart today and commit yourself to Him totally. Obey His Word, seek Him first, and acknowledge Him in all you do. Then pray for our country, for we truly need it!

August 25

Reason Not to Fear #238: We Listen to God and Live in Reality

"Why have I seen them dismayed and turned back? Their mighty ones are beaten down; they have speedily fled, and did not look back, for fear was all around,' says the LORD." Jeremiah 46:5

The other day, I went to watch my nine year old grandson, Luke, play soccer. Every Thursday night, he practices with his team for their upcoming game on Saturday. He lives in Indonesia in the jungle with his missionary parents and plays soccer with his team there. When they come home on furlough, he joins the team here.

As Saturday drew near, I reminded him that only one team would win the game and the other team would lose. He understood this concept, yet his hopes were high that his team would win. On Saturday, the day of his game, I repeated my warning. Yet even as I spoke, I knew that while he understood my words, he didn't want to deal with the prospect of reality.

In the above verse, the word of the Lord came to Jeremiah concerning God's plan for the nation of Egypt. "Your warriors will run and hide. You will be defeated. You will have terror on every side," God said through His prophet.

This once victorious nation would be overthrown by a nation more bold and powerful than themselves. All their earthly prosperity, wealth and power sapped their spiritual strength. They were proud and lifted up against God. They refused to worship God and now they would be punished. What is interesting is that they did not listen to warning after warning given by the Lord, and they continued to trust in their own strength and power. They would not face reality, nor would they obey God.

My grandson played well that day, yet his team lost. He was greatly disappointed. I tried my best to ready him for this defeat, but he was set on winning.

How like Luke I am. I do not heed the Lord's warning when it comes to being defeated by sin, and if I continue a certain wrong behavior, attitude, or action, I will experience God's judgment on my life. My prayer is that I will hear, listen, and act on what the Lord reveals to me.

Pray that you will be prepared for reality, that you will obey God and walk in His ways today and every day. Even on days when you team loses the game.

August 26

Reason Not to Fear #239: The Lord Rescues the Righteous

*"But do not fear, O My servant Jacob, and do not be dismayed, O Israel!
For behold, I will save you from afar, and your offspring from the land of their
captivity; Jacob shall return, have rest and be at ease; No one shall make him
afraid. Do not fear, O Jacob My servant," says the LORD, "For I am with you;
for I will make a complete end of all the nations To which I have driven you,
But I will not make a complete end of you. I will rightly correct you, for I will
not leave you wholly unpunished."* Jeremiah 46:27, 28

From 605 BC to 586 BC, the powerful nation of Babylon conquered the
nation of Judah, destroyed her capitol city, and plundered the people, taking
them as slaves. In 605 BC, Egypt engaged Nebuchadnezzar (king of Babylon)
at the Syrian city of Carchemish north of Damascus, and Egypt was defeated.
This tipped the balance of world power to Babylon. The armies then marched
south and took all of Palestine, Gaza, Edom and Egypt. This was all predicted
ahead of time by the prophets Isaiah and Jeremiah.

The Assyrians had already decimated the northern kingdom of Israel and
taken them slaves. Then Babylon rose as a world power, destroyed the
Assyrians, and came against God's people. Eventually Judah was destroyed,
Jerusalem was captured, the temple was burnt to the ground and the Jews were
taken into captivity.

Yet in the midst of this, God acted mercifully and did not allow the nation
of Israel to be completely annihilated. God will preserve a remnant of people
and bring them home, Jeremiah declares.

When all seems utterly impossible, there is always hope in God. All the
afflictions that touch God's people did not come upon them to destroy them;
rather the afflictions came to purify them. The Israelites would never again
worship idols. To this day, they revere and honor Yahweh God. There is
coming a day when they will also recognize and worship Jesus Christ as their
Messiah. God's kingdom is continually advancing, and He is telling His people
not to be afraid. He is going to bring us home. Are you longing for your
heavenly home?

For today, give your heart and soul to Him and He will restore you, comfort
you, and give you peace no matter what your circumstances are right now. In
closing, read John 14:1-6 and think about the heavenly home He is preparing
for all who believe in Him.

August 27

Reason Not to Fear #240: God Can Change the Heart of Your Enemy

*"Fear and the pit and the snare shall be upon you, O inhabitant of Moab,"
says the LORD. "He who flees from the fear shall fall into the pit, and he who
gets out of the pit shall be caught in the snare. For upon Moab, upon it I will
bring the year of their punishment," says the LORD.* Jeremiah 48:43, 44

Presently we are living with my daughter and her family. The reason is that
I sold our home and have not been able to find another one yet. So my husband
and I are using their living room as our bedroom. It is quite an interesting
situation. We have been here for almost two months, but hopefully we will find
a house to buy soon. We have gotten to know the neighbors and had some brief
conversations with them, but the friendly conversations changed last week.
Several of my grandchildren were playing basketball outside and the ball went
into the neighbor's backyard and broke an item.

The man was furious and remained furious despite every apology we
extended. It is strange how some people start out being friendly, but when
something threatens them, they are suddenly angry.

The Moabites were neighbors with the Israelites. In fact, these two groups
of people were related. However, like all relatives, they had conflicts. When the
children of Israel came north to enter the Promised Land, the Moabites refused
to allow them to go through their land. The Moabites also turned their backs on
God and refused to worship Him. Their disobedience and worship of idols led
God to punish them and judge them. They became fierce enemies of the
Israelites, to the point of rejoicing when the Babylonians overran Judah. God
would judge the Moabites for their sin, as our verse for the day states.

What makes you fearful? Is it a situation that you have caused because of
your disobedience, pride or stubbornness of heart? Are you refusing to give
Him first place in your life? Are you hanging onto guilt, bitterness, anger or a
grudge?

In your prayer today, ask forgiveness if you are living in sin. Come back to
God. Then turn all your situations in life over to Him and watch Him work. He
can give you peace. He can give you love. He can even change the heart of an
angry neighbor.

August 28

Reason Not to Fear #241: God Is Able to Save Me from Fear

"'Behold, I will bring fear upon you,' says the Lord GOD of hosts, 'From all those who are around you; you shall be driven out, everyone headlong, And no one will gather those who wander off.'" Jeremiah 49:5

This morning I took an hour or so for myself and went out to the garage sales. It happens to be one of my favorite activities, looking for that perfect money-saving find. At one particular sale, which was huge, I overheard the couple speaking a foreign language. Being who I am, I inquired what language they were speaking, to which they replied Babylonian. They then clarified that it was Aramaic, the language spoken during Bible times. I told them I was Armenian and that my family spoke both Armenian and Turkish.

Slowly the man rose up from his chair and said, "We are neighbors and friends to your people."

Most of the time, when I tell someone I am Armenian, they have no idea what I am talking about. The truth is, a lot of people have never heard of the Armenian people or our country and background, so when a connection is made it brings joy to my heart.

People do not generally know who the Ammonites were, either. They were a nation descended from Abraham through his nephew Lot, the children of an incestuous relationship with Lot and his daughter. They became enemies of the Israelites. This verse declares that the Ammonites were fearful of Nebuchadnezzar and rightfully so, because he defeated them.

However, out of God's mercy, those taken captive would have an opportunity to return to their homeland. God had to judge the Ammonites (now their territory is the nation of Jordan) for their sin in not worshipping Him. They had the truth and knew the truth, yet they turned against God and chose to worship idols.

It is not a big deal if you don't know what an Armenian is, or an Ammonite. What is important is that you allow no group of people to bring fear over you that interrupts your relationship with the Lord. What is important is that you walk in obedience and the fear of the Lord, and that you teach your children this same kind of faith and walk.

How are you doing on that score today? Close this time by praying to God, seeking His face and His will.

August 29

Reason Not to Fear #242: God Is Bigger Than Terror

"Damascus has grown feeble, she turns to flee, and fear has seized her; anguish and pain have taken her like a woman in labor.... Their tents and their flocks they shall take; they shall take for themselves their curtains, all their vessels and their camels; and they shall cry out to them, 'Fear is on every side!'" Jeremiah 49:24, 29

Presently in our country there is some fears and concerns surfacing about North Korea and their missile programs. The North Koreans have made numerous threats toward the United States and some of our leaders have begun to take them seriously. Even more than the threat from outward enemies, we should be in dread of the sin that is eating away at the core of our national foundation and faith in God, because it is judgment on sin that causes God to rise and bring calamity on a people who have rejected Him.

In this verse, Jeremiah was preaching against the nation of Syria to the north and uses their capitol city, Damascus, to typify the whole country. Because of their sin in disobeying God, because of their persecution and warfare against Israel, God is prepared to destroy them and bring them low. He will use the mighty army and nation of Babylon, whose king was Nebuchadnezzar, to be His instrument of judgment.

I find it interesting to notice that in v. 25, God says, "the town in which I delight". God loved these people and wanted them to worship Him. He delighted in their beautiful city and wanted it to be a place of praise and honor to His name. But the people would not listen to the warnings His prophets gave concerning what God was intending to do to them.

Could it be that those who threaten us are also a tool in the Lord's plan to get our country to become faithful and obedient again? Never forget God has a sovereign plan He is carrying out in this world of ours, whether we understand it or not. The key issue is: whom do you fear? Do you fear sinning against God more than you fear North Korea or any other threat to your security?

If you believe God is in control and bringing about His plan, you will fear Him and trust Him. Put aside your fears and trust only in God. He is able to deliver you from all fear.

August 30

Reason Not to Fear #243: We Don't Forget Whose We Are

"And lest your heart faint, and you fear for the rumor that will be heard in the land (A rumor will come one year, and after that, in another year a rumor will come, and violence in the land, ruler against ruler), therefore behold, the days are coming that I will bring judgment on the carved images of Babylon; her whole land shall be ashamed, and all her slain shall fall in her midst."
Jeremiah 51:46-47

Have you ever heard a rumor and after you listened to it, fear began to take over your heart? Rumors can be dangerous. They can also be harmful and hurtful. They can damage your reputation and destroy a ministry. They can breed fear and division among Christians.

Do you remember the fear that was prevalent during the 60's and 70's about open warfare with Russia? Many people believed that Russia would invade America and take over the government and our way of life as free individuals. Because of this fear, many people put in underground bomb shelters and stocked these shelters with food, water, blankets and other necessities. Yet they didn't think beyond surviving the nuclear bomb. How would they survive in the after-math of such devastation when they emerged outside again?

The verses for today were written to the Jewish exiles who had been taken from their homeland in Judah and carried into captivity in Babylon. They were far from home, in a new culture and surrounded by people who hated them. They were cast deeper into despair each day that passed, for they saw no way to return home. Rumors were plenteous and the more they listened to them, the more their fears grew. That is what rumors do. They cause you to lose your hope. They cause you to lose your vision. They cause you to lose your rationality.

All things lie in God's control, even the idols of the nations. What will you do when fear knocks on your door? Who will you send to answer it? Send the Lord. He knows how to deal with rumors and with fear. Put your trust in Him alone. He will give you peace instead of fear.

August 31

Reason Not to Fear #244: God Is With Us When We Cry

"I called on your name O Lord, from the lowest pit. You have heard my voice. Do not hide Your ear from my sighing, from my cry for help. You drew near on the day I called on You and said, 'Do not fear!'" Lamentations 3:55-57

Jeremiah was the author of the book of Lamentations. His heart was broken because God's chosen people, the Israelites dishonored Him. The Israelites displayed arrogance, pride, and rebellion toward God. Their sinfulness broke Jeremiah's heart and God's heart, too. Therefore, he wept.

As Jeremiah witnessed the destruction of his beloved city and its people, as he saw the suffering, starvation, despair and misery all around him, he could not help but cry out to God for relief. He wept until there were no tears left. Six hundred years later, Jesus Christ walked the earth, and He, too, wept over the sins of his people, over the sins of *all* people.

Some people today rarely, if ever, weep. Yet the Bible is full of people who wept. Abraham, Joseph, Elisha, Hezekiah, Ezra, Nehemiah, Job, Isaiah, Jesus and many others expressed their pain and grief through this means. What keeps us from crying? I believe it is pride. We cannot allow others to see that we are broken and hurting. And so we dam up the flood of tears and put on a stony face even when inside we are dying.

God gave us tears as a way to release the sorrow and grief we bear. Tears are a blessing. Tears show that we care, that we love, that we need God. Confess your pride and ask God for a spirit of humility to sweep over your soul.

James 4:9 says, "Be miserable and mourn and weep; let your laughter be turned into mourning and your joy to gloom. Humble yourselves in the presence of the Lord, and He will exalt you." This verse tells us that we should weep over our sins in humility and repentance.

What has been your deepest, darkest sorrow? What has cast you into utter despair? Jeremiah realized that the only hope for the Israelites was in God's mercy, compassion and goodness. In the gloomiest of circumstances God says to you, "Do not fear."

He will not forsake His children; He will comfort you when you repent of your sin. When you weep, you allow God's Spirit to comfort and strengthen you, and you can face your heartache with His help.

September 1

Reason Not to Fear #245: We Proclaim the Truth Without Fear

"And you, son of man, do not be afraid of them nor be afraid of their words, though briers and thorns are with you and you dwell among scorpions; do not be afraid of their words or dismayed by their looks, though they are a rebellious house." Ezekiel 2:6

As a soldier and government official in SE Asia, Boun became a Christian when he heard the gospel through a radio message. A little later, he found a man in Thailand who would talk to him about Christ. After he believed in Christ and was baptized, he returned to Laos and proclaimed the gospel in his village and wherever he went. The authorities warned him to stop preaching and finally fired him, but this did not stop him from witnessing. He was arrested on June 8, 1999 and was sentenced to 15 years in prison.

On Feb. 2, 2012, he was released, two years early. During his imprisonment, he was locked in a dark room for over a year. He asked his wife to send him a Bible, and she did. In all, during the 12 years in prison, he had six Bibles, five of them confiscated by the police. Despite the torture and interrogations he endured, Boun never recanted his faith. He thanked God for the time he had in prison.

Much like Ezekiel, Boun found that he could be hard as nails when it came to the persecution others gave him when he spoke the Word of God. His daughter, Sangdara, also accepted the Lord. She said, "Because my father was put in jail, we experienced the goodness, love and mercy of the Lord. Many people cried with us, prayed for us and supported us. If we didn't have God, prayer, and support, we would have been in trouble."

Ezekiel was called on by God to give his message to a group of people who were hard-hearted, cynical, and insensitive. Yet it did not matter to Ezekiel how much he was threatened or how many were the scowls on their faces. In his commissioning, God told him he would have courage, wisdom and perseverance to preach the Word to his people without backing down.

Ezekiel and Boun faithfully proclaimed God's Word to their generation without fear. You, too, are God's messenger to the world. You, like Ezekiel, need to have a thick skin and give out God's truths despite the reactions of those around you. Proclaim the truth. It's your responsibility.

September 2

Reason Not to Fear #246: We Do Not Walk in Pride

"Thus says the Lord God, 'I will also destroy the idols and cause the images to cease from Noph; there shall no longer be princes in the land of Egypt; and I will put fear in the land of Egypt.'" Ezekiel 30:13

Ezekiel prophesied against the land of Egypt. Did you know that the people of Egypt had over 2,000 gods? They worshipped everything from the sun to the River Nile to grasshoppers and frogs! The cities and locations mentioned in this chapter are still there in Egypt today. Pi-beseth (v. 17) was about 30 miles NE of Cairo and was a center of worship of the cat-headed goddess, Tehaphnehes. Noph was modern Memphis.

The plagues, recorded in Exodus 7-11, were a direct hit against one of the gods or idols of Egypt. Yet they had the truth. For over four hundred years, the Israelites lived with the Egyptians, giving them a witness of the true God in heaven. The Egyptians knew the truth and the way to God, but they rejected it and followed after their own gods. Pharaoh hardened his heart and would not repent or turn to the God of the Israelites. This resulted in his death and the total destruction of the nation.

Today Egypt is a center of the Muslim religion, having been taken by Arab caliphs around 640 AD from the Byzantium nation. Nebuchadnezzar, the Babylonian king, was the arm that the Lord used to break Egypt's power in Ezekiel's day.

Nebuchadnezzar had a problem with pride, too, and had to be taught a lesson from God about it. Daniel predicted that unless he humbled himself and worshipped God alone, he would be humbled by God's hand. It came true. When he boasted about his mighty works, his power, his wealth, God struck him and he became like an animal for seven years, eating grass like a cow. (Daniel 4:19-37)

Pride is an offense to God. Pride says I can do it myself. It will not bend the knee to God or to anyone. It is the root of all sin. How much pride do you have? Can you say you are sorry? Can you take second place and be at ease? Can you watch others succeed and not lust after their success, or be jealous? Confess your sin and experience purity, humility and faith.

Walk in the light and in God's wonderful fellowship, care and comfort.

September 3

Reason Not to Fear #247: Stay Loyal to God and He Will Help You

"And the chief of the eunuchs said to Daniel, "I fear my lord the king, who has appointed your food and drink. For why should he see your faces looking worse than the young men who are your age? Then you would endanger my head before the king." Daniel 1:10

It takes most young people awhile to figure out who they are and what they want to eventually become in life. In June, my first grandchild will begin college in Illinois. Many have asked her what she wants to become when she graduates, but she has no idea yet. Teenagers oftentimes cannot make decisions about what they want to study or what career they want to pursue.

That was not the case with Daniel. Here was a young man, taken captive to a foreign land, whose name had changed and whose whole life had changed. He was taken into slavery when he was young, leaving behind his family, his nation, and his religion. But Daniel did not change. He knew his mission on this earth. It was to follow God no matter what the cost, and to glorify God even in a strange, foreign country.

Daniel was forced to live in a system that was totally hostile to the Lord's people, one in which idols were worshipped and the Law of God was not considered. Yet he faithfully sought to please the Lord despite spiritual opposition. Therefore, he had no fear whatsoever of the king.

He stood up for his principles and did not compromise. Perhaps the king thought if he surrounded these boys with worldly items and food, then they would shed their Jewish identity and their faith in the Lord. Maybe he thought Daniel would drop his guard and fold under the temptation. He was wrong.

Daniel spoke out to the steward and asked to be given food that was lawful for them to eat. The steward, while fearing the king, agreed to Daniel's request and God blessed the four young boys for their faith.

Daniel's outward circumstances may have changed, but his heart did not. Remember the mission God has given you on this earth. It is not to please and be in fear of an earthly king or president. It is to fear God alone. Like Daniel, stay loyal to God and to your faith no matter who opposes you. Be a Daniel today.

September 4

Reason Not to Fear #248: We Do Not Fear In A Shaky World

*"I make a decree that in every dominion of my kingdom men must tremble
and fear before the God of Daniel. For He is the living God, and steadfast
forever; His kingdom is the one which shall not be destroyed, and His dominion
shall endure to the end." Daniel 6:26*

In the nearby town of Sun City, Arizona, a man took a gun and killed his
wife of over 66 years. She had been sick since 1977 and in a wheelchair,
needing constant care. When she discovered that her feet needed to be
amputated because of gangrene, she told her husband, "I cannot do this
anymore." She asked him to end her life.

He refused, but she pursued the topic. Finally he took a gun and killed her.
The judge decided that the man would be on a two year probation period. After
receiving the judgment, he said, "I still love my wife very much."

I tell you that story to remind you we live in a very shaky world. Whether
you agree or disagree with this man's decision, these are the issues we have to
wrestle with in the world in which we live. Yet Christians must always go back
to the Word of God for our choices, and the Bible tells us it is a sin to take a
human life, no matter what the situation.

Daniel was an old man and had lived a long life of serving God. He now
served under King Darius, the Persian. Because of an evil plot, he had to spend
the night with a bunch of hungry lions. He would not bend to the commands of
the king even when his life depended on it. He obeyed God and His Word and
because of this, he was unshakable. God protected him and used the incident to
teach Darius a lesson. The king made a proclamation that the people in all the
nations he ruled would fear and reverence the God of Daniel.

Daniel determined not to defile himself no matter how shaky the new world
was that he was now a part of. Because of this decision, he became a respected
leader. However, when you are living for God and doing the right thing, there
will always be some who will not like or respect you.

Perhaps you find yourself today in some new and scary surroundings. Live
out of your faith. When you decide to obey God and do things His way, not
yours, you will find an amazing comfort and strength that you never
experienced before. It is the unseen power of God. It is the reality of your
unseen Companion. So do not fear, not even in a shaky world.

September 5

Reason Not to Fear #249: We Listen to God from His Word

"Then he said to me, 'Do not fear, Daniel, for from the first day that you set your heart to understand this and to humble yourself before your God, your words were heard, and I have come because of your words.'" Daniel 10:12

Daniel was eight-five years old, an old man for those days. He had served under a number of heathen kings in the land of Babylon and had been faithful all the days of his life to give a witness to these kings and the people. After a lifetime of service, we find Daniel deeply concerned about the spiritual condition of his people, the Israelites. He fasted for three entire weeks, mourning for the sins of his people. He had not returned with the first group of people to the land, for he was too old. Yet he longed to be with them and he prayed for their safe arrival.

It is while he was in prayer, sitting along the banks of the great river, Tigris, that he saw another vision. In this, an angel revealed to Daniel a prophetic message that would span centuries and millennia. This vision reassured the prophet that God was in control and all things would come about as He has planned.

I pray for my children and grandchildren regularly. I pray that they will hear God, that they will listen to Him, and that they will grow into His image. These three things depend on each other. You cannot be conformed to the image of Christ if you do not hear Him. Oh, you can do spiritual disciplines, you can bear fruit for Him, but your trust level and your obedience will be affected if you do not hear Him. Your heart is changed when you hear Him through His Word.

Do you know why Daniel received this visit? Because he truly longed to hear from the Lord. All of his other desires became second to hearing God. He didn't want to eat, sleep, drink or even bathe. Do you know why he wanted to hear from the Lord? Because he knew the children of Israel were missing the blessing of God. They had gotten comfortable there in Babylon. He wanted them to return to the land and experience all that God had for them.

What about you? Do you desire to hear the Lord? What priority do you give reading His Word, spending time in prayer, and worshipping Him in church? Consider your ways. Become a Daniel today and give Him all of your heart, your mind and your soul. *Listen to people and your life will change. Listen to God and your heart will change.*

September 6

Reason Not to Fear #250: God Will Show Us the Way

"And he said, "O man greatly beloved, fear not! Peace be to you; be strong, yes, be strong!" So when he spoke to me I was strengthened, and said, "Let my lord speak, for you have strengthened me." Daniel 10:19

If you read the entire tenth chapter of Daniel, you will discover that having visions is no picnic, and neither is being a prophet.

God gave visions to the Old Testament prophets, and to the Apostle John, to communicate and reveal His will, His nature, and His mind to mankind. Once the written Word of God was completed, and with the revelation of His Son, Jesus Christ, there is no need for further prophetic messages from God. (Hebrews 1:1-3) I am not discounting the Word given to people who cannot know, nor those who do not have the Bible. God is able to miraculously give these people His Word to bring them into His Kingdom by the means of special revelation.

Yet when people receive dreams or visions, they can become puffed up with spiritual pride, and when they give out the interpretation of the dream, they may claim to speak for God. Yet many times, these visions are not from God because they contradict or stray from the Word of God.

Daniel was extremely exhausted from the last vision he had received. Then here comes another one in answer to his prayer. This angel tells the prophet that he had to fight a wicked spirit from Satan to arrive and deliver his message. Through it all, Daniel experienced this in total weakness of his flesh. The angel had to touch him to revive him. In the verse we read today, the heavenly messenger told Daniel to not be afraid and to be courageous. Then he begins to reveal God's plan for the nations down through the centuries.

Rather than longing for special spiritual gifts, why don't you spend time with the book God has written just for you: the Bible. All that you need to know for your life, for your relationship with God, and for wisdom to know God's will is found in the pages of this marvelous book. You will never plum the depths of it, and the more you study it, the more you will fall in love with its author, God Himself.

Strengthen yourself and have courage as you study the Bible. Take it to heart. Obey it and love it. You will not be sorry you did!

September 7

Reason Not to Fear #251: Turn Your Eyes to Jesus

"Afterward the children of Israel will return and seek the LORD their God and David their king. They shall fear the LORD and His goodness in the latter days." Hosea 3:5

Psalm 2:11 and 12 says "Worship the Lord with reverence and rejoice with trembling. Do homage to the Son, that He not become angry, and you perish in the way." In the King James Version, it reads, "Kiss the Son, lest He become angry.

How would you feel if the President of the United States came to visit in your home? Or what if someone you admire greatly came to visit you? We could name hundreds of people in our world today who are incredibly wealthy and who hold whole nations in their hands. Yet they are nothing compared to the glory, power and honor we should give our King, Jesus Christ.

Hosea had an extremely difficult job to do as he prophesied to the nation of Israel prior to the time when they would be judged by God and taken into bondage by the Assyrians. God told him to go and marry a woman who was a prostitute. This woman, Gomer, left him after they were wed to run after other men. She ended up being a sex slave and Hosea was instructed by God to redeem her, bring her back to his house, remarry her, and love her.

This became a powerful object lesson to the people of their own sin against God. Jehovah God of the Israelites had brought about the nation of Israel and claimed them as His own. He redeemed them from bondage in Egypt and gave them their own land. Yet they turned against Him, went after other gods and idols, rejecting his repeated messages of love and warning to return to Him.

After a time of judgment, God's plan was to bring them back to their land, Israel, and eventually Jesus Christ would be their King. They would come, then, as this verse says, in trembling to the King of kings and Lord of lords to seek His blessing. They would honor Him, love Him and worship Him.

Instead of running after the rich and powerful people of this world who are nothing compared to the majesty of Jesus Christ, I challenge you today to turn your eyes to Him. Honor Him. Obey Him. Love Him. Worship Him. Do it right now.

September 8

Reason Not to Fear #252: God's Amazing Unfailing Love

"The inhabitants of Samaria fear for the calf of Beth-Aven. For its people mourn for it, and its priests shriek for it -- because its glory has departed from it." Hosea 10:5

Hosea was a prophet of God who lived in the northern kingdom of Israel. Material prosperity and spiritual bankruptcy characterized the time under Jeroboam II when Hosea began his ministry. Judgment seemed remote, but already the powerful nation of Assyria had taken Syria and Damascus in 732 BC, and they were threatening Israel.

The theme of this book is God's steadfast love for Israel despite her continued unfaithfulness. The prophet traveled to the city of Bethel, just north of Jerusalem, where Jeroboam I, the king after the division of the nation, had set up a golden calf for the people to worship. He also set one up in the northern territory of Dan, for the people of the that area to come to worship. He did this so the people would not have to travel south to Jerusalem for their religious ceremonies and thus be lured back to Judah.

The worship of these calves resembled the Israelite worship of Yahweh. Jeroboam appointed priests, erected temples, and had sacrifices and feast days for the golden calf god. Yet it was all a sham. This false religion became like the worship of the gods of that day which included human sacrifices and gross immorality. It led the people away from God.

Hosea wept when he looked upon the golden calf god. He called Bethel "Beth-aven," which means House of Wickedness, a slur on the name of Bethel, which means House of God. Hosea declared that when the Assyrians came to conquer Israel, they would take this calf god with them, and the people would mourn over it. They had fallen so far from God that they cried over an idol!

It is very easy to slide away from God. You can forget the Lord God who created you, who redeemed you and who loves you. He stands at the edges of your life, watching you descend a treacherous path away from Him. You no longer desire to worship in church. You no longer have time to serve Him. You can't even find time to read your Bible or to pray.

Hosea would weep over you, too. Come back to God today. Give Him your time, your money, your love, your devotion, your honor, your life. Give it all to Him and you will be blessed.

September 9

Reason Not to Fear #253: On Your Knees You Will Find God

"Before them, the people are in pain (fear); all faces are drained of color."
Joel 2:6

My mom used to say that she could tell by my facial expressions if I was telling the truth or not because my face gave me away. It is true -- your face speaks to people. Beyond the words you might utter, your face gives you away. Are you bored with the company and yawn behind your hand? Guess what. They know what you are thinking.

Are you angry, yet you put on a front of civilized cheerfulness, thinking people don't know? Think again. They know you are angry. Are you peeved, excited, sad, tired or ready for a fight? The people you are with know what is going on behind your carefully made up face. You do not need to use words. People can read your facial expressions.

In this verse, the minor prophet Joel preaches about a day when an invading army will march into Judah and cause anguish and fear. This invading army will, he says, completely devastate the nation. Just prior to his prophecy, a severe drought and a plague of locusts came into the land, bringing the ruination of the crops and starvation for the people. Joel saw these natural events as the judgments of God for the nation's sins.

He also saw this invasion of locusts as a picture of an invasion by a foreign army that would completely destroy them unless they repented of their sins. He says that when the people saw this great army, their faces would grow pale because of their fear. When life gets overwhelming, it shows on your face.

What are you supposed to do when you repeatedly find life beating you up? What are you supposed to do when you find yourself faced with circumstances that are devastating, with a situation that doesn't go away and is inescapable?

Look up to your Father, even when you are blown away with the grief that is tearing you apart. Repent of any sins God convicts you about. Tell people you need their prayers. Be transparent. When things are bad, don't hide it. Seek God in prayer.

Stop everything and talk to Him right now. When you are at the end of your rope with no resources left, when there is no one left to turn to, then drop to your knees. On your knees, you will find forgiveness, comfort and hope. It is the only position to take when your face turns pale.

September 10

Reason Not to Fear #254: The Lord Has Done Great Things!

"Fear not, O land; be glad and rejoice, for the LORD has done marvelous things! Do not be afraid, you beasts of the field; for the open pastures are springing up, and the tree bears its fruit; the fig tree and the vine yield their strength." Joel 2:21, 22

The prophet Joel called the people of Judah to repentance in this little book. He preached these sermons about 123 years before the northern nation of Israel was taken into bondage by the Assyrians and about 246 years before Judah was conquered and taken by the Babylonians.

God gave them a warning that they needed to repent of their sins of idolatry, pride and greed. Joel used an invasion of three kinds of locusts, and the famine and starvation that went with that, to warn the people. To paraphrase what Joel meant we would say, "This is God's judgment on the land. In a small way, this is what is going to happen to you if you do not repent."

In 2:12, he writes, "'Yet even now,' declares the Lord, 'return to Me with all your heart, and with fasting, weeping and mourning; and rend your heart and not your garments.' Now return to the Lord your God, for He is gracious and compassionate, slow to anger, abounding in lovingkindness and relenting of calamity."

We need to heed this warning and pass it on to our children, grandchildren, and even great-grandchildren. God has allowed America to suffer in many ways, and we need to repent and come back to Him. In the passage for today, Joel looks ahead to the blessed fact that one day God will restore His people to their land and to a right relationship with Himself. But it all hinges on the individual's response to God.

It is a Biblical principle to pass on to the next generation our faith and our walk with the Lord. It is vital that we pass on what the Lord has done. Think back over your walk with the Lord. I am sure you can name several great things the Lord has done for you. Pass that information on.

As you share your memories, you will equip the next generation not only to walk with the Lord, but to fear Him in the right way. Share your stories of faith with the next generation and see what great things He will do in their lives, too. Teach them the Word of God. Repent of your own sins and get right with God, then pass your faith on to your children.

September 11

Reason Not to Fear #255: The Lord Will Not Tolerate Sin

"If a trumpet is blown in a city, will not the people be afraid? If there is calamity in a city, will not the LORD have done it? Surely the Lord GOD does nothing, unless He reveals His secret to His servants the prophets. A lion has roared! Who will not fear? The Lord GOD has spoken! Who can but prophesy?" Amos 3:6-8

It was never on my bucket list to work in the inner city of Chicago for fifteen years. Nor was it on my bucket list to teach for Bible Study Fellowship in Pennsylvania for ten years. The truth is, I simply wanted to be a housewife and mother. Being around people and holding lengthy conversations was and is not one of my strong points. God had different ideas for my life. When my life crossed Bob's life, my plans totally changed. While he attended Moody Bible Institute, he felt the call of God on his life for full time Christian service and my life followed a new path.

Don't you love it when God chooses the unexpected, the unnoticed, and the unpredictable one to do His work? Boy, I sure do.

Amos was not an acclaimed prophet. He came from Tekoa, a small village in Judah during the days of the kings (around 755 B.C.). He felt the call of God on his life to leave his vocation of sheep breeding and master shepherd to preach God's Word. He traveled north to Israel, to Bethel, which was foreign soil to him. Bethel was the residence of King Jeroboam II and a center of idol worship. You can imagine that his message was not well received!

Amos announced loudly and fearlessly that the Israelites, from the king downward, should tremble and be fearful because the Sovereign Lord Jehovah had roared against their iniquities. The people did not like Amos' message, so they banished him from their country. But God's voice could not be silenced. Even in Judah, Amos continued to preach and write against the sins of the nation of Israel and warn them that if they did not turn from their wicked ways, they would suffer the judgment of God.

The Lord will not tolerate sin forever. This was true in Israel, and it is true in America today. If you are God's child, you should live a holy life style. You cannot live like you used to live before you came to know Christ. Search your heart and get it right before God. Put away your idols. Don't ignore the voice of the Sovereign Lord. It has come for a reason.

September 12

Reason Not to Fear #256: We Don't Run Away from God

"Then the mariners were afraid; and every man cried out to his god, and threw the cargo that was in the ship into the sea, to lighten the load." Jonah 1:5

Jonah was called by God to go to the great city of Nineveh, which was the capitol of the nation of Assyria. There he was supposed to preach His Word. But Jonah did not want to do it. He became, as is known today among the Israelites, "the indigestible prophet." Why did he not want to fulfill this commission?

I believe it was because the Assyrians were the ancient, bitter enemies of God's people and he flat-out refused to go there and preach a message of God's grace and love to them. They were deeply involved in idolatry, which included human sacrifice and immorality. In Jonah's opinion, they deserved God's punishment, not His grace.

Jonah did not do things by halves; we have to give him that. He boarded a ship that was sailing in a totally different direction than Nineveh, heading west across the sea. He went down into the hold and fell asleep so soundly asleep that even a great storm did not awaken him. He was totally oblivious of the trouble and misery he was causing by his disobedience.

Have you ever run away from God? How do you respond when God gives you an assignment to do for Him? Does it bring fear to your heart? How would you feel if He asked you to go to a nation that had declared war on our country? Would you come up with a dozen excuses why you could not do it? Would you run from it as Jonah did?

Can you really run away from God? When you decide to run away from the Lord's will, you may be risking the safety of the people around you. Such was the case with Jonah. In the process of our disobedience, we can risk the lives of the people around us. Your decision can affect others. It can bring a fear into their lives like it did with the sailors.

It is a high privilege to work for and with God. Therefore, when He calls you to do something for Him, humble yourself and obey. God will bless your life if you walk in obedience to Him each day. What has He given you to do today? Do it and praise Him for the opportunity to serve Him.

September 13

Reason Not to Fear #257: Disobedience Leads to Failure to Witness for God

"So he said to them, 'I am a Hebrew; and I fear the LORD, the God of heaven, who made the sea and the dry land.' Then the men were exceedingly afraid, and said to him, 'Why have you done this?' For the men knew that he fled from the presence of the LORD, because he had told them." Jonah 1:9

I teach two Bible studies a week. The study of Jonah was our topic last week. His book makes me feel uncomfortable because I relate to Jonah on many levels. Why do we run away from God? And what happens when we run? In the case of Jonah, he evaded the will of the Lord. He had the wrong attitude, and did not want to obey God.

Yet God was not about to let him get away. He prepared a great storm, a great fish, a people prepared to hear God's Word, a plant, and a worm for the sake of His prophet.

When a massive storm struck the ship that Jonah was aboard, he was forced to admit his fear of the living God. Catch it. A prophet of God was being questioned by unbelieving sailors as to his belief, and they had to *wring* out of him this confession of his faith in Yahweh God. His disobedience had a huge effect on others besides himself.

Jonah did not want to talk about God because he was running from God. He slipped to the bottom of the ship and went to sleep when he should have been testifying to these pagan sailors about the glory, love and majesty of his God. I hope you do not have to have the truth of God wrung out of you by those who do not know Christ!

In the book of Jonah, God is mentioned over thirty-eight times. God is in control, and whether we like it or not, He will never leave us or forsake us. God did not let His reluctant prophet go his own way. He brought him back to repentance and set his feet on the right path. Jonah's eight-word sermon produced a great revival in the city of Nineveh, right up to the king!

You can either run away from God or you can run to Him. My advice is to run to Him. Don't be disobedient, stubborn or resistant to God's will. Don't run away from the mission God has given you to do. He will give you joy when you do His will above your own.

September 14

Reason Not to Fear #258: The Future Is Rosy for Those Who Fear God

"Each of them will sit under his vine and under his fig tree, with no one to make them afraid for the mouth of the Lord of hosts has spoken." Micah 4:4

There is cause to be afraid in a nation and society that has left God out in the cold.

There was a news story of a young woman in Oklahoma who noticed two strange men prowling her neighborhood. She was alone most of the day and had a small child. The sight of these two men alarmed her. She knew she should be prepared if they attempted to break into her home.

The next evening, it happened. She heard men on the steps and saw that they were trying to force their way in. She called out to them and told them she was armed and not to come in, but they did not listen. They broke the lock and entered the home. She was ready. She fired a blast of rifle fire that killed the first man and frightened the other one away.

Why do these kinds of things happen in our country? Because people have lost their fear of the Lord. As a nation, we have excluded God from our schools, our government, our businesses, our entertainment, our songs, our way of life. People choose to worship the god of money, sex, food, pleasure or prosperity.

Micah was a prophet in Judah. He directed his words against the leaders of Jerusalem and Samaria and warned them of using their position and power to take advantage of poor people.

The people living in Judah and Israel were deeply troubled at this time, for they had left God out of their lives. Judges, priests and prophets all put their services up for sale, deteriorating their services. They were hypocritical. They worshipped false gods. They were cruel and unfeeling to the poor.

In this type of atmosphere, Micah offered words of hope to people who were full of fear. He envisioned a time of peace when the fear and love of God would prevail among all nations and they would once again enjoy prosperity, peace, and plenty.

Micah's words offer each of us encouragement, too. In a time when fear is prevalent in our society, we need to trust the Lord for our needs, for our strength and for our hope.

September 15

Reason Not to Fear #259: God's Judgments on the Wicked Make Them Fear

"The nations shall see and be ashamed of all their might; they shall put their hand over their mouth; their ears shall be deaf. They shall lick the dust like a serpent; they shall crawl from their holes like snakes of the earth. They shall be afraid of the LORD our God, and shall fear because of You."
Micah 7:16, 17

While Hosea and Amos prophesied to the northern nation of Israel and Isaiah prophesied to the court in Jerusalem, Micah, a Judean from the town of Moresheth in southwest Judah, preached to the common people of his nation. He began his prophetic ministry in 742 B.C, only nine years before Tiglath-Pilsear, the Assyrian king, invaded Israel the first time, and only twenty years before the Assyrian general, Sargon II, conquered it and took the people captive.

Micah preached a message of coming judgment that would soon fall upon God's people for their sin and idol worship. He spoke to people who were downtrodden, poor and needy. These people lived in times of hardship, for the armies would march through and destroy crops, take slaves and burn villages.

Micah warned the people that they needed to forsake their idols and return to the Lord God Jehovah. Idol worship swept the land. Evil crept into the society from the top down, but even the poor people knew and practiced the worship rites of the pagan nations. They sacrificed their children to the heathen gods. They prayed to these gods. They gave of their wealth and money to the idols. They participated in the worship of demons.

Micah says that the rulers reversed things. They hated what was good and loved what was evil. He and his message was despised and rejected. God was left with the awful decision to bring judgment on these people. They would not listen to His voice.

Do you see our beloved nation following these same tactics today? Instead of trust in Jesus Christ and in God, our nation and leaders trust in military might, wealth and the alliance with other countries. We need to pray for our leaders and pray for ourselves. We need to see revival come to our nation. Revival starts with you. Plead with God right now for salvation and renewal for the people of our nation.

September 16

Reason Not to Fear #260: Revival Comes With Prayer

"O LORD, I have heard your speech and was afraid; O LORD, revive Your work in the midst of the years! In the midst of the years make it known; In wrath remember mercy." Habakkuk 3:2

Is there the possibility of true revival in America today? Or are the revivals just a thing of the past?

Habakkuk can tell us something about real revival. He was a puzzled prophet, and he was not afraid to pose his questions to God. His two questions to God in this book are: why does God permit evil to go unpunished? (1:2-4), and how can a holy God use the Babylonians, a people more wicked than the Jews, as an instrument to punish the Jews? (1:12-2:1). Good questions! God answers them, too. If you want to know the answers, read the book.

Habakkuk was looking for revival among his people. The northern nation of Israel had been taken captive by the Assyrians. Now war was imminent with the Babylonians, and he knew God was going to use them to judge the Israelites. Yet despite the bad news that was looming on the horizon, Habakkuk urged the people to repent of their sins, turn from their wicked ways, and return to God.

We live in a society that is no longer influenced by Christian faith. Many people today think that God is dead or never existed. In this post-modern era, people are no longer interested in a vibrant, growing and meaningful relationship with the living God. But I do believe there is still a chance that revival can occur in our land in this day and age.

What is revival? It is God's work, not ours. Revival begins with one sinner on his knees crying out to God for forgiveness, pardon and mercy. God begins to move in the hearts of others, and the repentance spreads because people have prayed. Revival starts with God, not a series of meetings. Each revival that has ever touched a country, a church, or an individual has been a unique work of God. Let God move in His own way to do a genuine work of revival in your church, your child's or spouse's life, in your life.

Repentance is the key that opens the door of God's mercy and love. It is not too late. Let the revival begin in your heart today. An unknown author wrote, "Mercy has no memory; grace has no regrets."

September 17

Reason Not to Fear #261: We Gather, Seek and Obey God

"I said, 'Surely you will fear Me, You will receive instruction'-- So that her dwelling would not be cut off, despite everything for which I punished her. But they rose early and corrupted all their deeds." Zephaniah 3:7

When I was raising my children, they fell under my authority and had to learn to abide by the rules in our home. However, sad to say, they didn't always obey. At times they needed my correction.

Zephaniah preached to the nation of Judah just prior to the Babylonian assault and conquest of the nation. His voice rang out as one of the last of the prophets to call people back to repentance and to obedience to the Lord. This is why, if you read the entire short book, you will notice the urgency in his tone. Judgment is the central theme of the book.

Despite his passionate plea, the people continued in their sinful behavior. They were corrupt, dishonest, disloyal, and deceitful. In chapter two, Zephaniah asks three things of the people: **gather** together for the purpose of revival and repentance; **seek** the Lord and His favor; **obey** the Word of God from their hearts.

Even in His declaration of judgment, God held out hope. "If only you will repent and turn back to Me," He said, "I will heal your land and will not have to judge you." Yet they continued to remain indifferent to Him. They lived in apathy, trusting in their gods, their wealth and their military might.

That, my dear friend, is the attitude of many people today. *God doesn't see me*, they say. *God will not judge me. God is love.* The people of Judah were facing the dark side of God's love, for His judgment fell on their nation with relentless justice. Many of them died. Many were taken into slavery. They lost all they had hoarded -- money, lands, position, fame.

The cost of disobedience is high, indeed. Where do you stand with the Lord and His Word? Do you trust in your wealth, your possessions, your job, your position, your insurance company, your abilities? Do you put God first place in your life? If you answer no to that question, you need to look at your priorities and put Him at the top of the list.

Do not be apathetic. God is going to judge His Church, and He is going to judge America. Get serious about your obedience to Him today.

September 18

Reason Not to Fear #265: God Keeps His Promises

"The LORD has taken away your judgments, He has cast out your enemy. The King of Israel, the LORD, is in your midst; You shall see disaster no more. In that day it shall be said to Jerusalem: "Do not fear; Zion, let not your hands be weak. The LORD your God in your midst, The Mighty One, will save; He will rejoice over you with gladness, He will quiet you with His love, He will rejoice over you with singing." Zephaniah 3:15-17

There is something tender and sweet about the comfort, protection, and guidance of God as revealed in the above passage. The judgment of God has ended for the people of Israel and now He can comfort them. This passage brings to mind a mother who gently rocks her child, crooning to him, perhaps singing a lullaby to sooth his fears.

"I am with you," God is saying to His people. "I will protect you. I will never let anyone attack you again. Be still. Know that I am God."

In a coming day of great joy, Zechariah describes the time when the people of Israel will be safe and secure without alarm. He says that at that time, God Himself will croon over them with the love songs of the Beloved. We will be part of those people over whom He sings the songs of Zion!

God still loves Jerusalem, despite the spiritual shortcomings of the people, and He loves the church. He loves you. After His discipline, God longs to comfort you. To give you joy. To bring you close to Himself. How has God been a comfort to you in recent days? *He will exult over you; He will rejoice over you.* He will rock you in His everlasting arms and wipe all tears away from your eyes. This is the blessed hope we have in the Lord.

Someday, and it might not be very far away, we will be with the Lord. Is it too hard for you to endure your hardships for this lifetime when you consider the eternity we will spend with Christ? Yes, you may face hard times, but you do not have to be destroyed by them.

Do not fear. Your God has the ability to deliver you and provide for you. He is mighty to save, and He is there to give you all that you need. Turn to Him. Love Him and give Him your total life, devotion, honor and glory. His love is all you need today.

September 19

Reason Not to Fear #263: God Helps Us Finish Our Projects

"Then Zerubbabel the son of Shealtiel, and Joshua the son of Jehozadak, the high priest, with all the remnant of the people, obeyed the voice of the LORD their God, and the words of Haggai the prophet, as the LORD their God had sent him; and the people feared the presence of the LORD." Haggai 1:12

I like this minor prophet. In fact, when I taught on this book a couple of weeks ago, he instantly became my boyfriend! The reason is that Haggai is a man of action. He wants to get things done, and I can relate to that. When I have an assignment, it bugs me if I do not do it or finish it.

Half-finished projects clutter most of our lives. We have the afghan that is only partially knitted in a bag in our closet, the cross-stitch embroidery project we started for Mary Jane's wedding sitting in a drawer, and she now has three kids!

When it comes to God, His Word, the church, our service to Him, and our obedience to Him, we need to clean up those unfinished tasks. We need to roll up our sleeves and do it.

Haggai, a prophet who preached after the people returned to their land, witnessed the half-finished temple sitting there in dust and disrepair. The temple to the Jewish faith was the very center of their worship, their salvation, their faith. This unfinished temple cried out that they had uncompleted business in their hearts as well.

God's call to them was to finish the temple. The Israelites responded to God's call and did it! They were enthusiastic, energetic, and eager to work. The fear of disobedience to the Lord brought a godly fear over them, and they finished the task with God's help.

What is it that is unfinished in your life? Did you start out eager to serve God, yet have you allowed a conflict with someone or a discouraging word stop you? Working for the Lord is never easy. We need to persevere past the difficult times and continue to serve God.

It is when we realize that God is in our work, then He will help us and give us strength, and it can be completed. Let me be clear about this. Laziness is something the Lord does not bless. Stop sitting on the side lines. Stop being a spectator. Make a decision to get in there and work. Do not be a quitter. Finish those projects God has laid on your heart to do.

September 20

Reason Not to Fear #264: We Apply Ourselves to Our Christian Faith

"According to the word that I covenanted with you when you came out of Egypt, so My Spirit remains among you; do not fear!" Haggai 2:5

The people who returned from Babylon after the captivity were poor, unarmed, unorganized and fearful. They began rebuilding their lives by throwing up shelters in the burned out city of Jerusalem, but there were no walls around the city, and their enemies were numerous.

Haggai, who was a contemporary of Zechariah, was the first prophetic voice to be heard after the Israelites returned to their land. To their credit, they were obedient to God's command, and in a record time (23 days!), they finished their new temple. Yet most of them remembered the glory of Solomon's magnificent structure, and in comparison, this new one was a poor copy.

When the new temple was dedicated, some wept for joy and others wept for sorrow as they remembered Solomon's temple, and this one was not nearly as grand. Yet God said, "I am with you, I will prosper you, and someday, my people, you will have a temple that will be the wonder of the whole world! Do not fear!" Why should they have been afraid?

They lived in an un-walled city, surrounded by enemy nations. They had to rebuild their houses, till the land and make a living from it. Were they frightened? Oh, yes. I imagine that every man in soldier's garb mounted on a horse that approached Jerusalem caused them consternation.

Whenever fear knocks on your door, whether it is because of something that is in the past or something in the future, this is a signal for you that you have taken your eyes off the Lord. You have feared this thing rather than fearing God.

Did God begin a good work in you, yet because of your busy schedule and pressures, you have forgotten Him? Is His work lying unfinished?

Close this time by reading Philippians 2:12. God will do His part if you apply yourself to a godly life. This means you must give time to study His Word, pray, and serve wherever He puts you. Think about it and then write down what He wants you to do to continue the good work He has begun in you.

September 21

Reason Not to Fear #265: We Roll Our Burdens on the Lord

"And it shall come to pass that just as you were a curse among the nations, O house of Judah and house of Israel, so I will save you, and you shall be a blessing. Do not fear; let your hands be strong." Zechariah 8:13

Why is it that throughout most of human history, the Jews have been looked down upon, despised and persecuted? Even in our day, there is much anti-Semitism to be found in America and around the world. There are those who have declared that they would like nothing better than to eradicate the Israelites and shove them off into the depths of the sea.

Satan wants to destroy them because he knows they are the instruments God used to bring about the birth of His Son, the redemption of all mankind, and the written Word of God. Satan tried his best to destroy them, all the way from the Egyptians, to Haman of Esther's day, to Stalin and Hitler, and on down to the extremist Muslim factions of our day.

Yet God has miraculously preserved them throughout all the ages. While He had to discipline them and judge them by sending them into captivity for seventy years, He brought them back. One of the greatest signs of His soon return to this earth is the fact that Israelites now live in their own country; Hebrew is spoken; children play on the streets of Jerusalem! In other words, Israel and the Jewish people are alive and well today.

It is the sovereign plan of God that despite nations coming against Israel, He will preserve them. Though they become fearful, the Lord assures them He will always be there for them. He will save them. He will bless them.

One day the Lord Jesus will return to reign and rule from the land of Israel. In that day, there will be world peace, and Israel will have no fears.

For those of us who have accepted Christ as our Savior, we share the same privileged position with God that the Israelites have. While the world may look at Christians and despise us, curse us and persecute us, we know what our destiny holds for us in God's plan. We, like the ancient Israelites, do not need to fear.

God will take care of you. Do not try to carry the load of the world on your shoulders. Do not even try to carry the load of your personal life. Turn it over to God. Roll the burden onto Him and He will give you peace. *Do not fear* -- these words were written to you, too!

September 22

Reason Not to Fear #266: God's Grace Is Wonderful

"So again in these days I am determined to do good to Jerusalem and to the house of Judah. Do not fear." Zechariah 8:15

This is the season when people are harvesting their gardens. Early crops, such as peas, radishes and lettuce are pretty well finished. Now we are reaping the good stuff -- corn, tomatoes, peppers, squash, pumpkins. My sister and brother both live in the Midwest and like to plant a garden. What they love most, though, is harvesting what they planted.

The prophet Zechariah, who lived in Judah around 520-518 BC, wanted Judah to have a harvest, too, a harvest of peace. The nation had their temple desecrated and destroyed, their leaders and people taken into exile, and the land desolated. After they served their foreign masters of Babylon for seventy years, the Persian king, Cyrus, allowed the Israelites to return to their land.

Zerubbabel and later, Ezra returned with a group of people to the land. Can you imagine how they felt when they turned the last corner and saw the place where the temple once stood? They must have wept many bitter tears. The godly leaders who returned with them encouraged them to rebuild the city, their homes, the temple, and finally, (under Nehemiah's leadership) the walls of Jerusalem.

However, the people had grown a little lax about finishing some of their projects. They forgot they needed to finish the temple. God's purpose was to bless them, prosper them and be with them if they would obey Him.

Yet they forgot God's Word and were edging toward a dangerous position of disobeying Him again. God reminds them that He wants to bless them. They might have despaired had it not been for these good words of Zechariah of God's grace and love. "Let your hands be strong," God says to them, "and finish the temple." (8:9) And they did!

This grace that God extended to the children of Israel is offered to you today. God still calls his people back with the intent to bless them even though they have rebelled against Him.

The wonderful grace of God is available today. Do you want to be blessed by God? Walk in obedience to Him and to His Word. Stay close to Him. Seek His face every day, and you will know the blessing of the Lord on your life.

September 23

Reason Not to Fear #267: God Protects His Own

"For Tyre built herself a tower, heaped up silver like the dust, And gold like the mire of the streets. Behold, the LORD will cast her out; He will destroy her power in the sea, and she will be devoured by fire. Ashkelon shall see it and fear; Gaza also shall be very sorrowful; And Ekron, for He dried up her expectation. The king shall perish from Gaza, And Ashkelon shall not be inhabited.... I will camp around My house because of the army, because of him who passes by and him who returns. No more shall an oppressor pass through them, for now I have seen with My eyes." Zechariah 9:3-5, 8

Tyre and her sister to the north, Sidon, were great cities of commerce, shipping and wealth during the days of the Old Testament. To think that they would be wiped from the face of the earth so completely that they would never rebuild to that place again was unthinkable. It would be the same as saying that one day New York City will be nothing but a cluster of fishing huts.

It must be noted that their great sin was not that they possessed much wealth, but that they left God out of their lives. They worshipped idols and refused to believe in the One God of All, Jehovah of the Jews. God said He would judge these cities, and it happened when Alexander the Great attacked the city of Tyre.

The people fled to an island off the coast, but this Greek general threw the stones of the city into the sea to build a causeway. Yet even this general had his moment of justly deserved punishment. Every city that he conquered he renamed after himself, which caused him to become more and more proud. One day, a priest even told him he was a god, which caused him to make his citizens worship him.

Alexander the Great had it in his mind that he would take Jerusalem. As he was marching towards the holy city, he was greeted by a priest who told him that it was predicted in their holy book that he would not come to their city. Alexander the Great was so impressed with their knowledge and their holy book that he changed his mind and did not pursue destroying Jerusalem.

The city of Jerusalem could not be destroyed because God promised He would redeem His people and make them live in the land forever. Nor can Jerusalem be destroyed in the future, because that is where Jesus will return and set up His kingdom. God protects His own. Are you His own? Then He will protect you. Do not fear.

September 24

Reason Not to Fear #268: God Knows All the Answers

"A son honors his father, and a servant his master. If then I am the Father, Where is My honor? And if I am a Master, Where is My reverence (fear)? says the LORD of hosts to you priests who despise My name. Yet you say, 'In what way have we despised Your name?'" Malachi 1:6

Some people are hooked on watching game shows. I must confess from time to time I have watched Jeopardy and, truthfully, I do not understand how the contestants know all the answers. I would never win. I do not know the answers.

In the book of Malachi, it seems like God was putting the Israelites on a quiz show. Malachi, the last of the Old Testament prophets, asked 23 questions in the book, and God made 8 accusations based on these questions. It seems the Israelites failed the quiz show!

The first group of people Malachi zeros in on are the priests. They were to be the nation's spiritual leaders. While they gave an outward show of spiritual superiority, they were dishonoring the Lord and despising His name and His service by offering blemished sacrifices. They were careless in their worship. Malachi asked, "How would your governor like to be given such animals?"

God was to be honored, feared, and reverenced, especially by the priests. The truth is, they did not honor God as their Father, nor did they have any fear of Him. The priests failed to listen to God. They failed to obey God's laws. They failed to teach the people the right way to live and worship. In their failing, they caused many to stumble.

You may not be a priest, a prophet or a preacher, but you have the same responsibility to honor God first and be obedient to Him. Remember God is your father and He deserves the very best service and dedication from you. God loved the people of Israel. It grieved Him immensely that they did not return His love.

What about you? Are you giving God your best, your first, your most precious? Are you using the gifts God has given you to serve, to reach the lost, to teach, or to comfort those who are hurting? Or are you casual and negligent when it comes to God's work?

Search your heart and change your ways, or you may be placed on God's quiz show and you may not like what the outcome will be. He is God. Fear Him.

September 25

Reason Not to Fear #269: We Give God Our Best

"But cursed be the deceiver who has in his flock a male, and takes a vow, but sacrifices to the Lord what is blemished-- for I am a great King," says the LORD of hosts, "and My name is to be feared among the nations." Malachi 1:14

Malachi, the last of the Old Testament prophets, gave a series of short sermons, "oracles," to the people who had returned to their land and were now living within the walled city of Jerusalem. It had been almost one hundred years since they were captives in Babylon. The new generation, those who had been born since the return, knew nothing but the peace and prosperity they now enjoyed as a province under the Persians. They had grown a little soft, a little complacent, a little lax in their worship of Jehovah.

Malachi came on the scene and bellowed out to them, "Thus says Jehovah God, 'You do not fear Me any longer!'" The people, with polite surprise on their faces and in the tone of their words, replied, "How have we shown contempt for God? How have we defiled the sacrifices? How have we not feared our God?"

Malachi replied that they were bringing crippled animals to the altar. They did not want to bring their best animals, for they figured they couldn't "afford" that much for God. They brought Him their leftovers, the animals they did not want.

They were giving their second best to the Lord of all creation. God demands our first, our best, and our all. I remember the story of a young boy in a developing country who heard about the Magi who brought precious gifts to Jesus, and honored Him as king. He didn't have anything to bring the Lord, and so as the offering plate was passed and he held it in his hands, he suddenly laid it on the floor and stepped into it, offering his whole body, soul, mind and spirit to the Lord as a gift.

Many of you dedicated your lives to the Lord, perhaps when you were young. How is your life today in regards to that? Have you grown complacent in your sacrifices to the Lord? Are you giving Him second best or the last best?

Search your heart. Listen to the call of God from the book of Malachi. Decide today to give Him first, best, and all.

September 26

Reason Not to Fear #270: We Renew our Commitment to God

"Then you shall know that I have sent this commandment to you, that My covenant with Levi may continue,'" says the LORD of hosts. "'My covenant was with him, one of life and peace, and I gave them to him that he might fear Me; so he feared Me and was reverent before My name.'" Malachi 2:4, 5

Life takes its toll. We are busy with work, family, community, and play. It is so easy to get sucked into the vortex of a busy life and find one day that we have left God entirely out of the picture. We feel driven to buy more things to impress others. As Dave Ramsey (a Christian author and speaker on finances) says, "We want to impress the guy in the car next to us at the stop light, someone we will never see again." We are trapped in a life style that demands more of us than we can give and when someone at church says, "Will you help in the nursery?" our immediate response is, "No, I am too busy."

After returning from exile in Babylon, the Jews were now comfortable in their situation and intent on building homes, farming the land, and setting aside wealth. As we mentioned in yesterday's devotional, they had grown apathetic about their worship of God Almighty. This affected every area of their lives. Malachi used the question and answer method of teaching and proposed 23 questions in this short book, designed to catch their attention and their hearts and to bring them to repentance.

What were they doing that was so offensive to God? They were bringing unworthy animals to the temple for sacrifices; they were unfaithful to the Lord Jehovah, turning to the love of money and a life of comfort as their gods instead of Him; they were marrying Gentile wives; they were practicing divorce. These things may not seem like a big deal to you.

But it *was* a big deal to God. He could see their hearts and He knew they needed to get down on their knees and repent of their sins. They needed to renew their commitment to Him and put Him first in their lives.

This is what we need today as well. The universal church of Jesus Christ in America is in the same danger of laxity, apathy and idol worship. How can we fix this problem?

Get on your knees. Confess to God your lack of devotion, your cold heart, your worship of other things. Don't get off your knees until you are forgiven, your heart is stirred by His love, and you are willing to accept His will for your life.

September 27

Reason Not to Fear #271: We Confess Our Sin Often

"'And I will come near you for judgment; I will be a swift witness against sorcerers, against adulterers, against perjurers, against those who exploit wage earners and widows and orphans, and against those who turn away an alien-- because they do not fear Me,' says the LORD of hosts." Malachi 3:5

Malachi stood at the temple, or in the market place, or at the city gates, preaching the message God gave him. It is easy to imagine the people frowning, snarling and spitting out their disgust and rejection as they turned away to go about their business, because Malachi was talking about money.

Most of these people rejected what he had to say, just as most Christians today would reject it.

"We have to make a living," they said self-righteously, and so they cheat, steal and defraud others in the business world to get that extra dime in their bank account. They steal things from their employers, pad the expense account, cheat on their tax returns, loan money at exorbitant interest rates, and justify not giving a tithe because they are retired and they get no "real" income. They know every tax loop-hole and government freebie out there. They might slip a dollar or five dollars into the offering plate, but they hold onto the bulk of their wealth with tight fists because they might need it someday, or they want to give it to their children when they die, who will fight over it.

Yes, just like the preacher or Malachi, I have gone from preaching to meddling. You might think I am exaggerating, but there are Christians who live like this. When wealth increases, so does their hold on their money. When it comes time to fill shoeboxes for the Christmas Child Samaritan's Purse project, they very carefully place five or six items in the box and call it good.

How are you doing with your money? Is God first in your thinking when you write out your bills and payments for the month? How much do you have saved or invested that could be used for His kingdom? These are hard questions and only you can answer them. Take some time and read James 5:1-5. Seriously consider where your heart is and where your money is.

Revival starts at home. My prayer is that you will be blessed abundantly because of your total devotion, love and commitment to God.

September 28

Reason Not to Fear #272: We Don't Rob God

"Then those who feared the LORD spoke to one another, and the LORD listened and heard them; so a book of remembrance was written before Him for those who fear the LORD and who meditate on His name. 'They shall be Mine,' says the LORD of hosts, 'On the day that I make them My jewels. And I will spare them as a man spares his own son who serves him.' Then you shall again discern between the righteous and the wicked, between one who serves God and one who does not serve Him." Malachi 3:16-18

Chapter 3 of Malachi is very interesting. It not only predicts the coming of the Messiah, but also the coming of John the Baptist, the "messenger" who would prepare the way for the Lord, v. 1. In verses 2-5, the Lord reveals the work of the Messiah in judgment of His own people, first the Levites, and then against all who sin and transgress God's law in the matter of sorcery, adultery, blasphemy and lying, oppression of the poor and rejection of God.

The first error God confronted them with was robbery of God. They were not bringing their tithes to the storehouses at the temple. There were those who were arrogant against God and would not be obedience in this. They said, in effect, *if we do not prosper materially when we obey God, we will not obey Him, for what use is that?*

Yet those who feared the Lord banded together and wrote their names in a book of remembrance. They wanted future generations to know that they were the ones who feared, obeyed and loved God. I love this!

"They will be mine," says the Lord, "on the day I prepare my own possession". In the King James Version, this verse reads, "in the day I make up my jewels." Not only will those who fear the Lord be His own special treasure, He will also protect them from the coming judgment that falls on the earth. Verse 18 is a great comfort to those who might be afraid of God's judgment.

Where do you stand today? Are you with those who are arrogant, disobedient to God, and disrespectful of His commands? Or are you with those who fear Him? Is your name written in the Book of Life? Will you be protected from God's judgment?

Make sure of your life today. Give your tithes. Obey what the Word says you should do. Then walk away from this time with the Lord with joy in your heart to the Lord.

September 29

Reason Not to Fear #273: Joy Comes With Obedience

"But to you who fear My name The Sun of Righteousness shall arise with healing in His wings; and you shall go out and grow fat like stall-fed calves."
Malachi 4:2

The Old Testament book of Malachi ends with a warning to the wicked. Verse one speaks of a great fire that will consume the evildoers and all the effects of their wickedness will be gone. See Zephaniah 1:14-18 and II Peter 3:7 for further information about this last "day of the Lord" which is a time of judgment when God answers the sin question once and for all.

Again we see a division of the people who fear God from those who are wicked, so that the righteous will not face the searing heat of God's anger and wrath. The picture we get from these verses is one of healing, joy, and release from the bondage of the sin nature.

For anyone who has lived on a farm, you know that in the spring, baby calves are born and begin to leap and run in the warm sunshine. With their little tails lifted, they jump joyfully, bounding with great abandon. Spring is a picture of the life that flows into God's people, bringing healing, joy and exuberance during the days of the Kingdom. This time will also be characterized by righteousness.

Even the bells on the horses in the Kingdom will have "HOLY" written on them! Everything will be dedicated and set apart for the Lord in that day. (Zechariah14:20)

Today, as pressed as we are on every side with the worries and cares of this world, we should be experiencing the joy of the Lord on a daily basis. Jesus said *don't worry*. In Matthew 6:25-34, He repeated that command four times! Read that passage for today and let it calm your heart. Lift your eyes to Him, and find your joy in Him.

We cannot find joy, love, peace or hope in this old world. John expressed it best by saying, "The world and its desires pass away, but the man who does the will of God lives forever." (I John 2:17) Are you doing the will of the Father with a calm heart, a steadfast mind, and a heart full of love for Him?

If not, confess your lack of the fear of God and lack of faith in Him. When you finish, His joy will fill your heart beyond anything that the world can understand. Allow the "sun of righteousness," Christ Himself, to heal your wounded heart and mind.

September 30

Reason Not to Fear #274: We Listen When God Speaks to Us

"But while he thought about these things, behold, an angel of the Lord appeared to him in a dream, saying, 'Joseph, son of David, do not be afraid to take to you Mary your wife, for that which is conceived in her is of the Holy Spirit.'" Matthew 1:20

How many of us could stand before a messenger from God, an angel, and not be afraid? In most cases when angels appeared to people as recorded in the Bible, the first words out of the heavenly messenger's mouth were "fear not." Ezekiel and Daniel had to be physically strengthened to stand on their feet and listen to the message that was given to them from God.

For centuries, the Jews waited for their Messiah. They believed that one day God would fulfill His promise and pledge. Over the years, many came claiming to be this promised one. But none lived up to the true Messiah's claims.

There is a gap in the Bible between the Old and New Testaments called the 400 Silent Years. During this time, there was no special revelation or word from God. Time went by and maybe people were beginning to think that God would never fulfill His promises to send a Messiah, a Savior, a Redeemer to this world.

Yet they were wrong. The long silence was finally broken one day when an older man, a priest named Zacharias, entered the Temple to offer the blood of a lamb on the altar. After that, the angel gave his message to a young maiden, Mary, who lived in Nazareth. Then Joseph, her betrothed husband, received this message in a dream.

Mary was the mother of the promised Messiah. Who of us could digest such news without fear? But as Joseph thought long and hard over this announcement, in the stillness of the night, his mind slowly and painfully accepted the angel's words. Though a dark cloud would hang over their heads for many years, Joseph would rise to the occasion and fulfill His responsibility in raising the Messiah.

You may not receive special dreams or messages such as Joseph did, yet we have the completed Word of God, and we can know what God wants us to do. Are you doing it without fear? Check your life and your obedience level. Make sure you listen when God speaks and then obey Him.

October 1

Reason Not to Fear 275: God Will Take Care of Me

"But when he heard that Archelaus was reigning over Judea instead of his father Herod, he was afraid to go there. And being warned by God in a dream, he turned aside into the region of Galilee." Matthew 2:22

The murder of the innocents by Herod the Great is still hotly debated today. Was this ruler truly a wicked man, was he mentally disturbed, was he led astray by evil counselors, or was he merely trying to protect himself as king over Judea? The Bible portrays him as paranoid, selfish, cruel and wicked.

This atrocity must have been sharp in Joseph's mind, even after living for two years in Egypt. He and Mary must have listened avidly to the reports coming from Judea, reports that said that Herod was dead and now Archelaus, his son, was ruler in his stead. This news did not give them much comfort, for they knew that this particular son was even more wicked and evil than his father. Both of them were Idumeans, from the ancient tribe of the Edomites, who were avowed enemies of the Israelites.

Then an angel appeared to Joseph in a dream and told him to return to Israel. Needless to say, it took courage on the part of Joseph to leave Egypt with his family and head toward Galilee. Yet he did just that and they came at last to their original home town of Nazareth.

Joseph exercised both common sense and faith, and was obedient to God. People may cause you to experience fear because they hold positions of authority, yet God is able to lead His children to safety. Joseph needed a direct revelation from God to help him know the way to go, when to go, and where to go.

How do you find the will of God for your life? Are you facing a choice today that might affect your life? God has given us His Word and within these sacred pages is the answer to all your questions for your life.

As you study the Word, write down verses that speak to you about the issues you are facing. Listen when you hear a sermon on the radio or in church and be aware that God can use these to guide you, too. Ask for wisdom. List your options and the pros and cons. Pray about it, and seek godly advice. Then move out with confidence and without fear, for God will certainly lead you just as He did Joseph.

October 2

Reason Not to Fear #276: I Will Trust When I Am Afraid

"And you will be hated by all for My name's sake. But he who endures to the end will be saved. When they persecute you in this city, flee to another. For assuredly, I say to you, you will not have gone through the cities of Israel before the Son of Man comes. Therefore do not fear them.... For there is nothing covered that will not be revealed, and hidden that will not be known."
Matthew 10:22-23, 26

Jesus gave instructions to His disciples before sending them out on a mission trip to proclaim the good news of His arrival to those who lived in Galilee. They preached the need to believe in Him and accept Him as their Messiah and Savior. I can see Jesus and His disciples standing under a tamarisk tree, listening intently as the Master speaks in a low voice.

I imagine that some of the disciples gripped their staffs a little tighter as the time to depart drew near. They had seen how some people hated Jesus and rejected His message. They had seen how his own people of Nazareth almost pushed Him off the cliff. They had seen how the Sadducees and Pharisees dogged his steps and took notes to report back to their chiefs in Jerusalem. Now it was their turn to face the animosity of the world.

Jesus' words were not altogether reassuring. "They will hate you," He said, "just as they hate me. But don't fear them." Why should they not fear those who would persecute them and give them trouble? Because God was leading them to this task, and He would be with them.

Down through the ages, we have the record of thousands of people who have looked their persecutors in the eye and said, "I do not care what you do with this body. My home is out of this world, and I am going there soon." And they died with those words still ringing off the cobblestones or walls.

These people leave us one clear message: fear God and Him alone, and all other fears will disappear. If you truly believe that God is in control of all things and that He has promised to be with you, then you don't have to fear the future.

There are so many uncertainties in our world today. We may face the loss of our jobs, our health, our finances, our homes. But Jesus' words ring down through the centuries to us in America today. "Do not be afraid."

Stand firm on His promises and He will be with you every step of the way.

October 3

Reason Not to Fear #277: Chose Your Fears Wisely

"And do not fear those who kill the body but cannot kill the soul. But rather fear Him who is able to destroy both soul and body in hell. Are not two sparrows sold for a copper coin? And not one of them falls to the ground apart from your Father's will. but the very hairs of your head are all numbered."
Matthew 10:28-30

You could smell their fear. Jesus knew that His friends were afraid to start out on their journey, yet He assured them that they would be okay because they were in the hands of His Father, the Lord of the universe, who takes care of the birds and knows how many hairs are on their heads. The opposition to Jesus' ministry and person had mounted to frightening proportions. The Pharisees and Sadducees and the rulers of Israel hated Jesus and were plotting to kill Him. Indeed, the more popular Jesus became with the people, the more urgent became His enemies' desire to destroy Him, for they were jealous of His position.

Yet Jesus healed the sick, walked from town to town freely, doing the will of the Father in complete confidence, peace of mind, and joy. He did not fear what these men, powerful though they were, would do to Him because He knew the Father's will. He knew nothing could harm Him as long as He stayed within that perimeter.

"Either fear God, or fear everything else." I heard this quote recently. If you fear God in the proper way, you will not fear anything else.

We often look to the future and wonder how we would do if persecution came to America for Christians. Could our faith withstand the loss of everything we have? Fear pokes its ugly head into our lives when we think of such things, robbing our peace and joy, yet we shouldn't be caught in that trap. Do not borrow trouble from tomorrow, Jesus counseled. Tomorrow has enough trouble of its own. (Matthew 6:34)

Are you facing severe health issues? Do you worry about the future for your children or your spouse? Are you in the middle of a family fight or a church fight? Do these things disturb you and cause you to lose your peace?

Consider this: when you've lost your peace of mind, this is a signal that you are engaging in fearing the wrong things. Focus on the Lord, set aside your other fears, and trust Him today. He will restore your peace of mind, and He will take care of you.

October 4

Reason Not to Fear #278: When I Am Tested, I Will Trust God

"And when the disciples saw Him walking on the sea, they were troubled, saying, "It is a ghost!" And they cried out for fear. But immediately Jesus spoke to them, saying, "Be of good cheer! It is I; do not be afraid." Matthew 14:26, 27

The Sea of Galilee is known for its violent, sudden storms, and many fishermen have lost their lives on this small lake. When it is placid, it is absolutely beautiful. Yet in a storm, the situation is very different. It is totally scary.

For the disciples that night, the storm appeared out of nowhere. They struggled against it for hours, gaining little ground, wearing themselves out. Jesus had spent the night on the hillside in prayer, so they didn't think they could look to Him for help.

Yet when their strength was spent, and they knew they might die beneath the angry waves, someone shouted, "Look! What's that?"

The disciple pointed frantically through the rain, wind and howling of the sea. The others wiped the water from their eyes and strained to see. It looked like a man ... a man who walked on the waves! As he approached, they shrank back. "It's a ghost!" they screamed in fear. Frantically they tried to row away, but of course they could go nowhere, for the sea was still turbulent.

We know that it was Jesus, and they soon recognized Him, too. Yet at first they did not recognize their deliverer. In fact, fear controlled them. Why didn't they recognize Jesus? The reason was they were not expecting Him and that caused them to jump to the wrong conclusion. You see, fear and faith do not work side by side. Fear will always blind your faith.

Do you understand the reason for the storm? It was to build their faith. Do you understand why storms touch your life? It is the same reason: to build your faith. Jesus knew His disciples needed a strong belief because eventually He would leave them. They needed to trust Him even when they did not see Him. They had to learn that when storms come, Jesus would be there with them, seen or unseen.

He may not come when you want Him to, or in the manner you expect, nonetheless, He will rescue you. In the storms of life, He is with you. Rest in that fact today.

October 5

Reason Not to Fear #279: I Step Out in Faith

"So He said, "Come." And when Peter had come down out of the boat, he walked on the water to go to Jesus. But when he saw that the wind was boisterous, he was afraid; and beginning to sink he cried out, saying, "Lord, save me!" And immediately Jesus stretched out His hand and caught him, and said to him, "O you of little faith, why did you doubt?" Matthew 14:29-31

In the movie, "We Bought A Zoo", the main character of the story is challenged to have at least one moment in his life when he exercises thirty seconds of raw courage. This was the motivator that caused him to speak to a beautiful woman, who became his wife, and to purchase a zoo.

But it takes more than raw courage to follow the Lord's leading. I admire Peter. He got out of the boat and stood on the water. That was his thirty seconds of raw courage. He did what Christ told him to do. He stood there, staring at the Lord, and suddenly began to wonder what in the world he was doing. Here he was, standing on water!

Maybe you have stepped out in faith, too, and began to be obedient to God. But at some point, the task became too difficult for you. Maybe it was a class of rowdy youngsters you said you would teach, and when you go to teach, nothing goes as you planned. Or maybe you decided to witness to your neighbor, but he throws your message back in your face and tells you to mind your own business. You become discouraged, cast down and want to quit.

When Peter took his eyes off the Lord and onto the stormy sea, he was afraid. Jesus was testing his faith and this meant his eyes needed to be totally on Jesus, not on his own abilities. He began to sink, but Jesus graciously rescued him, taking him into the boat.

The good news is that Jesus wants to come to you in the storms of life. They are not easy or enjoyable, but they are necessary. Each storm you pass through teaches you to trust in Christ alone, no matter what the circumstances. Jesus will rescue you, too. You may not be buying a zoo, but you are walking on water when you minister in Jesus' name.

It is His strength, His faith and His love that must flow through you to others. Remember that the next time you want to give up. Turn to Christ. Ask Him for help, and He will give it to you.

October 6

Reason Not to Fear #280: I Will Obey God's Voice

"While he was still speaking, behold, a bright cloud overshadowed them; and suddenly a voice came out of the cloud, saying, 'This is My beloved Son, in whom I am well pleased. Hear Him!' And when the disciples heard it, they fell on their faces and were greatly afraid. But Jesus came and touched them and said, 'Arise, and do not be afraid.'" Matthew 17:5-7

Peter distinguished himself among the disciples as the most outspoken of them all. Jesus took three of His most intimate friends, Peter, James and John, up on a high mountain. At the top of the mountain, they saw Jesus changed before their eyes to His heavenly glory. He was accompanied by two men, Elijah and Moses. In great zeal and passion, Peter burst out, "We should build three tabernacles here to commemorate these two men who have come!"

A loud, booming voice spoke from the bright light that enveloped Christ, "This is My Son with whom I am well pleased! Listen to Him!"

All three of the disciples fell flat on their faces onto the ground! The message was clear: you are not to worship created beings, even if they are shining brightly, or even if they appear out of heaven. You are to worship, fear, and be in awe of Christ alone.

My dad had a distinct voice. It was deep, forceful, and influential. I can still hear it in my head today. Whenever he spoke to me, his voice always captured my attention. But, despite the fact that my dad and I often talked and even disagreed about issues, I still loved to hear his voice. However, there were a few times when his voice ignited fear in me.

All three of the disciples realized they were in the presence of Almighty God. I would have been afraid, too, and I would also have fallen on my face to the ground. Isn't that what happens to you when you finally become fully aware of God's majesty? Of His Lordship? A reverential fear falls over you when God's voice speaks to you.

Refuse the worship of other gods and idols in your life. What are you trusting in today? Your financial portfolio, your status, your bank account, your insurance policies, your possessions, your education, intellect, charm, or abilities? Everything of this world can be wiped away, gone, in an instant. Only Christ is the "everlasting Rock." (Isaiah 26:4)

Just as my dad's voice was distinct, so is God's. Listen for it. Recognize it. Obey it.

October 7

Reason Not to Fear #281: I Will Use My Talents and Gifts for God

"Then he who had received the one talent came and said, 'Lord, I knew you to be a hard man, reaping where you have not sown, and gathering where you have not scattered seed, and I was afraid, and went and hid your talent in the ground. Look, there you have what is yours.' Matthew 25:24, 25

Jesus told a story about a landowner who went away from his property holdings and left them in the care of his servants. To each servant he entrusted a sum of money to invest, bank, or use however he wanted, with the express purpose of earning him more money. The landowner was not cruel as the third servant thought him to be. In fact, he was fair and just, as shown by his treatment of those who served him well.

When the landowner returned, he found that the third servant had not used his money wisely. He had dug a hole in the ground and buried it! The master turned the unwise servant's words against him and said, in effect, "If you knew, or supposed, that I was such a man, shouldn't that knowledge have motivated you to try harder? Even if you had just banked it, it would have returned some money to me. So will take your money and give it to the wise servants who knew how to use what I have given them. And you I will throw you outside my kingdom where there is darkness and weeping and gnashing of teeth."

The landowner is Jesus Christ. He went away, leaving His servants to care for His kingdom on earth. To each of His servants He entrusted talents, which are natural gifts and abilities. Like these servants, we will be judged how we have used these gifts, whether they are in the areas of music, the arts, writing, speaking, building and crafting, administering, showing mercy, or serving.

How are you using your talents and abilities today for His kingdom? Are you cringing in fear saying God surely is a hard taskmaster and I must hide my talents, for He will never be pleased with anything I do? If you are like that, I feel sorry for you.

My advice for you today is to use what you have for Christ. Teach a Sunday school class, use your music to glorify Christ and minister to others, serve Him gladly in whatever task He has given you to do. You will be like the wise servants of the master, and He will say, "Well done, thou good and faithful servant, enter into the joy of the kingdom."

October 8

Reason Not to Fear #282: When Catastrophe Knocks on My Door, I Will Trust

"So when the centurion and those with him, who were guarding Jesus, saw the earthquake and the things that had happened, they feared greatly, saying, "Truly this was the Son of God!" Matthew 27:54

A number of events occurred the moment Jesus died. The veil in the temple was torn from top to bottom. There was a great earthquake in which the rocks split apart and the graves were opened of righteous people who were long dead. These people were raised to life again and walked in the city streets (v. 51-53).

I don't know who these righteous people were but can you imagine this happening? Golgotha is located directly across from the Mount of Olives where many people were buried. In those days, they used cave-like tombs for family burial plots. After the body decayed, the bones were placed in jars and the jars kept on shelves. This way many people could be buried in the same place. A stone was rolled across the opening.

Suddenly when Jesus died, the earth shook and these graves came open. People emerged from them -- people who had lived long ago and were now brought back to life! As the Roman centurion saw these things taking place, he gazed on the body of the Lord and said that he was amazed. "I think this man must have been the Son of God!"

Did he believe in Christ as the Savior for the forgiveness of sins, or was he just merely in awe of the things he had seen that day? We will not know until we reach heaven, yet the fear he felt is something we should carefully note.

How many times have we been amazed, afraid, and astounded of natural events without thinking once about God? Do you see God's hand in the things that occur around us which our secular society terms "nature"? An earthquake happens in Indonesia. How many saw God's hand in that? A hurricane and flood decimates much of New Orleans, yet we are hesitant to say that this was God's hand of judgment on a city in which there was much wickedness.

It is natural to be afraid when things like earthquakes and hurricanes and tornadoes rip our world apart. Yet how much more should we be in awe of God! Turn to Him today and acknowledge Him as Lord of your life. Commit your life to Him. Be in fear of Jesus Christ today and He will change your life.

October 9

Reason Not to Fear 283: I Believe That Jesus Rose from the Grave

"And behold, there was a great earthquake; for an angel of the Lord descended from heaven, and came and rolled back the stone from the door, and sat on it. His countenance was like lightning, and his clothing as white as snow. And the guards shook for fear of him, and became like dead men."
Matthew 28:2-4

I have to smile when I read Matthew's account of the resurrection story, beginning with chapter 28. I wonder if he smiled, too, as he wrote it.

The Romans had killed Jesus. They knew how to do that; in fact, you could say that each man in the Roman army was a killing machine. When a person took a cross on their shoulders and started down the street with it to the place of execution, there was only one outcome at the end of that road: death.

After Christ died, the Jews demanded that a contingent of Roman soldiers be placed at the tomb, and Pilate went along with it. The men stood at the tomb throughout the night, keeping watch. They thought they were guarding the tomb against fanatical believers who might raid it and steal the body, but they actually stood there under the command of God Himself as a witness to the whole world forever that no one stole the body, for no one could get past them.

They were godless men who worshipped the Roman gods, and they thought the Jews with their one invisible God were preposterous. They did not believe in life after death, and they most certainly did not believe that the man they crucified was the Son of God, or that He had any life in Him when they left Him on the cross. They were going to get the surprise of their lives.

The arrival of an angel and an earthquake shook their world to the core. They trembled like men taken with a violent illness, their legs collapsed and they fell flat on their faces, fainting. These strong warriors, who thought they were invincible, could not stand before one angel who rolled the rock from the mouth of the tomb and sat on it, smiling.

Dead people stay dead. Except Jesus. His resurrection brought fear to His enemies and consolation to others. It really took place. Believe in the risen Christ today and live your life as one who has hope beyond the grave. Don't faint at the news that Jesus is really alive today!

October 10

Reason Not to Fear #284: Death Has Been Conquered

"So they went out quickly from the tomb with fear and great joy, and ran to bring His disciples word. And as they went to tell His disciples, behold, Jesus met them, saying, 'Rejoice!' So they came and held Him by the feet and worshiped Him. Then Jesus said to them, 'Do not be afraid. Go and tell My brethren to go to Galilee, and there they will see Me.'" Matthew 28:8-10

Most of us at some point will attend a funeral or a memorial service. Just two weeks ago, my family had a memorial service for my dear son-in-law, James Poarch. James was my daughter, Nicky's husband. They were missionaries in Indonesia for 10 years. A month ago, James had a heart attack and died. Life for my daughter and her children has not been the same. The impact of James' death has caused us as a family to draw closer to each other and to our God. We have wept, sobbed, and groaned together.

James was only 36 years old. His life was spent telling the DaAn tribal people about Jesus. We miss him deeply and fervently pray that the Lord will be known, seen, and glorified through his life.

In just minutes James died. He never regained consciousness. And the phone call that day from my daughter was unbelievable. I was in shock over the news. Death has a way of doing that to us.

We grieve. We have sad heavy days. We have questions. We feel depressed. But we do not mourn as those who have no hope. James went to heaven instantly and that truth has been our strong rock to cling to when the waves of grief roll over us. We hang onto the fact that since Jesus was raised from the dead, we will someday be with the Lord and with James.

Death causes us all to fear. The women who went to the tomb, who saw the angel, and who spoke to the resurrected Lord, were tempted to fear. Jesus said, "Do not be afraid." Yes, for those women, as well as for us today, these things are beyond our natural scope of understanding. However, Jesus says to you today, "Do not be afraid."

We believe and serve a risen Savior. He is not dead. Because Jesus rose from the dead, so will all who have put their faith and trust in Him. Therefore, you can look your enemy straight in the eye and declare that you are not afraid. You, dear child of God, will not stay in the tomb when you die. You will live forever. Jesus calls you out of the tomb. He calls you to life.

October 11

Reason Not to Fear #285: Jesus Can Still My Storm

"Then He arose and rebuked the wind, and said to the sea, 'Peace, be still!' And the wind ceased and there was a great calm. But He said to them, 'Why are you so fearful? How is it that you have no faith?' And they feared exceedingly, and said to one another, 'Who can this be, that even the wind and the sea obey Him!'" Mark 4:39-41

A boat was discovered in Israel that is much like the one in which Jesus and His disciples sailed on the Sea of Galilee. It was found beneath many feet of mud along the shore of the Sea of Galilee in 1986 by two brothers , Moshe and Yuval Lufan. It is 26' long and 7' wide, and is preserved for visitors to view at the small seaside village of Migdal, and its small dimensions makes a person wonder how thirteen men could have fit in it!

When the disciples went fishing that night, Jesus, totally exhausted by the day's events, curled up in the stern where there was a little spare room and promptly fell asleep.

Suddenly a storm was upon them. They struggled against it, but the storm increased, and they knew they would soon die. In desperation, they cried out to Jesus. Upon waking, He sat up and calmly looked around. Then, hanging onto the main mast that held the limp sail, he gained His feet and spoke to the storm. "Be still!" It was like a parent speaking to a disobedient child.

To the disciples' astonishment, the storm stopped. Just little bubbles appeared on the surface of the glistening water. Absolute silence followed, a silence broken only by the gentle lap of the waves against the boat and the panting breath of the fishermen.

Jesus looked at them sternly, wiping water from His face. "Why are you so afraid? Don't you have any faith at all?" It was the same tone He'd used to calm the storm.

If your faith could be measured, how much would you have? How much do you depend upon your own strength, wisdom, and wealth to get you by every day? If you'd been in that boat, would you have believed that Jesus could calm the storm?

Take stock of your heart today. If you are facing an impossible situation, thank God for it and exercise your faith. Faith and fear do not go together. Either you will face it with faith or with fear. It's your choice.

October 12

Reason Not to Fear #286: Satan Is A Conquered Foe

"Then they came to Jesus, and saw the one who had been demon-possessed and had the legion, sitting and clothed and in his right mind. And they were afraid. And those who saw it told them how it happened to him who had been demon-possessed, and about the swine. Then they began to plead with Him to depart from their region." Mark 5:15-17

Satan and demons are real. Throughout the New Testament we are told of times when Jesus or the Apostles cast out demon's from people. But nowhere in the Bible is the description of demon possession more graphic or horrifying that here in Mark 5.

This guy is scary. He lives in a graveyard. He is unshaved. He is scarred from chains and ropes that have been unable to hold him. His face had a dark, haunted look to it. His body bears the marks of cuts he has made on it with sharp stones. Every night and every day he roams around the graveyard, howling in the crazed torment of a man who is possessed by demons who will not allow him to rest.

If you had the courage to get close enough to talk with this man, you would have heard him shout at you with different voices from the demons who lived within him. Jesus confronted this man and his legions of demons. He expelled the demons and sent them into a herd of pigs.

The response to that amazing miracle was that the people of the town urged Jesus to leave them. They didn't want Him doing any more miracles that would endanger their income and mode of living.

Are you bound by the chains of sin and death that Satan tries to put on you? You might not be a raving lunatic, but there are many other ways that he can live with the chains of Satan. Fear is one of them. Holding a grudge in unforgiveness is another. Jealousy is definitely of Satan, too.

Look to Jesus today for help. He will deliver you from whatever it is that binds you. He is the victor over Satan, over demons, over sin. You must confess your sin, repudiate the demons, and tell them to be gone in the name of Jesus. Do it today and find the freedom Christ has won for you!

October 13

Reason Not to Fear #287: We Chose to Fear God and Not People

"For Herod feared John, knowing that he was a just and holy man, and he protected him. And when he heard him, he did many things, and heard him gladly." Mark 6:20

Even though Herod feared John, and maybe he feared God in some remote sense, he did not fear enough. As the story goes, his wife, Herodias, who was his sister-in-law, hated John. The prophet had been bold enough to criticize Herod for taking his brother's wife, and the woman wanted John's voice silenced for all time.

So on Herod's birthday, they threw a big party for him. They invited all his friends, hired musicians, jugglers and other entertainers, and settled down to a good time of eating and drinking. Yet Herodias had a scheme in mind. When Herod was drunk, and when his guests were thinking that this party was going downhill fast and was pretty boring, Herodias stepped forward with her plot.

This involved her pretty little daughter, Salome, who could dance. The act that Salome performed for this sodden group of lecherous men was sensuous. At the end of it, Herod was so pleased with her that he made her an offer she could not resist. "I will give you half the kingdom," he said, "just tell me what you want."

She hurried off and found her Mamma, who instructed her to ask for a very unusual thing: the head of John the Baptist! Herod felt he couldn't renege on his promise, even though it was a cruel and unjust thing to do. So he ordered for John's head to be cut off and brought in on a platter. He has gone down in history as an oaf who kept a foolish promise. He killed a prophet of God whose only fault was to confront him with the truth.

What do you fear? If you fear the opinion of others, you are fearing the wrong thing. If you fear rich and powerful people, you are fearing the wrong thing. If you fear those who can destroy your body and take away your money, you are fearing the wrong thing.

Fear God only, and you will keep your feet on the solid rock. "Choose you this day whom you will serve," was Joshua's charge to Israel in his final address to the people. "As for me and my house, we will serve the Lord." Josh. 24:14-15

October 14

Reason Not to Fear #288: He Is Greater Than Any Storm

"And when they saw Him walking on the sea, they supposed it was a ghost, and cried out; for they all saw Him and were troubled. But immediately He talked with them and said to them, 'Be of good cheer! It is I; do not be afraid.'"
Mark 6:49-50

I love the picture of Jesus walking on the water of the Sea of Galilee. If you read the previous verse, it says that Jesus was taking a stroll across the lake, and He was about *to pass them by* when they spotted Him. Would He have gone right on by if they hadn't noticed Him?

I believe that Jesus would have tapped them on the shoulder if He had to, to get their attention that night! Jesus knew the distress of his friends. He had seen them pulling uselessly on the oars. He found them in a dark, stormy sea, and He walked on the water to get to them! On that dark night, on that rough sea, the voice and person of Jesus dispelled every fear. Jesus went to them. He saw their trouble and came to their aid.

Have you ever felt abandoned of God? There have been many instances when I have prayed earnestly, frequently, and with what I have thought was sufficient faith, yet God did not answer my pleas. People urged me to have more faith and said that if I did, God would answer the way I wanted.

But nothing worked. I tried fasting and only got hungry. I tried praying on my knees and only got sore knees. I promised God everything I could think of and only ran out of breath. No, there was something I needed to learn. God is sovereign and there are some things to which He answers *wait*, or *no*. I needed to learn to trust God even when I didn't get what I wanted.

This miracle of Jesus walking on the water was a private one for the disciples alone. On the troubled Sea of Galilee, Jesus revealed to those closest to Him his power over nature and the laws of gravity. He also revealed His love and tenderness.

Maybe you need to learn those lessons of faith and trust, too. Commit your way to God today, fear Him and relinquish your control over the issue that is troubling you. Rest in Him. No boisterous sea or dark night can keep Him from you. He will come, and He will answer.

October 15

Reason Not to Fear #289: Jesus Knows What He Is Doing

"For He taught His disciples and said to them, 'The Son of Man is being betrayed into the hands of men, and they will kill Him. And after He is killed, He will rise the third day.' But they did not understand this saying, and were afraid to ask Him." Mark 9:31, 32

I wonder why the disciples were afraid to ask Jesus what He meant. Was it like being afraid of going to a doctor about a chronic pain because you have the nagging fear it could be something really bad, like cancer? Do we avoid knowing the truth, and deliberately walk in the darkness of ignorance just so we won't have to deal with harsh reality? Fear is what motivates us in those moments, not faith.

Jesus was purposeful in telling His disciples about the coming events, things He was going to have to face in the near future.

Many people in Holland deliberately refused to believe the horror of what was happening in Nazi Germany, making the choice to live in ignorance about what the Fuhrer and his great army were doing to people who opposed him. It seems incredible to me that there were people who denied the existence of the concentration camps and the gas chambers and made themselves believe that Hitler was a good leader. *Let him take control of our government and our lives. If he promises prosperity for us, we are all for him.*

Jesus knew that life changing, earthshaking things were right around the corner for His friends and loved ones. He wanted them to know what was coming so they could prepare their hearts and minds. Yet they stubbornly refused to believe and were afraid to ask Him about it.

This story is found in three of the Gospel accounts: in Matthew, Mark, and Luke. This was not the first occasion that Christ said this. He had mentioned this fact to them many times, perhaps because He wanted these truths to impact His disciples' lives deeply.

Steps were already taken to bring about His death. There was danger ahead for them all. The authorities were determined to do away with Jesus, and He was crucified. Yet He did not stay dead! He kept His promise and arose!

His resurrection offers great hope to believers who are experiencing fear in the difficult places of their lives. In the midst of your darkest fear, Jesus can and will sustain you. Don't avoid the truth. With courage and faith, step out to face whatever God has for you today.

October 16

Reason Not to Fear #290: I Will Trust God Even When I Don't Understand

"Now they were on the road, going up to Jerusalem, and Jesus was going before them; and they were amazed. And as they followed they were afraid. Then He took the twelve aside again and began to tell them the things that would happen to Him." Mark 10:32

We often say that we would have liked to actually see Jesus and walk with Him, and we think smugly that we would have done so much better than the people He dealt with. Yet I wonder. How would we have reacted to the many things Jesus did and said?

Jesus taught so radically different from the other rabbis that people were often astounded at His teachings. In chapter 10 of Mark, we see that reaction three times -- in verses 24, 26, and 32. Jesus taught that it was very hard for a wealthy person to get into the kingdom of heaven, and they were astonished. Jesus taught them that for such a person, it was harder than to get a camel through the eye of a needle than a rich man to get saved, and they wondered how anyone could be saved.

Then, to everyone's surprise, Jesus started up the road toward Jerusalem.

They had all tried to warn Him of the dangers awaiting Him in that city, yet He would not be swayed. They all knew that the religious leaders had determined to put Him to death. They knew that they, too, could experience something dismal ahead. Yet Jesus forged on ahead of them, His face set to accomplish His Father's will. And they followed, yes, but they were shaking their heads and meeting each other's eyes with dread and trepidation.

Fear swept over their souls when they thought of what lay around the bend of the road. Christ's determination and courage caused the disciples to be filled with dread and wonder. He went before them all. He led the way. He had no fear, for He knew what He was doing, and He was willing to face anything to be obedient to His Father.

Is this true in your life? Or are you fearful as the disciples were? Jesus walks ahead of us, and knows the fear and dread we may have as we follow Him. Nevertheless, it is our obligation to follow Him and do His will, wherever that will take us. He will be with you and help you each day.

October 17

Reason Not to Fear #291: I Will Not Be Jealous of Others

And the scribes and chief priests heard it and sought how they might destroy Him; for they feared Him, because all the people were astonished at His teaching.... 'But if we say, 'From men' --they feared the people, for all counted John to have been a prophet indeed. So they answered and said to Jesus, 'We do not know.' And Jesus answered and said to them, 'Neither will I tell you by what authority I do these things.'" Mark 11:18, 32-33

The chief priests and the teachers of the law feared Jesus' influence on the crowds. They were jealous of His ministry with them, for they knew the common people of the land loved Him for all He had done for them. The leaders wanted to kill Jesus, but they couldn't just arrest Him in front of the people. In one of the last discussions Jesus had with them, the priests plotted to trap Him with a question.

The priests thought they would come up with a difficult question for Jesus by which they could trap Him. "By whose authority are you doing these things? Who gave you authority to do this?"

Jesus didn't blink. "I will answer you, if you will answer my question. Concerning John's baptism, was it of God or of men?"

With much wagging of heads and mumbling together, they knew He had them. If they said "of men," the people would be angry; if they said "of God," Jesus could claim the same authority. So they took the middle road and said, "We don't know."

Do you see where fear takes a person? The religious leaders were ensnared by their own fears and doubts. They hated Jesus and wanted to kill Him, but they feared the people.

Jesus, on the other hand, feared nothing. He moved about the country freely and did the will of God in the face of such opposition that it would have rocked our world. Yet He cheerfully healed the sick, preached to the masses, loved them and showed them mercy. He did not fear the religious leaders. He only feared God.

Are you in a situation today in which you are tempted to fear? Do you fear the opinion of others? Do you have jealousy and hatred in your heart? If so, confess this to the Lord and have Him cleanse you. Fear God only and set your eyes on His will. Be obedient to Him no matter what opposition you face.

October 18

Reason Not to Fear #292: We Confess Our Sin

"And they sought to lay hands on Him, but feared the multitude, for they knew He had spoken the parable against them. So they left Him and went away." Mark 12:12

Vineyards are lovely places to be. Armenians love grape vines. The reason is we use the leaves to make our special food. My grandmother as well as my mother each had large grape vines growing in their yards. Every year during the month of July we would pick the leaves and make wonderful stuffed grape leaves.

The vineyard was a well-known figure of speech in Israel. So when Jesus began telling a parable to the religious leaders who had come to accuse Him about a vineyard, they understood what He was talking about.

Read verses 1-11. What would the owner do to these wicked tenants of his vineyard? He killed the tenants and gave the vineyard to others. Then Jesus quoted Psalm 118:22, 23, "The stone the builders rejected has become the capstone; the Lord has done this, and it is marvelous in His eyes."

The teaching was clear: Israel rejected the Son of God and wanted to kill Him. Now God would bring judgment on them and give their inheritance to others. This incensed the spiritual leaders. They wanted to kill Christ. But they could do nothing because they feared popular opinion. So they left Jesus alone and went to confer together, plotting when and how they could do this deed.

They could have repented and believed in Jesus as their Messiah and the Son of God, but they were too proud, too hungry for control and power, and too caught in their own ideas of what the Messiah would be like.

How about you? Confession of sin is a blow to pride, but if pride is standing in your way of accepting the Lord and His forgiveness, you are in danger of becoming like these men who were foolish, stubborn and arrogant against the truth. Don't fear the crowds. Don't fear losing your pride. Don't fear tomorrow. With simple faith, place your life in the nail-scarred hands of the One who died for you. Do it today. Now.

October 19

Reason Not to Fear #293: Because He Lives I Have No Fear of Tomorrow

"And entering the tomb, they saw a young man clothed in a long white robe sitting on the right side; and they were alarmed. But he said to them, "Do not be alarmed. You seek Jesus of Nazareth, who was crucified. He is risen! He is not here. See the place where they laid Him. But go, tell His disciples--and Peter--that He is going before you into Galilee; there you will see Him, as He said to you." So they went out quickly and fled from the tomb, for they trembled and were amazed. And they said nothing to anyone, for they were afraid."
Mark 16:4-8

I had only seen pictures in a National Geographic magazine when it came to what a jungle looked like. On my first visit into the jungle to visit my daughter and her family, the pictures in the magazine really did not prepare me. The beauty of the jungle cannot be truly captured in a photograph. As I walked through the jungle with my family, there were many times we stopped to admire its majesty and wonder. We were overcome with the splendor of the land. It took our breath away. We were speechless.

When Mary Magdalene and Mary, the mother of Jesus, arrived at the tomb where Jesus was buried, they saw an angel sitting inside who gave them a message. After they heard his message, they fled with trembling and bewilderment. Why? Because this was something far beyond what they were prepared to see. Planning to wrap Jesus' body correctly (maybe thinking the men hadn't done it right!), they found no body -- only an empty tomb and an angel. Now, that is something to be shocked about!

Once you truly see Jesus and encounter Him like these women did, you will never be the same. People, places, and things will change. You may find your commitment enhanced, your call to excellence elevated, your allegiance to Him more complete. You may find yourself no longer living to impress people, but living for the Lord to honor and praise His name.

We can all encounter Jesus Christ in our prayer times. We can see Him with spiritual eyes, speak with Him, and listen to Him speak with us. Who knows, in your encounter with Him, you, too, may be too speechless for awhile!

October 20

Reason Not to Fear #294: We Don't Give Up Praying and Hoping

"But the angel said to him, "Do not be afraid, Zacharias, for your prayer is heard; and your wife Elizabeth will bear you a son, and you shall call his name John. And you will have joy and gladness, and many will rejoice at his birth."
Luke 1:13-14

Most of us have a burden that we carry to the Lord on a regular basis. Perhaps it is in regard to your mate, your child, your health, or your grandchild. I prayed for my mother for over twenty-five years to come to Jesus as her Savior. Her comprehension of salvation was not correct. She was confused and did not believe the truth. My only option was to pray repeatedly for her.

In August, 2013, my mother died. I am happy to say that she died knowing Jesus. I am so thankful the Lord answered my prayer. Her decision to believe has re-enforced my commitment to pray regularly for certain people.

Zechariah and his wife, Elizabeth, also had a burden they carried to God regularly. They wanted a child, and for years prayed for this. Recently they had accepted the fact that they would *not* have one, for they were both getting on in years.

You can imagine Zechariah's shock and fear when an angel tapped him on the shoulder as he was in the Holy of Holies that day! He probably almost jumped out of his skin!

"Don't be afraid," were Gabriel's gracious words to him. "Your prayers have been heard."

Now, we can't be too hard on Zechariah for entertaining some doubts, for we have all experienced that moment of awe mingled with fear when God attends to our needs and meets with us personally. God was glorified, Elizabeth had a child, and they named him John.

Have you prayed for something, and the skies were dark, and God seemingly closed His ears to your cries? Remember Zechariah and Elizabeth. When the circumstances were hopeless, God answered. When you least expect it, God will come to you and answer.

Don't give up. No matter how long you have been waiting for an answer to your prayer, continue to believe God. Raise your expectation level and anticipate an answer soon.

October 21

Reason Not to Fear #295: We Move With God's Will

"But when she saw him, she was troubled at his saying, and considered what manner of greeting this was. ³⁰ Then the angel said to her, "Do not be afraid, Mary, for you have found favor with God. ³¹ And behold, you will conceive in your womb and bring forth a Son, and shall call His name JESUS."
Luke 1:29-31

In the community where I live, everyone is over fifty-five. Therefore, for those who drive, there are two speeds, slow and fast. They either pound the gas pedal to the floor, or they gently ease out into the street, hoping that the car coming will slow down. We've all been behind cautious older drivers, yet it is terrifying scary to be in the car with an older driver who goes extremely fast.

Sometimes God seems to be moving at mach speed, and at other times it seems He appears to move slowly. Four hundred years had elapsed between the Old and New Testament. People had not heard from God for that length of time, and maybe there were those who were thinking He would never utter another word.

Then He spoke, and everything changed. The angel, Gabriel, appeared to a girl in Nazareth one day as she was going about her business of living. He gave her an astounding message. It rocked her world. She was betrothed (engaged) to be married, and her life seemed set to follow the normal patterns, yet now she would give birth to the Son of God!

Her initial reaction was one of fear. When her fears subsided, she accepted the Lord's will humbly, not knowing where this path would take her. "Don't be afraid." Those words must have echoed in her mind throughout her life, even as she saw her Son on the cross one day in the far future. Both she and Joseph would experience the loss of home, reputation, and a normal life after the angel made his appearance to her that day, yet she moved out with faith instead of fear. Perhaps this is the greatest legacy this woman can give us -- her faith despite her fears.

Do you have some fears about the future? God wants to take them away. If you trust Him, as Mary and Joseph did, you will have nothing to fear. Commit your way to Him today and release your fears into His hand. He loves you and He will take care of you.

October 22

Reason Not to Fear #296: We Live With Vibrant Faith

"So they made signs to his father--what he would have him called. And he asked for a writing tablet, and wrote, saying, 'His name is John.' So they all marveled. Immediately his mouth was opened and his tongue loosed, and he spoke, praising God. Then fear came on all who dwelt around them; and all these sayings were discussed throughout all the hill country of Judea.
Luke 1:63-65

When I say my age, I feel it is old. My mind plays tricks on me but my body does not. They say you know you are getting older when you and your teeth don't sleep together anymore; when you hear snap, crackle, pop and realize you aren't eating cold cereal.

Zechariah and Elizabeth, both senior citizens, had received unexpected news. God promised them a child, despite their age, much like He had Abraham and Sarah. Zechariah was so astounded by this news that the Lord took his speech away until after his son was born. Once he declared that their son's name was to be John, his tongue was loosed, and he was able to speak again. This verse tells us that when this happened, fear, or a sense of awe, filled all the people in the village.

Elizabeth and Zechariah were just regular people like you and I, but the Lord gave them a once in a lifetime experience. Do you know why the angel appeared to this man? Because he was a faithful priest. God took their faith seriously. He knew they could be entrusted with raising this boy to love and serve Him. Jesus said that John was the greatest person to ever be born, and I believe it was his parents' devotion to God that molded him to become such a man.

It does not matter what your age, your life should reflect the Lord. If you are getting older, like me, take a deep breath and throw your shoulders back. Live your faith even more vibrantly than you did when you were in your twenties. Like they say, "It doesn't matter how many moments you breathe, but how many moments have taken your breath away."

This moment was a breath-taking time for these two older people, and the whole village shared their sense of awe. When you give glory to God and praise Him, others see your faith and will fear the Lord God.

October 23

Reason Not to Fear #297: We Serve Him Without Fear

"To grant us that we, Being delivered from the hand of our enemies, might serve Him without fear, in holiness and righteousness before Him all the days of our life." Luke 1:74-75

What do Colonel Sanders, Laura Ingalls Wilder, Ronald Reagan, George Bernard Shaw, Mother Theresa, and Julia Child have in common? They began their careers and became celebrities after the age of fifty! Julia Child didn't even know how to cook until she was 40!

Oscar Swahn proved that, even in sports, age does not matter as much as the desire to succeed. He won a gold medal during 1912 Olympics, becoming the best shooter in the world. He was 64 years old. He went on to compete in two more Olympics, winning silver at the 1920 Olympics. At age 72, he was not only the oldest Olympian ever, but also the oldest medalist.

Zechariah and Elizabeth raised John when they were older. They began their career in childrearing when they were past the age to bear children, and they did an incredible job of it! They had more excitement in the next twenty years than in all their previous years.

Their greatest days were their older days.

While it is important to give God your life and energies in your youth (Eccel. 12:1), we tend to think in our "youth culture" that the best days of our lives are our early years and that getting old is bad. We rarely think that a person's greatest work will be done after retirement age.

John the Baptist had a mission to accomplish and was a miracle child. He paved the way for the coming of the Messiah who would save His people from their sin. Many came to John in the wilderness and many people thought seriously about his message of repentance. He served God without fear and God blessed him for it, even though he was martyred by Herod later on in his life. John served because he was a servant of God.

God wants you to live your life so that you can serve him without fear. What are you afraid of today? Cast aside those fears and begin to witness of God's saving grace, of His mighty power to save from sin, and His holiness. Try it and see what joy God brings in your life because you are obedient to Him, as were John and his parents.

October 24

Reason Not to Fear #298: God's Message to Mankind Is One of Peace

"Then the angel said to them, 'Do not be afraid, for behold, I bring you good tidings of great joy which will be to all people. For there is born to you this day in the city of David a Savior, who is Christ the Lord.'" Luke 2:10-11

In the middle of an ordinary night, God met with a group of shepherds on a hillside in Palestine to deliver an earth-shaking message.

My days since the death of my daughter's husband, James, are filled with helping Nicky and her children. Truthfully, I never guessed that at my age I would be doing this. I thought for sure by now He would have me be a well known speaker! But these days I do not have a lot of fanfare or challenging conversations.

Simple, common days. Sometimes I cry over the death of my son in law. I speak to the Lord about my confusion and bitterness, usually in the early morning hours, and I sit and wait for Him to speak to me. It finally happened today. It's Thursday and on Thursday's I travel two hours to teach a women's Bible Study. The lesson was on the disciples in the storm on the Sea of Galilee. It is a very familiar story. But today the Lord had the Holy Spirit give it to me in a fresh manner. As I taught the lesson, the Holy Spirit took these words that Jesus spoke and applied them to my heart. "Fear not, it is I."

I have no idea what the future is for any of us now, but this I do know: the Lord is with us in the unexpected storm.

It was the same for a small group of shepherds on the hillside that night outside the small village of Bethlehem. They were going about their job of taking care of sheep, gazing up into the sky, and possibly wondering when the Messiah would come when suddenly the dark sky was rolled back, and they saw into heaven. The message they received was one of peace to all the inhabitants on earth, unspeakable joy, and love.

The way to pardon and peace with God was now thrown open to all people. The knowledge about Jesus as God's Son was no longer to be confined to the Jews, but eventually offered to the whole human race. That indeed is good joyful news for everyone. This good news was full of hope. Do not be afraid to hope. You belong to a God who is full of hope and good news, as the message conveyed to the shepherds that night so long ago.

October 25

Reason Not to Fear #299: Get Up and Follow Christ Without Fear

"When Simon Peter saw it, he fell down at Jesus' knees, saying, 'Depart from me, for I am a sinful man, O Lord!' For he and all who were with him were astonished at the catch of fish which they had taken; and so also were James and John, the sons of Zebedee, who were partners with Simon. And Jesus said to Simon, 'Do not be afraid. From now on you will catch men.'"
Luke 5:8-10

Beware of stopping your ears from hearing the call of God.

Peter and his friends had been up all night fishing. They returned to shore with empty nets. They were tired, having worked hard all night and had not caught one single fish. That morning, while they were cleaning the nets, Jesus came by and asked to borrow Simon's boat. After Christ preached to the crowds on the shore, He requested that Simon row out into the deep water for a catch of fish. Simon was reluctant to obey, as he knew Jesus wasn't a fisherman. Yet, to be polite, he obeyed. The result? Their nets were filled so full they almost broke, and the boats were swamped as they pulled to shore.

Simon fell down at Jesus' feet, afraid and trembling. He knew what he had witnessed was a miracle and that Jesus was something more than a rabbi with an unusual message. Simon Peter suddenly realized he was in the presence of God and that knowledge shook him to the core. It would require of him something that he was unwilling to give at that moment -- his entire soul, heart, mind and life.

Jesus announced that Peter, from this point on, would be no longer fish for fish but for people. He would become an instrument of life to a lost world, and his business from now on would be to spread the truth about Christ.

Today God is looking for people who will get up and follow Him without fear. He is calling you, dear friend. The call may not be convenient or suitable to your liking, but if you want to advance as a fisher of men, you will submit.

Have you ever experienced an encounter with God that made you fall down and worship Him in reverent fear? May the Spirit of God create in your heart something of the respect and fear Peter experienced when he realized that God is God over everything and that he needed to obey Him. Hear His call and obey Him in your life today.

October 26

Reason Not to Fear #300: We Share God's Blessings with Others

"And they were all amazed, and they glorified God and were filled with fear, saying, 'We have seen strange things today!'" Luke 5:26

This is an interesting and humorous story. Jesus was sitting inside a house, probably resting. The house was full of people -- the religious leaders who had come to snare Him into saying or doing something they could accuse Him with; the curious, and those who hoped Jesus would heal them; the disciples and their families. In fact, it was so crowded some of them had to stand outside.

You know the story of how the men tore a hole in the roof to get their friend, who was paralyzed, to Jesus. This probably wasn't as hard then as it would be now, but nevertheless, it was a desperate and startling thing to do. I can imagine the sounds of the blows on the roof, the pieces of tile and mortar and bits of straw starting to drift down into the room. Maybe some of religious leaders looked up, annoyed at the ruckus.

When the hole was large enough, they lowered the man down in front of Jesus, who looked at the man and said, "Take heart, son; your sins are forgiven you." Now the man might have replied, "But I don't want my sins forgiven. I want my legs healed.." But he didn't.

The scribes and Pharisees jumped on Jesus' statement and accused Him of blasphemy. But Christ's question set them back on their heels. "Which is harder, to forgive sin or to restore a paralyzed man's legs to him?" And to demonstrate, He went ahead and healed the man. They were furious, but what could they say? The people were filled with awe and the fear of God as they witnessed the power and compassion of the Lord. They not only observed a physical miracle but also a spiritual one. Sins were forgiven, and health was restored.

What is God doing in your life? Has He forgiven your sin, healed your heart, and given you joy and peace? If so, you should be telling others about it, so they can find that same kind of healing. Make it a point to tell someone the marvelous things that God has done for you today.

Do not live in fear, live in faith and believe God for miracles. He is able to save you from sin and to heal your heart!

October 27

Reason Not to Fear #301: Christ Meets Us on the Dusty Paths of Our Lives

"Then He came and touched the open coffin, and those who carried him stood still. And He said, 'Young man, I say to you, arise.' So he who was dead sat up and began to speak. And He presented him to his mother. Then fear came upon all, and they glorified God, saying, 'A great prophet has risen up among us'; and, 'God has visited His people.'" Luke 7:14-16

Omnipresence means that God is everywhere. For an unbeliever, this might be a fearful thing to think that wherever I go, God is there. Yet for a Christian, this truth is a comfort and encouragement. While Jesus was on earth, He was limited to a human body and had to be in only one place at a time. Yet when He was needed, He often showed up to meet people's need.

Jesus might have known the young man who had died in the village of Nain, for it is just a few miles from Nazareth. Perhaps they had played together, attended the synagogue school together, enjoyed playing in the woods outside of town.

One day, Jesus was traveling on a dusty road with a crowd of people and passed through the village of Nain, His old stomping grounds. He sees a funeral procession coming down the hill toward the cemetery, and to His sorrow, He sees it is the mother of the young man He once played with, a widow woman whose only son now lay dead.

Jesus had compassion for this woman, and His compassion moved Him to comfort her far beyond what she could have ever possibly imagined. The procession stopped, and the men lowered the casket. Christ addressed the corpse as if he could hear Him, and said, "Okay, friend. Get up!"

The man obeyed the Word of God and sat up! Can you imagine being one of those who witnessed this miracle? The widow must have stood there in shock at first, then tearfully and joyfully welcomed her son back to the land of the living.

Notice the result: great fear came over the crowd, and they glorified God. There was a mixture of fear and worship. This is our Savior. This is the One who is everywhere, and who can meet us on the dusty paths of our lives. He brings His Word to bear on our grief, distress, sadness and suffering. Turn to Him today and allow His Spirit to minister to your heart.

October 28

Reason Not to Fear #302: We Take A Leap of Faith

"And they came to Him and awoke Him, saying, "Master, Master, we are perishing!" Then He arose and rebuked the wind and the raging of the water. And they ceased, and there was a calm. But He said to them, "Where is your faith?" And they were afraid, and marveled, saying to one another, "Who can this be? For He commands even the winds and water, and they obey Him!"
Luke 8:24-25

I get a little annoyed when I share a problem I'm facing with someone and they come back with the flippant answer, "You should have more faith." This answer is often given with the idea that you can get what you want from God and your prayers will be answered if only you have enough faith. The reality lies in the fact that God is sovereign and sometimes it isn't His will to immediately remove me from distress and trials.

The disciples were facing something they couldn't remove and couldn't get away from -- a storm that threatened to swamp their boat and take their lives. When Jesus calmed the storm with a word, they were amazed and frightened. *Who is this*, they asked themselves. *Only God can do this kind of thing! Is God in our boat with us right now?* Yes, He was!

How strong is your faith? Do you need to grow in this area? Many of us desire stronger faith, yet we don't know how to get it. Our faith must begin in the confidence that God is who He is and that He is in charge of our lives.

When your world and situations press upon you with more demands than you can meet, how do you respond? In quiet, trustful faith? Or in despair, panic, worry, or over-control?

"Consequently, faith comes from hearing the message, and the message is heard through the Word of Christ." Rom. 10:17 How much time do you spend in study, memorization, and reading God's Word? In direct proportion to that, you will find how much faith you have. The more you understand the Word, the more you will understand God and His will for your life.

We forget that the Lord has deep interest in _our_ welfare. Despite the financial, emotional, or physical stress *you* may be under, He can still command the winds in *your* life to be still. By reading the Word, or hearing it, your faith was born. By reading the Word now, your faith will increase. The Creator of the universe wants to have a word with you, so read His Word.

October 29

Reason Not to Fear #303: We Put Our Trust in Christ Alone

"Then they went out to see what had happened, and came to Jesus, and found the man from whom the demons had departed, sitting at the feet of Jesus, clothed and in his right mind. And they were afraid. They also who had seen it told them by what means he who had been demon-possessed was healed. Then the whole multitude of the surrounding region of the Gadarenes asked Him to depart from them, for they were seized with great fear. And He got into the boat and returned." Luke 8:35-37

Fear does funny things to a person. There was a man who lived across the Sea of Galilee in a village. He was so crazy he had to live among the tombs. Now men from the village came out and saw him dressed and in his right mind. Yet their herd of pigs had been drowned. Why would they demand Christ leave their country? The Bible says they were overcome with fear, and I imagine this meant terror, dread and panic.

We have a similar incident in Acts 16. Paul and Silas, who had traveled to the Macedonian city of Philippi and were preaching in that city, found themselves followed by a demon-possessed slave girl who cried out, "These men are servants of the Most High God!" While this statement was true, they did not need this kind of publicity, nor did they want to be associated with those who consulted demons, spiritists, and fortune tellers.

Paul commanded the demon to leave her and that is when the trouble began. Because they could no longer profit from the girl, her owners stirred up the city against Paul and Silas and ordered them to be thrown into prison, beaten and placed in stocks. The Lord intervened for them and sent an earthquake to free them, but they had to leave the city.

In both instances, fear sprang full blown into the minds of the people because they were afraid of financial loss. When the Gospel is preached and people begin losing money, watch out! When you are brave enough to confront a sinful society, you will not be welcome with open arms by them.

Jesus left a stalwart witness behind when He left. He said to him, "Return and tell how much the Lord has done for you." How about you? Are you telling everyone the Good News of what God has done for you? Spend a little time this morning and ask God to give you one person to share with today. Then go out and do it without fear.

October 30

Reason Not to Fear #304: We've Gotta Tell Somebody!

"But when Jesus heard it, He answered him, saying, 'Do not be afraid; only believe, and she will be made well.'" Luke 8:50

Don Fransisco, a Christian song writer and artist, highlighted this story with a song he entitled, "I've Gotta Tell Somebody". In the last stanza, Fransisco builds suspense and tension when he repeats the phrase several times. You can almost feel the frustration of this father who wanted so desperately to share the good news of this breathtaking miracle that happened in his life with others.

In our age of publicity and making money as the bottom line, we are urged to let as many people know about us and our product as possible. We have Facebook, Twitter, Linkedin, Pinterest, and many other forms of social media outlets that connect us with an assortment of people. To market a product, we are told we must be number one on the Google search page, or at least number nine, so the searcher will find our name and product without having to go to the second page. Most people dream of putting a video on YouTube and having it go "viral".

Yet in this story, Jesus urged the people *not* to talk about His amazing miracles. He did not want publicity for the message He was giving to the world. Even the angels, when they announced Jesus' birth, went to a bunch of poor shepherds huddled on the hillside with their sheep. Today, we would have made a video of it and put it on YouTube. We would have sent it to all our friends by Facebook with a score of pictures. We would have emailed it to hundreds on our email list. In our world today, the more people you have on your lists or as your "friends", the more important you are.

Jesus did not demand or seek publicity, prominence, or prosperity. He was content to do His Father's will and to meet the needs of others, like raising this little girl from the dead. To avoid the crush of the crowds, and to forestall pride that comes with fame, Jesus asked them not to spread around the news of what He had done.

The lesson I want you to take with you from this time in the Word is to stop seeking the things of the world and begin doing only what your Heavenly Father wants you to do. Seek to know His will for your life. Then do it without all the fanfare, stress, and unhappiness that this world brings. Today's lesson: do not puff yourself up, but tell others about Christ!

October 31

Reason Not to Fear #305: If We Fear God, We Won't Fear Others

"And I say to you, My friends, do not be afraid of those who kill the body, and after that have no more that they can do. But I will show you whom you should fear: Fear Him who, after He has killed, has power to cast into hell; yes, I say to you, fear Him!" Luke 12:4-5

Jesus' words to His disciples may be easy to read, yet they are very hard to do. When it comes to suffering, pain, and persecution, most of us do not even want to go there in our thinking. We have become so accustomed to ease, freedom, and prosperity, we can't imagine what it would be like to suffer for our faith.

Yet many in our world today are paying the ultimate sacrifice for believing in Christ and teaching others to do that, too. Jesus knew that most of the men who stood around Him that day as He taught them would die for the sake of the Gospel. Peter would be hanged upside down on a cross in the Roman coliseum, James would be beheaded by the order of Herod, John would suffer banishment and deprivation as an old man on the island of Patmos. Historians reveal that every one of the disciples died for the cause of Christ except John.

Jesus said, "Do not fear those who kill your mortal bodies." Read the book, *Foxes Book of Martyrs*, if you want to be astounded at the faith, joy, and peace that characterized Christians in their last moments of life, even though they experienced death at the hands of their tormentors.

Who, then, should we fear? Fear God, for only He has the power to send you to hell, or to forgive your sins and accept you into heaven. It is only God who has your soul's eternal destiny in His hands. When we fully grasp this principle, there is no hold that Satan can have on our lives, minds, or souls.

Think about the things or people that you fear today. These things chain you more securely than any prison can. To be free, allow God control of all things in your life. Fear Him, give Him your reverence and admiration. The more you fear others and the adverse situations of life, the less you will fear God. The more your fear God, the less these others fears will control you.

Make this a matter of your prayer as you close this time with the Lord today.

November 1

Reason Not to Fear #306: God Takes Cares of Us

"But the very hairs of your head are all numbered. Do not fear therefore; you are of more value than many sparrows." Luke 12:7

Clocks. I collect clocks and love them. I love to hear them chime, tick, and cuckoo. In fact, as I was typing this, one of my cuckoo clocks just played its melody. It is my intention to have these clocks dispersed to my children and grandchildren, and I have told them which clocks they can have. However, I do not allow them to touch my clocks, and when they dare forget that rule, I remind them rather forcibly. Yet I know and try to keep to the rule that we should not value the things of this world too highly.

Jesus reminded His disciples in this verse that people are of the highest value to God. He pointed out that even small sparrows, which sold for a few pennies, do not escape His attention. Since God cares for these insignificant birds, how much more does He care for us? He knows the number of the hairs on our heads. He knows that people are more valuable than sparrows and clocks.

Our Lord was giving His disciples instructions on how to live in a hostile world, a world ruled by Satan, governed by evil and opposed to God. How could they possibly carry on His work in this world if they were controlled by fear? He wanted to impress upon them their value in God's sight. How much does God value His children? How much does He value you?

Think about the sparrows, chickadees, and finches that twitter in the branches of the trees near your house. I love to feed birds close to my windows so I can watch them. It cheers my heart. God's concern and love for me goes far beyond anything I can understand. His loving care for me goes beyond my imagination. He knows when I lie down and when I get up. He knows what bothers me and what makes me happy. Every tiny detail of my life is His concern.

Therefore, we need not fear whatever is ahead. Do not live in fear of the future. Release that fear to God and trust Him instead. Your sighs, your tears, your heartaches are all known by Him. All of your losses are known and God knows how to work them for your advantage. Be comforted, you are of great value to Him. You are worth more than clocks!

November 2

Reason Not to Fear #307: Our Treasure Is In Heaven

"Do not fear, little flock, for it is your Father's good pleasure to give you the kingdom. Sell what you have and give alms; provide yourselves money bags which do not grow old, a treasure in the heavens that does not fail, where no thief approaches nor moth destroys. For where your treasure is, there your heart will be also." Luke 12:31-34

How can a disciple of Christ live in a hostile world and do God's will with a cheerful heart and steadfast mind? How can we face persecution, trouble, difficulties, an aging body, and ill health with a focus set entirely on Christ?

These were the issues Jesus addressed when He spoke to His disciples that day. "Do not be afraid, little flock," He said as He looked around at each one of them in turn, His love piercing their hearts with its tenderness. They knew what it meant to be a shepherd. Jesus assured them that God the Father would give them the kingdom. That was good news!

But He continued with instructions that were (and are) hard to accept. In this world, as they traveled through life, they were to sell their possessions, carry a light backpack, and not accumulate treasures on earth; rather, they were to send them on ahead to heaven.

Now, I do not think He wants each of us to sell everything we have. He has given us many things that we can share with others and use for His kingdom. But the principle is this: we must let go of our earthly desire for things to focus more completely on His will.

The Shepherd not only provides food and clothes for His flock, but also His kingdom. In our world, we often crave comforts, pleasures, and material items. We tend to forget that our Father has provided a kingdom for us in the future. Never forget God has a kingdom in store for His little flock, His children.

If you cannot let go of your possessions, you are in trouble, indeed. This is where fear may take hold of your heart. You fear the loss of your things, not thinking that your real treasure lies in heaven. Send your hoarded treasures on ahead of you by giving them away.

That is hard to do. Yet God will reward you and give you freedom from the curse of having to keep and protect all your hoarded treasures. Trust God and do not fear, for He will take care of you. This is the key to living life successfully in God's kingdom.

November 3

Reason Not to Fear #308: Focus On Eternal Values

"Then one of the criminals who were hanged blasphemed Him, saying, "If You are the Christ, save Yourself and us." But the other, answering, rebuked him, saying, "Do you not even fear God, seeing you are under the same condemnation? And we indeed justly, for we receive the due reward of our deeds; but this Man has done nothing wrong." Then he said to Jesus, "Lord, remember me when You come into Your kingdom." And Jesus said to him, "Assuredly, I say to you, today you will be with Me in Paradise." Luke 23:39-43

The thief on the cross next to Jesus rebuked the other criminal by saying, "Do not you fear God?" Obviously, the man did not, not even when his life was ebbing from him. But the first thief feared God and knew he should ask Jesus Christ to forgive his sins. Christ turned his tortured gaze upon the man, and in His grace and mercy did not see a despised thief, a criminal. He saw a repentant sinner. He said, "Today you will be with Me in paradise."

This story shows the tender love, grace, and concern Christ had for others even as He died for the sins of the world. He looked at His mother, Mary, and saw that she had a son and a home with John. He forgave the Roman soldiers and all mankind who were responsible for the ugly deed of crucifying Him.

Often when trouble hits, our first thought is how to get out of it. Recently my oldest daughter lost her job. It has been a very trying experience for her. Money is tight for their family right now and only necessities are brought. The kindness of God's people has been evident. They will not starve. They will survive this hard experience, and hopefully through this ordeal, their trust and faith in the Lord will become stronger and deeper. They, like many of us who are older, will realize that God has lessons for us to learn during this time.

Jesus knows and cares about each issue in your life. If you are desperate, in need, and praying hard for Him to resolve a situation, rest easy, my friend. He knows, and He will answer you, just like He did the thief on the cross. Wait for His time. Commit your way to Him, and He will see you through.

November 4

Reason Not to Fear #309: I Believe God's Word

"And it happened, as they were greatly perplexed about this, that behold, two men stood by them in shining garments. Then, as they were afraid and bowed their faces to the earth, they said to them, 'Why do you seek the living among the dead? He is not here, but is risen!'" Luke 24:4-6a

Jesus had a following of some special women. These women provided materially for Jesus and His disciples. Even though the rabbis were not to speak to women in public, Jesus never discouraged any woman from following Him. The two Marys, Joanna, Susanna, Salome, and others listened to Jesus teach and stood at the foot of the cross when He was crucified.

They came early that Sunday morning to the tomb where Jesus was buried, and when they got there, they were not only perplexed, but frightened. They stood before an empty tomb, and they were afraid. Afraid of what? Death or life?

Their first moment of surprise came when they saw the great stone that was sealing the tomb. It was rolled away, and they could enter. So they did. But the tomb was empty. Maybe they went back outside, wondering where the body of their Lord had gone. They did not really expect the tomb to be empty; if they had, they would not have brought the embalming spices with them.

Their second moment of surprise burst upon them as brilliant strokes of lightning. Two angels stood beside them in glowing, white robes. They asked the women a shocking question. "Why do you seek the living among the dead?" It is not, "Why do you seek the dead man who was buried here." The angels knew He was already risen and alive.

Are you expecting God to show up today – suddenly, unexpectedly? It is usually when we confess we can no longer handle our life or situation that He comes to us! Just as God had a *suddenly* planned for these women, He has a *suddenly* planned for you, too. He moves in your life in unexpected ways. Watch for Him and do not be afraid when He comes to you.

Are you confused, weak and unable to carry on? This, then, is the very moment when He will manifest Himself to you. Hold tight to the promises of God; securely grasp His Words. They will soothe your fears away, and you will move out with joy into what God wants to do in your life.

November 5

Reason Not to Fear #310: We Live in the Light

"And this is the condemnation, that the light has come into the world, and men loved darkness rather than light, because their deeds were evil. For everyone practicing evil hates the light and does not come to the light, (for fear) lest his deeds should be exposed." John 3:19-20

Light is a picture to us of the truth and of Jesus Christ. Later in the book of John, He said, "I am the light of the world. Whoever follows Me will never walk in darkness, but will have the light of life.'" John 8:12

It is sad that people love darkness rather than light. I think it is interesting that most taverns are dark places with few windows, and even the windows that are in the building are usually boarded up. It is dark inside, a picture of the darkness that dwells in each heart without God.

My daughter and her husband, who spent eleven years in Indonesia, saw this truth every day. People do love darkness rather than light. Over and over, James and Nicky would present Christ to their neighbors and to the tribal people. Stepping out of the kingdom of darkness was difficult for the majority of them. Yet for my children, the burden was real, to bring the kingdom of light to people in the dark. Slowly a few of the tribal people listened and some of them allowed James and Nicky into their homes to teach.

The kingdom of darkness is controlling, commanding, and powerful. The truth is that many will not leave it. Nonetheless, we should be burdened for those who dwell in this kingdom and carry the light to them faithfully.

When you believe in Jesus, you step out of the kingdom of darkness into the kingdom of light. It is like leaving a dark room where everyone is groping around in fear and confusion and suddenly you walk into the light. We continue to walk in the light by being obedient to His Word and by continuing to ask Him to cleanse us from sin. "If we walk in the Light as He Himself is in the Light, we have fellowship with one another, and the blood of Jesus His Son cleanses us from all sin." I John 1:7

Where are you walking today? Have you put your trust and faith in Christ for salvation? If so, great! But how are you doing in your daily walk with Christ? Ask Him to cleanse you of sin and be obedient to His Word. Walk in the light. It is the only way to go!

November 6

Reason Not to Fear #311: Even In the Storm, I Will Trust God

"So when they had rowed about three or four miles, they saw Jesus walking on the sea and drawing near the boat; and they were afraid. But He said to them, 'It is I; do not be afraid.'" John 6:19-20

We can see some storms approaching from a long way off, and we are warned. It doesn't make the going any easier, but at least we have some knowledge that they are coming. There are other storms that hit us like a moving train and with about the same force, coming upon us suddenly and without warning.

It was like that for some missionary wives in Ecuador in 1956. One of them was Elizabeth Elliot, who waited with her little daughter for the return of her husband, Jim, from a plane trip he was taking with four other missionary men into the jungle. Jim never returned alive and Elizabeth was left to weather out the storm of sudden grief and death. Yet there are many other Christians who die long, tortuous deaths that can be seen and anticipated for months or years ahead of time. Which is the most difficult to endure? Storms of any nature are hard to deal with, especially when you feel your very life is in danger.

The disciples found themselves in a storm as they were in a small boat on the Sea of Galilee. One moment it was calm, the next moment, the storm raged. Jesus had told them to get in the boat and go across the sea. The disciples had no idea where Jesus was, but He knew where they were. Maybe they thought he forgot about them. Though Jesus did not come immediately, He did come, yet in the way they did not expect.

He came walking on the water. In the midst of their fears and confusion, they mistook Him for a ghost. They cried out in terror. Jesus identified Himself and there was no mistaking His voice. Just as suddenly as the storm came, it was gone, and peace reigned again.

In a storm, it is the presence of Christ that will calm your soul. His voice will speak words of encouragement to you. If you find yourself in the middle of a stormy situation, rest assured you are never out of the Lord's sight. You may be experiencing some of the same fears the disciples felt. Or you may be wondering where the Lord is and if He even knows about your predicament. Yet the One who never slumbers or sleeps watches over you.

He is saying to you today, "Do not be afraid, my child, I am with you."

November 7

Reason Not to Fear #312: I Am Not Afraid of People

*"And there was much complaining among the people concerning Him.
Some said, 'He is good'; others said, 'No, on the contrary, He deceives the
people.' However, no one spoke openly of Him for fear of the Jews."*
John 7:12, 13

Have you ever been the brunt of gossip, discussion, or controversy among those whom you were serving or leading? It is not a comfortable feeling. I think, for me, the worst thing I can experience is to know that others have been talking about me for quite awhile, and I have just found out about it.

The majority of the Jewish leaders wanted to extinguish the name of Jesus as well as the fame of Jesus. Those who were true believers lacked the confidence to speak in favor of Jesus because they feared what might be done to them or their families. It seems rather odd that the enemies of Jesus were not afraid to speak boldly, but His followers were. Even though they really believed Jesus was the Messiah, they remained silent and did not speak on His behalf.

Jesus, too, was the object of much talk, speculation, gossip and slander as He ministered in Galilee and Judea. The fact that He attracted great crowds, healed many people, and brought some back from the dead stirred the people to wonder and interest. The religious leaders hated Him because they were jealous of Him. They were plotting to kill Him, so they spread rumors and lies about Him.

There will always be people who desire to speak up, but do not because their fear of the consequences overtakes them. Do not let the fear of people silence your voice for Christ. There is power in confessing Jesus as your Savior. When presented with the opportunity, speak up and be counted as a redeemed child of God.

When you are prompted by the Holy Spirit to witness to others, are you afraid of what others will think? Are you afraid you will lose your job? Or your influence? Fear makes you shut up; faith encourages you to speak up. As Christians in America in this time in history, we are not being the salt and light to our culture that we should because of our fear. It is time we shed our fear and begin making bold statements about our faith in Christ to our generation.

It might cost you something. But consider this: it cost Christ His life!

November 8

Reason Not to Fear #313: I Will Do What Is Right

"His parents answered them and said, 'We know that this is our son, and that he was born blind; but by what means he now sees we do not know, or who opened his eyes we do not know. He is of age; ask him. He will speak for himself.'" His parents said these things because they feared the Jews, for the Jews had agreed already that if anyone confessed that He was Christ, he would be put out of the synagogue." John 9:20-22

In the movie, *Last Ounce of Courage*, the main character, Bob, is the mayor of a small town in Kansas. He loses a son to the war in Afghanistan. Fifteen years later, he is challenged by his grandson and wife to become active in defending the religious freedom in this country. Since Christmas was approaching, he decided to make Christmas the issue, and he erected a huge tree in front of the courthouse, along with other decorations.

The government agencies waded in and accused him of breaking the laws concerning the separation of state and religion. He ended up in jail. Yet the overwhelming support he received from the people showed that the people were behind him. His last ounce of courage helped him win the fight to display Christmas decorations and was a clarion call to all Christians to stand up for their rights.

The parents in this Bible story were afraid of the Jews, meaning the ruling authorities, and therefore they refused to speak up for their grown son who had been healed by Jesus. The ruling religious leaders of that day controlled every aspect of the common citizen's life. To be cast out of the synagogue was to be refused the right to worship God, to have your sins forgiven, to fellowship with others, even your own family and friends, and to be an outcast as far as trade and business. Who would not fear someone with this kind of power?

Yet Jesus casts out all fear and darkness. He opened the eyes of this man and also opened the way for this family to enjoy a life without fear, walking in the light of His love.

The choice is yours. Will you cast aside fear and do what is right, or will you be intimidated, manipulated and oppressed? What or who do you fear today? Confess your fear, move out in faith, and wait to see what God will do as you walk in the light of His love.

November 9

Reason Not to Fear #314: I Am Looking Forward to the King's Appearance

"Fear not, daughter of Zion; Behold, your King is coming, sitting on a donkey's colt." John 12:15

Why should the people of Israel, the "daughter of Zion," be afraid of their king when he comes? John quoted Zechariah 9:9 which says, "Rejoice greatly, O Daughter of Zion! Shout, Daughter of Jerusalem! See, your king comes to you, righteous and having salvation, gentle and riding on a colt, the foal of a donkey....He will proclaim peace to the nations. His rule will extend from sea to sea and from the River to the ends of the earth."

While other kings come in great pomp and splendor, in might and with an array of power, this King comes on the foal of a donkey, riding gently down the slope of the Mt. of Olives into the city with a sad, almost forlorn look on His face. We know this event happened on what we celebrate as Palm Sunday when Jesus entered Jerusalem and the people hailed Him as their king.

The reason for that type of entrance is because God commanded the kings of Israel not to multiply horses. Jesus did not break this law or any other part of the law; rather He came to fulfill the law. He obeyed the command of His Father, God; therefore, He rode on a donkey's colt. He fulfilled the prophecy spoken about His coming in the book of Zechariah.

Notice that His coming forbids and dispels fear. Jesus did not want people to be afraid of Him, for He was not going to be like all the other human kings. Perhaps that is why He did not come with pomp and power. Jesus deliberately presented Himself as a humble, meek, approachable king who did not want to be dreaded.

We know that Jesus will come to this earth again to rule as King. Our King is the Righteous One who came in a peaceful and lowly manner. We do not need to fear His second coming, nor shy away from studying about prophecy that speaks of it.

We should rejoice in the fact that someday the King we revere and honor in our hearts will actually reign on this earth and that we will reign with Him! Put aside your fears and be glad in this today. Fear the Lord and put Him first in your heart, always looking for the blessed time when He will come.

November 10

Reason Not to Fear #315: I Am Trusting in Jesus

"Peace I leave with you, My peace I give to you; not as the world gives do I give to you. Let not your heart be troubled, neither let it be afraid." John 14:27

Death is a very heavy topic. I have never thought about it so much or so deeply until my daughter's husband, James, died two months ago. I have read this verse over and over because my heart has become extremely troubled since the death of James. In the Greek, this verse literally means, "stop letting your hearts be troubled." Jesus knew that we would become troubled, for we often experience conflict, disappointment and extreme pain in this world. It is during those times one must remember the Lord is with us.

I have tried to be of some comfort to my daughter and her children after the death of their father and husband, but I cannot be their "all." Jesus can. He can be whatever my daughter needs and whatever her children need, too. I love this wonderful promise, "In my Father's house are many dwelling places, if it were not so, I would have told you."

Going Home to heaven will not be like going to a giant, unfamiliar place. We will be going to our Father's house. It will be indescribably beautiful and glorious. The walls are made of jasper, the streets are made of gold, the foundation stones are of every kind of precious stone, and the each of the twelve gates has a single pearl. In our home, there will be the purest, brightest, and the most fabulous flashing jewels. The gates will never be shut. Jesus is preparing a place that is filled with dazzling beauty.

Augustus Toplady, who wrote "Rock of Ages," died in London at the age of 38. When death drew near he said, "It is my dying vow that these great and glorious truths which the Lord in rich mercy has given me to believe and enabled me to preach are now brought into practical and heartfelt experience. They are the very joy and support of my soul. The comfort flowing from them carries me far above the things of time and sin."

Then he said, "Had I wings like a dove I would fly away to the bosom of God and be at rest." About an hour before he died he seemed to awaken from a gentle slumber, and his last words were, "Oh! What delight! Who can fathom the joys of heaven! I know it cannot be long now until my Savior will come for me." And then bursting into a flood of tears he said, "All is light, light, light, light, the brightness of His own glory. Oh, come Lord Jesus, come. Come quickly!" And he closed his eyes.

I cannot wait to go, too.

November 11

Reason Not to Fear #316: I Walk in Integrity and Truth

"The Jews answered him, "We have a law, and according to our law He ought to die, because He made Himself the Son of God." Therefore, when Pilate heard that saying, he was the more afraid, and went again into the Praetorium, and said to Jesus, 'Where are You from?' But Jesus gave him no answer."
John 19:7, 8

Pontius Pilate was caught in an impossible situation. He ruled the Judean province as prefect from 26-36AD. Historians report that he repeatedly caused insurrections among the Jews because of his insensitivity to Jewish customs. He ran into trouble with the Jews several times because he brought shields and ensigns into the city of Jerusalem with effigies on them that were offensive to the people. When they asked him to remove them, he put soldiers among the crowd. The soldiers surrounded the demonstrators and killed many of them.

Philo, a Greek historian, wrote that Tiberius sent a letter to Pilate with a host of reproaches and rebukes for his audacious violation of precedence and bade him at once take down the shields and have them transferred to Caesarea. Historians say that Pilate had "vindictiveness and a furious temper," and was "naturally inflexible." He was afraid that the Jews would send a delegation to Tiberius because they might also expose the rest of his conduct -- the briberies, insults, robberies, outrages and wanton injuries, the executions without trial, and many other crimes.

Pilate was a man elevated to an important and delicate position, yet one who could not make wise decisions. When he came face to face with Jesus, he couldn't understand Him. If you read John's account carefully, you will see they were speaking on two levels, as if in different languages. Pilate's verdict to scourge Jesus and later have Him crucified was utterly without justice. He wanted this problem to go away, and he didn't mind how or where it went. For that, he has gone down in history as the most foolish, incompetent and unjust ruler of them all.

What are the fears that inhabit your mind and soul today? Are they brought on because your conduct is not what it should be? Decide today that you will not be like Pilate. Clean up your heart and your behavior, then set aside your fears. God is with you.

You do not need be afraid of anyone.

November 12

Reason Not to Fear #317: Bold Faith Brings Confidence

"After this, Joseph of Arimathea, being a disciple of Jesus, but secretly, for fear of the Jews, asked Pilate that he might take away the body of Jesus; and Pilate gave him permission. So he came and took the body of Jesus."
John 19:38

How bold is your faith? How strong is it? Have there been times in your life when your faith was rather shallow?

I love being around people who have brave daring faith. They challenge me. I have a friend like that in my life. She is always confident as she speaks about her belief in Christ. It does not matter where she is she is ready, willing, and able to speak up. Through the years, her fearless faith tested mine. Slowly, I began to inform my parents, siblings, aunts, uncles, and cousins of my decision to follow Christ.

I was raised in the Armenian Church and coming to believe in Christ as your Savior was unique. I was fearful to reveal my discovery to my family. But this woman encouraged me to face up to my faith. I did. It was not an easy confrontation but it definitely was a needed one.

Bold faith comes from within. It is based on a Person -- the Person of Jesus Christ. When our faith is firm in Christ, we find ourselves doing, acting and thinking in a different realm. We find ourselves unafraid of the world or the consequences of speaking out for our Savior and God. Joseph of Arimathea was a rich man, a member of the Sanhedrim. He did not consent to the death of Jesus. This verse tells us that he had the boldness to approach Pilate and request the body of Jesus. Take note of his courage because from this moment on, he would be publicly identified as a disciple of Jesus.

It is interesting that while Jesus was alive, Joseph did not have the courage to be identified with Jesus' followers. It seems that the death of Christ awakened him, and his faith became heroic. His devotion to Christ was far more important than how the Jews (the ruling class of Pharisees and scribes) thought of him or regarded him. Joseph of Arimathea did not allow his fear to enslave him.

What about you? Do you need to seek God and ask Him to enable you to be bold? There is no reason to live in fear when you have the Holy Spirit within you.

November 13

Reason Not to Fear #318: Christ Dispels My Fears

"Then, the same day at evening, being the first day of the week, when the doors were shut where the disciples were assembled, for fear of the Jews, Jesus came and stood in their midst, and said to them, "Peace be with you."
John 20:19

What strikes me in this story is the terrible fear that the Jewish religious leaders instilled in the people, even the disciples. The text does not read that they feared the Romans, those who ruled them with an iron fist. The Romans were the military force that had just crucified their Lord, the powerful nation that massacred thousands of them with so little notice that it was like stamping out a nest of ants. No, they feared the Jews, the ruling class, the Sanhedrin.

Why would they be in such fear? What power did the Sanhedrin hold over them that they would cower in the upper room, lock the doors and quake at every sound? At the time of Jesus, the Jewish Sanhedrin had their own police force and could arrest people. They could not execute them, however, for the Romans held that dubious privilege.

This ruling group of men held the fate of life and death over millions of their own people. To be excommunicated from the faith of the Jews, to be kicked out of the temple and the sacrifices, meant spiritual and emotional death. The Jews wielded their power with a strong, ruthless hand. Anyone who did not obey their decrees paid the consequences. And the Sanhedrin also had influence with the Roman emperor, Tiberias.

We find the disciples trembling behind locked doors; not a very complimentary picture! However, they witnessed the crucifixion of Jesus and thought they could be the next victims. Fear was present in that room as they gathered together. Yet Jesus appeared and it was like sunshine dispelling darkness. They rejoiced to see Him and flocked around Him, touching Him, laughing, tears of joy streaking their faces.

Do you have moments of fear? Do some people frighten you?

Be assured at the right time God will show up and will say the right words to you like He did to His disciples. Listen to Him when He speaks to you. Set aside your fear of people and circumstances. Rejoice with great joy in Christ.

What specific fear is keeping you behind locked doors? Let Christ in and watch your fears evaporate.

November 14

Reason Not to Fear #319: Walk in the Light and Fear No Evil

"'While it remained, was it not your own? And after it was sold, was it not in your own control? Why have you conceived this thing in your heart? You have not lied to men but to God.' Then Ananias, hearing these words, fell down and breathed his last. So great fear came upon all those who heard these things.... Then immediately she fell down at his feet and breathed her last. And the young men came in and found her dead, and carrying her out, buried her by her husband. So great fear came upon all the church and upon all who heard these things." Acts 5:4-5, 10-11

This is a story that takes place in the early days of the church, during the time of its formation and early practices. It may be hard to understand why lying or deceit is a sin worthy of death, and we are surprised when this drastic measure was taken by Peter as the leader of the church.

When God begins something new, He often uses extreme measures to ensure that the coming generations will live according to His standards of holiness. The story of Acts is the history of the church, and at its very beginning, we see God setting a standard of righteous behavior for all generations to come.

Ananias and Sapphira sold some of their property and brought the money from it to the disciples. On the outside, they appear very spiritual and generous. On the inside, they are full of pride and jealousy (Barnabas had just donated the sale of his entire property to the church, Acts 4:36-37). They attempted to deceive God because they wanted to appear something they were not. They did not expect to be exposed, but they were met with sudden death. Great fear came over those who witnessed this and heard about it. Their sins, insincerity and dishonesty cost them dearly, yet it was the pride and greed in their hearts that God had to judge.

God judged them as an example for all the rest of us who would come later. What is the lesson we can learn from the lives of Ananias and Sapphira? We cannot hide our inner thoughts, attitudes and sins from God. He sees all. He sees your heart. He sees your sin.

What are you hiding from others that God can see? David prayed, "Forgive me from presumptuous or willful sins." Psalm 19:13. Confess your sin to God today and then rejoice in His mercy and love.

November 15

Reason Not to Fear #320: Do What Is Right and Trust God

"Then the captain went with the officers and brought them without violence, for they feared the people, lest they should be stoned." Acts 5:26

"No good deed goes unpunished" is an old axiom that should get the ax, but it sticks around because we all know how true it is. Have you ever done something with the purest of motives, yet been castigated for the very thing you did out of love and concern?

Peter, John, James and the others must have felt unjustly persecuted when they were called on the carpet before the Sanhedrin to give account of what they had been doing and saying. They had just participated in a huge revival among the common people. Many had been healed and many turned to God through Jesus Christ and embraced Christianity. Acts 5 records for us the amazing ministry these men had with the people. They even brought their sick so that Peter's shadow could fall on them and they were healed!

The religious leaders were jealous. They arrested the apostles and put them in jail. Yet God had the final say. He sent an angel who delivered them from prison and told them to go and publicly teach the people from the courtyard of the temple! And they did.

When the Sanhedrin discovered what had happened, they were furious, but they were afraid of the people. So the religious leaders politely asked the Apostles to accompany them to the meeting room and told them they could not speak of Jesus or of the Gospel anymore. Peter and the others did not feel threatened, and even though they were flogged, they rejoiced that they had been found worthy to suffer for Christ's sake.

How do you react when you are attacked, persecuted and criticized for doing what is right? Are you gracious and forgiving, or do you lash out in anger? I confess, sometimes I am discouraged and ready to give up. But God gives us the strength to overcome all things. He is the One to whom we answer. If we are told to disobey God, we must choose to obey God. Let the chips fall where they may. You have done the right thing.

As you close this time of prayer and meditation, recommit yourself to obedience to God and His Word, no matter what the cost. Thank Him for His many blessings. Begin this day with joy in your heart, even if you feel unjustly accused and persecuted.

November 16

Reason Not to Fear #321: We Encourage and Help Others

"And when Saul had come to Jerusalem, he tried to join the disciples; but they were all afraid of him, and did not believe that he was a disciple. But Barnabas took him and brought him to the apostles. And he declared to them how he had seen the Lord on the road, and that He had spoken to him, and how he had preached boldly at Damascus in the name of Jesus. So he was with them at Jerusalem, coming in and going out." Acts 9:26-28

Faithfulness is a high standard to keep.

Rev. Billy Graham is not perfect. He is only a man, and I imagine he makes many mistakes and sins as regularly as you and I. Yet he has been faithful to the call of God on his life.

One time, after a crusade, he was driving with his team back to the motel where they were staying. But there was a roadblock ahead. A long line of cars ahead were stopped and people were milling about as if on a holiday, drinking and carousing in the street. Rev. Graham got out of the vehicle and climbed onto the hood to see what was holding up the line.

Suddenly he and the others on his team saw something being passed toward them over the heads of the people. It looked like a body wrapped in blankets, and they realized it was a woman. Rev. Graham said he was instantly alerted by the Holy Spirit that something very evil was afoot. They got off the car, got in it, and locked the doors. The crowd eventually dispersed when the police arrived. They found out later that the woman was nude and people were prepared to take pictures of Rev. Graham with a nude woman.

The scriptures call us to be faithful to our Lord. Despite all the major challenges in his life, the Apostle Paul remained steadfast and faithful. Believers turned their backs on him and were afraid of him. The religious rulers plotted to kill him. Nonetheless, Paul never gave up. When Paul went to Jerusalem, he tried to join the other disciples, but they were all afraid of him and would not give him the time of day. Thank God for Barnabas who stood by him and endorsed him, allowing Paul entrance into the church and the ministry.

Can you be like Barnabas today? Can you encourage someone who might be rejected? Can you be like Paul and stick to your ministry even when others turn their backs on you? Determine to be like both of these men of God and do your work today for the Lord without fear, without shame, without regret.

November 17

Reason Not to Fear #322: God Gives Us Peace When We Fear Him

"Then the churches throughout all Judea, Galilee, and Samaria had peace and were edified. And walking in the fear of the Lord and in the comfort of the Holy Spirit, they were multiplied. Acts 9:31

There has been much debate about what a successful church looks like. Some people want to go back to the first century and do things exactly as they did. Some people think of success in terms of great crowds of people attending church and a huge, fancy building. Some people look at success as meeting the physical needs of those in their communities.

But the first century church had none of this. The church met secretly in homes, and the people were poor and persecuted. This is not the picture of what many in our society today deem as a successful church. After being persecuted for years, the church had a time of peace. They could breathe again, because Paul, the bitterest persecutor of the church, was converted to Christ. Note that even in this time of peace, the believers continued to walk in the fear of the Lord. The astounding truth is this: the way to tell a successful church is by this very measure. Do the people fear God? Do they live as if they fear Him?

This group of believers had their consciences awakened to sin. They now detested it above anything else. They did not want to offend their Lord. Without this type of invigorating fear of the Lord, we cannot experience success. The fear of the Lord changes a person. We want to study the Bible, obey what God says to us, and leave our idols and sins to walk in obedience to Him. We must put our faith totally in the Lord -- not in money, jobs, possessions, and not our education, social standing, or insurance policies.

These Christians were walking on the right path now. The fear of the Lord points to a **holy walk**, and the comfort of the Holy Spirit points to the **silent operation of peace**. So this group of believers had an excellent mixture of inward and outward peace which the fear of the Lord presided over.

It still is true for me and you. If we fear the Lord, we will have both inward and outward peace. Will you obey God, trust in Him completely, and walk in the light of His fellowship? Is this what you want for your life? Start today. Start right now. Confess your sin, put away any idols, and then you will begin to experience the peace of God.

November 18

Reason Not to Fear #323: My Faith Leads Me to Fear God

"There was a certain man in Caesarea called Cornelius, a centurion of what was called the Italian Regiment, a devout man and one who feared God with all his household, who gave alms generously to the people, and prayed to God always." Acts 10:1-2

What are the indications of a person who fears God? What does he do or not do? Cornelius was a Roman soldier, a centurion with the Italian Regiment. He lived in Caesarea, a Roman city on the Mediterranean Sea of the Italian Regiment. Where he learned his faith in the true God of the Israelites no one knows, but that he was a true believer in God was quite clear.

The soldiers and officers of the Roman army were trained killing machines. As they stood together as a fighting force with their regiment and cohort, they were invincible in the ancient world. Before Jesus was born, they conquered the entire known world, and some of it that was not so well known, bringing back to Rome the spoils of war -- gold, jewels, silver, slaves, and captives who would be killed in the arena in a great display of military might. Wherever the Roman soldiers marched with the eagle at the top of their banners, they fought and conquered, showing no pity or mercy.

Yet Cornelius was different. We read that he gave generously to those in need and he prayed to God regularly. He feared the God of the Israelites, and this fear changed his life from the inside out. God honored his faith and brought new revelation to him of Jesus Christ's death on the cross and the new era of grace.

A person who fears God and worships Him sincerely are those whose faith translates into doing good deeds. They are willing to accept instruction from others. They are not proud, haughty, smug or critical. They earnestly seek to know more about God and become more like Christ. Are you like this?

Do you worship God sincerely and regularly? Do you do good deeds for others as a result of your faith? Do you accept instruction from the Word, or are you smug and proud?

Search your heart. Ask God to show you where you stand on this issue of fearing God. Turn, change, and accept His correction in your life. Be like Cornelius today.

November 19

Reason Not to Fear #324: We Can Change According to God's Word

"About the ninth hour of the day he saw clearly in a vision an angel of God coming in and saying to him, "Cornelius!" And when he observed him, he was afraid, and said, "What is it, lord?" So he said to him, "Your prayers and your alms have come up for a memorial before God." Acts 10:3-4

We learned yesterday that a person who fears the Lord is able to accept instruction and is willing to change his life in accord with the Word of the Lord. We see that not only in Cornelius, but also in Peter's life, too.

Peter was having quite a day. It seemed normal enough until he went up on the rooftop (maybe the only place where he could escape the smell of the tannery!) to pray and to take a little nap. After awhile, he became hungry and called down to the women and asked when lunch was going to be ready. "In a little while," they called back.

Sitting down again, he started to pray and suddenly he fell into a trance. He saw a sheet coming down from heaven with all sorts of animals, birds, and serpents in it. Some were clean and lawful for a Jew to eat, and others were unclean and forbidden by the law to eat. The command came to rise and eat. "No," he protested vigorously, "I've only eaten clean animals all my life! I cannot eat unclean things."

God's voice spoke to him from heaven. "Do not call anything impure that God has made clean." This happened three times! Peter woke up and tried to figure out what this strange dream was all about. Suddenly there came the sound of a brisk knock on the door down below. Cornelius' men had arrived and asked for Peter. When he discovered he was supposed to go and preach the Gospel to a Gentile family, he understood the meaning of the dream. God wanted His good news preached to all the people of the earth! Peter obediently went with the men, and as he preached the next day to Cornelius and his household, he was able to witness God's great work among Gentile people.

He was willing to change and embrace something new because he feared God. Can you do the same? What new thing has God brought into your life that is stretching you? Trust Him with it today. Change and broaden your horizons. Give this new thing to Him and watch to see what He will do with it.

November 20

Reason Not to Fear #325: We Fearlessly Share the Gospel

"Then Paul stood up, and motioning with his hand said, '"Men of Israel, and you who fear God, listen.'" Acts 13:16

Wherever Paul and his friends went to preach the Gospel, they sought out the Jewish synagogue first, even though he was commissioned by God to preach to the Gentiles.

In this passage, Paul was on his first missionary journey with Barnabas and they had arrived in Asia Minor (now Turkey) at the city of Pisidian Antioch. It was first Greek, then Roman, and is now Turkish. It was situated in a strong position on a plateau close to the western bank of the river Anthios, which flows down from the Sultan Dagh to the double lake called Limnai. The plateau on which Antioch stood commands one of the roads leading from the East to Meander and Ephesus.

It seemed that whenever there was an opportunity to preach the Gospel to the Jews, Paul could not pass it up. He was invited to speak, so he stood up and addressed the Jews in that place and to the devout Gentiles (proselyte Jews). These people were eager to learn more about their new belief, and Paul was more than delighted to accommodate them.

In this discourse, Paul introduced both these groups of people to the truth that Jesus is the Messiah. Boldly Paul declared, "Therefore, my brothers, I want you to know that through Jesus the forgiveness of sins is proclaimed to you. Through Him everyone who believes is justified from everything you could not be justified from by the law of Moses." v. 38-39 Some believed, others did not, but for those everyday people who did, they were filled with reverence and power as they lived out their faith daily.

The people flocked to hear Paul and Barnabas speak, but the leading Jews became jealous and threw them out of the city. Yet the Gospel found good soil there in Antioch of Asia Minor, and the disciples were filled with joy and the Holy Spirit.

When was the last time you spoke the amazing truth to someone that Jesus is the Messiah? How about doing that today? Think of someone right now and ask God to open the door for you to speak of His marvelous love and grace. You might be surprised what God will do through you.

November 21

Reason Not to Fear #326: We Sing Praises to God

"Then he called for a light, ran in, and fell down trembling before Paul and Silas.... And the officers told these words to the magistrates, and they were afraid when they heard that they were Romans." Acts 16:29, 38

On Paul's second missionary journey, he went across the Aegean Sea to Macedonia, visiting the cities of Philipi, Thessalonica and Berea. They came to the city of Philipi and found some devout women praying alongside the river. In this way, they met Lydia and after she was converted to Christianity, they met in her home.

As was true in every town they visited, they had good success in preaching the Gospel and many were saved. But the leading Jews became jealous and stirred up trouble. Pretty soon Paul and his buddy found themselves being whipped and put in stocks. They spent the night in a dank, dark prison. The amazing thing is that they sang songs of praises to God in the midst of their desperate situation.

Now, I don't know about you, but if I found myself in a similar situation, I doubt very much if I would feel like singing. Yet God was with them in that foul place, and He caused an earthquake that broke their bonds. The other prisoners became free, too, and Paul urged them all to stay where they were. Surprisingly, the men obeyed him. Do you think it was because they had heard the singing and knew that God was with these two men? Yes, I think that was the case. By remaining where they were, they saved the life of the jailer.

Paul led the jailer and his whole household to the Lord that night. They were taken to his home (which might have been right there at the prison), their wounds were tended, they were fed, and in the morning they were freed. The Roman officers were afraid when they heard that these two Roman citizens had been unlawfully detained and punished.

When adverse things happen to you, what is your first response? If you were arrested, beaten, and put into stocks, would you sing praises to God? Or would you do a little bit of complaining? The next time you are in a trying situation, stop and praise God. Sing a song. Think of all the positive things that are going right. You might not experience an earthquake, but you will be surprised to see God working in your life and through your life to reach someone else.

November 22

Reason Not to Fear #327: God Takes Care of Us

"Now the Lord spoke to Paul in the night by a vision, '"Do not be afraid, but speak, and do not keep silent; for I am with you, and no one will attack you to hurt you; for I have many people in this city.'" Acts 18:9, 10

C.S. Lewis wrote in his biography, *Surprised by Joy*, "I did not know that grief felt so much like fear." This was after he had suffered the loss of his beloved wife, Joy, to whom he had been married only four years.

Grief and fear have much in common. Grief looks down the long years ahead and is fearful at the thought that one must live alone without their loved one. Grief looks inward and says, "I can't do this." Grief sometimes becomes very selfish and angry, an anger that can turn into deep bitterness. Grief then refuses to love or to live again while nursing its own hurt feelings. But God is above all grief and fear. He has conquered death and He is victorious over sin, Satan, evil and defeat of any kind.

When Paul was living in Corinth and preaching the Gospel, he might have become a little discouraged when the Jews stirred opposition and persecution against his ministry. Paul may have been so fearful that he entertained thoughts of not preaching any longer. Then the Lord spoke to Paul in a night vision. He comforted him, encouraged him, and assured him that he need not be afraid or be silent.

Paul was reassured from above with the words, "Don't be afraid." We know that he continued to do God's work, and eventually gave his life in the Roman coliseum. He did not allow grief over the death of many of his friends, persecution, hard times, or opposition to get him down permanently. He was able by God's grace to continue on until the very end.

Work in ministry is not easy and the prospect of being successful can become uncertain, but the presence of God will take away any fear you may encounter. By persevering you will disarm your anxieties and hear God reassure you with the words, "Don't be afraid."

What are you facing today? Don't give in to grief, fear or worry. God is able to care for you, just as He did for Paul. Commit your way to Him and He will give you what you need for today -- and for every day for the rest of your life.

November 23

Reason Not to Fear #328: We Fear His Holy Name

"This became known both to all Jews and Greeks dwelling in Ephesus; and
fear fell on them all, and the name of the Lord Jesus was magnified."
Acts 19:17

To stir a whole city and region with the Gospel of Jesus Christ is an amazing feat. The story that precedes our verse for today comes from such an event in which the Holy Spirit used Paul and the other men with him to bring a great revival to the city of Ephesus. During the course of the his ministry, the Apostle Paul healed many people who were ill, cast out demons, and proclaimed with confidence the power of God over Satan.

Some people at that time believed in magic. They believed if they invoked a certain name or said a certain incantation, they would get the results they desired. Seven men, sons of the one of the Jewish priests, had been watching Paul and the other disciples and figured they could make some money if they followed the same procedure that Paul used, calling upon the name of Jesus Christ to release people from demonic bondage.

So the seven men went to a man's house one night and tried it. The demon inside the man cried out, "I recognize Jesus, and I know about Paul, but who are you?" Then the man, energized by the demons, attacked the seven men, tore off their clothes and left them wounded and bleeding, fleeing for their lives.

The lesson is that Jesus Christ is to be honored, feared and obeyed above all. The demons know who is the Lord's child, and they do not obey any other. Unbelievers may not use His name for their purposes. Fear fell on the people of the city of Ephesus and many turned away from evil and their belief in magic.

How do you use the name of Christ? Do you lightly call upon God in His name and ask for things that are not His will? Do you judge others in His name without searching your own heart for wickedness?

Fear His name and use it carefully. It is common, even for Christians, to glibly say, "Oh, my lord" or "Oh, my god." Don't do it! Revere His name and honor Him. If you do, you might see revival happen in your own heart and in the hearts of others.

November 24

Reason Not to Fear #329: God Will See You Through

"For there stood by me this night an angel of the God to whom I belong and whom I serve, saying, 'Do not be afraid, Paul; you must be brought before Caesar; and indeed God has granted you all those who sail with you.' Therefore take heart, men, for I believe God that it will be just as it was told me." Acts 27:23-25

Traveling as prisoners, Paul and his companions, including Luke, were sailing from Caesarea to Rome under the supervision of a Roman guard. They encountered inclement weather and were forced to land on the island of Crete. The sailors were determined to sail on, hoping to reach Phoenix, another large harbor. Yet as they set sail, the storm lashed their ship mercilessly for many days in the Mediterranean Sea, and they gradually lost hope that any of them would survive.

The captain and all the men aboard had not eaten for many days, fasting and praying to whatever gods they served. Yet this further imperiled them, for now they had little energy and strength. In the midst of this dire circumstance, Paul had an unusual experience one night. An angel of the Lord appeared to him and gave him a message for all the men.

The next morning, he stood up and announced the message. He urged them to take courage and to eat, and to demonstrate, he ate some food in front of them. He declared that his God, Yahweh, would see them safely to a harbor and that not a single soul would be lost.

Why wasn't Paul afraid like the others? What gave him hope and peace in the middle of a desperate situation? It was this simple fact: he placed his trust and hope utterly in God and in His Word. He knew that he had more to do, that he was bound for Rome and would stand before Caesar to declare the Gospel. His trust and faith in God kept him from the fear that paralyzed his shipmates, helped him minister, and saw him through to the end of his life.

You may not have an angel appear to you with a message of hope, yet you have the Word of God.

Can you trust this Word and apply it to your life today? I don't know what you are facing, but whatever it is, there are many promises for you to claim in His Word. Find them and place your hope and faith entirely in Christ. He will see you through.

November 25

Reason Not to Fear #330: We Remember to Reverence God Every Moment

"As it is written: 'There is none righteous, no, not one; There is none who understands; There is none who seeks after God.... There is no fear of God before their eyes.'" Romans 3:10-11, 18

In a society that has left God out almost entirely, we see many problems arising. The basic difficulty is outlined for us here in Roman 3 where the Apostle Paul gives a stinging, inclusive verdict on the moral condition of the human race apart from God. "There is no one who is righteous," he says. "Not even one."

Before I was married, I dated several young men. I am sad to admit that some of them were not Christians. One of those young men was a Mormon. We dated for quite awhile and enjoyed each other's company. One evening, while we were out for dinner, the conversation flowed into our beliefs. As we discussed them, it was evident we were not united. I shared how I believed that Jesus Christ is the only way to heaven and that each person must accept and confess their sin to Him. He did not believe that he needed to confess his sin to Jesus and be forgiven. We made a decision that evening that we would no longer continue our relationship.

Many people in our world today refuse to believe that we are all sinners. You do not have to look very far to realize that people have no fear of God. They do not know His Word or His will and refuse to believe in Him.

As a result, we have people walking into a kindergarten classroom and shooting the children and their teacher. We have young men at the Boston Marathon who place a bomb near two children and walk away, knowing they will die. But it is not only these who are godless. It is your neighbor who appears good and kindly, yet has no knowledge of God and does not recognize Him as having authority over their lives. It is your relative who sneers at God and shows disrespect for His Word. We need a revival to restore the fear of God in human hearts.

Don't be among those who have no fear of the living God. Hold Him in reverence always. Let the fear of the Lord keep you from sin and evil. Let the fear of the Lord transform you. Let the fear of the Lord guide you in all your decisions. Grow in that fear daily.

November 26

Reason Not to Fear #331: We Respond to God with Love and Obedience

"For you did not receive the spirit of bondage again to fear, but you received the Spirit of adoption by whom we cry out, '"Abba, Father."'
Romans 8:15

Adoption. For a believer, this means the act of God, placing a person as an son or a daughter into His family. s family. When we accept Christ as our Savior, we are born into the family of God as a child who needs to grow and develop. We also often require discipline and correction. Our **position** in the family is one of full privileges; our **practice** involves growth in grace.

Over thirty-five years ago, we adopted a little girl while we lived in Chicago. It was such a special day when my husband, son and I drove to pick up our baby girl. At the time, my husband was attending Moody Bible Institute, and I was working to put him through college. I will never forget the phone call that came to my desk on a Monday morning. The woman on the other said, "After three years of waiting, Chris, on Thursday you may come and welcome your new child into your family."

From Monday to Tuesday I did not sleep. This adoption was such a positive experience in our lives that several years later we did it again. Through the years, I have never distinguished between the children we adopted and the children I birthed. They are a part of our family and joined to us.

Paul, in writing this marvelous chapter to the Roman believers, described the fullness of life and joy we experience when we accept Christ and are adopted into His family. He states that we have the Spirit of God, not the spirit of slavery to sin and fear. We should grow, walk and live in the joy the Spirit of God gives us.

Yet many Christians walk according to the world and the flesh and give little heed to the Word of God or to the Lord. They are like the children of my friends. They do not ask God for direction in their lives, give little time to reading or memorizing the Bible, and are not cleansed of their sins. They walk in slavery to sin and in fear. Their position is secure, but their practice is on shaky ground.

Don't go back to slavery and fear in your life as a Christian. Live in the fullness of what it means to be a child of God, both in practice and position.

November 27

Reason Not to Fear 332: We Humble Ourselves Before God

"You will say then, 'Branches were broken off that I might be grafted in.' Well said. Because of unbelief they were broken off, and you stand by faith. Do not be haughty, but fear. For if God did not spare the natural branches, He may not spare you either." Romans 11:19-21

There is a debate raging throughout Christian churches today. It centers around the so-called "replacement theology," which states that the Israelite nation and people have been replaced by the church, those who have been saved by grace in this present age. The teaching is that the Israelites are no longer the "chosen people of God" as they were in the Old Testament, and that since they broke the covenant with God, God has abandoned them, and the church is now the recipient of all the promises He gave to the Jews.

The other side teaches that the universal church of Jesus Christ has not replaced the Israelites, and that the Israelites are still the chosen people of God and will one day enjoy the promises God gave to them in the Old Testament in regards to their land of Israel, to the part they will play in the kingdom of Christ, and to their privileged position as recipients of the covenant blessings.

Replacement theology leads people to support the Arab cause against the Israelites today. They say the Israelites have no just claim on the land and that they have been rejected by God.

Paul addressed this question in Romans chapter 11. Read the whole chapter if you are confused about this verse. The apostle asserts that Gentile believers in Christ have been grafted into the vine of God's people, and as such, they share (not replace!) the blessings of God on their lives. Note that he goes on to say that this knowledge should not cause us to become puffed up in pride against our Jewish brothers and sisters. *No*, he says. We should be afraid that somehow we might disobey God, and He would cut us off for a time, too.

There is no place for pride when we fear God. Yet we should be afraid that we will fall into disbelief, disobedience and laxity in our walk with God. Cleanse your life of sin and determine to walk humbly before God. Entrust your soul to Him who can keep you until the day of Jesus Christ. Only when we fear God can we find our correct place in His plan.

November 28

Reason Not to Fear #333: We Obey the Laws of the Land

"For rulers are not a terror to good works, but to evil. Do you want to be unafraid of the authority? Do what is good, and you will have praise from the same. For he is God's minister to you for good. But if you do evil, be afraid; for he does not bear the sword in vain; for he is God's minister, an avenger to execute wrath on him who practices evil." Romans 13:3-4

We have all become annoyed at certain laws and chaff at obeying them. I'm thinking of wearing seat belts, helmets for motorcyclists, not talking or texting on the cell phone when you're driving, and many others we could name. As the government grows stronger, we don't like the rules that would seem to take away our personal freedom and privacy.

In a Bill Gaither video, Mark Lowry spoke about the laws of Texas, his home state. Evidently they don't (or didn't at that time) have helmet laws. He stated, "Here in Texas, we don't care about stupid people. If they don't want to wear a helmet, that's fine with us. They can just go ahead and get hurt."

We smile at that, yet underneath we know it is true: most of the laws such as the ones I mentioned are passed to protect us, not to harm us. Yet we find it very difficult to keep our speed down in a residential area or at the edge of town.

Even when living under a repressive government, as Paul was at the time he wrote this, the injunction for all Christians is to obey the laws of the land unless they go against what God has said in His Word. The law holds terror and fear for those who disobey it. A friend of mine told me that she makes it a point to drive in accordance with the speed limits. "That way," she said, "I don't have to be worried or afraid of getting a ticket."

Where do you stand when it comes to keeping the law? To paying your taxes? To being scrupulously honest in all your business dealings and payment of debts? To fulfilling your responsibility when called for jury duty? Can others look at your life and see a person who keeps the laws, is honest and above-board, and can be trusted?

That officer who comes to your car window and asks to see your license, yes, he is there for your good. Determine today that you will keep the laws of the land. Then go out with joy and peace, for God will go with you.

November 29

Reason Not to Fear #334: We Seek After God's Wisdom

"I was with you in weakness, in fear, and in much trembling. And my speech and my preaching were not with persuasive words of human wisdom, but in demonstration of the Spirit and of power, that your faith should not be in the wisdom of men but in the power of God." I Corinthians 2:3-5

In the days of Paul, they had no TV, movies or computers. Their main source of entertainment was the theater, plays, and oratorical speeches performed by men of great vocal prowess. They enjoyed hearing these men expound and act. Yes, they were as besotted with sin and passion as we are today.

It was shocking to read about a church in the Seattle area that canceled their Sunday morning service to watch a big Seattle Mariners game on their huge TV screens. They served refreshments and had everything but "beer and babes," as someone who was not a Christian said about the affair. These people got the best of two worlds. They could say they went to church, and they also got to see the game.

When Paul appeared on the scene and began preaching, the people expected a dose of the same stuff they heard at the theater. They thought he would be a powerful, witty, and entertaining speaker, making them feel good. But he disappointed them. His sermon was delivered in a plain monotone and he spoke in simple language. They criticized him for this. His rebuttal? He had none. He declared that he came to them in fear and trembling, that he did not possess great oratorical abilities, and could only speak the simple message that God had given him.

He goes on to say that the wisdom of the world is foolishness to God, and that God's wisdom seems like foolishness to the world. If you are a spiritual person, you can discern and be wise in God's wisdom, not the world's way of thinking.

How about you? Are you wise in the world but foolish in the things of God? If you are spiritual, you will seek God's wisdom and not the world's. Transform your mind, Romans 12:2 says, by the Word of God to think and judge and act according to God's wisdom. Refuse the world. Choose God.

November 30

Reason Not to Fear #335: We Are Not Jealous of One Another

"Now if Timothy comes, see that he may be with you without fear; for he does the work of the Lord, as I also do. Therefore let no one despise him. But send him on his journey in peace, that he may come to me; for I am waiting for him with the brethren." I Corinthians 16:10, 11

Paul knew what it was like to be rejected and refused fellowship. After he came to know the Lord, Barnabas brought him to Jerusalem, but in Acts 9:26-28, we read that they were all fearful of him and refused to have company with him. It was only much later, after he had returned to his home city of Tarsus and spent nine years there making tents, that Barnabas again sought him out and restored him to fellowship with the other apostles and believers.

Have you ever felt ostracized, marginalized and rejected? Most of us have been in those shoes, and I can tell you, they are not comfortable. There are people in the church who are jealous of leaders, of anyone who lifts their head above the others and tries to do a ministry, and who are successful in it. Jealousy is a knife that can cut a person out and cut a person to the heart. It separates, divides, and sets up a whole atmosphere of distrust and competition.

Jealousy among God's people is a cancer and it needs to be killed. It is not a virtue, and it has no value. Yet if I would be honest with you, I have fallen into those negative feelings. There have been times I have been jealous over other speakers, authors, and even those with normal, loving husbands. However, the jealousy did not change my circumstances. Truthfully, jealousy caused me to become a miserable person in the inside. I do not want to be envious, or resentful, or covetous to anyone.

Paul wrote to the Corinthian church and tried to ease the way for Timothy's arrival. It is interesting to note that he says very pointedly, "Receive him, and see that he has nothing to fear from you." Evidently Paul knew there were some who had jealousy in their hearts.

Are you jealous of others and when the opportunity comes do you ostracize them and make them miserable? Confess this attitude as sin to God and make sure you are not guilty of this in your walk, in your church, or with your friends. Make sure that no one has to fear or step carefully when they are around you. You will not only have more friends, you will also please God.

December 1

Reason Not to Fear #336: We Reflect the Fruit of the Spirit

"Knowing, therefore, the terror of the Lord, we persuade men; but we are well known to God, and I also trust are well known in your consciences.... For the love of Christ compels us, because we judge thus: that if One died for all, then all died; and He died for all, that those who live should live no longer for themselves, but for Him who died for them and rose again."
II Corinthians 5:11, 13-15

When I was growing up in Milwaukee, Wisconsin, my dad was one to be feared. I did not want to disobey him, nor did I want to break his rules. I learned at an early age that my life went much smoother if I followed his instructions. And truthfully, fear of him kept me in line. I loved my dad and wanted to bring him happiness through my behavior. Down through the years, I have often shared that truth with my children, hoping they in turn would understand that truth and that it would help them in their lives, too.

The Apostle Paul totally loved the Lord. His fear of the Lord did not terrorize him; rather, his fear was a reverential awe which caused him to give his utmost efforts in his service for Christ. Paul yearned to win others to Christ. He wanted to have an honest life and a pure ministry. You see, every Christian who truly fears the Lord must reflect qualities of the Spirit in their life. You are accountable to God for every word, thought, and action. Just like I did not want to disgrace my dad and his name, so it is with the Lord. Remember you are on a mission while you are here on earth. You are no ordinary citizen. You belong to the King.

Sadly, many Christians have lost this sense of awe and fear of the Lord. Many are too content in this world. The fear you have for the Lord should inspire you, motivate you, and stir you to live a life that is pleasing to Him. Fear Him, and you will avoid evil. You will stay on the path of righteousness. Others will notice, and your conscience will be clear.

A little farther down in this passage, Paul wrote, "Christ's love compels us..." The Greek word for *compel* means "to constrain, contain, hold, keep in, press, be taken with." The love of Christ, Paul said, pressed him forward, motivated him onward and controlled him inwardly to the extent that he had to share the Gospel with others.

The fear of the Lord and the love of Christ can motivate you to walk in the way of holiness and commitment. Be genuine. Be holy. Be Christ's light today.

December 2

Reason Not to Fear #337: We Work at Being Holy

"Therefore, having these promises, beloved, let us cleanse ourselves from all filthiness of the flesh and spirit, perfecting holiness in the fear of God."
II Corinthians 7:1

What does a person who fears God look like, act like, and talk like? What are the characteristics of one who fears the Lord?

To find the answer to this question, we have to go back to chapter 6 of II Corinthians and discover what the Apostle Paul was talking about. In verses 14-18, Paul admonishes the believers to come out from among the people of the world (unbelievers) and be separate from them, for "what partnership has righteousness and lawlessness, or what fellowship has light with darkness?"

One of the main characteristics of a person who fears God is that he is willing to disassociate himself from the world and from unbelievers in the area of partnership with them in marriage or business. If we do this, we can experience the fullness of God's presence in our lives. "'I will welcome you, and I will be a father to you, and you shall be sons and daughters to Me,' says the Lord Almighty." v. 18

Paul goes on to say that having this mighty and wonderful promise of the living God's Spirit dwelling in our bodies, we should purify ourselves from everything that would contaminate us with sin. The second characteristic of a God-fearing person is that they will ruthlessly destroy anything that brings sin into their lives and turn away from it completely. This means you will get rid of any sinful thing you see on TV, computers, magazines, movies, or anything else. You will get rid of bitterness, jealousy, pride or criticizing others.

Then the apostle states that we should "perfect holiness" in our lives. The third characteristic of a God-fearing person is that they work at becoming more and more holy in their walk, talk, heart attitudes, and thought patterns.

How do you rate when you consider the importance of fearing the Lord? Are you working at holiness in your life, or are you just coasting? Get serious with God today, and find the joy of the fullness of His presence within you.

December 3

Reason Not to Fear #338: We Honor One Another in Love

"Therefore we have been comforted in your comfort. And we rejoiced exceedingly more for the joy of Titus, because his spirit has been refreshed by you all.... His affections are greater for you as he remembers the obedience of you all, how with fear and trembling you received him." II Corinthians 7:13, 15

I have some exceptional friends in my life. Some live here in Arizona near me, while others live in Pennsylvania, Illinois, and Indiana. Over the course of time, I have been able to introduce these dazzling friends of mine to each other. Every time I have been able to connect my friends with other friends of mine, they have always been welcomed, accepted, and made to feel comfortable.

Little is written or even preached about Titus. However, he was an outstanding friend to Paul and an excellent worker for the Lord. No matter what assignment was given to him, he proved himself faithful. Paul trusted Titus to continue to preach, teach, and maintain sound doctrinal truths in his ministry in Corinth.

While Paul was in Ephesus, he received disturbing news regarding the church in Corinth. He wrote them some letters and decided to send Titus to the church there. The reason he sent Titus was because he was very concerned for this church. It is amazing that Paul entrusted this important ministry to a young man. Yet he did and Titus was God's man of the hour. He was able to bring peace to this troubled church.

In Macedonia, Titus met the anxious Apostle Paul and shared with him the good news that the church at Corinth had repented. Paul was overjoyed. It is a wonderful feeling to entrust a big job to a younger person and see them fulfill it and do it well.

Titus was no novice; he was a man who knew how to complete tough tasks. He was a blessing to the brethren in Corinth. He loved the people. He became a good role model for us today when we are asked to do difficult tasks for the Lord.

Can you delegate responsibility to younger people after you have trained them? Can you do your task with excellence and without fear? Decide today that wherever you are on the spectrum of service, that you will be the one God can use.

December 4

Reason Not to Fear #339: We Are Not Deceived by Satan's Tricks

"But I fear, lest somehow, as the serpent deceived Eve by his craftiness, so your minds may be corrupted from the simplicity that is in Christ."
II Corinthians 11:3

The Apostle Paul, in this third letter (the second one was lost) to the troubled church at Corinth, finds himself in the undesirable position of having to defend himself and his ministry as an apostle of Christ and a preacher of the Gospel. Evidently these Corinthian believers prided themselves on their open-minded policy of accepting men who came to them preaching a "different Jesus" and false doctrines. These men were trained speakers who could ensnare others to follow them.

They were false teachers who not only gloried in themselves and taught others to walk in the way of pride, they also found it necessary to criticize Paul and "bring him down" in the eyes of the church. They demanded money for preaching their version of the Gospel. They were "deceitful workmen, masquerading as apostles of Christ." (v. 13)

Paul was afraid for his friends and fellow believers, his children in the faith, in Corinth. This is the kind of feeling you have when you watch your kids make the wrong decisions, decisions you know will lead them down the wrong paths. It drives you to your knees. It makes you speak out to them in love and fear, hoping they will heed your advice.

Paul's fear was that just as Eve was led astray in the garden, so they, too, would be deceived in believing Satan's lies. The false teachers in the Corinthian church fed the pride and egos of the people. Perhaps they taught that you could get to heaven by doing good deeds. Perhaps they taught that if you just follow my teachings and give me money, you will find righteousness with God. Perhaps they taught that it doesn't matter what you believe -- you only need to feel good to achieve heaven.

What can you do when you see someone you love goes the wrong way? Pray for them. Speak to them. Write a letter to them. And while you are at it, be on guard against false doctrine. Know the Bible. Study it every day. Memorize it. Get involved in a Bible study and learn the Word so you can be a guide to others.

December 5

Reason Not to Fear #340: We Confess Our Sin and Keep Our Lives Holy

"For I fear lest, when I come, I shall not find you such as I wish, and that I shall be found by you such as you do not wish; lest there be contentions, jealousies, outbursts of wrath, selfish ambitions, backbitings, whisperings, conceits, tumults; lest, when I come again, my God will humble me among you, and I shall mourn for many who have sinned before and have not repented of the uncleanness, fornication, and lewdness which they have practiced."
II Corinthians 12:20-21

There is nothing new under the sun, the Preacher says in Ecclesiastes. This is so true in the life of a church. We have recorded for us in bold and honest detail the problems the Corinthian church faced and the spiritual bankruptcy of its people. We might be shocked by this, that these kinds of things can go on in a church made up of people who are supposedly born again Christians. Yet it happened in Corinth, and it happens today.

Everything of the flesh can be found in our churches today. Many pastors resign the ministry after a few years because of being beaten down, gossiped about and frustrated in their administration. They are discouraged because of petty jealousies, playing games, wars over control, divisions over money matters, and choosing sides and fighting it out in business meetings. All of this takes place in the very church that should provide a haven of peace, unity, and grace to a dying world!

The church in Corinth was no exception.

Paul was fearful when he considered a visit to the church he had planted in Corinth. He admitted honestly that he was afraid that when he arrived, he would find things not as he liked, and that they would find him not as they wanted him. He was concerned that he would find many of the old problems he had tried to correct still in their midst, like ghosts from the past, lingering around and ready to spring to the fore.

Leave the past, dear friends, and begin a new way of behavior. The only way to do this is to repent of your sin and turn away from it. Don't be like the Corinthians, or like the man enslaved to his sinful passions. Christ wants you to live without fear, without guilt, without regrets. Start on this new path today and you will not be sorry.

December 6

Reason Not to Fear #341: We Listen to Godly Advice

"But then, indeed, when you did not know God, you served those which by nature are not gods. But now after you have known God, or rather are known by God, how is it that you turn again to the weak and beggarly elements, to which you desire again to be in bondage? You observe days and months and seasons and years. I am afraid for you, lest I have labored for you in vain."
Galatians 4:8-11

Have you ever despaired that the advice you've given to someone goes unheeded and that despite your best efforts to help this person or group of people, they continue on their own way, heedless of the danger and folly that they are walking in and toward?

We often feel like this with our children. How many parents have warned their teenagers and early twenties children that the path they are taking will lead to much misery, distress and trouble? Many young people disregard their parents' advice and continue the path they have chosen to walk, only to find years later that their parents were right after all!

The writer of Proverbs addresses this problem when he writes to his son. "Hear, my son, your father's instructions and do not forsake your mother's teaching; indeed, they are a graceful wreath to your head and ornaments about your neck." Proverbs 1:8-9

Some people never grow up enough to receive instruction and listen to godly advice. They have too much pride and think they know the right way to go. They often go to counselors, but they carefully chose these people to give them the advice they want to hear.

The Apostle Paul was nearly tearing his hair out when he wrote this very pointed letter to the Galatians. These people believed in Christ and were saved, yet they were going back to the old ways of keeping the law and adding to the purity of faith in Christ with good works. "I fear for you," Paul wrote with anguish of soul.

How carefully do you listen to advice? Does it take something drastic before you heed good counsel and the Word of God? Make sure your heart is open and tender to receive what God has to tell you today. Don't be like the Galatians. Be willing to change. Listen to godly advice and you will be glad you did.

December 7

Reason Not to Fear #342: We Submit to One Another in Love

"Submitting to one another in the fear of God. Wives, submit to your own husbands, as to the Lord." Ephesians 5:21-22

In prefacing his remarks on the relationships of life in the home, Paul lays down an important concept. If we do not heed this truth about how we relate to one another, we are heading for trouble. It is very succinct. "Submit to one another."

Paul goes on to say that the fear of the Lord and submission principle should be practiced by wives to their husbands. Let me share with you some facts about marriage. #1-- There are over 18 million single parents in the United States alone who have children under 18 in their home. #2-- 46% of new marriages involve one spouse who has been divorced. (from US Statistics, 2010)

Someone has said, "One thing I know is that marriage is made in heaven, but then again, so is thunder and lightning." The fact is, it does not take long to learn that if the Lord did not help us in our marriages, we would all be in hot water. A lot of people are in difficult marriages because they simply have not chosen to obey God. This is the only way a marriage can last. It is up to both partners to give and sacrifice. That's the attitude Christ wants from us.

In this verse, Paul is describing what the ideal marriage looks like. Wives should submit to their husband as to the Lord. Husbands should love their wives as Christ loved the church, giving themselves to their wives unselfishly. The marriage relationship should mirror how you relate to Christ, with love, respect and submission.

Now, keep your pants on. I am not saying wives are second class citizens, nor should they be doormats. When the husband loves his wife with the love of Christ, and when she submits to him in that same love, they find peace, joy and harmony in the home. Their home becomes a living example of what it means to be a follower of Christ.

How do you measure up in this regard? Take careful note and change your behavior. Confess where you have sinned, and get it right with God and with each other. This is the only way we as believers in Christ can show to the world what it means to be a Christian. Therefore, out of reverent fear for our God, we obey this command.

December 8

Reason Not to Fear #343: We Are Thankful

"Bondservants, be obedient to those who are your masters according to the flesh, with fear and trembling, in sincerity of heart, as to Christ; not with eye service, as men-pleasers, but as bondservants of Christ, doing the will of God from the heart, with goodwill doing service, as to the Lord, and not to men, knowing that whatever good anyone does, he will receive the same from the Lord, whether he is a slave or free." Ephesians 6: 5-8

My daughter is the principal in a large Christian school here in Glendale, AZ. She loves her job and some of the people she works with. Even in Christian work there are some unsavory people. People who gossip, steal, and do not obey her. They do not like some of my daughter's decisions and that can lead to being stabbed in the back.

You don't have to go far to find a complaining spirit in our world today. The workplace is full of it, and it grows with each bitter, ugly comment. Paul was writing here to a group of people who were slaves.

Americans have become unappreciative and spoiled. The complaints, bickering, and hard feelings in the work world increase all the time, even though it is hard to find a job, and many have lost their homes, retirement plans, and savings when a company cuts back or shuts down. You would think people would be thankful for their jobs. But they are not.

Paul wrote to a group of slaves, "Obey your masters as if they were Christ Himself with respect and fear." While we are not slaves, we can take these words to heart. What should a Christian act like on the job?

We should not participate in the gossip, back-biting, complaining, and comparing that so many people engage in today. Paul instructed the young pastor, Timothy, to be content. In I Timothy 6:6, 8, he wrote, "But godliness with contentment is great gain.... But if we have food and clothing, we will be content with that."

How are you doing in this area? Do you find yourself complaining about your work conditions, the pay, the schedule, or the benefits? Stop your gripes and try to have a thankful heart. Obey your boss, not only when he is looking, but when he is not looking. You will be the one who benefits from this attitude. Remember the 3 B's: **Be** content. **Be** thankful. **Be** glad.

December 9

Reason Not to Fear #345: We Witness to Others Without Fear

"And most of the brethren in the Lord, having become confident by my chains, are much more bold to speak the word without fear." Philippians 1:14

Ribur is a young girl who grew up in a Christian family in Indonesia. During high school, she became interested in mission work. After studying for five years in a Bible school, she joined a community-development group that was teaching agricultural methods to villagers. Teaching this class gave the team an opportunity to hear about people's lives and share their Christian faith if asked.

Ribur started a small Bible study in a nearby village. She and a friend from the development group, Roy, began speaking with a woman in the community named Maria. They visited her on a Monday and the next day, they learned that she was ill. They visited with her, and Maria prayed and asked Christ into her life.

Ribur and Roy went back to check on Maria, but she left soon after they arrived. A crowd gathered and began beating them and accusing them of being unfaithful to Islam. After forty-five minutes, the police arrived and took them to jail where they were beaten again and questioned. Ribur prayed that the Holy Spirit would give her the strength to stand strong and testify to the truth. "I wasn't frightened," Ribur said, "because I had already been beaten in the other office. Also, the Bible says you will have persecution."

Roy and Ribur were arrested on May 29, 2012, and three days later were charged with abusing Islam. Ribur was alone during the 60 days she spent in jail. She used the time to read the Bible and pray. "Prison was a learning process for me," she said. She was released after two months. "After I was released, I felt that the same God who helped me in the prison was helping me still," said Ribur.

You may not be imprisoned for your faith, but you might face some kind of persecution today as you go about your day. Be encouraged to share Christ even in hard times. He is coming soon, and we must ready to give an answer to all who would ask us about our faith.

Remember the Apostle Paul. Remember Ribur. She is still active, eager to serve Christ, and ready to go to prison again if she must. She lives without fear because she fears the Lord.

December 10

Reason Not to Fear #346: We Stand Firm for Our Faith

"Only let your conduct be worthy of the gospel of Christ, so that whether I come and see you or am absent, I may hear of your affairs, that you stand fast in one spirit, with one mind striving together for the faith of the gospel, and not in any way terrified by your adversaries, which is to them a proof of perdition, but to you of salvation, and that from God." Philippians 1:27-28

Are you alarmed or fearful of those who oppose the preaching of the Gospel? We hear on every side about persecution coming to the church of Jesus Christ. There are many who blatantly oppose the Word of God and the preaching of the Cross and the blood of Christ.

Paul wrote to the Philippian believers to encourage them to stand firm against opposition for their faith. These followers of Christ faced the loss of their careers and jobs, properties, and lives. They were marginalized, despised, and rejected from the mainstream of life. In the nearby city of Smyrna, there lived a man whose name was Polycarp. He was a godly man, a bishop of the church, one who was known and respected by the governing officials.

He had no fear of man or of death when the state of Rome made a law saying that each person must make reverence to the likeness of Caesar, declare him as their god, and sprinkle a little incense on the altar. This godly man refused to do this.

When then he was brought before the proconsul, the official said, "Swear the oath, and I will release thee; revile the Christ." Polycarp replied, "Fourscore and six years have I been His servant, and He hath done me no wrong. How then can I blaspheme my King who saved me?" As a result of his refusal to declare Caesar as his god, he was burned at the stake with the people assisting in his death, clamoring eagerly to provide the wood and the fire to burn him.

How do you view your life? Are you willing to sacrifice everything to serve Christ? Or do you fear the opposition? Search your heart. Set your priorities and affections on things above, my dear friend. Only then can you be fearless toward the persecution against believers and focused on Christ alone.

Be a Polycarp today.

December 11

Reason Not to Fear #346: God Has Given Us Power, Love and A Sound Mind

"Therefore I remind you to stir up the gift of God which is in you through the laying on of my hands. For God has not given us a spirit of fear, but of power and of love and of a sound mind." II Timothy 1:6-7

In the New American Standard Bible, the word *fear* is translated *timidity*, and when you think about it, these two words have a lot in common! In other places, timidity is translated cowardice, weakness, apprehensive, or shyness. Cringing like a dog with its tail between its legs, this person is afraid of what others think of him; they are afraid of speaking their mind; they want to maintain a low profile and keep under the radar. They are the "yes" men in the corporate world who do whatever the CEO says to do. They are fearful of censure, fearful of criticism, fearful of the gossips. Even in church, they will not offer to head up a ministry for fear they might fail. They will not offer a comment in the small group Bible studies. They will not pray aloud.

In the last letter Paul wrote before he died, he admonishes young Timothy to kindle afresh the gift of preaching and ministering that God gave to him, not being afraid of what others think, not to be craven or cowardly in his proclaiming the Gospel message, not ashamed or smitten with fear of what man could do to him.

Some people I know are employed by the school district. They are totally afraid to be a witness on their job because the school board prohibited any of their employees to mention the name of Jesus or to give out any kind of witness to their faith.

Instead of fear and timidity, what kind of a spirit does God give us? He gives us power, love, and a spirit of discipline, or, as the King James Version puts it, *a sound mind*. I like that -- power instead of fear, love for all who would persecute us, and a disciplined and sound mind that is controlled by the Spirit of God. These three can get you through any situation life can throw at you.

But the choice is yours. You can live fearful and worried of everything. Or you can live in power, love, and with a sound mind. Which will you chose today? I hope it is to walk in the Spirit and reject fear. Fear the Lord. It is the only way to go.

December 12

Reason Not to Fear #347: We Do Not Fear Death

*"Inasmuch then as the children have partaken of flesh and blood, He
Himself likewise shared in the same, that through death He might destroy him
who had the power of death, that is, the devil, and release those who through
fear of death were all their lifetime subject to bondage. For indeed He does not
give aid to angels, but He does give aid to the seed of Abraham."*
Hebrews 2:14-15

Do you have a fear of death? Most of us have a natural, God-given desire to keep alive, and that is good. What is bad is to fear death to the point that you avoid the topic, avoid those who are going through it, avoid visiting in the hospital, and avoid attending funerals.

If you were to visit hospital waiting rooms, especially the ICU unit, or sit in homes where someone is dying, or been with someone who has just received news of a terminal illness, you would find out in a hurry that there is a marked difference between those who have faith in God and those who do not.

In the former case, the surviving family members know peace and joy in the belief that they will see their loved one again. This faith keeps them safe as they journey through the long dark valley of the shadow of death and grief.

To live with the fear of death is slavery. I can see how death would terrify an unsaved person. People spend millions of dollars each year on drugs and alcohol, and in other pursuits, to keep the thought of death from their minds. Yet as those redeemed, forgiven, justified, and on the way to heaven, we have something better. Death holds no power over us anymore, for we know we will not really die, but we will be taken to a place that is beyond our wildest imaginations of delights, joy, and peace.

If you live with a fear of death, now is the time to become free of that fear. God does not want you to be tormented with it any longer. Ask God to forgive you for not believing what He says about life after death for the Christian. Ask Him to set you free. Read I Corinthians 15 to get a new view of what it means to pass through the valley of death, but not be held there.

You can live with joy in your heart for the awesome future God has for you in heaven! If you believe that, thank God for what He has done for you right now.

December 13

Reason Not to Fear #348: We Do Not Hesitate to Enter His Rest

"Therefore, since a promise remains of entering His rest, let us fear lest any of you seem to have come short of it." Hebrew 4:1

Do you like to rest? The older I get, the more welcome that topic becomes. Rest is a wonderful subject in the Bible, and there are different kinds of rests that it speaks about. There was the rest of creation, when God *rested* from His work. He sat back and enjoyed His creative work. The Jews, in obedience to the law of Moses, celebrated the Sabbath to commemorate that event.

There was the *rest* that the children of Israel enjoyed when they entered the Promised Land of Israel under Joshua's leadership. Entering the Promised Land involved battles, hard work and many tears and struggles. The rest of entering the land promised by God to His children foreshadowed the rest we have as Christians when we believe in Christ and grow up in Him in grace and knowledge. When the children of Israel came to Kadesh-barnea, they did not believe God and they were not allowed to enter His rest. Instead, they had to wander for forty years in the desert. What hinders our rest in Christ? Unbelief. When we doubt God and His Word, we cannot find peace of heart or mind and we suffer the consequences.

The last *rest,* which Hebrews speaks of, is the rest Christ won for us at the Cross. This is *salvation rest*. Christ paid for our sin, and when we believe in His name and His finished work on the cross, we find rest in Him. The resurrection guarantees our rest, and so we commemorate His resurrection on the first day of the week, Sunday, when we gather together.

The writer of Hebrews was concerned that some of his readers, those who worshipped together and called themselves Christians, might have missed or fallen short of this rest. Only a true believer can enter the rest that Christ has won for us, yet there were many in that day (and in this day!) who slip into our churches and fellowships who have not been born again. To these people, the writer of this book addresses these comments.

Beware that you do not miss His rest! Do you want rest? Rest from your burdens, from your anxieties, from your struggles? Come to Christ today. If you are a believer, commit your way to Him and lay aside your burdens and your worries. He wants to carry them. Rest in Christ today.

December 14

Reason Not to Fear #349: We Set Aside Our Little Gods and Fear God

"By faith Moses, when he was born, was hidden three months by his parents, because they saw he was a beautiful child; and they were not afraid of the king's command." Hebrews 11:23

Have you been star-gazing? We have stars, heroes, and celebrities in abundance in our society today. People worship these people. We see their beautiful (air-brushed) faces on TV, in magazines, and on the computer.

I am saddened and sickened by the display of magazines at the check-out stands. These magazines show the poor people of Hollywood who are our celebrities. I say *poor* with intention, for if you were to follow their lives, you would see they are miserable, conflicted, tortured, and hounded. Yet people make gods of them simply because their faces and bodies are beautiful, because they are in movies and on TV, because they can play football or sing fairly decently or because they are rich and powerful.

This 11th chapter of Hebrews gives us some of God's heroes. This chapter can be called the Hall of Faith, and we honor and revere these who have gone before us in the walk of humble faith. Moses' parents, Jochebed and Amram, are in this hallowed hall. They were merely slaves, yet they feared God more than they feared the king. They hid their third child, protecting him from being killed along with all the other Hebrew children. Because of their faith, Moses lived and became the one God used to redeem His people from Egypt and slavery.

Walking by faith requires the fear of God. Sometimes it also requires us to step out into the dark, into a place where we do not know what will be the outcome. Someone has said that when we do this, one of two things will happen. We will either find something solid under our feet, or we will learn how to fly.

Stop looking at and worshipping the little gods of this world. When you are asked by God to take a step of faith, fear Him and do it, believing He will go with you and either give you a firm foundation or wings. What is He asking you to do today? Remember Jochebed and Amram. They feared and trusted God and God honored their faith. Can you walk in their footsteps today?

December 15
Reason Not to Fear #150: We Are Citizens of Heaven

"For you have not come to the mountain that may be touched and that burned with fire, and to blackness and darkness and tempest, and the sound of a trumpet and the voice of words, so that those who heard it *begged that the word should not be spoken to them anymore. (For they could not endure what was commanded:* 'And if so much as a beast touches the mountain, it shall be stoned or shot with an arrow.' *And so terrifying was the sight* that *Moses said,* 'I am exceedingly afraid *and trembling.')"* Hebrews 12:18-21

For eleven years my daughter and her husband and their three children lived in Indonesia. Every day they were challenged to live out their faith in front of those they had come to serve. How does one do that? What does living out your faith in daily life look like? I saw my family have people into their home for meals, take and make special food to their neighbors, and share material items with them. Living out your faith is supposed to be sensible.

James often squatted next to a man as he explained how to repair something. My daughter, Nicky, would invite a woman into her home to teach her how to make American food. Living out your faith is meant to be practical.

The writer of Hebrews progressed in his exhortation to the Jewish believers from the examples of faith found in chapter 11 to the practical working out of their faith in chapter 12. Now he wrote that Christians should live out our faith in practical ways, for we were redeemed and have become a nation and tribe of God's chosen people.

I love the contrasts he brings out between Mt. Sinai and Mt. Zion. Read through verse 24 and see for yourself. No longer do we have to fear a dark, noisy, fiery mountain and a Voice booming from it that threw them all to their faces. Our heritage is Mount Zion, the city of our God. We enjoy angels, a great assembly of believers, the church of the firstborn, God Himself, Jesus the mediator of our new covenant, and the sprinkled blood of Christ. What a blessing awaits us! We have all of eternity to bask in the light of His love, yet we can begin right now.

Right now God is calling you to live like a citizen of that heaven. You are a child of the King! Rejoice in all His blessings and don't let Satan defeat you with fear, worry, anger, idolatry, or greed. You are redeemed. Live like it!

December 16
Reason Not to Fear #351: We Have Been Given Grace

"Therefore, since we are receiving a kingdom which cannot be shaken, let us have grace, by which we may serve God acceptably with reverence and godly fear. For our God is a consuming fire." Hebrews 12:28, 29

The writer of this amazing book concludes with an appeal to show gratitude and to offer God an acceptable offering of the service of our lives in fear and awe. We should remind ourselves continually that our God is one to be feared, honored, respected and obeyed. He is all powerful, always present, all knowing, and holy. He cannot sin, nor can He endure its presence. He is a just judge. He is sovereign over the affairs of the world and the nations.

Yet He is also loving, kind, full of grace, and mercy. He longs for each individual to come to Him in repentance. This passage states that because we know all of these truths about God, we should act in a certain way. Our behavior and the daily choices we make reflect how we feel and think about God.

What does it mean that He is a consuming fire?

The first time this phrase is used to describe God in the Bible is Deuteronomy 4:24. In this passage, God is instructing His people to avoid making graven images or idols as gods to serve as the nations who surrounded them did. "For the Lord your God is a consuming fire, a jealous God." Fire, we understand, is a symbol of God's holiness. As fire purifies metals, so God's holiness purifies our lives (see I Peter 1:7).

God is also a jealous God. Jealousy in this case has the connotation of a God who maintains His rights and longs for what is truly His. God longs for us with an intense desire because He made us and redeemed us. We belong to Him, and He has every right to want us back from sin and Satan.

Where do you stand on this? Have you given your entire life to Him without holding back anything? Do you fear Him because He is a jealous God? If you have been flirting with other gods, now is a good time to get things right with your true Owner. Confess your sin and ask Him into your life. Don't give Him just a "nod" when you begin your day and have your daily devotions. Invite Him into every detail of your life because you love Him and long to serve Him. Fear Him because He is a consuming fire!

December 17

Reason Not to Fear #352: We Have Been Redeemed by the Blood of the Lamb

"And if you call on the Father, who without partiality judges according to each one's work, conduct yourselves throughout the time of your stay here in fear; knowing that you were not redeemed with corruptible things, like *silver or gold, from your aimless conduct received by tradition from your fathers, but with the precious blood of Christ, as of a lamb without blemish and without spot."* 1 Peter 1:17-19

I have mentioned before that if you fear God and honor Him, it will change your life and your behavior. Many of the Israelites in the days of the judges and the kings slipped into idolatry and sin because they did not believe that God could see them, and if He could, He would do nothing to punish them for their wayward behavior.

Peter writes to the scattered Jewish Christians, telling them to live their lives in fear. Fear? But I thought we weren't supposed to fear. Notice what he says: fear God because He will judge you for your conduct on this earth. Fear because you were redeemed by the precious blood of the Lamb, a costly price! Fear because you will stand before Him some day and give an accounting for every deed and every word that proceeded from your mouth.

In our society, we tend to dress up sin and call it by other names. They say that most things are disorders or conditions a person is born with, and even psychopathic behavior, occurs because of an inherited gene and has nothing to do with the choices we make. The obvious answer to all deviant behavior, the authorities tell us today, is to take a drug or to call it a life style.

I am not saying that these diseases of the mind do not exist or that they are all caused by demons or satanic influence. I am saying that when we give sin a different name, we are walking in darkness, depression, and death. We must not call sin by anything but what it is, and we must confess sin before God and others to be rid of its' effects.

Conduct yourself in fear as you live on this earth. The fear of God will keep you from sin. It will lead you into holiness, peace, and joy. Take the high road today and live in the fullness of all God has for you. Live in the fear of God.

December 18
Reason Not to Fear #353: We Submit to the Government

"Honor all people. Love the brotherhood. Fear God. Honor the king."
I Peter 2:17

If you fear God, you will conduct yourself in a certain way while you live on this earth.

Peter gives a list of instructions for the Jewish Christians who have fled persecution and now live scattered throughout Asia Minor and Greece. Life was not easy for these Christians. They had left their homes, their jobs, their families and friends, and everything else that was familiar. They were looked down upon and ridiculed by the society in which they lived, and for many of them, they would face increasingly severe persecution under the Roman government.

Yet Peter says that they should submit to the government's authority over them (v. 11-15). He states that it is the will of God for them to do this. In submitting to those over them, these Christians would silence the ignorance of foolish men. They were to act as free men, not using their freedom to cover up their sin, but as a testimony to all.

"Keep your behavior excellent among the Gentiles, so that in the thing in which they slander you as evildoers, they may because of your good deeds, as they observe them, glorify God in the day of visitation." v. 12

We may not like everything our government, president, or congress does, or the laws they pass, yet if it does not conflict with our conscience or go against God's Word, then we must submit to it and honor those over us.

By keeping the law and not complaining about our government, we show the world a different way to live. As they observe our behavior and our speech patterns, they realize we have something they do not. And they may ask us why we are different. They may ask us why we have hope and peace in days such as this. We will have the opportunity to tell them of Christ who lives within us, of the hope we have of eternal life, of the peace that passes all understanding, of a love that never ends.

The choices you make affect not only your life but those around you. Make a conscious decision to walk in the way of love and respect today. Obey the laws. Pray for our governmental officials. Love your brother and sister. Fear God. This is the only way to go.

December 19

Reason Not to Fear #354: We Should Live Chaste Lives with the Fear of God

"Wives, likewise, be submissive to your own husbands, that even if some do not obey the word, they, without a word, may be won by the conduct of their wives, when they observe your chaste conduct accompanied by fear."
I Peter 3:1-2

One of the most difficult situations in life is to be married to a person who is not a believer. There are so many issues that arise from this that we should be counseling and instructing our children from a young age that they should avoid this and marry only a believer. Yet what if they are both unsaved and one comes to Christ, yet the other does not?

As I have spoken at many different women's retreats and events, frequently someone in the audience will come and discuss with me the problem of being married to an unbeliever. I remember one particular woman in Texas coming to talk with me. She was frustrated and torn up inside about this issue. She told me that some of the entertainment her husband wanted her to join him in was sin.

She said, "What should I do, Chris? My husband wants me to go with him. When I do, I am miserable and feel I am in the wrong place. I am exhausted."

Do you have some advice you would have given this woman? My advice was simple. If the activity makes you sin, then do not do it. Obey God. Discuss the issue with your husband and explain why you made your decision.

The issue is not the activity, rather the issue is who to obey. God or man. Be consistent. If you need to, change your behavior and follow what God tells you to do in His Word.

Peter addressed this topic in our passage for the day. He said the wife of the unbelieving husband should first of all be submissive to her husband in the fear of God. She should honor him, respect him, and obey him when he tells her what to do or not to do. Peter goes on to say that if a wife would do this, she might win her husband to the Lord without speaking a word. Without nagging him about going to church or being the kind of man she wants him to be, he will be won by the sweet, loving attitude of his wife as she exhibits Christ-like love.

How is your attitude today? Get your heart right, change your behavior, and follow God's Word in all you do.

December 20
Reason Not to Fear #155: We Live In Obedience to God

"For in this manner, in former times, the holy women who trusted in God also adorned themselves, being submissive to their own husbands, as Sarah obeyed Abraham, calling him lord, whose daughters you are if you do good and are not afraid with any terror." 1 Peter 3:5-6

It seems strange that Peter would use the example of Sarah as a woman who obeyed her husband, calling him *lord*. Wasn't Sarah the lady who persuaded him to take the serving girl, Hagar, and to have a child with her because she was tired of waiting for the promised son? Wasn't Sarah the gal who flared up at Abraham and blamed him for all her trouble with Hagar when her plan worked and the girl actually got pregnant? Yes. This is she.

Why did Peter use her as an example for us to follow? You have to understand that all of the people in the Bible were flawed human beings with a sin nature. They failed God, walked out of His will, and sinned. Yet when they repented (and this is the key!) of their sin, and sought to please God and keep His Word, they were forgiven and they got their second chance.

Sarah was one of these who won a second chance. It is not recorded that she asked forgiveness from God or from her husband, but we see a different Sarah when Isaac's birth is announced. The verse above says that she called her husband lord and that she ended her life well, raising Isaac to fear and love Yahweh.

We would do well to follow in her footsteps and be called her daughters. I am not suggesting you go around and call your husband lord! I am suggesting that your heart attitude be one of the "incorruptible qualities of gentleness and quietness," which comprise what true beauty is all about. Our bodies are going to deteriorate. We will get wrinkles and brown age spots, and our hair will turn gray and fall out. Yet we can have a beauty that never dies or diminishes. This is the inner beauty of a spirit that loves without conditions, gives without thought of return, shows kindness without thought to ourselves.

Do you have these qualities? As the busyness of the Christmas season presses upon you, and you are stressed, tired, and anxious, can you display this attitude? It is only through Christ that we can achieve this. Call out to Him and He will help you. He will give you that quiet and gentle spirit that is so precious in the sight of God.

December 21
Reason Not to Fear #356: We Are Not Afraid of Persecution

"But even if you should suffer for righteousness' sake, you are blessed. And do not be afraid of their threats, nor be troubled. But sanctify the Lord God in your hearts, and always be ready to give a defense to everyone who asks you a reason for the hope that is in you, with meekness and fear." 1 Peter 3:14-15

Our society is trying to divorce Christ from Christmas. They are striving to delete the religious aspect of what this celebration is truly all about, the birth of Jesus Christ. In place of Christ, we have the materialistic god of Santa Claus who delivers to all children good gifts, who knows the hearts of all, and who can accomplish miracles. This god does not demand that we keep the Ten Commandments or any commandments at all. We just need to crawl up onto his large lap and tell him our wishes, and he fulfills them.

Someone once asked Leonard Bernstein, famed conductor of the New York Philharmonic, which instrument was the most difficult to play. His immediate response was, *"the second fiddle."* Joseph as second fiddle, played an essential part in the Nativity Story, and he played it well.

His is a story of courage and patient, quiet faith. He was the man to whom God entrusted the task of protecting the mother and her child from the time she conceived Jesus. He was the rugged and brave man who led Mary safely along the dangerous roads to Bethlehem, to Egypt, and eventually back home to northern Israel. God selected this man to protect the infant Jesus in the dangerous first years of his life. This story of Joseph was included in our Bible to encourage each of us to live courageously, even if it means living dangerously, in doing God's will. Yet Joseph was an ordinary, flesh and blood man like us. Life isn't easy. It requires courage.

Peter tells his readers that they should not be persecuted as evil-doers who deserve punishment, but they should count it a blessing to suffer for righteousness sake. We should set Christ apart in our hearts and be ready to give an answer to those who ask us about our faith.

Make Christ the center of your own Christmas celebrations, and let His love and joy shine through your eyes, your actions, your heart and your life this year. If you are persecuted for speaking His dear name, then be a good testimony through that. He will bless you. Rejoice! Be glad! Jesus Christ was born!

December 22
Reason Not to Fear #357: We Guard Against False Teachers

"Then the Lord knows how to deliver the godly out of temptations and to reserve the unjust under punishment for the day of judgment, and especially those who walk according to the flesh in the lust of uncleanness and despise authority. They are presumptuous, self-willed. They are not afraid to speak evil of dignitaries, whereas angels, who are greater in power and might, do not bring a reviling accusation against them before the Lord." 2 Peter 2: 9-11

In this second short letter that Peter wrote to the dispersed Christians, he addressed the problem of false teachers who by that time (66 AD) were infiltrating the church and leading many astray with erroneous doctrines. He warned that these evil people would come to them and bring in destructive heresies, denying the Lord Jesus Christ's virgin birth, His atoning death, His resurrection, and the validity of the Word of God. The reason they did this was for their gain. They sold on the open market the precious Gospel of Christ which was free to every human being!

He went on to describe the judgment of God on such men and women as these, citing the fall of angels with Satan, the flood, and Sodom and Gomorrah. In each case, God rescued out of the judgment those who were righteous in Him. The Lord God is able to deliver His people, those who truly love Him, obey Him and follow Him with all their hearts, souls and minds from the judgment that falls on the wicked.

The false teachers, he says, are bold, strong willed, and daring. They are not afraid to revile and curse powerful, angelic beings. Peter says these men, who are like brute animals, will perish when God judges them.

We have had these kinds of people in the church since the first day. We still have them today. They flaunt their "freedom" in sexual exploits, demean godly teachers of the Word who have gone before them, and spout forth their folly of having "secret" and "special" ways to know God. There are those who have torn our precious Word of God apart and said it is all just myth and stories.

Be careful to whom you listen and to what you put your faith in. You should be so grounded in the Word that you can tell when someone is teaching contrary to it. Be sure, even in this busy Christmas season, to stay in the Word, in your faith, and in your courage to stand against all those who would deny Jesus Christ.

December 23
Reason Not to Fear #358: We Live in God's Love

"There is no fear in love; but perfect love casts out fear, because fear involves torment. But he who fears has not been made perfect in love."
1 John 4:18

I am always amazed by the horror movies out there today. Why would someone want to be terrified out of their skins through a movie? What appeal does horror hold for people? Yet fear is a big business. I guess people love the thrill they get from being afraid, yet I must tell you that there is no love in this kind of fear.

What the world calls love is not love. God's love nourishes, protects, enriches, and enhances the person who is loved.

We have learned about the fear of the Lord and its opposite, the fear that brings torment and despair. The Apostle John writes this wonderful little book in which he explains and depicts God's agape love.

Since this is the Christmas season when we're thinking so much about God's love in sending His Son Jesus to this earth, why don't you read I John 3-4 today and contemplate on His love?

During the hippie uprising in the Haight-Asbury district of San Francisco several years ago, an editorial hit the paper titled, "Love Menaces the City." Yet it was not love. It was lust and selfishness that fueled that movement, destroying lives and properties.

Fear has punishment is the correct way to translate this passage. Fear enslaves and puts a person in prison. There is no love in fear because love sets free its beloved. You have God's Spirit and His love dwelling within you if you are a child of God, but because of fear, you may not be experiencing all that love can do for you and others through you.

Fear shuts you up; love sets you free. Fear makes you focus on yourself; love reaches out to others and meets their needs.

Try living in God's revolutionary love today. When you feel fear creeping up on you in the form of worry, anxiety, stress or dread, refuse it. Recognize it for the evil that it is, and allow God's love to flood your heart. Love those who are different. Reach out to those you would naturally avoid.

Pray and ask God to give you love. *Agape* love. It will change your life.

December 24
Reason Not to Fear #359: We Reject False Teachings

"Woe to them! For they have gone in the way of Cain, have run greedily in the error of Balaam for profit, and perished in the rebellion of Korah. These are spots in your love feasts, while they feast with you without fear, serving only themselves. They are clouds without water, carried about by the winds; late autumn trees without fruit, twice dead, pulled up by the roots." Jude 11-12

Jude was a brother of James and the half-brother of Jesus. He was influential in the early church in Jerusalem. He writes like one of the Old Testament prophets, very scathing in his remarks, and he draws deeply from the tradition and the history of the Israeli nation. The danger he is confronting is starkly true of our day and age. We, too, have false teachers who appear on our TV screens, and on YouTube, and in large churches. In his book, *Love Wins*, Rob Bell declared that there is no hell, that God would not punish living souls in this way, and that we will all make it to heaven. This is clearly not what the Bible teaches.

There were many so-called spiritual teachers invading the newly born church in Jude's day. New believers flocked to these lively, attractive men like bees to honey. One of the main false teachings came from the Gnostics who believed in two realms -- the physical and the spiritual. These two never mixed, they said, and they taught that a person could cultivate the spiritual life and not worry what you do with the physical. This led to great sin in the area of sexual activities.

Jude doesn't pull any punches when he confronts these false teachers. He charges them with the sin of Cain (rebellion and murder), the error of Balaam (greed and pride), and the rebellion of Korah (pride, rebellion, and jealousy). They were like clouds without water. If you've ever lived through a drought, you know how awful it is to see clouds forming and come overhead, only to dissipate and leave without any life-giving water. These men promised to deliver the water of life, but they were trees without fruit, hidden reefs, doubly dead, uprooted and withered.

Be careful who you listen to, what you watch, and what you believe in the books you read. Know the Word and measure everything (even this devotional!) by it. That way you cannot go wrong. Jude said, "But you, beloved, ought to remember the words that were spoken beforehand by the apostles of our Lord Jesus Christ." v. 17 Heed the warning today.

December 25

Reason Not to Fear #360: God Gave His Son

"Keep yourselves in the love of God, looking for the mercy of our Lord Jesus Christ unto eternal life. And on some have compassion, making a distinction; but others save with fear, pulling them out of the fire, hating even the garment defiled by the flesh." Jude 21-23

Merry Christmas!

I love Jude's closing remarks, especially his great doxology at the end of this book. I also love his admonition given here to "keep yourselves in the love of God."

We focus a lot at Christmastime on the love of God. God gave His Son. For those of us who have believed in His Son for eternal salvation, we should heed the appeal to keep ourselves in His love. I think Jude was exhorting us to watch our daily walk. Be careful to obey His commands, to fear Him, to love Him and to keep close to Him. This is a daily, moment by moment task. A good way to accomplish this is by doing just what you are doing right now -- reading His Word, meditating on it, applying it to your life, and obeying it.

When we do that, we also need to watch out and help our fellow Christians, our brothers and sisters in the faith. We are to have mercy on those who are doubting (and which of us hasn't been there a time or two in our lives?), and to others, who are not yet believers, we should snatch them from the fire, having mercy on them, too.

Yet we should be involved in this rescue work with an attitude of fear. Why fear? I think the fear comes because, knowing our own weakness and sinful nature, we must acknowledge that we might be caught in the same kind of sin.

If you are ministering to people involved with drugs, pornography, the sex trade or alcohol, you know how easy it is to become casual with the way they talk, their life styles, and their dysfunctional habits. It is easy to accept their sin as a way of life rather than something that should be shunned and discarded. We need to fear that we might become tainted by their sin and become unable to lead them to the light.

On this Christmas day, worship the Christ in the cradle and the Lord in the heavens and in your heart. Keep yourself in the love of God. Help others who need to see Jesus in you.

December 26
Reason Not to Fear #361: Jesus Conquered Death for All Time

"And when I saw Him, I fell at His feet as dead. But He laid His right hand on me, saying to me, 'Do not be afraid; I am the First and the Last. I am He who lives, and was dead, and behold, I am alive forevermore. Amen. And I have the keys of Hades and of Death.'" Revelation 1:17-18

If you are like me, you would admit that you do not understand all the truths that are contained in the book of Revelation. However, I like to read it since it provides me with glimpses into my future. If you are a Christian reading this, if Jesus is your Lord and Savior, then this verse instructs you that you do not need to be afraid of the future. Here are some reasons why you do not need to be afraid.

#1-You do not need to be afraid because of the power of the touch of Jesus. If you read this verse carefully, notice John says that he fell at the feet of Jesus as a dead man. But take note of what happened next. "He (Jesus) placed his right hand on me and said, 'Do not be afraid.'" There is a calming power when it comes to fear in the gentle hand of Jesus touching you. Catch it. Jesus reaches down and touches you and instructs you to be calm, composed, and quiet. He has the situation under His control.

#2- You do not need to be afraid because Jesus is the first and the last. At the dawn of creation when the world was without form and void, there was Jesus. His hands made everything. As the crowning act of creation, He took dust and formed man, and breathed into life into Adam and all humans. But not only is He is the First, He is also the Last. He is the final end of all things. You end your search when you find Him. And you can also find an end to your fears when you find Him.

#3-You do not need to fear because Jesus has conquered death for all time. Because He lives, we can have that same encouragement and hope. Because He lives, we do not mourn at the graveside of a loved one like those in the world do. Jesus is the only one who can set you free from your fears and give you everlasting life. Because He lives, we can persevere and walk the road He has given us to walk in this life with joy and peace.

He is the First and the Last and the Giver of Life. Trust in Him and do not be afraid!

December 27
Reason Not to Fear #362: Christ Is With You, Even to the End

"Do not fear any of those things which you are about to suffer. Indeed, the devil is about to throw some of you into prison, that you may be tested, and you will have tribulation ten days. Be faithful until death, and I will give you the crown of life." Revelation 2:10

Jesus addressed His churches in Asia Minor, seven of them, and gave specific instructions on how they should change, what they should repent of, and what reward awaited those who were faithful. In Smyrna, Jesus did not need to send any word of reproof or correction, only of hope and encouragement, for these people were suffering persecution from the Roman government and were about to enter a time period of even deeper suffering. "Hang on," Jesus seems to say to them, "be faithful until you die, and I will give you the crown of life."

Presently my daughter is home on furlough. She and her husband and their three children are missionaries in Indonesia on the island of Borneo in a very remote tribe. They have been there for quite a long time now, and through the years there have been all sorts of challenges and sufferings they have had to face. Let me tell you about one.

My daughter has struggled with extreme loneliness in the jungle. Before I go any further let me interject that she knows she is where the Lord has called her. However, she gets very lonely being away from family, friends, and the outside world. The jungle can be very dark. Loneliness has been her pain and her affliction. How does she handle it? Truthfully, sometimes it gets the best of her, and she encounters depression and despair. Yet God always lifts her up to serve Him for another day.

God has a purpose for every obstacle and every frustration, pain and affliction that touches your life. However, your love for the Lord should stay constant. It should not waiver, no matter what your trial and difficulty might be. You see, Satan wants to stamp out my daughter's work in Indonesia, and the same is true for you. Yet I believe that through suffering and hardships we often bear a deeper testimony for Christ.

It is from your suffering that faithfulness will spring, and you will grow as a Christian. Take hope and encouragement. He is with you always, even to the end of the world.

December 28
Reason Not to Fear #363: God Is Victorious in the Face of Opposition

"Now after the three-and-a-half days the breath of life from God entered them, and they stood on their feet, and great fear fell on those who saw them."
Revelation 11:11

As I write this in August 2013, my mother is almost 89 and her health is deteriorating. In fact, we have had to contact hospice because the end of her life is drawing to an end. But the best part of her life is just beginning. The song *This World Is Not My Home* is a great reminder of that truth.

This verse in Revelation is referring to the two witnesses who some people believe are Elijah and Moses. As the world nears its end, these two men will possess great power, and they will be strong witnesses for Christ. Day after day in front of the temple in Jerusalem, they preach righteousness to a world given over to evil. When their enemies come against them to kill them, fire comes out of their mouths and they destroy their enemies. All the bullets, bombs, and weapons built by man cannot overcome them. They go on preaching to a world that hates them.

The great world dictator at the time, the one the Bible designates as the Anti-Christ, hates them and makes war against them. After three and a half years, he is able to kill them. Their dead bodies are displayed for all the world to see in the public square in front of the temple.

Those who live on this earth will celebrate because these two witnesses are dead. It will happen in real time and I think people will be glued to their televisions like never before. For three and a half days, the Anti-Christ will be very proud of himself. But these two men will come back to life, and people everywhere will be overcome with great fear.

Our responsibility as Christ-followers is to testify unceasingly about Jesus Christ. You may be attacked, slandered, and insulted, but if you remain a true and faithful servant, you will receive the reward Christ gives you. You will be taken to heaven and hear from Christ's lips, "Well done, good and faithful servant."

When your life is finished, what awaits you? Consider giving what you have left of your life to Him who is our coming King and Lord.

December 29
Reason Not to Fear #364: God's Will Is Done on Earth and In Heaven

"Then I saw another angel flying in the midst of heaven, having the everlasting gospel to preach to those who dwell on the earth--to every nation, tribe, tongue, and people-- saying with a loud voice, 'Fear God and give glory to Him, for the hour of His judgment has come; and worship Him who made heaven and earth, the sea and springs of water.'" Revelation 14:6, 7

The other day, several of my grandsons came over to my house. One of the many things they like to do here is play baseball in the back yard. I have a brick wall the goes around my entire yard, and they love to throw a ball against the wall and made up a game with a point system of some sort. However, on this particular afternoon, one of them was crying. Within a few moments, I was outside having a question and answer discussion with him. It seems his older cousin always got the ball ahead of him because he is taller, stronger and faster.

As the little boy dried his tears, he muttered, "It's not fair!"

I can relate to those feelings of things not being fair, cannot you? But in the end, no one will be able to accuse God of unfairness.

I find it interesting that God is so purposeful about redeeming lost mankind that at the end of all things, He sends angels to proclaim a message of grace and love to the world. While the judgments of God in the book of Revelation are horrific, He graciously extends His grace up until the last minute and the last breath.

The message the angel gives is very simple. **Choose Door #1**: fear God and worship Him and here is what you will receive: forgiveness and eternal life. **Choose Door #2:** rebellion against God and sin and here is what you receive: sin and eternal death. What is so sad is that even with such a clear choice, many during the days of final judgment against wickedness on this earth will decide to go against God.

Therefore, He is not unfair; rather He is just because they choose their judgment. As this old year winds down and you contemplate what might lie ahead in the New Year, it is important for you to think about which door you choose. Is it the door of life or the door of death? Think through your decision carefully; it is a costly one.

December 30
Reason Not to Fear #365: Jesus Christ Reigns!

"They sing the song of Moses, the servant of God, and the song of the Lamb, saying: 'Great and marvelous are Your works, Lord God Almighty! Just and true are Your ways, O King of the saints! Who shall not fear You, O Lord, and glorify Your name? for You alone are holy. For all nations shall come and worship before You, for Your judgments have been manifested.'"
Revelation 15:3, 4

Read this chapter from the beginning. It is absolutely marvelous! I love the book of Revelation because it gives us God's view of the events on earth. In heaven we see a throne; we see angels with the bowls of the wrath of God, ready to be poured out on the earth; we see a great sea like glass and glowing like fire with millions gathered around it who sing the praises of God with harps. They praise God for His greatness, His powerful works, His great name, and His judgments against sin.

The older I get, the more aware I am of the battles, burdens, and heartaches I have faced in my life. And like you, I have found myself saying, "Why, Lord? Why did this happen to me? When will this weight leave me?"

Yet I am also more and more aware of another truth. God is great and marvelous. God is just and true in all His ways. God is to be feared, reverenced, and adored. God is love incarnate. I have to admit that I do not understand His ways. In Isaiah 55:9, the Lord declares, "For as the heavens are higher than the earth, so are My ways higher than your ways and My thoughts than your thoughts."

God created us. We are His sons and daughters. Therefore, your life is precious. It is a gift from the Lord, and you need to treasure it. You need to live it as best you can to His glory. As I mature in my faith, I become more aware that I am to not to live by explanations but by promises found in the Word of God. I have learned that fearing Him and bringing glory to His name sometimes comes through battles, burdens, and heartaches.

Perhaps as this year trickles away like sand in an hourglass, you need to stop and take stock of your life before God. Commit your life to Him. He will give you joy as you contemplate living another year for His glory. Don't forget what awaits you in heaven. If you need a reminder, read chapter 15 of Revelation again!

December 31
Reason Not to Fear #366: Our Redemption Draws Near!

"Then a voice came from the throne, saying, 'Praise our God, all you His servants and those who fear Him, both small and great!' And I heard, as it were, the voice of a great multitude, as the sound of many waters and as the sound of mighty thunderings, saying, 'Alleluia! For the Lord God Omnipotent reigns! Let us be glad and rejoice and give Him glory, for the marriage of the Lamb has come, and His wife has made herself ready.'"
Revelation 19:5-7

While you may be looking out your window on a world of white today if you live in the northern part of the country, I am writing this in the month of May, the time of the year when a lot of people decide to get married. I like weddings. I like the music, food, and even the family chaos! Oriental weddings sometimes lasted up to a week of feasting, revelry, and celebrations.

There is one wedding I cannot wait for and that is the one that will take place in heaven, the one described in this verse between Jesus Christ and His bride, the church.

Marriage is one of the greatest events in our lives, and that is the image God wants to place in your mind when it comes to the wedding awaiting us in heaven. When we are taken to heaven either by death or the Rapture, there is going to be a great wedding feast. It will be the greatest event in your life. Thousands, possibly millions, of people and angels will come to celebrate this spectacular event. Bible scholars believe the guests are the Old Testament saints.

We will wear white robes of the finest material, and we will eat heavenly food that does not run out. There will be music, laughter, singing, food, and celebrating. Best of all, you will be with those you know and love. Truly, nothing you have even known will even begin to compare to what you will experience on that day.

Those who attend this wedding banquet are those who fear, honor, and adore Him. All of God's plans from the beginning of history to its end have this one goal, to worship Him alone.

It is your privilege to do that now and in eternity.

II Peter 3:11, 12 reads, "Since all these things are to be destroyed in this way, what sort of people ought you to be in holy conduct and godliness..." How does your life measure up to God's holiness in your conduct, words, thoughts, and attitudes?

As the New Year comes, focus on the wedding event of the ages and all that God has for you. "Look up, for your redemption is drawing near!" (Luke 21:28) *Hallelujah!*

A Note from the Author:

It is funny how a book comes about. Sometimes the story behind the book can be even better than the book! Fourteen years ago, my husband had a cardiac arrest. For one week he lingered in a coma, between life and death. In an instant, a new normal entered my life that I was totally unprepared for. One by one each of my four children gathered together at the hospital. Over coffee, late at night, my oldest son and I began an intimate conversation about the possible death of his father. As we talked, I revealed my fears for the future.

What would it be like to be a widow at age 52? Where would I live? If Bob survived, how would I take care of him? Why did this unexpected interference enter our lives?

My son listened, then responded, "Mom, don't you know that there are over 250 *fear not's* in the Bible?"

I replied, "What mother knows that? Certainly I don't."

As our coffee was finished, my son said, "You need to find those verses, Mom. You need to read them and hold on to them."

Thus began my search and writing on one fear not a day. In my personal life, they have been overwhelmingly important and vital. May the Lord strengthen you on your journey by knowing you do not have to face your fears alone.

Please feel free to correspond with me and contact me for any speaking opportunities.

My email address is: **boelterchris@gmail.com**

***

Virginia Ann Work is an accomplished author of seven fiction novels. She is also a pastor's wife, a mother to three grown children and a grandmother to six of the most beautiful children in the world (so she says!). She has been writing stories, Bible studies and devotionals for 35 years and found it a delight and joy to work with Chris Boelter on this project after meeting her at a ladies' retreat five years ago. Virginia's great passion is the study of God's Word and a desire to write books that lead others to know Christ and live for Him. To find out more about her and the books she has written, check out her website at: **www.VirginiaAnnWork.com**

Made in the USA
San Bernardino, CA
20 July 2016